PORTRAIT OF THE ASSASSIN

BY

GERALD R. FORD

AND

JOHN R. STILES

SIMON AND SCHUSTER · NEW YORK

TO OUR RESPECTIVE FATHERS—
GERALD R. FORD, SR.
FREDERICK E. STILES

FOREWORD

PORTRAIT OF THE ASSASSIN is a narrative that grew out of the reactions of one member of President Johnson's Commission that was
set up to report upon the assassination of President John F. Kennedy.
Not all members of that Commission would necessarily interpret
everything they heard the same way, but the material here presented is factual and accurate. As the authors of this book worked
together daily for ten months they became more and more persuaded that the Report itself, while it could tell only the bare facts
of the tragedy, convinced most readers that the Commission did its
work thoroughly and well. The present account is not intended to
take issue with the conclusions of the Commission.

It is hoped, however, that this book will reach many readers who,
for lack of time or other reasons, may not have read and analyzed
the massive content of the Report and the 26 volumes of testimony
and exhibits. The narrative is organized in the style of a novel. It
lives and breathes with the emotions of those who suffered through
the events. The witnesses speak—the dialogue comes directly from
the statements of real people.

The authors have taken the liberty of omitting some paragraphs
and sentences that were repetitious, or irrelevant to a given incident,
and in order that the sequence should move smoothly, footnotes
indicating these omissions have not been used. Spelling and grammatical corrections have been made in documents that would otherwise be difficult to read. However, the meaning of all statements
and quotations has been faithfully guarded, and these minor changes
or deletions can easily be checked against the record.

There is a common saying that everyone's life story would make
a dramatic novel but that only the fiction writer who can invent
his own characters, situations and dialogue normally succeeds in

7

selecting the right materials. From real life we seldom garner and retain enough details of our experiences to create our personal stories. But the Report of the Warren Commission is so voluminous that here—perhaps for the first time in history—everything essential to a nonfiction novel is available. As the authors listened day by day to the unfolding of this narrative from real life, they came to feel that it was essential that the story be written in a form in which any reader could participate in the surprise, suspense and privilege of being a member of the Commission himself.

Those who served did so only to discover the truth. In writing this narrative the authors hope they have furthered that purpose.

We wish to thank many who voluntarily labored in the production of this book. Special thanks go to former Congressman John H. Ray, who, although retired, came to Washington and worked uncounted hours helping to analyze and check the record. His private efforts added much to the character of this book. Special acknowledgment of the work of Francis X. Fallon, Jr., is also made. His keen and perceptive reading of the testimony assured a degree of accuracy that might otherwise have been lacking. The authors have enjoyed a unique experience in their collaboration, and although specific words or phrases may have been those of one individual or the other, the final product is the result of mutual effort and thought.

—GERALD R. FORD
—JOHN R. STILES

8

CONTENTS

9

Office of the White House Press Secretary

- -

THE WHITE HOUSE

EXECUTIVE ORDER
NO. 11130

- - - -

APPOINTING A COMMISSION TO REPORT UPON THE
ASSASSINATION OF PRESIDENT JOHN F. KENNEDY

Pursuant to the authority vested in me as President of the United States, I hereby appoint a Commission to ascertain, evaluate and report upon the facts relating to the assassination of the late President John F. Kennedy and the subsequent violent death of the man charged with the assassination. The Commission shall consist of--

The Chief Justice of the United States, Chairman;

Senator Richard B. Russell;

Senator John Sherman Cooper;

Congressman Hale Boggs;

Congressman Gerald R. Ford;

The Honorable Allen W. Dulles;

The Honorable John J. McCloy.

The purposes of the Commission are to examine the evidence developed by the Federal Bureau of Investigation and any additional evidence that may hereafter come to light or be uncovered by federal or state authorities; to make such further investigation as the Commission finds desirable; to evaluate all the facts and circumstances surrounding such assassination, including the subsequent violent death of the man charged with the assassination, and to report to me its findings and conclusions.

The Commission is empowered to prescribe its own procedures and to employ such assistants as it deems necessary.

Necessary expenses of the Commission may be paid from the "Emergency Fund for the President".

All Executive departments and agencies are directed to furnish the Commission with such facilities, services and cooperation as it may request from time to time.

LYNDON B. JOHNSON

THE WHITE HOUSE,

November 29, 1963.

CHAPTER I

THE COMMISSION
GETS ITS FIRST SHOCK

No SOONER had the Commission investigating President Kennedy's assassination assembled its staff and tentatively outlined methods of operation than it was plunged into an astounding problem. On Wednesday, January 22, the members of the Commission were hurriedly called into emergency session by the chairman. Mr. J. Lee Rankin, newly appointed General Counsel for the Commission, had received a telephone call from Texas. The caller was Mr. Waggoner Carr, the Attorney General of Texas. The information was that the FBI had an "undercover agent" and that that agent was none other than Lee Harvey Oswald, the alleged assassin of President Kennedy!

Prior to that day the newspapers had carried an inconspicuous article or two speculating on whether Oswald could have been an agent of any United States Government agency. Mrs. Marguerite Oswald had made statements that she thought her son must have been tied in with the CIA or the State Department. But now the alarm had been sounded by a high official; and the Dallas prosecutor, Mr. Henry Wade, who had also reported the rumor, was himself a former FBI man.

Individual members of the Commission got their first inkling of the seriousness of Carr's report when they met in emergency session late in the afternoon of the twenty-second of January. Each had received an urgent message to come at 5:30 P.M. to the Commission's offices in the Veterans of Foreign Wars Building. My secretary had contacted me immediately. I happened to be in a subcommittee hearing in connection with my normal duties on military appropriations. The other members of the Commission—Chief Justice Earl Warren, Senators Richard B. Russell and John Sherman Cooper, Congressman Hale Boggs, John J. McCloy and Allen W. Dulles—were going about their busy schedules.

On the arrival of the members, each took his place around the eight-foot oblong table. The late hour and the complete disruption of everyone's personal plans added to the atmosphere of tension. I was already overdue to leave the office, go home, change to evening clothes and attend the dedication of the new Museum of History and Technology. The Chief Justice had the same problem. He was the scheduled speaker at this important event.

J. Lee Rankin, General Counsel of the Commission, then reported the startling allegations to the members. They looked at one another in amazement.

The session that followed lasted until after seven. I cannot recall attending a meeting more tense and hushed.

The Commission made the decision to ask the Texas Attorney General, District Attorney Wade and any other Dallas officials who had knowledge of these allegations to come at once to Washington and secretly present what they had heard. There should be absolutely no publicity.

The Texas officials slipped into the nation's capital with complete anonymity. They met with Lee Rankin and other members of the staff and told what they knew. The information was that Lee Oswald was actually hired by the FBI; that he was assigned the undercover-agent number 179; that he was on the FBI payroll at two hundred dollars a month starting in September 1962 and that he was still on their payroll the day he was apprehended in the Texas Theatre after having gunned down Officer J. D. Tippit! The officials returned to Dallas after their visit on Friday, January 24. Their presence in Washington was unknown to the press or the public.

Meantime, a story broke over the weekend in *The New York Times*. The *Times* had got wind of part of the speculation that Oswald was an agent and point-blank asked the FBI if it was true. The FBI denied any possible connection with Oswald.

Then Harold Feldman's article in *The Nation* magazine hit the newsstands at the moment the Dallas officials were consulting with the Commission on Friday. No one could have known the consternation among the Texas officials and the President's Commission, but Mr. Feldman had laid down four pages of hard-to-answer questions in his article, "Oswald and the FBI," in the January 27, 1964, issue. Fortunately, the public did not know how serious the matter appeared to be at the moment. Although the speculations in Feldman's article were enough to arouse a good deal of public interest, the theories had no official basis and they did not create the panic they might have if it had been known that even the Attorney General of Texas was afraid that some of them might have a basis in fact. The Commission itself had no grounds at the moment for rejecting or accepting. Members simply knew that the whole business was a most delicate and sensitive matter involving the nation's faith in its own institutions and one of the most respected federal agencies. Harold Feldman set forth a formidable sequence of circumstantial evidence pointing to the same things the Attorney General and Mr. Wade had brought up in telephone conversations with Lee Rankin. His speculations were elaborate.

Feldman began his hypothesis with the observation that the day after the assassination the Dallas chief of police had stated on television that the FBI had interviewed Oswald about a week earlier and had failed to inform the Dallas authorities of the fact. If this was true—that the FBI had interviewed Oswald a week before the shooting—why would they have failed to let the agencies in charge of the President's security know that this dangerous man was near Dallas?

"In Washington the FBI denied they had interrogated Oswald recently," Feldman said.

Oswald had taken a mysterious trip to Mexico City in October and had returned on the third of that month. Feldman pointed out that William M. Kline, chief of the U. S. Customs Bureau investigative services in Laredo, Texas, stated on November 25 that Oswald's movements when he went to Mexico were watched at the request of a "federal agency at Washington." It was very apparent that the FBI knew a good deal about this former defector Lee Harvey Oswald. How could they be keeping such close tabs on him and still overlook the fact that he was working in the Texas School Book Depository Building, directly on the route of the President's motorcade?

Feldman went on to gather more of the published material that made the circumstances curious. He cited an article by one Joe Golden in the Philadelphia *Inquirer* of December 8, 1963, two weeks after Kennedy's death, that flatly stated:

"The FBI attempt to recruit Oswald as an informant, an informed law enforcement official said, was made in September, just after he had moved to Dallas from New Orleans.

"Oswald's mother said an 'agent named Hosty' came to the Irving house and talked to the young man at length in his car.

"An FBI agent named Joseph Hosty handles investigations of subversives for the Dallas field office.

"The source said he did not know if the FBI succeeded in hiring Oswald; and the federal agency would not discuss the matter."

In addition to the above article by reporter Golden, Harold Feldman cited another important story. It was an article written by Lonnie Hudkins in the Houston *Post* on January 1, 1964, "Oswald Rumored as Informant for U.S." There was indeed an agent Hosty in Dallas, and Hudkins alleged that Oswald knew him. William Alexander, an assistant prosecutor to Henry Wade, apparently affirmed this, because he stated that during the interrogation of Oswald which he attended after the assassination it had been brought out that in his address book Oswald had both the phone number of Hosty's office and the license number of his car. Why? In Hudkins' article he quoted Wade as commenting on the possibility of Oswald's connection with the FBI, "It may be true, but I don't think it will ever be made public."

Seeming to justify this point of view, Feldman pointed out that the FBI had asked witnesses not to talk to reporters about evidence they might have given that agency. In many cases witnesses later contacted by reporters did refuse to talk and, when asked why, were reputed to have said, "Well, the FBI told me to keep my mouth shut."

Shortly after the assassination a story gained currency in Dallas that Oswald had lived well for a man who couldn't hold a job. He was reputed to have had money to spend on projects his salary couldn't justify. Then a story was printed that the Western Union office had received small but regular money orders from an unrevealed source for Lee Oswald. Could this be the FBI's way of paying him off for his reputed "undercover" work? Reporters who tried to run this down collided with a brick wall. Western Union refused to make any of its records public—this could be done only by an order from Washington. Again, had the FBI told Western Union to bottle up the truth? Whom were they trying to protect if not themselves?

Despite the fact the FBI allegedly told witnesses to clam up and that they refused information to reporters, major news leaks were deliberately let out not by the FBI but by even higher federal authorities. It was as if they first opened the hatch to let out a puff of smoke and then suddenly slapped it down again. Two examples of this Feldman found tantalizing. It was said that Marina Oswald knew her husband kept a rifle in the Paine garage and that she noted it was missing the morning of the assassination. Then this was denied. Next the story was allowed to leak out that Marina knew Oswald had taken a "pot shot" at Major General Edwin A. Walker; the FBI was even said to have a document in Oswald's own handwriting admitting it. This information could only have come from some official source, but when reporters asked to see the document the matter was quickly cloaked in mystery and the FBI wasn't talking.

On the subject of the Walker shooting and the Kennedy assassination, had the authorities wanted to give the impression that the same gun was used in both cases? Feldman pointed out in this instance what would seem to be another inconsistency. The "experts" had said at the time the general was shot at that the bullet dug out of the wall had been fired from a .30-06 rifle. The rifle found in the Texas School Book Depository, after considerable contradiction, was reputed to be a 6.5 millimeter gun, equivalent to about .270 caliber. Someone had his "facts" mixed up or again there was a deliberate effort to confound the truth.

Going deeper into the subject of Oswald's income and the free-wheeling way he seemed to spend money, he was supposed to have earned eighty rubles a month while he was in Russia. According to authorities, this would be a bare subsistence level, and still he was able to raise the cash to come back to America in 1962 with a wife and child. A single passage from Moscow would be expensive enough; somehow he managed to pay the boat fare for three and then fly from New York back to Fort Worth.

And what about the $1,500 he was reputed to have put aside during his enlistment in the Marine Corps? It was this money he was supposed to have used to pay for his trip to Helsinki when he defected to the Communists. This was, to be sure, a substantial savings for an ordinary soldier, and one shouldn't overlook the possibility that he was subsidized in some way by the Soviets, or perhaps by the CIA and the FBI working together to plant an observer in Russia. There had been a fair number of American GIs who had "defected" to Russia. Likewise, some Russian defectors to the United States were suspected of posing as defectors in order to gain inside positions in this country. Turn about is fair play, and it would be hard to devise a more logical way to put a man behind the Iron Curtain.

Feldman pointed out that Oswald paid Miss Pauline Bates, a public stenographer, to type parts of a manuscript he was writing about his experiences in the Soviet Union. This was money he could ill afford to spend. He "hinted he had gone to the Soviet as a U.S. Secret Agent." Furthermore, he was alleged to have told her, "When the State Department granted my visa, they stipulated they could not stand behind me in any way," which could imply that they knew he was taking a desperate chance acting as an agent and would have to repudiate him if he was caught.

His activities in the Fair Play for Cuba Committee must have been costly. He was rumored to have rented at his own expense an office for thirty dollars a month; he arranged to have leaflets printed and recruited helpers to distribute them; and when he was arrested he promptly came up with payment of his fine. These activities did not sound like the work of a "loner."

The police were said to have found $150 in his room when he was arrested for the shooting of Officer Tippit. Some time previously he had purchased a rifle with a telescopic sight and a revolver and had supposedly spent other money on rifle-range practice and bore sighting of the weapon. Practice rifle shooting is not inexpensive.

And where did he get the money for a quick trip to Mexico City? His meanderings around the world sounded more like the journeys of a well-heeled globetrotter than the restricted life of a sometimes employed laborer without a skill. It was said that if he had obtained a visa from the Cuban Embassy in Mexico City he intended to junket over to Havana and then perhaps on to Moscow once more for a little sight-seeing. This was almost too much to believe. *Pravda* had recently explained it by stating that without a doubt Oswald had been an American spy from the beginning. Again there was the possibility he could have been a CIA agent, perhaps trained by the FBI, and upon returning to the USA was used to penetrate such groups as the Fair Play for Cuba Committee. With his background as a defector, he could have made a perfect counteragent to spy on Castro's supporters.

Feldman recalled that on November 30 the Dallas *Times Herald* had carried this Associated Press dispatch—again the allegation that Oswald had received money via Western Union: "Someone telegraphed small amounts of money to Lee Harvey Oswald for several months before the assassination of President Kennedy, it was reported today. The unidentified sender telegraphed Oswald $10 to $20 at a time."

The writer of "Oswald and the FBI," after examining some of the threads in the web, stated what every American would agree to: "The Warren Commission should, if possible, tell us how President Kennedy was killed, who killed him, and why. But beyond that it must tell us if the FBI or any other government intelligence agency was in any way connected with the alleged assassin, Lee Harvey Oswald." The same day on which the Commission was confronted with this challenge by Attorney General Carr, Feldman summed up the impressions of most laymen with the observation, "At this moment the possibility of such associations in the young man's life is intolerably a subject for speculation."

Discussions among members of the Commission on Monday, January 27, indicated they couldn't agree more—but just how to go about uncovering the facts was not an easy matter.

Because of the background of Mr. Allen Dulles, other members turned to him for suggestions on how best to handle this touchy matter. What were they to do with a story like this?

"This is a terribly hard thing to disprove," he told the others.

"Let's take a specific case," Representative Hale Boggs suggested. "That fellow Powers was one of your men."

"Oh yes, but he was not an agent. He was an employee."

"There was no problem in proving he was employed by the CIA?"

"No, we had a signed contract."

In the case of the U-2 incident and Powers, he was not an undercover agent, as Mr. Dulles pointed out. The problem was far more difficult with a true undercover agent, where there is nothing in writing.

Mr. Boggs observed with some uneasiness, "What you do is to make out a problem, if this be true—make our problem utterly impossible, because you say this rumor can't be dissipated under any circumstance."

These observations by Allen Dulles pinpointed the difficulty the

Commission would face in dealing not only with the possibility that Oswald might be an FBI agent but also with all the myriad rumors that the imaginations of thousands of writers would create in the next thousand years. They dramatized the complexity of the Commission's charge. A free society must have some secret agencies to defend itself against the deception of its potential enemies. On the other hand, secrecy is the enemy of truth, and the Commission was appointed by the President of the United States to find out *all* the circumstances surrounding the assassination of President Kennedy.

Mr. Rankin, chief counsel for the Commission, explained why Dallas' District Attorney Wade was so troubled. Wade had told Rankin about his wartime experiences as a former FBI man.

"He did say he had considerable experience with the FBI and knew their practices, that he handled as much as $2,000 a month during the war period in which he paid off informers and undercover agents in South America, and he knew that it wasn't revealed on any records he ever handled who he was paying it to and he never got any receipts, and it wasn't the practice to get receipts; that he would have a list of numbers in his office—that was one of the most closely guarded records that he had—and he would put down the amount he paid off.

"He was frank, however, about stating that he didn't know whether that practice continued; he didn't know how they were doing it; that was a long time ago and how the FBI would handle any such transaction now, he didn't know.

"He thought that the postal box was an ideal way to handle such transactions and was a way he had used at various times in the past too.

"He didn't indicate that he was sure this was the case at all. He just indicated that it was a possibility, and some of the things that happened he thought were curious."

In mentioning the use of postal boxes, Wade was thinking of the habit Oswald had of using these blind addresses wherever he went—again, why?

The dilemma of the Commission was how to go about checking the allegation that the FBI was involved in this matter. For more than thirty years the FBI had been one of the most highly respected agencies of the United States Government. Not that the members of the Commission would be awed by the prestige of the bureau or of its almost legendary director, J. Edgar Hoover, but certainly it would not be justified in plunging into the matter in some irresponsible manner that might jeopardize the effectiveness of an important agency's future operations.

The President's order creating the Commission implicitly authorized it to look into the security policies of the Secret Service. Every intelligence agency of the Government also had to be scrutinized. The Commission would have to devise an approach that was independent of all these agencies, and yet obviously the President's Commission could not create a "scientific crime bureau" of its own just for the purpose of this inquiry. They would need trained men from the CIA, the Secret Service, local police and certainly the FBI. They would need fingerprint experts, ballistics experts, handwriting analysts and dozens of other professional helpers. Thus the matter of determining at the outset how to handle the rumor that Oswald was connected with the FBI was a test of the ability of the Commission to execute its mission. Its members approached this challenge carefully. Senator Russell asked chief counsel Lee Rankin, "What steps, if any, have we taken to clear up this matter, Mr. Rankin, if it can be cleared up, to determine whether there is anything to this or not?"

Mr. Rankin: "Well, we have discussed various possibilities—that is, the Chief Justice and myself have—and I want to tell you about them, and I think you will have to instruct us what you want us to do.

"We thought, first, about approaching the Department with a request that the Attorney General inform us as to the situation, not only as to what he would say about whether Oswald was or was not an undercover agent, but also with the supporting data that the Commission could rely upon.

"I suggested the possibility for the Commission to consider that I should go over and see Edgar Hoover myself and tell him this problem and that he should have as much interest as the Commission in trying to put an end to any such speculations, not only by his statement, which I would be frank to tell him I would think would not be sufficient, but also if it was possible to demonstrate by whatever records and materials they have that it just couldn't be true, and see if we couldn't get his cooperation to present that with the understanding that the Commission—and stated understanding, at the time —the Commission would have to feel free to make such other investigation and take testimony if it found it necessary, in order to satisfy the American people that this question of an undercover agent was out of the picture."

Representative Boggs asked, "What other alternatives are there?"

Mr. Rankin replied, "Well, the other alternative would be to examine Hudkins, the reporter. Also to examine Hosty, the FBI agent who was working in that area, and to examine the Special Agent in charge of the area, and to examine Mr. Hoover, under oath, right up the line.

"We do have a dirty rumor that is very bad for the Commission, the problem, and it is very damaging to the agencies that are involved in it and it must be wiped out insofar as it is possible to do so by this Commission.

"So it seemed to me in light of the way I would treat it, if I were in their position, would be to have someone approach me, tell me the problem and see what I frankly could do to clear my skirts, if there was a way to do it, and as long as the Commission didn't agree not to go further, if they felt that would not satisfy them, I don't see how the Commission would be prejudiced."

Chairman Warren: "Well, Lee and I both agreed that we shouldn't leave this thing in this present posture, that we should go ahead and try to clear the matter up as best we can.

"Now, my own suggestion was to Lee that we find out first from these people as far as we can if there is any substance to it or whether it is just plain rumor.

"It may be that Hudkins would claim privilege. If he did, I thought that after we tried to get him to see that it was in the interest of his country to state the facts that we might go to the publisher of his paper and see if we couldn't get—enlist him to have this man tell us where he got his information.

"Lee, on the other hand, felt it would be the better part of cooperation to go over and see Mr. Hoover and tell him frankly what the rumor was, state that it is pure rumor—we haven't evaluated the facts—but ask him, first, if it is true, and secondly if he can supply us with information to establish that these facts are not true, and they are inconsistent with what would be the way of operation of their bureau."

Mr. McCloy observed, "If we got a statement from the Department that the Attorney General and perhaps from Mr. Hoover, or from Mr. Hoover himself, which said, 'I am telling you that this man was not in any way employed by the FBI,' or in the case of John McCloy or the CIA, I think that probably stops us, unless we run into something . . ."

Mr. Rankin: "Allen, how would you feel about it, if you were head of the CIA now, and the same claim was made and this Commission was worried about the claim being believed by the public, and they would ask you, would you want the Commission to come to you directly?"

Mr. Dulles: "Oh, yes, certainly I would."

Mr. Rankin: "Or would you want us to go out and examine witnesses first?"

Mr. Dulles: "I think I would want you to come so I could give you leads as to how you could examine witnesses if you wanted to."

Mr. Rankin: "If you had us out examining witnesses about whether you had the man in your employ, would you feel that we were not very fair to you?"

Mr. Dulles: "No. I don't think I would."

Mr. Rankin: "That wouldn't bother you."

Mr. Dulles: "No."

Senator Russell: "There is no man in the employ of the Federal Government who stands higher in the opinion of the American people than J. Edgar Hoover."

Mr. Dulles: "That is right."

Senator Russell: "Of course, we can get an affidavit from Mr. Hoover and put it in this record and go on and act on that, but if we didn't go any further than that, and we don't pursue it down to Hudkins or whoever it is, there still would be thousands of doubting Thomases who would believe this man was an FBI agent and you just didn't try to clear it up and you just took Hoover's word.

"Personally, I would believe J. Edgar Hoover. I have a great deal of confidence in him."

Mr. Dulles: "I do, too."

Senator Russell: "But the other people—I would believe, a simple statement as Holy Writ, this one statement without being under oath, but you can't try cases that way, and you can't base the conclusions of this Commission on that kind of material."

Senator Cooper: "I would like to have your idea about what I suggested."

Mr. McCloy: "State it again."

Senator Cooper: "We know these people have been here, so this speculation or rumor is somewhat official—we will not say it has their approval, but they don't disapprove it."

Mr. McCloy: "They have taken cognizance of it."

Senator Cooper: "That being true, since we are under a duty to see what Hudkins says about it, where he got that information, my suggestion was we do that but apprise Mr. Hoover about the facts—where this information comes from, that we have to inquire into it, that we will inquire into it, and then later talk to him further about it and see if there are any facts which he ought to know about, and it would be a matter of justice to him instead of having him disprove it from the beginning."

Mr. McCloy: "What is your objection, John, to going to Hoover or the Department of Justice, or the CIA, John McCone, or Under Secretary of Defense—he has an intelligence unit too—and ask them if they can give us any information which would prove or disprove this rumor?"

Senator Cooper: "I haven't got any objection to it, but even if—if we are dealing with the FBI now—if Mr. Hoover makes his statement, I think still by reason of the fact you have heard these people and they have said that Hudkins does have some information about the truth of it, whether it is so or not, you still are under a duty to examine them."

Chairman Warren: "We must go into this thing from both ends, from the end of the rumormongers and from the end of the FBI, and if we come into a *cul de sac*—well, there we are, but we can report on it.

"Now that is the way it would appeal to me. These are things where people can reasonably disagree. Whatever you want to do I am willing to approach it in that manner."

Mr. Rankin: "Would it be acceptable to go ahead and find out what we could about these—"

Mr. McCloy: "Hudkins' sources."

Mr. Rankin: "Then if he [J. Edgar Hoover] reacts and says, 'I want to show you that it couldn't be,' or something like that, beforehand, what about that kind of an approach?"

Chairman Warren: "Well, Lee, I wouldn't be in favor of going to any agency and saying, 'We would like to do this.' I think we ought to know what we are going to do, and do it, and take our chances one way or the other.

"I don't believe we should apologize or make it look that we are in any way reticent about making any investigation that comes to the Commission."

Mr. Rankin: "I don't think the country is going to be satisfied with the mere statement from, not to use Mr. Hoover's name, but just examine about any intelligence agency that Oswald wasn't hired, in light of this kind of an accusation, a rumor.

"I think that the country is going to expect this Commission to try to find out the facts as to how those things are handled to such an extent that this Commission can fairly say, 'In our opinion, he was or was not an employee of any intelligence agency of the United States.' "

It was the consensus of all seven men that the only way to proceed was to conduct extensive and thorough hearings of as many witnesses as was necessary to exhaust not just this rumor but dozens of other rumors. Where doubts were cast on any United States agency, independent experts would be hired and the investigation conducted in such a way as to avoid reliance on a questioned authority. No matter what the cost in time or money, every facet of the events in Dallas had to be explored. The Commission drew up an exhaustive list of witnesses and collected for analysis all pertinent books and magazines and newspaper articles. The staff compiled a directory of names of all persons said to have had any part in the matter. Then began months of hearings, hours of taking sworn testimony, which led from one skein of facts to another. Seldom has a crime appeared to be more complicated and mysterious. Never has a crime been so thoroughly investigated. From that investigation comes this biography of an assassin.

MARINA IN WASHINGTON

THE FIRST WITNESS to come before the Presidential Commission investigating President Kennedy's assassination was Marina Prusakova Oswald. In the weeks between the assassination and her appearance in Washington, the world had come to know some of the general facts of her life. She was twenty-two years old, having been born July 17, 1941, in Severo-Divinsk, Russia; her mother had died in Leningrad when she was sixteen; she had been trained as a pharmacist and had worked in that profession prior to marrying Lee Oswald; and, most important—from the public standpoint—she seemed like a very decent person. If Lee Oswald's appearance and manner were antagonistic to the television audience, public impressions of Marina were just the opposite. My reaction was that she was awed, quiet-spoken and humble. It struck me that she looked a little frightened by the events that had engulfed her. Furthermore, unlike her outspoken mother-in-law, Marguerite Oswald, she seemed to realize that the evidence against her husband Lee was overwhelming. She shared the sad feelings the American people had for another gracious young widow, Jacqueline Kennedy, and, as she sat those long hours in the witness chair, there was something to be pitied in her plight. Marina Oswald volunteered to come before the investigating Commission and tell all she knew about the events leading up to the President's assassination. There was no need to issue a subpoena. She would come voluntarily and would try to be as helpful as she could.

Marina Oswald took the stand on Monday, February 3, 1964. As her narrative of the tragic story began to unravel I noted that she was not overly dressed or made up, yet her personal appearance had been Americanized when I compared the young woman sitting an arm's length from me with the photographs of her I had seen before.

Chairman Warren: "Well, Mrs. Oswald, did you have a good trip here?

"The Commission will come to order, and at this time I will make a short statement for the purpose of the meeting. A copy of this statement has been given to counsel for Mrs. Oswald, but for the record I should like to read it.

"On November 29, 1963, President Lyndon B. Johnson issued Executive Order No. 11130 appointing a Commission 'to ascertain, evaluate and report upon the facts relating to the assassination of the late President John F. Kennedy and the subsequent violent death of the man charged with the assassination.'

"On December 13, 1963, Congress adopted Joint Resolution S.J. 137, which authorizes the Commission, or any member of the Commission or any agent or agency designated by the Commission for such purpose, to administer oaths and affirmations, examine witnesses and receive evidence.

"The purpose of this hearing is to take the testimony of Mrs. Marina Oswald, the widow of Lee Harvey Oswald, who, prior to his death, was charged with the assassination of President Kennedy. Since the Commission is inquiring fully into the background of Lee Harvey Oswald and those associated with him, it is the intention of the Commission to ask Mrs. Marina Oswald questions concerning Lee Harvey Oswald and any and all matters relating to the assassination.

"Mrs. Marina Oswald has been furnished with a copy of this statement and a copy of the rules adopted by the Commission for the taking of testimony or the production of evidence.

"Mrs. Oswald, do you have an attorney, a lawyer?"

Mrs. Oswald: "Yes."

Chairman Warren: "And your lawyer is Mr. Thorne?"

Mrs. Oswald: "Yes."

The chairman administered the oath to the witness, Mrs. Oswald, through the interpreter.

Chairman Warren: "Now, Mr. Thorne, and Mrs. Oswald, I want to say to you that we want to see that Mrs. Oswald's rights are protected in every manner, and you are entitled to converse with her at any time that you desire. You are entitled to give her any advice that you want, either openly or in private; if you feel that her rights are not being protected you are entitled to object to the Commission and have a ruling upon it, and at the conclusion of her testimony if you

27

have any questions that you would like to ask her in verification of what she has said, you may feel free to ask them.

"After her testimony has been completed, a copy will be furnished to you so that if there are any errors, corrections or omissions you may call it to our attention. Is that satisfactory to you?"

Mr. Thorne: "Very satisfactory, Mr. Chairman."

Mrs. Oswald: "Thank you."

During most of Marina's original week-long testimony I sat next to her lawyer, John Thorne, who, like others in the drama, had been drawn into the web of events by pure circumstance. I had previously asked Lee Rankin, our counsel, about Mr. Thorne's reputation as a lawyer, and the response had been favorable. I noted his close attention to the questions asked and the responses given by Marina. My feeling was that this rather quiet and apparently typical Texas lawyer was cooperating fully with the Commission.

Chairman Warren: "The questions will be asked of you by Mr. J. Lee Rankin, who is the General Counsel of the Commission.

"I think now we are ready to proceed, are we not, Mr. Rankin?"

Mr. Rankin: "Mrs. Oswald, you be at your ease, and the interpreter will tell you what I ask and you take your time about your answers.

"Will you state your name, please?"

Mrs. Oswald: "Marina. My name is Marina Nikolaevna Oswald. My maiden name was Prusakova."

"Where do you live, Mrs. Oswald?"

"At the present time I live in Dallas."

"And where in Dallas?"

"Mr. Thorne knows my address."

Mr. Thorne: "11125 Ferrar Street, Dallas, Dallas County, Texas."

Mr. Rankin: "Do you live with friends there?"

"I live with Mr. Jim Martin and his family."

"Mrs. Oswald, do you have a family?"

"I have two children, two girls. June will be two years old in February, and Rachel is three months old."

"Are you the widow of the late Lee Harvey Oswald?"

"Yes."

"Since your husband's death and even back to the time of the assassination of President Kennedy, you have had a number of interviews with people from the Secret Service and the FBI, have you not?"

"Yes, I did."

"We have a record of more than forty-six such interviews, and I assume you cannot remember the exact number or all that was said in those interviews, is that true?"

"I don't know how many there were."

"As far as you can recall now, do you know of anything that is not true in those interviews that you would like to correct or add to?"

"Yes, I would like to correct some things because not everything was true."

"Will you tell us—"

"It is not just that it wasn't true, but not quite exact."

"Do you recall some of the information that you gave in those interviews that was incorrect that you would like to correct now? Will you tell us that?"

"At the present time, I can't remember any specific instance, but perhaps in the course of your questioning if it comes up I will say so."

"Do you recall the date that you arrived in the United States with your husband, Lee Harvey Oswald?"

"On the thirteenth of June 1962."

"How did you come to this country?"

"From Moscow via Poland, Germany and Holland, we came to Amsterdam by train. And from Amsterdam to New York by ship and New York to Dallas by air."

"Do you recall the name of the ship on which you came?"

"I think it was the S.S. *Rotterdam* but I am not sure." [Commission research identified it as the S.S. *Maasdam*.]

"How long did you stay in New York at that time?"

"We stayed that evening and the next twenty-four hours in a hotel in New York, and then we left the following day by air."

"Do you recall the name of the hotel where you stayed?"

"I don't know the name of the hotel but it is in the Times Square area, not far from the publishing offices of *The New York Times*."

"What did you do during your stay in New York?"

"That evening we just walked around the city to take a look at it. In the morning I remained in the hotel while Lee left in order to arrange for tickets, and so forth."

"Did you visit anyone or have visitors at your hotel during that period?"

"We didn't have any visitors, but I remember that with Lee we visited some kind of an office, on official business—perhaps it had something to do with immigration or with the tickets. Lee spoke to them in English and I didn't understand it."

"Would that be a Travelers Aid Bureau or Red Cross?"

"I don't know."

"Do you know whether or not you or your husband received any financial assistance for the trip to Texas at that time?"

"I don't know exactly where Lee got the money, but he said that his brother Robert had given him the money. But the money for the trip from the Soviet Union to New York was given to us by the American Embassy in Moscow."

"Did you go to Dallas or Fort Worth at that time?"

"In Dallas we were met by the brother, Robert—he lived in Fort Worth—and he took us from Dallas to Fort Worth and we stopped at the house."

"Who else stayed at Robert's house at that time besides your family?"

"His family and no one else."

"What did his family consist of at that time?"

"He and his wife and two children, a boy and a girl."

"How long did you stay at Robert's?"

"About one to one and a half months—perhaps longer, but no longer than two months."

"Were your relations and your husband's with Robert pleasant at that time?"

"Yes, they were very good. His brother's relationship to us was very good."

"Would you briefly describe what you did during that time when you were at Robert's?"

"The first time we got there we were, of course, resting for about a week, and I was busy, of course, with my little girl, who was then very little. And in my free time, of course, I helped in the household."

"Did your husband do anything around the house or did he seek work right away?"

"For about a week he was merely talking and took a trip to the library. That is it."

"Then did he seek work in Fort Worth?"

"Yes."

"And when did he find his first job there?"

"While we were with Robert. It seems it was at the end of the second month that Lee found work. But at this time I don't remember the date exactly, but his mother, who lived in Fort Worth at that time, rented a room and she proposed that we spend some time with her, that we live with her for some time."

"Did you discuss with your husband this proposal of your mother-in-law to have you live with her?"

"Well, she made the proposal to my husband, not to me. Of course, I found out about it."

"Did you and he have any discussion about it after you found out about it?"

"Yes, of course."

"You recall that discussion?"

"No. I only remember the fact."

"Did he find work after you left Robert's then?"

"Yes."

"You did move to be with your mother-in-law, lived with her for a time?"

"Yes, about three weeks. And then after three weeks Lee did not want to live with her any more and he rented an apartment."

"Do you know the reason why he did not want to live there any more?"

"It seemed peculiar to me and I didn't want to believe it, but he did not love his mother—she was not quite a normal woman. Now I know this for sure."

"Did he tell you that at the time?"

"He talked about it, but since he spoke in English to his mother, I didn't understand it. There were quite a few scenes. When he would return from work he didn't want to talk to her. Perhaps she thought I was the reason for the fact that Lee did not want to talk to her. And, of course, for a mother this is painful, and I told him that he should be more attentive to his mother but he did not change. I think that one of the reasons for this was that she talked a great deal about how much she had done to enable Lee to return from Russia, and Lee felt that he had done most of . . . the greatest effort in that respect and didn't want to discuss it."

"Where did he find work at that time?"

"Of course, if I had been told now I would have remembered it because I have learned some English, but at that time I didn't know; but Lee told me that it wasn't far from Mercedes Street where we lived, and it was really common labor connected with some kind of metal work, something for buildings."

"Did he ever say whether he enjoyed that work?"

"He didn't like it."

"Do you recall how long he stayed at that job?"

"I don't know but it seemed to me that he worked there for about three or four months. Perhaps longer. Dates are one of my problems."

"Do you know whether he left that job voluntarily or was discharged?"

"He told me that he had been discharged but I don't know why."

"Did your husband work a full day at that time on this job?"

"Yes, sometimes he even worked on Saturdays."

"What did you do when he came home? Did he help you with housework?"

"Yes. He frequently went to a library. He read a great deal."

"Do you recall any of the books that he read at that time?"

"No. I only know that they were books more of a historical nature rather than fiction or literature."

"Did he go off by himself to read or how did he handle that?"

"He would bring a book from a library, sit in the living room and read. I was busy with housework, and that is the way it happened."

"Did you have differences between you about the time that he spent reading rather than devoting it to you or the other members of the family?"

"No. We did have quarrels about his relationship to his mother, the fact that he didn't want to change his relationship to his mother. I know that he read so much that when we lived in New Orleans he used to read sometimes all night long and in order not to disturb me he would be sitting in the bathroom for several hours reading."

"Did your quarrels start at that time when you were at Mercedes Street the first time?"

"Yes, we didn't have many quarrels."

"When you were at Mercedes Street did you have Robert visit you or did you visit him?"

"No, he came to us sometimes."

"Do you recall seeing any guns at Mercedes Street while you were there?"

"No."

"Did your mother-in-law come to see you at Mercedes Street?"

"Yes."

"Will you describe the relationship between your husband and your mother-in-law while he was at Mercedes Street?"

"She did not want us to move away to Mercedes Street, and Lee did not want to remain with her and did not even want her to visit us after that. Lee did not want her to know the address to which we were moving and Robert helped us in the move. I felt very sorry for her. Sometime after that she visited us while Lee was at work and I was quite surprised, wondering about how she found out our address. And then we had a quarrel because he said to me, 'Why did you open the door for her? I don't want her to come here any more.'"

"During this period did your husband spend much time with the baby, June?"

"Yes. He loved children very much."

"Were you still at Mercedes Street when he lost his job with the welding company?"

"Yes."

"Did he try to find another job in Fort Worth then?"

"Yes."

"Do you know how much he looked for jobs before he found one then?"

"He looked for work for some time but he could not find it, and then some Russian friends of ours helped him find some work in Dallas."

"How long was he out of work?"

"It seems to me it was about two weeks; hard to remember—perhaps that long."

"Where did he find work in Dallas? Do you remember the name?"

"I know it was some kind of a printing company which prepares photographs for newspapers."

"Was he working with the photographic department of that company?"

"Yes."

"Was he an apprentice in that work, trying to learn it?"

"Yes, at first he was an apprentice and later he worked."

"Do you know what his income was when he was working for the welding company?"

"I think it was about two hundred dollars a month—I don't know. I know it was a dollar and a quarter an hour."

"Did he work much overtime at that time?"

"Not too much, but sometimes he did work Saturdays."

"Do you recall how much he received as pay at the printing company?"

"A dollar forty an hour."

"How many hours did he work a week, do you recall?"

"He usually worked until five P.M. But sometimes he worked later and on Saturdays too."

"The ordinary work week at that time was the five-day week, then, and the Saturdays would be an overtime period?"

"Yes."

"When you moved to Dallas, where did you live the first time?"

"I did not move to Dallas together with Lee. Lee went to Dallas when he found the job, and I remained in Fort Worth and lived with Mrs. Hall."

"For how long a period did you live with Mrs. Hall?"

"I think that it was about a month and a half."

"During that month and a half what did your husband do?"

"He had a job, he was working. He would call me up over the telephone, but how he spent his time, I don't know."

"Do you know during that month and a half where he lived?"

"At first I know that he rented a room in the YMCA, but very shortly thereafter he rented an apartment. But where I don't know."

"During that month and a half did he come and see you and the baby?"

"Yes, two or three times he came to see us because he had no car. It was not very easy."

"Were these trips to see you on the weekends?"

"Yes."

"When he came did he also stay at the Halls'?"

"Yes."

"When you were staying at the Halls' did you pay them for your room and your meals?"

"No. No, she was very friendly toward us and she tried to help us."

"What did you and your husband do when he came to see you? Did he spend his time with you there in the home or did you go some place?"

"No, we didn't go anywhere."

"Did he do any reading there?"

"No. I remember that it was only a couple of times that he came for a weekend. Generally, he only came for a very short period of time. Because he would come together with our friends, and they could not stay very long."

"When he came during that period did he discuss what he had been doing in Dallas, his work and other things?"

"He liked his work very much."

"After this month and a half did he find a place for you all to live together?"

"Yes, but it wasn't a problem there to find a place, no problem there to find a place."

"Did you then move to a home in Dallas?"

"Yes, on Elsbeth, Elsbeth Street in Dallas."

"How did you move your things from Mrs. Hall's to the place on Elsbeth Street?"

"A friend who had a car helped us. I don't remember his name— Taylor, Gary Taylor."

Chairman Warren: "Suppose we take a recess now for about ten minutes to allow Mrs. Oswald to refresh herself."

All during the sessions of interrogation, which began daily at 9 A.M. and continued until late afternoon with an hour or so break for lunch, Marina held up well physically. Not until late Thursday morning, during her fourth successive day in the witness chair, did we on the Commission note any weariness. As the Commission recessed on this particular morning I vividly recall thinking of the world-wide consequences if Marina should collapse on the stand, followed by an ambulance ride in the full view of television cameras in the lobby downstairs. As she faltered a bit I could visualize the Communist propagandists building up the Commission's hearings as a "star chamber" operation. Fortunately, the Chairman was always solicitous of how she was holding up as question followed question hour after hour.

Mr. Rankin: "Did that require one or more trips to move your things from Fort Worth to Dallas when you went to Elsbeth Street?"

"One trip was enough."

"Did you observe any guns in your things when you moved?"

"No."

"What kind of place did you have at Elsbeth Street? Was it rooms or an apartment?"

"An apartment."

"How many rooms in the apartment?"

"One living room, a bedroom, a kitchen and the bathroom. It sounds very small for all of you but for us it was quite sufficient."

"Did you have a telephone there?"

"No."

"Do you recall what rent you paid?"

"It seems to me that it was sixty dollars, plus the utilities."

"That would be sixty dollars a month?"

"Yes, and electricity and gas, but the water was free. Sixty dollars a month including water."

"What about his reading habits there? Were they the same?"

"Yes, about the same."

"Can you tell us a little more fully about his reading? Did he spend several hours each evening in this reading?"

"Yes."

"Do you recall any of the books that he read at Elsbeth Street?"

"No. He had two books, two thick books on the history of the United States."

"Did your husband come home for a midday meal?"

"No."

36

"Did you go out in the evenings?"

"Yes."

"Where did you go?"

"Sometimes we went shopping to stores, and movies, though Lee really went to the movies himself. He wanted to take me but I did not understand English. Then on weekends we would go to a lake not far away or to a park or to a café for some ice cream."

"When you went to the lake or the park did you take food with you and have a picnic?"

"Yes."

"How did you get to the lake or the park, by bus or car or what means of transportation?"

"It was only ten minutes away, ten minutes' walking time from us."

"Were either you or your husband taking any schooling at that time?"

"Lee took English courses or typing courses."

"During what days of the week were these typing courses?"

"It was three days a week. I don't remember exactly what the days were. It seems to me it was one day at the beginning of the week and two days at the end of the week that he took these night courses."

"Would it help you to recall if I suggested they were Monday, Tuesday and Thursday?"

"It seems to me that is the way it was. I know it was on Monday."

"Do you recall what hours of the evening he was supposed to be at these classes?"

"It seems that it was from seven until nine."

"About what time would he get home from work?"

"About five to five-thirty."

"Then would you eat your evening meal?"

"Yes."

"How soon after that would he leave for the class?"

"When Lee took his courses he generally did not come home for dinner—usually he didn't."

"Did he practice his typewriting at home at all?"

"At home, no. But he had a book, a textbook on typing, when he was at home."

"How soon after the class was over did he come home ordinarily?"

"Nine o'clock."

"Did he tell you anything about friends that he met at these classes?"

"No."

"While you were at Elsbeth Street do you recall seeing any guns in your apartment?"

"No."

"When did you move to Neely Street from the Elsbeth Street apartment?"

"In January after the new year. I don't remember exactly."

"Do you remember why you moved from Elsbeth to Neely Street?"

"I liked it better on Neely Street. We had a porch there and that was more convenient for the child."

"Did you have any differences with your husband while you were at Neely Street?"

"No. Well, there was always some reasons for some quarrel between a husband and wife. Not everything is always smooth."

"I had in mind if there was any violence or any hitting of you. Did that occur at Neely Street?"

"No. That was on Elsbeth Street."

"Do you recall what brought that about?"

"Not quite. I am trying to remember. It seems to me that it was at that time that Lee began to talk about his wanting to return to Russia. I did not want that, and that is why we had quarrels."

"Did you have discussions between you about this idea of returning to Russia?"

"Yes. Lee wanted me to go to Russia. I told him that if he wanted me to go, then that meant that he didn't love me, and that in that case what was the idea of coming to the United States in the first place. Lee would say that it would be better for me if I went to Russia. I did not know why. I did not know what he had in mind. He said he loved me but that it would be better for me if I went to Russia, and what he had in mind I don't know."

"Do you know when he first started to talk about your going to Russia?"

"On Elsbeth Street."

"Do you remember any occasion which you thought caused him to start to talk that way?"

"No, I don't."

"Do you know why he started to hit you about that time?"

"Now I think that I know, although at that time I didn't. I think that he was very nervous and just this somehow relieved his tension."

"Did you observe sometime when you thought he changed?"

"I would say that immediately after coming to the United States Lee changed. I did not know him as such a man in Russia."

"Will you describe how you observed these changes and what they were as you saw them?"

"He helped me as before, but he became a little more of a recluse. He did not like my Russian friends and he tried to forbid me to have anything to do with them. He was very irritable, sometimes for a trifle, for a trifling reason."

"Did he tell you why he did not like your Russian friends?"

"I don't know why he didn't like them. I didn't understand. At least that which he said was completely unfounded. He simply said some stupid or foolish things."

"Will you tell us the stupid things that he said?"

"Well, he thought that they were fools for having left Russia, they were all traitors. I would tell him he was in the same position being an American in America but there were really no reasons but just irritation. He said that they all only like money, and everything is measured by money. It seems to me that perhaps he was envious of them in the sense they were more prosperous than he was. When I told him, when I would say that to him, he did not like to hear that.

"Perhaps I shouldn't say all these foolish things and I feel kind of uncomfortable to talk about the foolish things that happened or what he said foolish things.

"This is one of the reasons why I don't know really the reasons for these quarrels, because sometimes the quarrels were just trifles. It is just that Lee was very unrestrained and very explosive at that time."

"Mrs. Oswald, we will ask you to be very frank with us. It isn't for the purpose of embarrassing you or your husband that we ask you these things but it might help us to understand, and even if you will tell us the foolish and stupid things it may shed some light on the problem. You understand that?"

"I understand you are not asking these questions out of curiosity but for a reason."

"Did your husband indicate any particular Russian friends that he disliked more than others?"

"He liked de Mohrenschildt but he—because he was a strong person, but only de Mohrenschildt. He did not like Bouhe or Anna Meller."

"Did you ever tell him you liked these people?"

"Yes, I told him all the time that I liked these people and that is why he was angry at me and would tell me that I was just like they were. At one time I left him and went to my friends because he put me into—put me on the spot by saying, 'Well, if you like your friends so much, then go ahead and live with them,' and he left me no choice."

"When was this, Mrs. Oswald?"

"On Elsbeth Street."

"How long were you gone from him then?"

"One week."

"Did he ask you to return?"

"Yes. I took June and I went to Anna Meller, took a cab and went there. I spent several days with her. Lee didn't know where I was, but he called up and about two or three days after, I came to and we met at de Mohrenschildt's house and he asked me to return home. I, of course, did not want a divorce, but I told him it would be better to get a divorce rather than to continue living and quarreling this way. After all, this is only a burden on a man if two people live together and fight. I simply wanted to show him, too, that I am not a toy. That a woman is a little more complicated. That you cannot trifle with her."

"Did you say anything at that time about how he should treat you if you returned?"

"Yes. I told him if he did not change his character, then it would become impossible to continue living with him. Because if there should be such quarrels continuously, that would be crippling for the children."

"What did he say to that?"

"Then he said that it would be—it was very hard for him. That he could not change. That I must accept him such as he was. And he asked me to come back home with him right on that day, but he left feeling bad because I did not go and remained with my friend."

"What did you say about accepting him as he was?"

"I told him I was not going to. Of course, such as he was for me he was good, but I wanted simply for the sake of the family that he would correct his character. It isn't that I didn't mean to say he was good for me. I meant to say that I could stand him, but for the sake of the children I wanted him to improve his behavior."

"Then did he get in touch with you again?"

"At that time there was very little room at Anna Meller's and it was very uncomfortable, and I left and went to Katya Ford, whose husband at that time happened to be out of town on business. I spent several days with Katya Ford, but then when her husband returned I did not want to remain with her. And it was on a Sunday morning then when I moved over to Anna Ray. Lee called me and said he wanted to see me, that he had come by bus and he wanted to see me, and he came that evening and he cried and said that he wanted me to return home because if I did not return he did not want to continue living. He said he didn't know how to love me in any other way and that he will try to change."

"While you were at Mrs. Ford's did she go to the hospital?"

"No. I think that you are confused. This was Mrs. Hall in Fort Worth. She was ill and went to the hospital. It is not very interesting to hear all that. Somewhat boring."

"Do you recall the manner in which Lee brought up the idea of your going to Russia alone?"

"Quite simply he said it was very hard for him here. That he could not have a steady job. It would be better for me because I could work in Russia. That was all."

"Did you understand when he suggested it that he proposed that you go and he stay?"

"Yes. Now I think I know why—he had in mind to start his foolish activity which could harm me—but, of course, at that time he didn't tell me the reason. It is only now that I understand it. At that time when I would ask him he would get angry because he couldn't tell me."

"What would you say to him at that time?"

"I told him at that time that I am agreeable to going if he could not live with me. But he kept on repeating that he wanted to live with me but that it would be better for me, but when I wanted to know the reason he would not tell me."

"Is there something that you have learned since that caused you to believe that this suggestion was related to trying to provide for you or to be sure that you wouldn't be hurt by what he was going to do?"

"At that time I didn't know this. I only saw that he was in such a state that he was struggling and perhaps did not understand himself. I thought that I was the reason for that."

"Did he have a job then?"

"Yes."

"Did you feel that you were getting along on what he was earning?"

"Of course."

"Were you urging him to earn more so that he could provide more for the family?"

"No. We had enough."

"You were not complaining about the way you were living?"

"No. I think that my friends had thought, and it was also written in the newspapers that we lived poorly because for Americans two hundred dollars appears to be very little. But I have never lived in any very luxurious way and, therefore, for me this was quite sufficient. Some of the others would say, 'Well here, you don't have a car or don't have this or that.' But for me it was sufficient. Sometimes Lee would tell me I was just like my friends, that I wanted to have that which they had. That I preferred them to him because they give me more, but that is not true."

"Did you understand when he suggested you return to Russia that he was proposing to break up your marriage?"

"I told him that I would go to Russia if he would give me a divorce, but he did not want to give me a divorce."

"Did he say why?"

"He said that if he were to give me a divorce that that would break everything between us, which he didn't want. That he wanted to keep me as his wife, but I told him that if he wants to remain in the United States I want to be free in Russia."

"During this period did he appear to be more excited and nervous?"

42

"Not particularly, but the later time he was more excited and more nervous but it was quite a contrast between the way he was in Russia."

"By the later time that you just referred to, what do you mean? Can you give us some approximate date?"

"When we went to Neely Street."

Chairman Warren: "I think this is a good time to take our luncheon recess now. So we will adjourn until two o'clock."

Mrs. Oswald: "Thank you."

Whereupon, at 12:30 P.M., the President's Commission recessed to reconvene at 2:00 P.M. the same day.

CHAPTER 3

ROMANCE IN MINSK

BEHIND THE EVENTS which Marina narrated calmly the first morning she testified was more than her casual manner would indicate. It is one thing to talk about quarrels and domestic differences just as passing incidents, but it is another thing to know all the facts.

In the first place, the quarrels had begun in earnest long before their move from Fort Worth to Elsbeth Street. When asked about her stay with Mrs. Hall, she had replied, "It is not very interesting to hear all that. Somewhat boring." The truth is that she and Lee had had violent differences for a long time prior to that, and some differences began in Russia. The seeds of trouble were in the circumstances of the marriage itself and may have had much to do with Lee's decision to return to America. There was a lot Marina did not know about Lee, and in turn there was a good deal about Marina that he had underestimated in the character of this Russian girl. If it puzzled her that Lee was so irritable and unstable, she did not have the advantage of knowing some of his actions and thoughts prior to the time she met him in Minsk.

Among the documents the Dallas police found in Lee's room subsequent to his shooting of Officer Tippit was a manuscript in English entitled "Historic Diary." Marina could not read English. It would have been a shock to her had she known the facts he had confided to this journal. One might question the authenticity of things he told about his working conditions, pay and relationships with the Russian Government in this account, but the personal incidents ring too true to be discredited.

Members of the Commission had been furnished photostatic copies of this document by the FBI. Those who had the patience to decipher the almost illiterate jottings of Lee Harvey Oswald began to see a pattern of circumstances that had a significant bearing on the case.

44

The original entries are full of grammatical errors and misspellings. In order to make clear the atmosphere in which this marriage between an American defector and a Russian girl came about, the diary has been edited. Lee Oswald's words tell their own stark story.

January 7, 1960

I leave Moscow by train for Minsk, Belorussia. My hotel bill was 2200 rubles and the train ticket to Minsk 150 rubles so I have a lot of money & hope. I wrote my brother and mother letters in which I said, "I do not wish to ever contact you again." I am beginning a new life and I don't want *any part* of the old.

January 8

I meet the city mayor, Comrade Shrapof, who welcomes me to Minsk. Promises a rent-free apartment, and warns me about "uncultured persons" who sometimes insult foreigners. My interpreter: Roman Detkof, head professor, Technical Institute, next door.

January 13

I visit Minsk radio factory where I shall work. There I meet Argentinian immigrant, Alexander Zeger. Born a Polish Jew. Immigrated to Argentina in 1938 and back to Polish homeland (now part of Belorussia) in 1955. Speaks English with American accent; he worked for American company in Argentina. He is head of department; a qualified engineer; is in late 40s, mild mannered, likeable. He seems to want to tell me something. I show him my temporary documents, and say soon I shall have Russ citizenship.

I work as "checker," metal worker, pay 700 rubles a month. Work very easy. I am learning Russian quickly now. Everyone is very friendly and kind. I meet many young Russian workers my own age; they have varied personalities and wish to know about me; even offer to hold a mass meeting so I can speak. I refuse politely. At night I take Rosa to the theatre, movie or opera almost every day. I'm living big and am very satisfied. I receive a check from the Red Cross every 5th of the month "to help." My check is 700 rubles. Therefore every month I make 1400 rubles, about the same as the director of the factory! Zeger observes me during this time. I don't like: picture of Lenin which watches from its place of honor; and physical training at 11:00 to 11:10 each morning (compulsory) for all. (Shades of H. G. Wells!!)

March 10

I receive a small flat, one-room kitchenette near the factory (8 minutes walk) with splendid view from 2 balconies of the river. Almost rent free (60 rubles a month). It is a Russian dream.

March 17–April 31

Work. I have lost contact with Rosa after my house moving. I meet Pavil Golovachev—my new friend and very intelligent; an expert radio technician. His father is General Golovachev, Commander of Northwestern Siberia—twice hero of USSR in World War II.

May 1

May Day came as my first holiday; all factories closed after spectacular military parade. Workers parade past reviewing stand, waving flags and pictures of Mr. Kruschev. I follow the American custom of taking a holiday by sleeping in the morning. At night I visit with Zeger's daughters, at a party thrown by them. About 40 come, many of Argentine origin. We dance and play around and drink until 2 AM, when party breaks up. Leonara, oldest daughter, 26, formerly married but now divorced. A talented singer. Anita Zeger, 20, very gay, but not so attractive. But we hit it off. Her boyfriend, Alfred, is a Hungarian chap, silent and brooding, not at all like Anita.

Zeger advises me to go back to USA. It's the first voice of opposition I have heard. I respect Zeger, he has seen the world. He says many things and relates many things I do not know about the USSR. I begin to feel uneasy inside, its true!

June–July

Summer months of green beauty. Pine forest very deep. I enjoy many Sundays in the environs of Minsk with the Zegers who have a car, "Moskvich" Alfred always goes along with Anita. Leonara seems to have no permanent boyfriend, but many admirers. She has a beautiful Spanish figure with long black hair, like Anita. I never pay much attention to her; she's too old for me. She seems to dislike my lack of attention for some reason. She is high strung.

I have become habituated to a small cafe where I dine in the evening. The food is generally poor and always exactly the same menu in any cafe at any point in the city. The food is cheap, and I don't really care about quality after three years in the U.S.M.C.

August–September

As my Russian improves I become increasingly conscious of just what sort of a society I live in. Mass gymnastics, compulsory, afterwork meetings, usually political information meetings. Compulsory attendance at lectures, and the sending of the entire shop collective (except me) to pick potatoes on a Sunday at a state collective farm. A "patriotic duty" to bring in the harvest. The opinions of the workers (unvoiced) are that its a great pain in the neck. They don't seem to be especially enthusiastic about any of the "collective" duties. A natural feeling. I am increasingly aware of the presence in all things of the shop party secretary. Fat, forty-ish, and jovial on the outside, he is a no-nonsense "Party" regular.

October

The coming of fall—my dread of a new Russian winter is mellowed in the splendid golds and reds of fall in Belorussia. Plums, peaches, apricots and cherries abound for these last fall weeks. I am a healthy brown color, and stuffed with fresh fruit. (At other times of the year unobtainable.)

October 18

My 21st birthday sees Rosa, Pavil, and Ella at a small party at my place. Ella is a very attractive Russian Jew I have been going walking with lately. Works at the radio factory also. Rosa and Ella are jealous of each other. It brings a warm feeling to me. Both are at my place for the first time. Ella and Pavil both give ashtrays (I don't smoke). We have a laugh.

November

Finds the approach of winter now. A growing loneliness overtakes me in spite of my conquest of Ennatachina, a girl from Riga, studying at the Music Conservatory in Minsk. After an affair, which lasts a few weeks, we part.

November 15

In November, I make the acquaintances of four girls rooming at the Foreign Language Dormitory in room 212. Nell is very interesting. So is Tomka, Tomis and Alla. I usually go to the Institute Dormitory with a friend of mine who speaks English very well. Erik Titovyets, 22, is in the fourth year at the Medical Institute. Very bright fellow. At the Dormitory we 6 sit and talk for hours in English.

December 1

I am having a light affair with Nell Korobka.

January 1

New Years I spend at the home of Ella Germain. I think I'm in love with her. She has refused my more dishonorable advances. We drink and

47

eat in the presence of her family in a very hospital atmosphere. Later I go home drunk and happy. Passing the river homewards, I decide to propose to Ella.

January 2

After a pleasant hand-in-hand walk to the local cinema we come home. Standing on the doorstep, I propose. She hesitates, then refuses. My love is real, but she has none for me. Her reason, besides lack of love: I am American and someday might be arrested simply because of the example of the Polish Intervention in the '20s. This led to the arrest of all people in the Soviet Union of Polish origin. "You understand the world situation. There is too much against you, and you don't even know it." I am stunned. She snickers at my awkwardness in turning to go (I am too stunned to think!). I realize she was never serious with me, but only exploited my being an American in order to get the envy of the other girls who consider me different from the Russian boys. I AM MISERABLE!

January 4

One year after I received the residence document, I am called in to the passport office and asked if I want citizenship (Russian). I say no; simply extend my residential passport to agree, and my document is extended until Jan. 4, 1962.

January 4–31

I am starting to reconsider my desire about staying. The work is drab. The money I get has nowhere to be spent. No nightclubs or bowling allys, no places of recreation except the trade union dances. I have had enough.

February 1

I mail my first request to American Embassy, Moscow, for reconsidering my position. I stated, "I would like to go back to U.S.!"

February 28

I receive a letter from Embassy. Richard E. Snyder stated I could come in for an interview any time I wanted.

March 1–16

I now live in a state of expectation about going back to the U.S. I confided with Alexander. He supports my judgment, but warns me not to tell any Russians about my desire to return. I understand now why.

March 17

I and Erik went to trade union dance. Boring, but at the last hour I am introduced to a girl with a French hair-do and red dress with white slippers. I dance with her. Then ask to show her home. I do, along with 5 other admirers. Her name is Marina. We like each other right away. She gives me her phone number and departs home with a not-so-new friend in a taxi. I walk home.

March 18–31

We walk. I talk a little about myself. She talks a lot about herself. Her name is Marina N. Prusakova.

April 30

We are going steady and I decide I must have her. She puts me off, so on April 15, I propose. She accepts.

April 31

After a 7 day delay at the marriage bureau, because of my unusual passport, they allow us to register as man & wife. Two of Marina's girlfriends act as bridesmaids. We are married. At her aunt's home we have a dinner reception for about 20 friends and neighbors who wish us happiness, in spite of my origin, which is in general rather disquieting to any Russian, since foreigners are very rare in the Soviet Union, even tourists. After an evening of eating and drinking, in which Uncle Wooser started a fight and the fuse blew on an overloaded circuit, we take our leave and walk the 15 minutes to our home. We lived near each other. At midnight we were home.

1st May Day 1961

Found us thinking about our future. In spite of fact I married Marina to hurt Ella, I found myself in love with Marina.

In his diary Lee says he adjusted himself "mentally" to his marriage and developed a love for Marina. The age-old pattern of a marriage on the rebound, however, seemed to show itself in his chronically erratic attitude toward Marina. At times it appeared he really did love her; then there were times when he behaved like a man who felt he had trapped himself, and it all seemed futile. He valued his life with Marina very lightly, as we shall see later, and still as time went by he needed her adulation and approval. These he did not always get.

49

How much Marina knew about Lee's proposal of marriage as the reaction of a rejected suitor—still in love with Ella when he married Marina—is hard to say. She told at least one of her American friends later that Lee in anger had said he didn't love her and never had, even before they left Russia. With her tendency to underplay the whole story of their chaotic married life, there may well have been black eyes, beatings and savage arguments right from the very beginning.

Marina testified that she had never read her husband's dairy, which, because it was written in English, she would not have been able to translate if she had come across it in his personal belongings. This language barrier hid some truths from her about Lee and their marriage that she never realized until after the assassination, when the diary was shown to her. On the other hand, locked in her consciousness will always be the face on the other side of the coin. If Lee's confessions in his diary of a lack of true love for Marina are true, what were her motives in marrying him? Later in his diary he evaluates Marina's feelings for him: "She is madly in love with me." But was she really? Was it love, as Lee flattered himself, or did she have purposes of her own? A number of their American friends commented on this question in their testimony before the Commission. One of the most outspoken was George Bouhe, unofficial leader of the so-called "Russian Colony" in Dallas. The Commission asked him about Lee's reasons for returning to the United States:

"Did he tell you why he decided to come back from Russia?"

"He did say once—and I hate to talk about a dead man—what I thought shedding a crocodile tear, 'It would be good for my daughter to be brought up in the United States.' "

"Is that the only reason that he ever told you about why he wanted to come back to the United States?"

"Substantially. I cannot think of anything else besides the fact that most of us who spoke with him have an impression—and the Russian people are very subject to easy impressions—is that Marina was hellbent to go out of the Soviet Union and into America.

"And I think one of the ladies said, 'Why,' and I remember through third-hand a report reached me, 'I always wanted to have a room of my own.' "

"Do you remember who told you that?"

"Mrs. Anna Meller."

"Did you get the impression that Marina married Oswald just to get out of the Soviet Union?"

"I cannot say that that was the only reason."

"Do you think it was one of the reasons?"

"Oh, yes."

"Did she tell you that?"

"She was saying Marina wanted to come to America."

"And you gathered the impression that that was one of the reasons why Marina married Oswald?"

"Only after."

"Well, did you gain an impression that that was one of the reasons why she married Oswald?"

"That is my impression. My impression. But I wasn't there."

"You don't remember anyone telling you that that was one of the reasons? That is to say, neither Marina nor Oswald told you?"

"Certainly not Oswald. But just a minute, much as I'd like to say, I do not recall a direct statement to that effect, but Marina liked to look at magazines, she said, and Cadillacs and iceboxes and this and that, and from what I understood her talk, she was just itching to get in on that.

"Now that is my impression, and God strike me if I say something wrong about her, but that is my impression."

"Did you form an impression as to the girl's character of Marina Oswald throughout the time that you knew her?"

"Yes, I did."

"What do you think of her general character? Tell us about that."

"It seemed to me that she was a lost soul, as I understood without investigating the girl, no papa, no mama, no home—I don't know who they were—brought up by probably an old grandmother, born perhaps at the time of the greatest holocaust that existed there from 1941, 1942 and 1943, when Leningrad was surrounded by Germans, and there was a great deal of privation, hunger, and, I heard, even cannibalism.

"Maybe she was thinking that this is an awful place and she would have to do whatever she could to get out.

"Maybe she was partly influenced by her grandmother, who, I would say, is of the old school, but I don't know.

"And I think she must have been looking for that opportunity which presented itself in Minsk.

"So I think she is a very thinking person, but what her ultimate goal was or is, I cannot guess even now."

"Did you tell the FBI that you thought Marina was a product of the Soviet machine and that all initiative had been removed from her?"

"I certainly don't remember if I said that, those specific words, but that is what I believe. If you are educated by the Soviet regime, in their schools, I think you don't think anything of your own, which is substantially what I said, isn't it, or is it not?"

"Yes. She had had all initiative removed from her."

"Except a romantic initiative to get a man and do something about it."

"Now let's go back a little bit. A few minutes ago I asked you about your judgment of Marina Oswald's character and we had an off-the-record discussion. Would you repeat for us that discussion, the statement you made off the record at that time, and recapitulate for us your thoughts on Marina Oswald?"

"I think she is a well-brought-up girl. By that I mean, from my calculation, that she had received a good care from some old person of the old regime. Religious, well mannered and such.

"She liked glitter, fun, maybe just like any young pretty girl of that age would, probably, but I think she was also a driver and ambitious about it.

"Even by looking at her, I would say that in the small size you would not think she would.

"And it seems to me that she followed that line by meeting Oswald, coaxing him to come to America, and so, as she told me herself, she could write a postal card to her old girl friends, 'Watch me sail to America.' "

"You mentioned in your off-the-record discussion that you had thought to yourself, Isn't it possible that Marina is a great actress?"

"There again she acts so natural that I was disarmed. But at this stage of the game, maybe I was a fool."

"Why do you say that, Mr. Bouhe?"

"Maybe she is a super-agent of some organization."

CHAPTER 4

MARGUERITE'S VIEWPOINT

I F THE DALLAS AUTHORITIES thought the case against Lee Harvey Oswald was closed, it soon proved that they were about the only Americans who thought so. Millions had watched the live melodrama—perhaps in a way had a closer view, through television, than the participants in the action—and they were a long way from satisfied that this was an open-and-shut case. In addition to the complexity of events, the freakish coincidences of fact the public was expected to accept at face value, there were just too many seeming inconsistencies. Witnesses at the scene seemed to disagree completely on the direction from which the shots came. The so-called murder weapon proclaimed to be a German Mauser suddenly changed its nationality and was identified as an Italian Mannlicher-Carcano, a rifle of different bore and characteristics. Rumor had it that Lee Oswald was trying to get to the apartment of Jack Ruby in his flight from the Texas School Book Depository. The people Lee and Marina had associated with were mostly of Russian origin, any one of whom could have been a Communist. Two aliases were involved: A. J. Hidell and O. H. Lee. These were just a few of the obvious incongruities which the world in its state of dumb bewilderment couldn't possibly accept with the matter-of-fact statement, "The case is closed." Closed! The rumors and speculations had just begun. A case of this magnitude might never be closed. How could one close a case when the two leading personalities were dead and obviously many of the unknowables were hidden behind the Iron Curtain during the period of Oswald's defection to Russia?

Among those who immediately raised the question of the responsibility of Lee Harvey Oswald was his mother, Mrs. Marguerite Oswald. She simply refused to believe that her son could be an assassin, that he would have shot the President of the United States. Others who knew Lee Oswald intimately found themselves unable to accept the proofs put forth by the Dallas police. How could a mother, who in her own way had always been proud of her sons, accept these facts?

They needed a scapegoat—that was Marguerite's reaction. She was well aware of the kind of criticism Lee had suffered for his independent actions. The newspapers had been full of censure when he went to Russia, but she had never blamed him for that. He had as much as admitted that he had made a serious mistake and of his own accord made the decision to return. Of course, he loved his country; like all the other members of her family, they not only loved America but they were even patriotic about it. Lee was a patriot and she had reasons of her own to believe this. At times she had been hard pressed to explain some of Lee's surprisingly independent actions, but he was not a bad boy, never had been, even though the newspapers were now trying to make out that as a child he had been some kind of psychotic misfit. Marguerite Oswald persistently told the newspapers that her son was not only innocent of the shooting of President Kennedy but she was also certain he was an agent of the American Government. She was the second witness called before the Commission and she was carefully interrogated. She claimed that she had been convinced for a number of years that her son was an American agent. In 1961 she had made a trip to Washington at her own expense in hopes the Government would help her bring her hero son back from behind the Iron Curtain. Her account of this trip gave the Commission the substance of her beliefs.

Marguerite made her presence felt the moment she entered the hearing room. If I had seen her walking down the street I think I would have said to myself, "Here is a strong, purposeful woman." Her manner of dressing was neat and tasteful. Her eyes had a forceful character made more emphatic by heavy black shell-rim glasses. Her black hair was drawn back from her forehead and gathered in a bun in back. She clutched an oversized black handbag which proved to be her portable filing cabinet. It bulged with letters, documents and clippings. Unfortunately in her nervous intensity it seemed that her filing system got scrambled in her bag from time to time, and she would become excited and distraught if she could not find the paper she was looking for when she wanted to prove a point. The strain of the recent pressures she had endured did not show on her face but in her quick gestures. It was not easy for her to keep in order the sequence of events she had to relate. She spoke with pent-up concern to tell the Commission all she knew.

"I arrived at Washington at eight o'clock in the morning. I took a train and borrowed money on an insurance policy I have which I have proof. I had a bank account of thirty-six dollars, which I drew out and bought a pair of shoes. I have all that in proof, sir, the date that I left for the train. I was three nights and two days on the train, or two days and three nights. Anyhow, I took a coach and sat up.

"I arrived at the station eight o'clock in the morning and I called the White House. A Negro man was on the switchboard, and he said the offices were not open yet, they did not open until nine o'clock. He asked if I would leave my number. I asked to speak to the President. And he said the offices were not open yet. I said, 'Well, I have just arrived here from Fort Worth, Texas, and I will call back at nine o'clock.'

"So I called back at nine o'clock. Everybody was just gracious to me over the phone. Said that President Kennedy was in a conference, and they would be happy to take any message. I asked to speak to Secretary Rusk, and they connected me with that office. And his young lady said he was in a conference, but anything she could do for me. I said, 'Yes, I have come to town about a son of mine who is lost in Russia. I do want to speak—I would like personally to speak to Secretary Rusk.' So she got off the line a few minutes. Whether she gave him the message or what I do not know. She came back and said, 'Mrs. Oswald, Mr. Rusk'—so evidently she handed him a note —and Mr. Boster was on the line—'that you talk to Mr. Boster, who is special officer in charge of Soviet Union affairs'—if I am correct. And Mr. Boster was on the line. I told him who I was. He said, 'Yes, I am familiar with the case, Mrs. Oswald.' He said, 'Will an eleven-o'clock appointment be all right with you?' This is nine o'clock in the morning. So I said—this is quite an interesting story—I said, 'Mr. Boster that would be fine. But I would rather not talk with you.' I didn't know who Mr. Boster was. I said, 'I would rather talk with Secretary of State Rusk. However, if I am unsuccessful in talking with him, then I will keep my appointment with you.'

"So I asked Mr. Boster, I said, 'Mr. Boster, would you please recommend a hotel that would be reasonable?' He said, 'I don't know how reasonable, Mrs. Oswald, but I recommend the Washington Hotel. It will be near the State Department and convenient to you.'

"So I went to the Washington Hotel. And as we know, Gentlemen, there were nothing but men. They asked me if I had a reservation. I said, 'No, I didn't, but Mr. Boster of the State Department recommended that I come here.' So they fixed me up with a room. I took a bath and dressed. I went to the appointment—because this is nine-thirty, I am on the phone, and I had to take a cab to the hotel. I arrived at Mr. Boster's office at ten-thirty.

"But before arriving at Mr. Boster's office, I stopped at a telephone in the corridor, and I called Dean Rusk's office again, because I didn't want to see Mr. Boster, and I asked to speak to Dean Rusk. And the young lady said, 'Mrs. Oswald, talk to Mr. Boster. At least it is a start.'

"So then I entered around the corridor into Mr. Boster's office. I have all the pictures of the State Department and everything to prove this story is true. I told the young lady, 'I am Mrs. Oswald. I have an eleven-o'clock appointment.' Mr. Boster came out and said, 'Mrs. Oswald, I am awfully glad you came early, because we are going to have a terrible snowstorm, and we have orders to leave early in order to get home.'

"So he called Mr. Stanfield—the arrangements had been made—now, the other man—I don't have that name here for you, Mr. Rankin."

"Is it Mr. Hickey?"

"Yes, Mr. Hickey. You are correct.

"So then we were in conference. So I showed the papers, like I am showing here. And I said, 'Now, I know you are not going to answer me, Gentlemen, but I am under the impression that my son is an agent.' 'Do you mean a Russian agent?' I said, 'No, working for our Government, a U. S. agent. And I want to say this: that if he is, I don't appreciate it too much, because I am destitute and just getting over a sickness'—on that order.

"I had the audacity to say that. I had gone through all of this without medical, without money, without compensation. I am a desperate woman. So I said that."

"What did they say to you?"

56

"They did not answer that. I even said to them, 'No, you won't tell me.' So I didn't expect them to answer that."

"Did you mean you were seeking money from them?"

"No, sir. I didn't think that my son should have gone—in a foreign country, and me being alone. What I was saying was that I think my son should be home with me, is really what I implied."

"Did you tell them that?"

"In the words that I said before—I didn't come out and say I want my son home. But I implied that if he was an agent, that I thought that he needed to be home."

"Did you say anything about believing that your son might know full well what he was doing in trying to defect to the Soviet Union, he might like it better there than he did here?"

"I do not remember saying this. I know what I did say, and they agreed with me. I said—because I remember this distinctly—I said, 'Now, he has been exploited all through the paper as a defector. If he is a defector'—because as we stated before, I don't know he is an agent, sir—and if he is a defector, that is his privilege, as an individual.

"And they said, 'Mrs. Oswald, we want you to know that we feel the same way about it.' That was their answer."

"Did you say anything about possibly he liked the Soviet way of life better than ours?"

"I may have. I do not remember, sir. Honestly. I may have said that. I recall that they agreed with me, and they said, 'We want him also to do what he wants to do.'

"So now this is January 21, 1961, is my trip to Washington. Approximately eight weeks later, on March 22, 1961—which is eight weeks—I received a letter from the State Department informing me of my son's address."

"Do you recall that they assured you there was no evidence he was an agent?"

"No, sir, there was no comment to that effect."

"And they told you to dismiss any such ideas from your mind?"

"No, sir."

"You are sure they didn't tell you that?"

"I am positive. I said to them, 'Of course, I don't expect you to answer me.' No, sir, there was nothing mentioned about the agent at all. And in fact, I would think, just as a layman, that the State Department would not even consider discussing that with me. But I mean it was not discussed. I am positive of that."

"If they recorded in a memorandum as of that date that they did say that to you, that would be incorrect?"

"That is incorrect, emphatically incorrect. That is incorrect. Because I said, 'I don't expect you to tell me. But if he is an agent,' I didn't think it was the thing to do.

"Well, on January 21, was my trip to Washington, 1961. Approximately eight weeks later, on March 22, 1961, I received a letter from the State Department informing me of my son's address, which you probably have—if you don't, sir, I have the copies. And also stating that my son wishes to return back to the United States—just eight weeks after my trip to Washington.

"Now, you want to know why I think my son is an agent. And I have been telling you all along.

"Here is a very important thing why my son was an agent. On March 22 I receive a letter of his address and stating that my son wishes to return back to the United States. You have that, sir?"

"Yes."

"On April 30, 1961, he marries a Russian girl—approximately five weeks later.

"Now, why does a man who wants to come back to the United States, five weeks later—here is the proof; April 30, 1961, is the wedding date—marry a Russian girl? Because I say—and I may be wrong—the U. S. Embassy has ordered him to marry this Russian girl. And a few weeks later, May 16, 1961, he is coming home with the Russian girl. And as we know, he does get out of the Soviet Union with the Russian girl, with money loaned to him by the U. S. Embassy. I may be wrong, Gentlemen, but two on two in my book makes four.

"I have many more things that can go to this, and that has been published. I will probably never know whether my son was an agent, because I do not expect to be told these facts. But isn't it peculiar that a boy is coming home, and the Embassy informs me of that—I have all this, Mr. Rankin, and you know I do. You will have the copies. And then five weeks later he marries a Russian girl. And the proof of it is that he does come home with the Russian girl in a short length of time. And Lee would have been home one year earlier. But because of the lack of money to come."

"Did you ever ask him whether he married the Russian girl because they ordered him to?"

"No, sir. I have never asked Lee any questions of that kind. The only question I asked Lee was when they were living with me that one month, I said, 'Lee, I want to know one thing. Why is it you came back to the United States when you had a job and you were married to a Russian girl?' and they sent me lovely gifts and photographs and everything. So they seemed to be well off.

"I have a beautiful scarf. They sent tea, boxes of candy, which the postage is terrific. He says, 'Not even Marina knows that.' And that is the only question I have ever asked my son. This may be hard to believe. But I have explained to you over and over that I think we, as individuals, have a right to our own life."

"You saw your daughter-in-law and your son living together with you, didn't you, for some time?"

"Yes. They lived with me one month."

"Did you think they were in love with each other?"

"Yes, they were definitely in love with each other. Yes, I think they were in love with each other."

"Did you think at that time it was just because he was an agent and ordered to marry her that he married her?"

"No. I would say this. This is purely speculation. He knew Marina, and he loved Marina. They met at a dance. So that was—he had a girl friend. We are saying if he is an agent—I have to say 'if.' Then he tells the Embassy that he is in love with a Russian girl. And so it is a good idea to bring the Russian girl to the United States. He will have contacts.

"Now, when I was in Mrs. Paine's home, on the table was a lot of papers from Lee. The *Daily Worker* I happen to know about. And many, many subversive—now, I say if Lee is going to assassinate a President, or Lee is anything that he is otherwise than an agent, Lee would not have all these things, he would not have his finger in everything.

"He would not be reading only Communism and Marxism, that he would be a fanatic about that one thing and have a cause to assassinate the President.

"But that is not the picture of Lee Harvey Oswald. Lee has his hand in everything."

"What do you mean by everything?"

"Well, Cuba—because we know in New Orleans he was arrested for Fair Play for Cuba. He read the *Daily Worker*. And the other ones I don't know. But it was in the paper. There is plenty of subversive material."

"What about books? Did he read books much while he was living with you?"

"Yes, he read continuously. He went immediately to the library upon coming to the United States. He read continuously. All kinds of books."

"Now, was there any time that Marina said anything to you to lead you to believe that she thought your son, Lee, married her because he was an agent?"

"No, sir, no, sir. Not at any time at all."

"You think she loved him?"

"I believe that Marina loved him in a way. But I believe that Marina wanted to come to America. I believe that Lee had talked America to her, and she wanted to come to America. I say this for a lot of little things that happened—that Marina wanted to come to America. Maybe she loved him. I am sure she did, anyway. She said that she did."

"I am not clear about this being ordered to marry her. You don't mean that your son didn't love her."

"Well, I could mean that—if he is an agent, and he has a girl friend, and it is to the benefit of the country that he marry this girl friend, and the Embassy helped him get this Russian girl out of Russia—let's face it, whether he loved her or not, he would take her to America, if that would give him contact with Russians, yes, sir."

"Is that what you mean?"

"I would say that."

"And you don't think it was because your son loved her, then?"

"I do not know whether my son loved her or not. But I am telling you why he would do this—in five weeks' time. Now, you have a five-week period in here."

"I understand that. But I think it is a very serious thing to say about your son, that he would do a thing like that to a girl."

"No, sir, it is not a serious thing. I know a little about the CIA, and so on, the U-2, Powers, and things that have been made public. They go through any extreme for their country. I do not think that would be serious for him to marry a Russian girl and bring her here so he would have contact. I think that is all part of an agent's duty."

"You think your son was capable of doing that?"

"Yes, sir, I think my son was an agent. I certainly do."

"Have you got anything more that caused you to think he was an agent?"

"Yes, I have things that have been coming out in the paper. And I am not the only one that thinks my son is an agent. There has been many, many publications questioning whether Lee was an agent or not because of circumstances, and so on, and so forth, through the newspapers."

"That is newspaper accounts you are talking about now?"

"Yes. And as I said about the FBI."

"What about your own knowledge?"

"Well, that is why I wanted to go into the story. I wouldn't have become emotionally upset had I started in sequence.

"I told you about him not wanting me to see that program. And then the letters. There is so much. About him being an agent—all of his correspondence with the Embassy in Moscow. I have the letters in the hotel. One of the letters states that the Russians cannot hold you—'the Russians cannot hold you. You are an American citizen. You are not a bona-fide Russian resident.' We have the letters. You have a copy of the letter, Mr. Rankin.

"And if you will show this letter to the Russians, they cannot hold you in Minsk."

"They would say that about you if you were over there, or anyone."

"The point I am trying to bring there is Lee has always been an American citizen—according to all of my papers from the State Department."

"Yes."

"And they would say that about anyone—all right, I will grant you that. You are probably right."

"So that doesn't prove he is an agent that I can see. Now, how do you feel it shows he was an agent, Mrs. Oswald?"

"Because he has the sanction of the American Embassy all through this affair."

"They would give that to any of us."

"All right—so you are telling me that. But this man is married to a Russian girl, and does come back within a short time, and could have come back sooner. It was the lack of money. And that is another thing.

"The State Department repeatedly kept writing me, and I have the letters for the money. I have copies of my letters also. I could not raise the money. I said I had a 'fifty-four Buick car, and all I could get a loan on was $250. They wrote back and said could you ask some friends, or do you have any relatives—"

"Didn't you understand that the State Department had to try to find out if they could—or you or your son could get the money from other sources before they could advance the money?"

"Yes, sir, I understand that. I am trying to tell you that I tried awfully hard, but with no success."

"So they were just trying to do their duty in that regard, were they not?"

"It could be, yes. It could be."

"You don't think that makes him an agent, just because they asked you—"

"I think—well, as you say, they would probably help anyone. And then again, because he is married to a Russian girl, and because all these documents and everything are handled through the U. S. Embassy. And because of my trip to Washington—which was red-carpet treatment. Let's say, Gentlemen, if a woman gets on the phone at nine o'clock and has an appointment at eleven o'clock with three big men, that is wonderful treatment.

"Now, they probably would do that to anybody. I don't know."

"They might have done that—"

"I haven't been that fortunate before."

"Well, that shouldn't be held against them, that they treated you nicely."

"No, I have told you, Mr. Rankin, they were most gracious to me. The Administration was most gracious to me."

"I don't see why you should think that because they treated you nicely that was any sign he was an agent."

"Well, maybe you don't see why. But this is my son. And this is the way I think, because I happen to know all of the other things that you don't know—the life and everything. I happen to think this. And this is my privilege to think this way. And I can almost back it up with these things.

"This is a stranger to you folks. But this is a boy I have known from a child."

"How much money do you think he received for being an agent?"

"That I do not know."

"You have no idea?"

"But I do know this, and I have stated this. I have approximately nine hundred and some odd dollars.

"Now, this is my position. You asked me the question. But Marina has thirty-five thousand dollars publicly.

"Now, Gentlemen, thirty-five thousand dollars is a lot of money in donation dribs and drabs—is a very large sum of money. I question where does that money come from. Yes, some of it could be coming from Lee's back pay. And she might have more than that. That was the amount made public—thirty-five thousand dollars. And here is a mother without a job. And everybody knows I have no money. And my contributions are nine hundred and some odd dollars."

"Now, when you say that money that Marina has might come from your son's back pay, what do you base that on? Just speculations?"

"I am basing all of this on speculation. Sir, if I had proof, I would not be taking my energy and my emotional capacity to bring all this out—if I had proof he was an agent."

"When they asked you to contribute some money to help bring him home from Russia, did it occur to you that if he is an agent the Government could just pay his way?"

"Yes. But they don't want the public to know he is an agent. They want me to have all of this. They don't want the public to know. I am going around to people—you brought up a very good point. I am going around trying to get money for this boy to come home, so the public knows. Sure, they could have given him the money to come home."

"Are you trying to get money now? I don't understand what you mean by that?"

"I think, Mr. Rankin, you asked me the question that if he was an agent, that the Government would have given him the money to come home without any trouble. I say just the opposite. That it was a very good point. If he was an agent, it would make it hard for him to get the money to come home.

"Remember, I am under the impression he is coming home with this Russian girl in order to continue his work. So he cannot be given the money immediately to come home, because his mother might tell the story to someone. Lee was almost a year coming home for lack of money. So then they have an excuse to loan him the money.

"Lee loved the Marines, Mr. Rankin. Even coming back—he was a military man. And that has also been stated in the paper, that he had a military manner about him. I think District Attorney Wade remarked something of that order. People have noticed that."

"What made you think he loved the Marines? Was there something he did when he came back?"

"Yes. He loved the Marines because his brother was a Marine, for one thing. And John Edward—that is his career—fourteen years. My brother was in the Navy. His father was a veteran. We are a serviceman family. And I know Lee loved the Marines. I told you how he read the manual before he left. And on leaves, coming home, Lee would brag. He even said when he came home from Japan, 'Mother, my stay in Japan, just the trip alone would have cost about two thousand dollars.'

"Now, Lee, I know also, was in the Air Force of the Marines, and he went to Biloxi, Mississippi, for schooling. Lee has had quite a bit of schooling. And Lee spoke Russian equivalent to one year when he defected to Russia. I have that on his application from the Albert Schweitzer College. And Lee spoke and wrote Russian fluently when he went to Russia. So Lee learns Russian in the Marines."

"Did he ever talk about re-enlisting into the Marines after he returned?"

"Well, when Lee returned he was with me three days, and then, of course, he went over to visit Robert's house. So actually we didn't talk. I was trying to find a home. And I didn't think he would go. I was hoping that Lee would not go on the ship and work. I was hoping he would stay home. We were interrupted before. When he said to me about, that he wanted to work on a ship in the import and export business, I started to tell you I agreed with him. And this is how you have to do—particularly when you are a woman. A father could tell the man, 'You are not going to do this.' But I went along with that. And then the next day I said, 'Lee, why don't you stay?'— and I went into that—'until I settle my claim, and I can baby-sit and we can get along.' He said, 'No, my mind is made up. If I stay, we will both be in these circumstances.' So on the third day—I knew he wanted to do this, but I didn't think he was going to do it for a month or two. But on the third day he came with his suitcase in the room and he said, 'Mother, I am off.' So since his mind was made up, I told him goodbye."

"He said nothing about re-enlisting in the Marines?"

"No, the three days he was home. That was the conversation, about him going on a ship. I saw his passport. And his passport was stamped 'import and export' on his passport."

"Did it say anything about Soviet Russia on it?"

"No. What I am saying is that I saw the passport with big writing 'export and import.' I think it was blue. I did not read the passport, because Lee was there, but I happened to see the passport, 'export and import' stamped.

"Whether he had another passport, I do not know. I didn't ask. I am saying this—and God knows I am telling you the truth. I am just this type person. It is because of my life."

"Did you know that he spoke Russian at that time, when he had this passport?"

"No, sir, I did not know. The only time I knew that he spoke Russian is what came out in the news. But when I really knew was Lee's application for the Albert Schweitzer College. Shall we go into that—the application?"

"Yes."

"Now, the first that I knew—no, I am wrong. It is not the first I knew. I had received a letter from Lee while in the Marines, before he knew of my trouble, stating that he was accepted by the Albert Schweitzer College. And that letter was in the sea bag that I told you about, that I do not have."

Mr. Dulles: "Would you give us the date of that letter?"

Mrs. Oswald: "The other letter would have been—let's see. Lee was told in July about my trouble. And the other letter I would say would be about May or June. This is March 22. I received this in care of Lee. And you see, sir, I have a lot of addresses, because I am now living in these homes."

Mr. Dulles: " 'Fifty-seven or 'fifty-eight?"

"Nineteen-sixty."

Marguerite began reading the letter from the Schweitzer College.

" 'Due to a number of circumstances, we found ourselves forced to make a slight change in the arrival and departure dates of the third term. The first lecture will be held on Tuesday afternoon 1600 o'clock, April 19, instead of taking place on the 21st with the arrival day on the 20th. It will mean that the students arrive either on the evening of Monday, the 18th, or before noon on April 19th. This change, however, makes it possible to end the term on the weekend of July 2. We hope that you will still be able to fit this change of dates into your travel plan. Should it not be possible for you to arrive on the earlier date we, of course, understand the difficulty. In the latter case, please drop us a line.'

"So that is how I knew that Lee—I opened his mail. I didn't know whether my son was living or dead, sir. And that is how I knew—I won't go into all this. He made a deposit. I have all of this for you.

"He made a deposit. And this is my copies to them.

"Now, one thing I have forgotten.

"While at the State Department, the State Department told me that Lee had gone to Finland before Russia. And I did not know that.

"Now, Lee had applied at a college in Finland, evidently, because on the application it states such a fact. I did not know—because the paper just said he arrived in Russia—until I went to the State Department.

"So what I am trying to say—I may be forgetting a lot of important things, because I am just now remembering what the State Department told me.

"I don't think I am forgetting too much.

"But, after all, I am going through a whole life, and it is very hard.

"This is Lee's original application, that you cannot possibly have had. This is the only application there is. So this is something new for you gentlemen. I am not going to go through it all, because you

66

have a copy. But I am going to show you the thinking of this young man.

" 'Special interests: religious, vocational, literary, sports and hobbies. Philosophy, psychology, ideology, football, baseball, tennis, stamp collecting.' Lee had a stamp-collecting book. 'Nature of private reading: Jack London, Darwin, Norman Vincent Peale, scientific books, philosophy, and so on.' "

Representative Ford: "That is an application to where?"

"This is an original application for the Albert Schweitzer School.

" 'Active part taken in organizations: Student-body movement in school for control of juvenile delinquency, member YMCA and AYA Association.'

"I don't know what that is."

Mr. Rankin: "Where did you get this copy?"

"I had contacted Congressman Jim Wright, that has helped me—helped me to locate Lee through the State Department. But Mr. Jim Wright was not successful.

"I was successful because of my trip to Washington, as you know.

"And from the trip to Washington, I went to the building where Mr. Jim Wright worked, and I went in to tell the secretary about the trip to Washington. And that I had heard from Lee.

"Well, I had information here that Lee had paid a deposit. So I had written the school and asked if we were entitled to the return of the deposit, since he didn't show up. But I did not get an answer.

"So Mr. Wright's secretary said that, 'Mrs. Oswald, I will write and see what we can do.'

"So she wrote, and then they sent the application and everything back to Jim Wright's office. And that is how I got the application."

Mr. Doyle: "They may be interested in knowing where the college is."

"It is in Switzerland. 'Albert Schweitzer College, Churwalden, Graubuenden, Switzerland. Application form. High school. Completed high school by correspondence.'

"I have that. His original correspondence in the service—completed high school."

Mr. Rankin: "Is that part of his Marine work—he finished high school that way?"

"Yes, sir.

" 'January 'fifty-eight, passing sixty-five on scale of one hundred, B plus. College: None.'

"And then I read his books.

"Now, we go down to here.

" 'Vocational interests if decided upon: To be a short-story writer on contemporary American life.'

"Now, 'General statement regarding reasons for wishing to attend the Albert Schweitzer College: In order to acquire a fuller understanding of that subject which interests me most, philosophy, to meet with Europeans who can broaden my scope of understanding, to receive formal education by institutes of high standing and character, to broaden my knowledge of German, and to live in a healthy climate and good moral atmosphere.'

"This is very good thinking, Gentlemen. We are getting a picture now of the boy which has been not told in the paper.

"I have read this one particular statement at three press conferences. The first press conference was about eighty members there, from foreign lands and everything. Nothing was printed. Then I had a second press conference with sixteen men and I said, 'Now, I am tired of the things that are being said about my family, myself and Lee. We are not perfect. But I know there is some good things. And I have read a particular statement that has not been printed. Let's see if one of you has the courage to print it.'

"There was sixteen there. That did not come out. I had a third conference, and I said the same thing and quoted this. That was not made public in the paper.

"I hold a lot of these answers, Gentlemen, as you know by now."

Mr. Rankin: "You notice the next paragraph, about his plans?"

"Yes, 'Plans to be pursued after the period at Albert Schweitzer College: To attend the short summer course of the University of Turkin, Turkin, Finland.'

"Now, I have a brochure—this I cannot understand—from this college, dated 1960. I have this for you, Mr. Rankin, dated 1960.

"Lee is in Russia.

"And the men in the State Department told me he went to Finland before Russia. But this is dated 1960. I have it for you.

"But I don't understand that.

" 'Then to return to America and pursue my chosen vocation.' "

68

Mr. Rankin: "I want to ask you about that. Do you think he meant this at the time?"

"I do not know. I am saying—and I am going to stick to my story —that Lee is an agent, then a lot of this is a lot of baloney. I cannot make it any stronger. I don't know, sir. The boy is gone, and I didn't hear from his own lips."

"You think that he decided to defect after this application, then?"

"I do not know, sir, because I have not had this from the boy. I am speculating. But I have a lot of documents to sustain my speculation."

"Now, this, you cannot tell one way or another about whether he is an agent by this."

"I cannot tell by anything he is an agent, if you want proof. I am becoming a little discouraged about this, because I keep telling you —I did not have proof, sir. But I am giving you documents leading to it."

"All I am trying to find out is what you have. You are giving us that. I am also trying to find out whatever proof you have about these various things that we can rely on."

"Well, I am going to state once and for all, because it upsets me very much emotionally. And I have stated before, I do not have proof, sir. I do not have proof of an agent. I do not have proof my son is innocent. I do not have proof."

"You don't have any proof of a conspiracy?"

"Of anything. It is just as I feel, like the Dallas police do not have proof my son shot President Kennedy. If they have anything, it is circumstantial evidence. I have as much circumstantial evidence here that Lee was an agent as the Dallas police have that he shot President Kennedy."

CHAPTER 5

ANOTHER SIDE
OF LEE HARVEY OSWALD

WITH A MOTHER's natural loyalty and pride in her son, Marguerite refused to accept the picture of Lee as a psychotic killer. Her real memories of him in recent years, however, were scanty, to say the least. Nevertheless, with an instinct to protect not only her son's image but indirectly her own, she tenaciously clung to the belief that there was nothing abnormal about the boy. Her contention that the psychiatrist in New York exaggerated the facts would prove to be right. His report on Lee Oswald when he examined him many years ago did not bear out the newspaper stories that the doctor had considered him dangerous—a potential killer or anything of the kind. Lee had been recommended for probation. Why should she consider it abnormal that the boy skipped school and was sometimes uncooperative with his schoolteachers? Is truancy the proof of incipient schizophrenia? Hardly. Lee was perfectly normal—an unusual boy, to be sure, but she most certainly couldn't bring herself to believe that he would assassinate a President. There *had* to be some other explanation to these terrible happenings in Dallas. Her testimony before the Commission, although confused and sometimes bordering on incoherence, raised questions that rightfully had to be answered. But the other side of Lee Oswald, the side she knew little or nothing about, does not convey the picture of a normal twenty-year-old. As intimately as a mother feels she knows a son, what happens to a young man in the critical years seventeen to twenty-one can obscure everything in the past.

The adult relationship between Lee and his mother was cold and remote. Lee wanted it that way. What did she really know about Lee from the time he had joined the Marine Corps seven years previously at the age of seventeen? She had had brief letters from him; now and then between transfers of duty or on furlough they had seen each other; but after coming home on a "hardship discharge" and staying for less than a week, he had picked up his duffel bag and disappeared behind the Iron Curtain. There had been that day when, urged by newspaper reporters, she had made a frenzied attempt to reach him by telephone at the Metropole Hotel in Moscow. She had momentarily heard him answer the phone, and then he had hung up on her. She was cut off then; she had been cut off in Fort Worth when she tried to help him find his way back to a place in American society. She had been cut off many years before by Lee's own judgment of the way she had treated him as a youngster. But during the period when Marguerite was not in touch with her son, Lee did a good deal of thinking and writing about himself. An important side of his personality emerges from his clumsy jottings. Here is a brief autobiographical sketch he composed (complete with grammatical errors and misspellings) as an introductory note to a book he was writing:

"Lee Harvey Oswald was born in Oct 1939 in New Orleans, La. the son of a Insuraen Salesmen whose early death left a far mean streak of indepence brought on by negleck."

This notation found among Oswald's papers after the assassination was apparently written while he was en route back from Russia. Whatever the truth of Lee Oswald's treatment as a youngster, there can be no question about how he had come to view his own childhood. Self-sympathy and bitterness gave the barbed point to these remarks, and in them is very little of the loving fondness of a happy youth. Lee Oswald had learned to dramatize what he imagined to be the hardships of his life. Did Marguerite ever understand how he felt in this respect?

Oswald continued his personal sketch (this portion of which has been corrected) in a way that mixes bitterness with an immature romanticism:

"Entering the Marine Corps at 17 this streak of independence was strengthened by exotic journeys to Japan, the Philippines and the scores of odd Islands in the Pacific. Immediately after serving out three years in the USMC he abandoned his American life to seek a new life in the USSR. Full of optimism and hope he stood in Red Square in the fall of 1959 vowing to see his chosen course through . . ."

He was soon to find that the personal paradise he had imagined he would find in Russia was blighted with many shortcomings, not the least of which appeared to be the complete indifference of the Soviet Government to the twenty-year-old Marine and his desire to become a Russian citizen. The account of this period of frustration and bitterness in Lee Oswald's life was something his mother knew nothing about. In fact he did not confide these events to anyone—not to his brother, Robert, not to his mother, not even to Marina, who admitted she was shocked to learn months later the bizarre way in which he behaved when the Soviet officials failed to welcome him with open arms. Fortunately for our understanding of Lee Harvey Oswald and the completeness of a biography of an assassin, the pages of his "Historic Diary" recount the events. Here is a vivid self-portrait of a young man who, when he couldn't have his own way, resorted to melodramatic and rash actions to call attention to himself. When thwarted by circumstances, an ordinary person might beat his fists on a table or, better yet, learn a lesson in reality from the reverses. But not Lee Harvey Oswald.

Day by day, Oswald's "Historic Diary" tells what neither Marguerite nor Marina knew about his arrival in Russia. These notations may not tell all the story of Lee's relationship with Soviet officialdom, but there is no reason to question that, as far as his personal conduct was concerned, here is the way it happened. His own narrative most certainly reflects an impetuous and emotional tendency to solve through extreme actions what he was otherwise incapable of facing—namely, hard reality and personal frustration. It apparently was the almost predictable pattern he followed in the adult years of his short life.

October 16, 1959

"Arrive from Helsinki by train; am met by Intourist Representative and in car to Hotel Berlin. Registered as a student. Met my Intourist Guide, Rimma Sherikova. I explain to her I wish to apply for Russian citizenship. She is flabbergasted, but agrees to help. She checks with her boss, main office Intourist; then helps me address a letter to Supreme Soviet asking for citizenship. Meanwhile boss telephones passport and visa office and notifies them about me."

October

"Rimma meets me for Intourist sightseeing; says we must continue with this although I am too nervous. She is sure I'll have an answer soon. Asks me about myself and my reasons for doing this. I explain I am a communist. She is politely sympathetic but uneasy now. She tries to be a friend to me. She feels sorry for me. I am something new."

Obviously Lee Oswald was conscious of doing a dramatic thing in not waiting a minute to tell Rimma his intentions. He records her manner of uneasiness. Why? Did she shrewdly sense she was dealing with a young man who could be erratic or even more extreme? Or was she just suspicious that he might be a "plant" of some kind and fearful of the complications which might result for her personally?

October 18, 1959, was Lee's twentieth birthday. He had had no response whatsoever to what he considered his important request to the Supreme Soviet. He was on a five-day visa just as any other tourist, and Rimma showed him the sights in Moscow—an exhibition and the inevitable visit to the Lenin-Stalin tomb. Apparently he had envisioned a grand and immediate welcome by the Soviet officials, and his disappointment in the delay of the recognition he craved upset him more and more. The third day he wrote, "Am anxious since my visa is good for five days only. No word from authorities about my request." He was chafing and not happy to be a mere tourist when his true mission was to glory in the achievements of the USSR.

October 21

"Meeting with single official: balding, stout, fairly good English. Asks what do I want? I say Soviet citizenship. He asks why I give vague answers about 'Great Soviet Union.' He tells me 'USSR only great in literature.' Wants me to go back home. I am stunned. I reiterate. He says he will check and let me know whether my visa will be extended. (It expires today.)"

Assuming that the narrative in Lee's "Historic Diary" is a full statement of all he really knew about his reception in Moscow, his being treated in such a prosaic fashion, like any other tourist, was a humiliation. It was worse than that: he had mentally burned his bridges behind him; he had made a heroic pilgrimage to the place of the holy of holies, and here was a balding bureaucrat making such shocking statements as the "USSR only great in literature" and in the next breath telling him in a bored fashion to go home.

Lee went back to his hotel to wait and hope that something would be done to correct this grievous error. It had taken every cent he had been able to scrimp together during those endless months in the Marine Corps. He had trained himself—pored over Marx, Engels and Lenin and even spent grueling hours trying to teach himself the Russian language. He felt that if he could only reach the right officials, not just a minor bureaucrat, and explain all this to them, certainly this wrong would be corrected. But to whom could he appeal? There was nothing to do but remain in his hotel room and wait. The afternoon dragged on. He paced the floor and studied the patterns in the frayed carpet of this shabby hotel.

If his appeal to the bald bureaucrat failed, what would he do? He hadn't counted on a return trip to America. His money was running short, and there was even a chance that U.S. officials would find out about his application for Russian citizenship and refuse his re-entry into the United States. He worked himself into a frenzy of apprehension and discouragement. Oh, this was heart-breaking, disillusioning! It seemed so long that he had been working to fulfill this ambition. He had hated the Marine Corps—its authority and autocracy— and yet he had patiently served out his time. He had expected to surprise Soviet officials with his knowledge of Marxist theory.

At 6:00 P.M. he received the final, crushing news from the police officials. He had been rejected. He must leave the country by eight o'clock that night; his visa would not be renewed! They had turned him down cold.

"I am shocked!! My dreams! I retire to my room. I have $100 left. I have waited for 2 years to be accepted. My fondest dreams are shattered because of a petty official; because of bad planning. I planned too much."

"7:00 PM. I decide to end it. Soak wrist in cold water to numb pain. Then slash my left wrist. Then plunge wrist into bathtub of hot water. I think, 'When Rimma comes at 8 to find me dead, it will be a great shock.' Somewhere a violin plays as I watch my life whirl away. I think to myself, 'how easy to die' and a 'sweet death' (to violins) . . ."

Lee's account of his attempt to commit suicide is complete with overtones of a Grade B movie, with violins playing in the background. He was just twenty years old at the time and understandably emotional about the miscarriage of his fine schemes, but he was

74

also characteristically incapable of dealing with rejection and hard disappointments.

"About 8 PM. Rimma finds me unconscious (bathtub water a rich red color). She screams (I remember that) and runs for help. Ambulance comes. Am taken to the hospital where five stitches are put in my wrist. Poor Rimma stays by my side as interpreter (my Russian is still very bad) far into the night. I tell her, 'Go home' (my mood is bad) but she stays. She is my friend. She has a strong will. Only at this moment I notice she is pretty."

With the siren horns of the ambulance wailing through the streets of Moscow, the distraught and curious swarming around the doors of the Hotel Berlin, people rushing with stretchers through the corridors, Lee was now getting the attention he felt he had deserved all the time. He had been willing to face death this time to prove how important he was, and it wouldn't be the first time. He might have died before Rimma got there to raise the alarm; he was willing to face that. But if he lived he was not going to live a rejected and unimportant person. They would know now in Moscow who Lee Oswald was, and that balding bureaucrat would have to account to higher officials for his near-mockery of Lee's idealism.

The next morning he awoke in the hospital. Medical reports furnished by the Soviets indicate that from a technical viewpoint the wound was superficial. Only if he had bled to death would it have been a matter of any consequence. Five stitches and the blood vessel closed and he was on his way to quick recovery. But momentarily there was another problem.

"I am in a small room with about twelve others. Two orderlies and a nurse. The room is very drab as well as the breakfast. Only after prolonged observation of the other patients, do I realize I am in the Insanity Ward. This realization disquiets me. Later in the afternoon I am visited by Rimma. She comes in with two doctors. As interpreter she must ask me medical questions. Did you know what you were doing? Answer: yes. Did you blackout? No. I then complain about poor food. The doctors laugh. Apparently this is a good sign. Later they leave. I am alone with Rimma, among the mentally ill. She encourages me and scolds me. She says she will help me get transferred to another section of the hospital, not for the insane, where food is good.

October 23. Transferred to ordinary ward. Airy. Good food, but nurses suspicious of me. They know. Afternoon I am visited by Rosa Agafonova, of the hotel who asks me about my health. Very beautiful. Excellent English. Very merry and kind. She makes me very glad to be alive."

The next two days in the hospital were routine with visits from Rimma.

October 26

"An elderly American at the hospital grows suspicious about me for some reason; because I told him I had not registered at the American Embassy as most Americans as a tourist, and I am in general evasive about my presence in Moscow and at hospital. Rimma visits."

The next day the stitches were removed from his wrist and on the following day he was discharged. He changed hotels, from the Berlin to the Metropole, obviously under the closer care and scrutiny of the higher Intourist officials, including the head guide at the Metropole office, Lyudmila Dmitrieva. It was now twelve days since Lee had arrived in Moscow. He had not as yet visited the American Embassy, and they knew little or nothing about his activities during that period. The $100 he had left the night he slashed his wrist wouldn't go far living in the Metropole, but he felt certain now the higher Soviet officials would have to listen to his wishes. He waited at the hotel, and his impatience was mounting again. The day he moved to the Metropole Hotel there had been some action.

"Rimma notifies me that Pass and Registration office wishes to see me about my future. Later Rimma and the car pick me up and we enter the offices to find four officials waiting for me. They ask how my arm is. I say O.K. They say, 'Do you want to go to your homeland?' I say, No I want to become a Soviet Citizen. I want to reside in the Soviet Union. They say they will see about that. Then they ask me about the lone official with whom I spoke in the first place. Apparently he did not pass along my request at all, but thought to simply get rid of me by not extending my Soviet visa. I described him; they made notes. What papers do you have to show who and what you are? I give them my discharge papers from the Marine Corps. They say, wait for our answer. I ask how long? Not soon. Later Rimma comes to check on me. I feel insulted and insult her."

At last Lee felt he had his case before a group of four higher officials who would certainly take more intelligent action. He felt sure of himself already. He was insulted because Rimma came to check on him, and that "mean streak of independence" was reasserting itself to the point that he dared to insult Rimma, who ten days before he had called his friend because she had sat by his bedside most of the night. Now that blasé "single" official who had turned him down and caused all the trouble would get what he deserved. Certainly there would be action now!

But Lee was deluding himself. Bureaucracy is bureaucracy wherever it exists—in the Marine Corps, in the diplomatic corps, in all nations and all levels of government. It was no different in Russia.

October 29

"I wait. I worry. I eat once. I stay next to the phone. I keep fully dressed."

But the telephone didn't ring. "I have been in the hotel three days. It seems like three years! I must have some sort of showdown." It was too much for him. A "showdown"—that was a word he liked. It indicated strength and independence. The kind of showdown he was contemplating took shape in his mind. So far he had gotten action only through dramatic moves. Well, he would make another one. He had another trick or two up his sleeve. They didn't think he meant business about giving up his American citizenship. He would show them.

October 31

"I make my decision. Getting passport I meet and talk with Rimma a few minutes. She says stay in your hotel room and eat well. I don't tell her about what I intend to do since I know she would not approve. After she leaves I wait a few minutes and then I catch a taxi. 'American Embassy,' I say."

At 12:30 he arrived at the Embassy. Two policemen were standing at the entrance and saluted him. As Lee approached the door, one of the officers said, "Passport." Lee recounts that he smiled and showed him his passport. He then went inside. Referring to the official, he says, "There can be little doubt I'm sure in his mind that I'm an American. Light overcoat, no hat or scarf, and non-Russian but-ton-down shirt and tie."

The remainder of the account is given in Lee Oswald's own words because the flavor of his sentences and word choices reflects his atti-tude. Only minor changes in sentence structure have been made, and atrocious spelling errors have been corrected:

"Entering I find the office of 'Consular' sign. Opening the door, I go in.

"A secretary busy typing looks up.

" 'Yes,' she says.

" 'I'd like to see the consular,' I say.

" 'Will you sign the Tourist Register, please,' she says dryly, going back to her typing.

" 'Yes, but before I'll do that, I'd like to see the Consular,' laying my passport on her desk as she looks up puzzled.

" 'I'm here to dissolve my American citizenship.'

" 'She rises and taking my passport goes into the open inner office where she lays the passport on a man's desk saying, 'There is a Mr. Os-wald here who says he's here to dissolve his U.S. citizenship.'

" 'O.K.,' the man says, 'Thanks,'—without looking up.

"As she comes out she invites me into the inner office."

The repressed annoyance Lee shows in writing this account, be-cause everyone didn't get excited and seemed little impressed by what he considered a most dramatic act, indicates the feeling he al-ways seemed to have. It was his temperament to expect everyone to be impressed with his courage and independence. Failing to get it, he smoldered with contempt, and a sense of his own superiority as-serted itself:

"Crossing my legs and laying my gloves in my lap, I wait. He finishes typing, removes the letter from his typewriter, and adjusting his glasses, looks at me.

" 'What can I do for you?' he asks, leafing through my passport.

" 'I'm here to dissolve my U.S. citizenship, and would like to sign the legal papers to that effect.'

" 'Have you applied for Russian citizenship?'

" 'Yes.'

"Taking out a piece of paper, he says, 'Before we get to that I'd like some personal information.' "

The standard questions of name, home address, occupation and so forth were then asked, followed by the obvious question:

" 'Your reasons for coming here?'

"I say, 'I have experienced life in the United States, American military life, and American imperialism. I am a Marxist, and I waited two years for this, and I don't want to live in the U.S. and be burdened by American citizenship.'

"He says, 'O.K. That's all, unless you want to expound your Marxist beliefs. You can go.'

"I said I requested that I be allowed to sign legal papers divesting myself of U.S. Citizenship. 'Do you refuse me that right?'

"He says, 'Ugh. No. But the papers will take some time to get ready. In the meantime, where are you staying?'

" 'Room 212, at the Metropole,' I state, angry at being refused a right."

Furious, Lee started to leave.

" 'You'll tell us what the Russians do next?' Snyder asked.

"I turn very mad. 'Of course,' I say, and leave."

As Richard E. Snyder, the consular official, sat in the witness chair describing this incident to the Commission nearly five years later, I could visualize how this circumspect, thoroughly trained career officer of the Foreign Service might have reacted to this brash youngster. Offensive as Oswald's behavior had been, I pictured Snyder thinking, How can I slow down this callow kid before he hurts himself and his country? Because it was Saturday, technically the office was closed. Snyder told Oswald the papers would take a while to prepare. He should come back on Monday if he wished to sign them.

"I leave Embassy elated at this showdown. Returning to my hotel I feel now my energies are not spent in vain. I'm sure Russians will accept me after this sign of my faith in them!"

Lee states that Rimma advised him to stay in his hotel and wait. He says he did not confide in her his plan to go to the Embassy and renounce his citizenship. This may be true; there is no way of knowing. Yet Lee Oswald was shrewd enough to have calculated that

79

when the Russians found out about his actions they would be impressed. But how would they find out? Would the American Embassy report to the Russians? He had set a series of reactions in motion that eventually served his purpose.

October 31 (continued from the "Historic Diary")
2 P.M.

"A knock. A reporter by the name of Goldberg wants an interview. I am flabbergasted.

" 'How did you find out?'

" 'The Embassy called us,' he said—the American Embassy.

"I send him away. I sit and realize this is one way to bring pressure on me: by notifying my relations in U.S. through the newspapers."

No doubt that was the purpose of the Embassy's call to the press. Perhaps they thought it might cause Oswald to give a more serious review to his intended course of action. Lee sat and considered how he should handle the matter. He wasn't about to change his mind.

"A half an hour later, another reporter, Miss Mosby comes. I answer a few quick questions after refusing an interview. I am surprised at the interest."

Lee makes a considerable point of his surprise at gaining attention at last. He may have been surprised, but he most certainly was not displeased. Later in the evening he received a phone call from another important American source—*Time* magazine. Long-distance calls later came in from America. He was "nonplussed," as he expressed it, and uncertain how to play the game now that he had generated the interest he had sought. The next day there were more reporters at his door, more long-distance calls, including calls from his frantic mother and his brother. The big news had broken in Fort Worth. Another American GI defects! Having received this attention, he wrote, "Now I feel slightly exhilarated—not so lonely."

It is almost too simple to point out that Lee Harvey Oswald had learned a way to extricate himself from obscurity that he would never forget. He was like a child who, failing to gain the attention he wants, finds that smashing a toy or making a mess is the easiest way to obtain recognition. But for a child it is an understandable recourse; for an adult it is the weakest kind of refuge.

There is sufficient evidence to prove that Lee Oswald was not a stupid fellow. When he wanted to he could learn things and he could even be cunning. But his mind groped within a framework of tangled logic. His logic was not helped by the shortcomings of his education, although he read a great deal. His spelling is simply unbelievable. In the last entry he actually wrote, "I feel slightly axzillarated." A few years later, after he had returned to America, he was asked by his Aunt Lillian Murret why he didn't go back to school and qualify himself for some gainful occupation and constructive future. Oswald's reply was: "No, I don't have to go back to school. I don't have to learn anything. I know everything." He was badly equipped to cope with the major intellectual problems he attempted.

After his first burst of notoriety, Lee remained in his room at the Metropole, struggling with a bad case of dysentery. Although he received more calls from reporters, he seemed to be undecided what to do. Gradually the attention lavished on him subsided, and he again became lonely. Certainly it would seem that by now the Soviet officials would realize that he was entitled to recognition as a true Marxist. The days dragged by—a week, and then nearly two weeks. The phone calls were fewer and fewer. With typical lack of interest in stale news, the American reporters lost interest. To them he was just another "nut" who had a lot to learn, and if he wanted to find it out the hard way, that was no skin off their backs. So Lee, now feeling recovered from his bout with sickness, decided he would have to go further. The mere fact that American newspapers had reported his defection might not be enough to call him to the attention of authorities. Why not give an interview? That would hit the front pages again. As he related the event in his diary, on November 14 he called Miss Aline Mosby, whose phone number he had jotted down. Lee Oswald wrote a personal version of this interview. It does not differ substantially from Miss Mosby's account, except that it gives more insight into his assertive disposition. His account begins with Miss Mosby's entering the room:

"I start by saying that I wish it understood that I wish to see the story before it is sent."

" 'All right,' she says. 'It's all the same to me what you do in regards to your life. I'm just taking down your words.' "

"O.K. I say, first the reasons for my coming. She asks about my military service, I answer questions, and then she asks why did you apply for Soviet citizenship? What are your reasons for coming here?

" 'I have waited two years in order to dissolve my American citizenship. I have seen too much hate and injustice in the U.S. I had served in the occupation forces in Japan and occupation of a country is imperialitic [sic], what the Russians would call "Imperialism." I have chosen a Socialist country since there are only two main systems in the world.'

" 'Why the USSR?' she asks, 'Why not Checosylvia, where the housing problem is not so bad?'

" 'I have chosen the USSR since it is the leader of the Socialist camp and the symbolic champion of the cause of communism.'

" 'What other reasons led you to change your loyalty?'

" 'In the U.S., as we know, there are many short-comings: racial segregation, and the suppression of the underdog, the US Communist Party.'

" 'How long have you been studying Marxism?'

" 'I first started studying Marxism when I was 15. I always had to dig for my books in the back dusty shelves of libraries, and old out-dated books were the backbone of my reading.' "

And then the next incredible phrase as actually spelled: " 'Books on phlosiphy, political encomy ect.' "

In order to get the stark effrontery of Oswald's academic pretensions, the brief remainder of his own account of the interview is printed in its original spelling:

" 'In any libary in its most obvious places their are the prominiat anticommunist books we know so well but as I say I allways had to dig for my book.'

" 'What were some impresations you go serving in the occupation forces.'

" 'I saw the american military hauling cannon up a montain side, the tools of war and oppristion. I learned to hate the US imperialistic military.'

" 'Thank you,' she says."

That was the end of Lee Oswald's own account of his interview with Miss Mosby. His "Historic Diary" continues to tell the tale of the immediate result when this interview reached the ears of Soviet officials. In winding up his account of the interview in his diary, he says, "Again I feel slightly better because of the attention."

These are his own words, and they shed more light on his personality than a hundred psychologists could have testified to. He pictured himself a product of "negleck," and he was going to get recognition no matter what he did.

The next day a Russian official came to his room and notified Lee that he could remain in the USSR until some solution was found to what to do with him. "It is comforting news to me." Then followed a long period of waiting—more than a month before he was given his final reward for denouncing the United States. He records the time from then to New Year's, and it furnishes an interesting picture of how he occupied himself:

"I have bought myself two self-teaching Russian language books. I force myself to study 8 hours a day. I sit in my room and read and memorize words. All meals I take in my room. Rimma arranged that. It is very cold on the streets so I rarely go outside at all for this month and a half. I see no one; speak to no-one except every now and then Rimma who calls the ministry about me. Have they forgotten?

"During December I paid no money to the hotel, but Rimma told hotel I was expecting a lot of money from the USA. I have $23 left.

"This month I was called to the passport office, and met 3 new officials who asked me the same questions I was asked a month before. They appear not to know me at all.

"New Years Eve—I spend in the company of Rosa Agafonova at the Hotel Berlin. She has the duty. I sit with her until past midnight. She gives me a small 'Boratin' clown for a New Year's present. She is very nice. I found out only recently she is married, has a small son who was born crippled. That is why she is so strangely tender and compelling."

Thus the New Year's of 1960 passed for Lee Oswald, but he had little longer to wait. Russian bureaucracy had at last ground out a decision.

January 4, 1960

"I am called to passport office and finally given a Soviet document, not even for foreigners but a paper called, 'for those *without* citizenship.' Still I am happy. The official says they are sending me to the city of Minsk. I ask,

" 'Is that in Siberia?'

"He only laughs. He also tells me they have arranged to receive some money through the Red Cross to pay my hotel bills and expenses. I thank the gentleman and leave . . ."

The next day Lee went to the "Red Cross," which in Russia is not the Red Cross at all but a special government agency set up to carry on some of the functions that our voluntary organization would normally handle. He received, according to his own testimony, the substantial sum of 5,000 rubles (old exchange rate), which in Russian terms would be a small fortune. Two days later he left Moscow for Minsk by train to take up what he thought would be his permanent residence.

It is almost impossible to see behind the motives of the Soviet officials in eventually reaching the decision of how to dispose of Lee Oswald. What considerations may have been involved remain a mystery. Some time later Oswald made these notations for himself:

"When I first went to Russia in the winter of 1959, my funds were very limited, so after a certain time when the Russians had assured themselves that I was really a naive American who believed in Communism, they arranged for me to receive a certain amount of money every month. O.K. It came technically through the Red Cross as financial help to a Russian political immigrant but it was arranged by the MVD.

"I told myself it was because I was broke and everybody knew it. I accepted the money because I was hungry and there were several inches of snow on the ground in Moscow at that time. But what it really was was *payment* for my denunciation of the U.S. in Moscow in November and a clear promise that for as long as I lived in the USSR life would be very good. I didn't realize all this, of course, for almost two years.

"As soon as I became completely disgusted with the Soviet Union and started negotiations with the U.S. Embassy in Moscow for my return to the U.S., my 'Red Cross' allotment was cut off.

"This was not difficult to understand since all correspondence in and out of the Embassy is censored. ⟶ .

"I have never mentioned the fact of these monthly payments to anyone.

"I do so in order to state that I shall never sell myself intentionally or unintentionally again.

"As for the fee of $——— I was supposed to receive for this ———, I refuse it. I made pretense to accept it only because otherwise I would have been considered a crackpot and not allowed to appear to express my views. After all, who would refuse money?"

Here the notations are quite incomprehensible. What fee is he referring to now—the 5,000 rubles he was given on leaving Moscow for Minsk, or is it some other consideration for some other duties he was to take up? These last two notations were evidently made en route home from the USSR. They were written after he had spent at least two years there.

This is the other side of Lee Harvey Oswald, the side Marguerite knew nothing about when she came to Washington to testify. For a year and a half she had not heard from Lee—from the time he wrote in his diary that he had been paid off by the Soviet officials and he boasted he was starting a "new life," until he decided to return to the United States.

CHAPTER 6

LEE DECIDES TO COME HOME

L EE HARVEY OSWALD'S DECISION to try to return to the United States had been generating for several months. As early as May 1960, Alexander Zeger had urged him to leave Russia. At first he appeared to be surprised that anyone enjoying Soviet citizenship would encourage him to go home. In his diary he says that Zeger "seems to want to tell me something." Eventually his department head at the factory came right out and said, "Go home." Lee did not elaborate on the whys and wherefores of his friend's advice, but obviously he gradually came to the same conclusion. There is nothing in the thousands of pages of Commission testimony to indicate that Oswald was influenced in his decision by official government pressure. If one is to believe his own writings and statements to friends and relatives on his return, it was his own decision. Gradually he became restless with his life in Minsk. Little by little he found his Russian dream disillusioning.

Shortly after his marriage to Marina, he records in his diary, "I still haven't told my wife of my desire to return to U.S. She is madly in love with me from the very start; boat rides on Lake Minsk, walks through the parks, evening at home or Aunt Valia's place mark May." This brief but pleasant picture of a young married couple's life in Minsk could not hide the fact that Lee, however, was restless.

Even though his marriage to Marina was by his own admission a gesture to spite the girl he really loved, the first glow of their being man and wife gave him personal pleasure. It was very important for him to believe that Marina loved him "madly," because according to his own view of his past life he had had very little love from anyone. In June he wrote, "We draw closer, and I think very little now of Ella. In the last days of this month, I reveal my longings to return to America. My wife is slightly startled, but then encourages me to do what I wish to do."

If the opinions of witnesses who knew the Oswalds ·after their return to the United States can be taken literally, Marina would not have been unpleasantly startled to know Lee wanted to go back home. Many of them felt that her love for Lee had been influenced by more than simple affection. They thought she wanted to find a way to get to America and married Lee hoping he would go. With Lee's intense egocentricity, it never dawned on him that Marina might have some of his own qualities of calculated purpose. He recorded in his diary, "I decided to take my two week vacation and travel to Moscow (without police permission) to the American Embassy to see about getting my U.S. passport back and make arrangements for my wife to enter the U.S. with me."

Technically, Lee was still a United States citizen. The Russian Government had given him a passport "for citizens without nationality." His status, as far as the American Embassy in Moscow was concerned, was indeterminate. They had his passport, which he had given them so dramatically two years earlier. He had been told that if he wanted to fill out papers to renounce his citizenship officially he should return on Monday when the Embassy was open. He had never returned until now—supposedly a changed person.

During the hearings, as the details of· Oswald's nationality problems unfolded, I—and I am certain other members of the Commission—often wondered how much better it would have been if Oswald had not been deterred in his willful efforts to expatriate himself from the United States. The Commission concluded, and I concurred, that State Department officials followed the law as it existed. But—and this is a big *but*—has our Government made it too difficult for those like Oswald—determined to give up the benefits and protection of U.S. citizenship—to carry out their wishes?

I strongly suggest that Congressional committees having jurisdiction of legislation bearing on citizenship determine whether the laws should be modified to better protect the security of the United States. I raise the question: Isn't there some practical way to determine whether a person who has once expressed an allegiance to a foreign government has had a bona-fide change of mind and whether the change is significant?

How much Lee Oswald had changed in those intervening months can be judged by excerpts from a series of essays he wrote on Holland-America Line stationery evidently en route home:

"I have often wondered why it is that the Communist, Capitalist, or even the Fascist and Anarchist elements in America, always profess patriotism toward the land and the people, if not the government, although their ideals must surely lead to the bitter destruction of all and everything.

"I am quite sure these people must hate not only the government but the culture, heritage, and very people itself, and yet they stand up and piously pronounce themselves patriots, displaying their war medals they gained in conflicts between themselves.

"I wonder what would happen if somebody was to stand up and say he was utterly opposed not only to the governments but to the people, to the entire land and complete foundations of his society?"

These reflections by Oswald would indicate that at least he had come to recognize that Communists could be as bad as the capitalists he loathed when he renounced his homeland and offered to give up his American citizenship.

Although he would soon be back in the United States, it would not appear he had gained any new admiration for the economic structure of his own country—just an equal contempt for other systems. He had also acquired a confused and highflown vocabulary, which he exercised in another essay:

"To where can I turn? To factional militants of both systems? To oddball Hegelian idealists out of touch with reality, religious groups, to revisionist, or to absurd anarchism? No!"

In a third essay he explained:

"I have lived under both systems. I have sought the answers and although it would be very easy to dupe myself into believing one system is better than the other, I know they are not.

"I despise the representatives of both systems whether they be Socialist or Christian Democracies; whether they be labor or conservative, they are all the products of the two systems."

In this obscure but earnest vein Oswald proceeds to expound theories which are a mishmash of revolutionary dialectics and dreams of a better society he could not put his finger on. The writings are typical examples of Lee Oswald's chronic state of mind: no system is very good; no leaders are worthy; neither Russian communism nor American democracy operates in the real interest of the people.

In setting himself up as a critic of Karl Marx and Friedrich Engels in these essays, he made a good deal of their "monumental mistakes." Oswald especially concerned himself with the fallacy of the "withering away of the state."

"Marx visualized that the abolition of classes would lead to the gradual reduction of state apparatus. However, this is not the case and is better observed than contemplated. The state, rather, becomes more extensive in that while the powers of central ministries are delegated, they are not reduced in the dividing of an organ of state power into smaller units at lower levels so although some ministers have actually disappeared in Moscow they have become more entrenched than ever at lower levels. Thus in dividing power you multiply units and in everyday life you become more and more dependent on these organs of state power. Wherever you turn you meet them and they touch the lives of the people more and more."

In this discussion of the tendency of government to complicate its own functions, Lee Oswald makes good sense. But with his lack of thorough mental training, he is utterly incapable of understanding why these things happen and what can be done about them. He had seen some of the weaknesses of Russian communism, but he was not even now willing to admit the merits of capitalism. Still he had decided to return to the United States, and he prepared himself to deal with the questions he might be asked—either at the Embassy or when interviewed by the newspapers.

Among the papers found in Oswald's effects were two particularly curious documents. These are in the form of Q. and A's. In each he asks himself a question and then proceeds to answer. For all practical purposes they are identical questionnaires with two different sets of answers. In the first self-directed interview, he seems to be answering the way he would say it if he were answering questions honestly. In the second interrogation of himself he is evidently rehearsing what he intends to say so as to please American officials and regain his full rights of citizenship.

The first interview seems to tell how he really felt about his defection.

"Why did you go to the USSR?"

"I went as a mark of disgust and protest against American political policies in foreign countries; my personal sign of discontent and horror at the misguided line of reasoning of the U.S. Government."

"What about those letters?" [The letters he wrote at the time of his defection, denouncing his country.]

"I made several letters in which I expressed my above feeling to the American Embassy when in October 1959 I went to legally liquidate my American citizenship and was refused this legal right."

"Did you make statements against the U.S. there?"

"Yes."

"What about that type recording?" [Meaning radio tapes in which he lauded Soviet policies.]

"I made a recording for Radio Moscow which was broadcast the following Sunday in which I spoke about the beautiful capital of the Socialist work and all its progress."

"Did you break the laws by residing or taking work in the USSR?"

"I did in that I took an oath of allegiance to the USSR."

"Isn't all work in the USSR considered State work?"

"Yes, of course, and in that respect I also broke U.S. law in accepting work under a foreign state."

"What about the statements you made to UPI agent, Miss Mosby?"

"I was approached by Miss Mosby and other reporters just after I had formally requested the American Embassy to legally liquidate my U.S. citizenship, for a story. They were notified by the U.S. Embassy, not by me. I answered questions and made statements to Miss Mosby in regard to my reasons for coming to the USSR. Her story was warped by her later but in barest essence, it is possible to say she had the truth printed."

"Why did you remain in the USSR for so long if you only wanted a look?"

"I resided in the USSR from October 16, 1959, to the spring of 1961, a period of two-and-a-half years. I did so because I was living quite comfortably. I had plenty of money, an apartment rent-free, lots of girls and so forth. Why should I leave all that?"

"Are you a Communist?"

"Yes, basically, although I hate the USSR and the Socialist system. I still think Marxism can work under different circumstances."

"Have you ever known a Communist?"

"Not in the USA."

"What are the outstanding differences between the USSR and the USA?"

"None, except in the USA the living standard is a little higher; freedoms are about the same; medical aid and the educational system in the USSR is better than the USA."

This was the first set of questions that Lee Oswald put to himself with candid answers by that personality who had once described himself as having developed through neglect "a mean streak of indepence." The answers to the questions reflect a disillusionment with the Soviet brand of communism, but he is frank to say that he is still a Communist, with a belief in its workability under other conditions. He is more skeptical about his citizenship status, on the technical basis of having in effect pledged loyalty to a foreign power, than the State Department officials who reviewed his application for reinstatement of his passport. But the State Department eventually concluded he had not given up his citizenship under prevailing laws. After examining all the evidence, the Commission had to concur.

His purpose in the second interview must have been to rehearse what he intended to tell American officials and reporters, not what he really felt. Note the tongue-in-cheek irony of the concluding sentence of the second interview when he says about himself, "Newspapers: Thank you sir, you are a *real* patriot!!"

"Why did you go to the USSR?"

"I went as a citizen of the U.S. (as a tourist) residing in a foreign country which I have a perfect right to do. I went there to see the land, the people and how their system works."

"What about those letters?"

"I made no letters deriding the U.S.!! In correspondence with the U.S. Embassy, I made no anti-American statements. Any criticism I might have made was of policies not our government."

"Did you make statements against the U.S. there?"

"No."

"What about the tape recording?"

"I made a recording for radio—the Moscow Tourist Radio Travelogue in which I spoke about sight-seeing and what I had seen in Moscow tourist circles. I expressed delight in all the interesting places. I mentioned in this respect the University, Museum of Art, Red Square, the Kremlin. I remember I closed this two minute recording by saying I hoped our people would live in peace and friendship."

"Did you break laws by residing or taking work in the USSR?"

"Under U.S. law a person may lose the protection of the U.S., by voting or serving in the armed forces of a foreign state or taking an oath of allegiance to that state. I did none of these."

"Isn't all work in the USSR considered state work?"

"No. Technically, only plants working directly for the state, usually defense, all other plants are owned by the workers who work in them."

"What about statements you made to UPI agent Miss Mosby in 1959?"

"I was approached at the time of my arrival in the USSR just after I had formally notified the U.S. Embassy in Moscow of my future residence in the USSR by the newspaper agencies in Moscow including the UPI, API, and Time, Inc., who were notified by the Embassy. I did not call them. I answered questions and gave statements to Miss Mosby of UPI. I requested her to let me OK her story before she released it, which is the polite and usual thing. I saw her version of what I said just after she sent it. I immediately called her to complain about this at which time she apologized but said her editor, and not her, had added several things. She said London was very excited about the story (there is how I deduced that she had already sent it) so there wasn't much else I could do about it, and I didn't realize that the story was even more blown out of shape once it got to the USA. I'm afraid the printed story was fabricated sensationalism."

"Why did you remain in the USSR so long if you only wanted a look?"

"I resided in the USSR until February 1961 when I wrote the Embassy stating that I would like to go back (my passport was at the Embassy for safe-keeping). They invited me to Moscow for this purpose. However, it took me almost a half year to get a permit to leave the city of Minsk for Moscow. In this connection I had to use a letter from the head consul to the Russian authorities in Minsk (the Russians are very bureaucratic and slow about letting foreigners travel about the country and, hence, the visa). When I did get to Moscow the Embassy immediately gave me back my passport and advised me as how to get an exit visa from the Russians for myself and my Russian wife. This long and arduous process took months, from July 1961 until—1962. Therefore you see almost one year was spent in trying to leave the country. That's why I was there so long. Not out of desire!"

"Are you a Communist? Have you ever known a Communist?"

"No, of course not, I have never even known a Communist, outside of the ones in the USSR but you can't help that."

"What are the outstanding differences between the U.S. and the USSR?"

"Freedom of speech, travel, outspoken opposition to unpopular policies, freedom to believe in God."

"Thank you sir, you are a *real* patriot!!"

This second imaginary interview was hardly written in the spirit of a man who recognizes that he has made a mistake and is truly contrite. It is just as cynical and supercilious as Oswald ever was when he went to Moscow and demanded that the Embassy consider his American citizenship "dissolved." Between the lines it said what Lee Harvey Oswald always seemed to say to acquaintances, relatives and society in general: "You are all fools. You are all dopes. This is my game and I will play it to get what I want."

In his December 17, 1959, letter to his brother Robert he had said his final farewell with a similar flourish of conceit:

"I will be moving from this hotel and so you need not write me here. I have chosen to remove all ties with my past, so I will not write you again, nor do I wish you to try and contact me. I'm sure you understand that I would not like to receive correspondence from people in the country which I fled. I am starting a new life and I do not wish to have anything to do with the old life."

It is very possible that the tone of this letter had been determined not so much for his brother Robert's benefit as for the censors, who at the time were most certainly reporting everything he said in his letters to the highest Soviet officials. This was after his suicide attempt, after his denunciation of the USA to Miss Mosby and while he was still negotiating with Russian bureaucracy to let him stay in the USSR. Lee Oswald, who loved the sense of power that deception gave him, knew how to write letters and interviews which would put him in whatever light served his purpose at the moment. Now he wanted to get back to the United States. He was ready with an interview neatly prepared that would reverse everything he had said in 1959, and he was enjoying the irony of his deliberate duplicity. He had also resumed his contact with his brother Robert. In his opening letter he did not bother with apologies for what he had said previously.

May 5, 1961

DEAR ROBERT,

It's been a long time since I have written you, more than a year. A lot has happened in that time.

I am now living in the city of Minsk which is located about 400 miles S-W of Moscow. Minsk is the capital city of the Soviet State of Bello-Russia.

I shall have been living here already a year and three months. I came to live in Minsk after I wrote my last letter to you. I have been working at the local radio-television plant as a metal-smith.

On April 30, of this year I got married. My wife is nineteen years old. She was born in the city of Leningrad, which is the second largest city in the USSR. Her parents are dead and she was living with her aunt and uncle here in Minsk when I first met her.

Not too long ago I received a letter from mother but I lost the address. I would like you to send it to me when you write.

We have a small flat near the factory and are living nicely. In general I have found the living conditions here to be good but there are a lot of things still to be done. I hope to send you something from here if you like. The Soviet nation is one of the most interesting countrys I have seen in my travels. You should try to visit us sometime. I sometimes meet American tourists here especially in the summer. Well, that's about all for now. Hope to hear from you soon.

Regards to Vada and Kathy,

LEE

According to his diary, by the time this letter was written to Robert—sounding his brother out for a resumption of friendship, and incidentally not asking forgiveness—Lee had already made up his mind that he wanted to return to America. On May 31 Lee wrote Robert again, dropping a hint that "maybe I'll be seeing you again."

DEAR ROBERT,

I was glad to hear from you, and really surprised that you have a new son. That really is great. Congratulations to you and Vada.

My wife's name is Marina. I am sorry I forgot to write it last time. Marina works is a pharmacy at one of the hospitals here (almost all girls and women in the USSR have some kind of profession and work at it). She sends her regards to you and Vada and the kids. . . .

I can't say whether I will ever get back to the States or not. If I can get the government to drop charges against me, and get the Russians to let me out with my wife, then maybe I'll be seeing you again. But you know it is

94

not simple for *either* of those two things so I just can't say for now. I am in touch with the American Embassy in Moscow so if anything comes up I'll know.

Well, that's about all for now. Say hello to Robert Lee, Jr. for me.

Your brother,

LEE

Step by step Lee was working toward the information he really wanted to know before making an all-out attempt to return to the United States. He wanted Robert to tell him whether the United States Government would prefer charges against him. What would be the official reaction back home to his having so emphatically denounced his own country, his own people, his own family? He was fishing for information. He continued to probe the matter, carefully appearing not to be overanxious.

June 26, 1961

DEAR ROBERT,

. . . I assume the government must have a few charges against me since my coming here like this is illegal. But I really don't know exactly what charges. . . .

Marina says she would like to see America and meet you and the family. I received a letter from ma yesterday. She is working on a ranch in Crowell, Texas. Do you see her?

Well, that's all for now.

LEE

Approximately two weeks after writing this letter to Robert, Lee noted in his diary:

"July 8, I fly by plane to Moscow on a IL-20. Two hours and twenty minutes later, after taking a tearful and anxious parting from my wife, I arrive in Moscow. Departing by bus from the airfield, I arrive in the center of the city. Making my way through heavy traffic, I don't come in sight of the Embassy until 3:00 in the afternoon. It's Saturday. What if they are closed? Entering I find the offices empty but manage to contact Snyder on the phone (since all Embassy Personnel live in the same building). He comes down to greet me. Shakes my hand after interview. He advises me to come in the first thing Monday."

The fact that Consul Snyder shook Lee's hand after this interview gave Lee a great sense of relief and confidence. Twice he had mentioned the possibility of U.S. charges against him, and he had stood prepared to face the consequences if that was the case. On a Saturday, when the Embassy was officially closed and Lee reached an official only by chance, no one was in a position to give him final assurance that he would be admitted back into the United States. However, the ready handshake at the conclusion of his little talk with Snyder had particular significance. Snyder, at any rate, seemed inclined to let bygones be bygones. Obviously the door was not slammed shut. He did not have long to wait for a decision which at least re-established his personal status. On Monday he was no longer a guest of the USSR with a "passport for persons without nationality." Promptly on Monday he was given his own passport back! He had proof—the most valuable in the world—that he was an American citizen. Snyder pointed out that the possession of this in Minsk would give him bartering power when dealing with the Soviet officials in his efforts to get an exit visa for himself.

In retrospect it may seem incredible to the layman that the American Embassy in Moscow and the State Department in Washington could have reached such a decision. The Commission concluded that no law had been violated, however, and authorities had no proper basis for denying him the return of his passport. Historians may well ask the question of how anyone could have made the fatal mistake of readmitting a defector who, a year and a half later, would murder the President of the United States. Those who insist on seeing a sinister plot behind these events after all the facts of the Presidential Commission have been published may never be silenced. Marguerite Oswald, Lee's mother, insisted that the fact Lee was able to return so readily indicated that he must indeed have been some sort of agent working for the USA. But after thousands of pages of testimony there is nothing in the record to indicate any significance beyond a more or less standard policy of the State Department to treat returning defectors with leniency. Those who had met Oswald when he visited the Embassy two and a half years ago to renounce his citizenship regarded him as a callow kid who would eventually learn from firsthand experience in Russia what a mistake he was making. It had happened many times before with pseudointellectual youngsters. So Oswald had learned his lesson? Just as they had suspected. Well, technically it might be said that he had not renounced his citizenship. They would return his passport. When Lee wrote his brother Robert on the eleventh day of July he no longer talked of "charges" against him. He was once again the cocksure Lee Harvey Oswald of old:

DEAR ROBERT,

On the 8th of July I and my wife went into the American Embassy. I cannot write you what went on there because the Russians read all letters going in and out. But anyway I have the American passport and we are doing everything we can to get out.

You don't know what a test this is. I could write a book about how many feelings have come and gone since that day.

The Russians can be crude and very crude at times. They gave a cross-examination to my wife on the first day we came back from Moscow. They knew everything because they spy and read the mails but we shall continue to try to get out. We shall not retreat. As for your package we never received it. I suppose they swiped that too, the bastards.

I hope some day I'll see you and Vada but if and when I come, I'll come with my wife. You can't imagine how wonderful she stood up.

                                        Write often
                                        Your brother
                                        LEE

P. S. Marina sends her regards to Vada and you and the kids.

Lee's ability to shift his allegiance and suddenly become righteously injured by the possibility that his "comrade" Russians might have confiscated a package from his brother seems almost comical. For more than two years he had been accepting a living subsidy of 700 rubles a month from the so-called Russian Red Cross; he had ruthlessly cut all his ties with the country of his birth, with his very flesh and blood, not to mention the scathing denunciation of his homeland, and now (having admitted in a mock interview that he really was still a Communist) he professed great indignation at the "crude" way in which Russian officials treated Marina. Was this letter prepared with the thought in mind that the FBI might intercept his correspondence with Robert and suddenly realize what an upstanding American he really was? The workings of Lee Oswald's mind in these areas and many others are simply without principle. When trying to understand what motive Oswald might have had

97

when he fired those shots from the Texas School Book Depository Building, one must appreciate his long-standing temperament from these previous acts. Did Lee Oswald need a motive? The answer becomes clearer as the course of his career unfolds.

Having been given back his United States passport, Lee was in a stronger position to press for an exit visa for Marina. However, this was not something that could be quickly obtained, and, aside from Russian red tape, Soviet officials continued to put pressure on Marina to change her mind. Lee records in his diary:

July 15–August 20 (1961)

"We have found out which blanks and certificates are necessary to apply for an exit visa. They number about twenty papers: birth certificates, affidavits, photos, etc. On August 20th we give the papers out. They say it will be three and a half months before we know whether they'll let us go or not. In the meantime, Marina has had to stand four different meetings at the place of work held by her bosses at the direction of 'someone' by phone. The Young Communist League headquarters also called about her and she had to go see them for one and a half hours. The purpose (expressed) is to disuade her from going to the USA. Net effect —make her more stubborn about wanting to go. Marina is pregnant. We only hope that the visas come through soon."

August 21–September 1

"I make expected trips to the passport and visa office. Also to the Ministry of Foreign Affairs in Minsk. Also Minister of Internal Affairs, all of which have a say in the granting of the visa. I extracted promises of quick attention to us."

Never one to be intimidated by authority, and especially now that he had regained possession of his American passport, Lee stated that he "extracted" promises of quick attention. This fact, however, did not seem to impress Russian bureaucracy. The days dragged on and he reported on October 18, "No word from the Ministry ('They'll call us')."

Lee and Marina had now been married a year and a half. There was no more mention of Lee's frustrated love for Ella. On the surface, the course of their marriage was going along smoothly, and there were times when Lee expressed real enthusiasm for Marina. Although Lee did not elaborate on his wife's personality, it is apparent that Marina was not a weak person. She had stood up to the Soviet officials. She had a will of her own, and if Lee had imagined that he was marrying a girl who was so "madly" in love with him that she would agree to anything he wanted, he was mistaken. Marina had a streak of independence that no doubt provoked occasions of tension. She was outspoken. It appears that about this time domestic squabbles occurred. With Lee's overbearing and demanding personality, his superior outlook that he was intellectually above everyone else, these quarrels could arouse hot reactions. Did the fact that Marina took a month's leave of absence from her job for a vacation in the Urals in October signal the beginning of those many separations between husband and wife which were to characterize their married life in the United States?

Lee reported: "Marina leaves Minsk by train on vacation to the city of Khar'kov in the Urals to visit an aunt for four weeks." In a letter to his mother he explained, "Marina is on her vacation now. She is spending it with her aunt in the city of Khar'kov about six hundred miles southeast of here. She is just relaxing and taking it easy from work and the house work. We both agreed that she should go to a new environment on her vacation."

It is hard to imagine Lee agreeing so amiably to Marina's taking off for a month's visit 600 miles away when every cent was needed to pay for their passage to the United States if they hoped to leave soon.

In his diary Lee commented on his feelings and activities while Marina was away:

"During this time I am lonely but I and Erik go to the dances and public places for entertainment. I haven't done this in quite a few months now. I spent my birthday alone at the opera watching my favorite *Queen of Spades*. I am 22 years old."

Is it possible that he went to "the dances and public places for entertainment" without thinking of, or looking for, Ella?

On November 2, 1961, he seemed happy that "Marina arrives back, radiant with several jars of preserves for me from her aunt in Khar'kov."

A drab and cold winter settled on Minsk. Preceding deep snows and leaden sky were days of freezing, penetrating rain. Apparently

Marina's radiance did not last for long, nor did the spirit of reunion endure to offset the gloom and tedium of those gray days before the winter solstice:

"Now we are becoming annoyed about the delay. Marina is beginning to waver about going to the U.S., probably from the strain and her being pregnant. Still we quarrel, and so things are not too bright, especially with the approach of the hard Russian winter."

In her testimony before the Commission, Marina categorically denied that she and Lee had had any serious domestic difficulties prior to coming to the United States. Lee, however, used the expression "Still we quarrel" as if these were frictions that had been going on for some time. From the pattern of their domestic life once they were in America, it would have been surprising if all had run smoothly in Russia. When asked whether Lee had ever shown any vicious or brutal qualities while they lived in Minsk, Marina said that she had never known him to be that way in Russia; he was immediately a "different" person on coming to the United States. However, Marina was also the person who testified that their differences in Fort Worth were just small affairs, petty quarrels common to all married folks. She testified to this despite the fact that witnesses—including Marguerite Oswald and others—saw her with bruises and black eyes little more than two months after they arrived in Texas. Lee Oswald was not a person who could abide opposition or authority from anyone. Even though Marina did not know it, he would resort to almost any action—even attempted suicide—to get his own way. He had lied to Marine Corps authorities to get an early discharge on a "hardship" basis allegedly to help his mother. Three days after getting home, he had walked out and left her, saying he was going to New Orleans to obtain work. He lied to his mother when he said he was going into the import-export business and wound up in Moscow, having spent money she direly needed for passage. He had written brave letters to his brother implying that in case of war between Russia and the United States he would shoot Robert as quickly as any other American.

The seeds of trouble were planted long before their arrival in the United States. But Christmas Day of 1961 turned out to be a very happy day for them. The year ended on a more cheerful and optimistic note:

> *December 25 Christmas Day, Tuesday.*
> "Marina is called to the passport and visa office. She is told we have been granted Soviet exit visas. She fills out the completing blank and then comes home with the news. It's great (I think!)."

There were still months of waiting ahead before Lee and Marina would finally be on their way to America. There was the matter of entrance permission for Marina into the United States on a non-quota basis and the problem of raising the money to make the trip.

CHAPTER 7

A LONG WAIT

Bᴀᴄᴋ ʜᴏᴍᴇ ʙᴏᴛʜ Lee's brother, Robert, and his mother were doing everything they could to hurry his return. The relationship between members of the family was not close, but they were drawn together by the correspondence with Lee. In families we choose to regard as "typically" American, we think of children and parents communicating with one another even though they may live miles apart. We expect that brothers and sisters see one another at least on holidays and take an interest in one another's activities. But for a combination of reasons this was not true of the Oswald family. Perhaps it is no longer true of as many American families as we would like to think. Marguerite Oswald had three children by two different husbands. She also had a third husband. As far as the Commission knew, none of the husbands was living. As each child had come of age, he had left home and joined the Marine Corps or Coast Guard. In effect, none returned to a family life, and thus each went his own way. John Pic had been in New York many years and was now in the Air Force. Robert had returned from the Marines, lived with his mother a short while and then, getting married, had set out to establish his own household. Lee had left the Marines to journey to Russia. There were few threads to hold the family fabric together.

In his letters at this time Lee asked members of his family about the others. He told his brother, "I received a letter from ma yesterday. She is working on a ranch in Crowell, Texas. Do you see her?" In letters to his mother he inquired about other members of the family.

Marina testified that when she had first met Lee in Minsk she had asked him whether he had a mother. He had told her at the time that his mother was dead and only later admitted that he had lied to her. This attitude is not surprising, considering his other qualities of heartlessness. However, it still seems unusual that Robert would find out the whereabouts of his mother through the roundabout route of letters to Lee in Minsk, Russia! But that was typical of the relationships in the Oswald family. The Commission was later astounded to discover that John Pic's father was very much alive in New Orleans, Louisiana. He testified that he had supported his son through payments to Marguerite until John was an adult. John Pic, however, had not seen his father or heard from him since he was an infant.

Now, through the prospect of Lee's return to America, the family drew together—but only momentarily. In understanding later events one has to appreciate that the Oswald family was not a family at all, in the sense of living together. They were individuals of common blood each of whom went his own way most of the time but now and then were drawn together by unusual circumstances. Marguerite was a person who sometimes tried to unite them but invariably failed. Robert had considerable affection toward his brother and tried to be helpful. Some family warmth revived in Lee. From Russia he had written Robert in part, "I received a package from mother a few days ago. She sent me a razor and pressurized can of shaving cream (which I asked her for) and a lot of other stuff. She is real good to me."

Occasionally Lee expressed himself as appreciative of his mother's affection:

"Received your letter today and was surprised that you are working on a ranch. Where is Crowell, Texas, anyway? How is it you decided to go there?

"I am glad you think Marina is beautiful and I shall be good to her. She doesn't have a mother and father. They are dead. But she has a lot of aunts and uncles here in Minsk and also in Leningrad where she was born. She was living at her aunt's place when I met her. They are real nice people. Her uncle is a major in the Soviet Army. She works as a druggist. She finished the University two years ago for that occupation.

"We are in good health and I am glad you are with good people also."

And then a few weeks later,

"I received your packet today. Thanks a lot for all those nice things. You really should not have bothered to send those little things—it's so expensive. I really now only need literature and every now and then some shaving cream like you sent before. In the future please send very light and necessary things.

"I wrote Robert and he was surprised that you are working at Crowell, Texas—don't you write at all to each other?"

Even Lee was surprised that his brother and mother were so completely out of communication. Marguerite took great pleasure in re-establishing contact with Lee and lavished presents on him.

"Received your package of books yesterday. Thanks a lot for them. I am very glad to have them.

"I hope you are feeling well and enjoying your stay in Vernon. . . ."

"Do you ever hear much from John [Pic—Lee's half-brother]? Where is he?

"I am receiving a letter from Robert almost once a month now. . . ."

Now that Lee had determined to think of himself once again as an American he was eager and happy with his correspondence. He warmed to Marguerite and her generosity:

"Sorry to take so long to write but I thought something might have come up but we're still waiting.

"I received your birthday card on the 19th—thanks for the thought. I'll be glad to get *any* books you send in the future. You might include some fashion magazines for Marina also if you remember it.

"You needn't worry about my losing American citizenship. I can only do that if I want to, and I don't want to.

"Marina unfortunately doesn't speak any English at all. I would like her to learn and I've bought some books for her on the subject but for now she doesn't want to learn. She speaks a little French already (she learned in grammar school) and she doesn't want to study another language for now. She really does not have time, you know, what with her working from 10-5 and then the housework but it doesn't matter for now."

This discussion regarding Marina's attitude toward learning English proved interesting for a number of reasons that came out in the testimony later. Most witnesses agreed that Lee never wanted Marina to learn English, and he systematically discouraged her. Even after he returned to the United States he insisted on talking nothing but Russian with Marina and would leap at an opportunity to speak

Russian whenever he met someone who spoke it. On the other hand, at least two witnesses—George Bouhe and George De Mohrenschildt—found Marina lazy about making any effort to teach herself. They gave her books and English teaching records which they claim she did little to make use of. As the witnesses tell their stories about Marina we see a many-sided individual who is hardly the simple, soft-spoken innocent portrayed by the majority of the press. In the course of the investigation, the witnesses spoke for themselves. Marina was not without her human frailties.

A little more than a month before Christmas Lee had announced to his mother:

"Well, at the end of February or the beginning of March we should have a baby. We want a boy. . . .

"If you have any old photos of myself and of you also, please send them.

"Do you ever hear anything from Aunt Lillian in New Orleans [Marguerite's sister, with whom Lee had once lived]?

"And how about John?

"Marina sends her love and asks do you want to be a grandmother again??

"Are you still working for those people? You have changed addresses again haven't you?"

Enclosed in the letter were some postal cards of Leningrad, the city where Marina was born.

Although Marina could not write English, she wrote a letter to Marguerite in Russian which Lee transcribed in English:

"DEAR MOTHER;

"Today we received your grand gift. I am very surprised you guessed my taste in color and fabric.

"Here it is already very cold so your wool stole will be very useful. It is nice to feel that you are so attentive to me, more so even than to Lee.

"I shall always remember your gift as a mark of our friendship.

"I hope you won't be nervous for us; you shouldn't worry about us too much.

"I have never seen you (except on a photograph) but I have a lot of affection for you already. . . ."

Having Marina write her in this warm manner no doubt pleased Marguerite very much. Lee's mother had lived a lonely and independent life for many years. The prospect of a daughter-in-law who might care for her—and a new grandchild—gave her a lift. Never one to lack energy, she was busy trying to set things up for her son's return. Perhaps things would be different with Lee now. Perhaps she would have a family again—a son and a daughter-in-law who would care for her and listen to her advice as children should listen to their parents. John Pic and Robert had long since shown that they wanted as little to do with their mother as possible. Perhaps there was still hope that one of her children would treat her as a real mother! Just before Christmas Lee wrote:

"I sure do appreciate your help.

"I think we'll get together if we finally get back to the States, and maybe we'll be able to do that in Texas.

"Marina is feeling fine and everything is OK with that.

"Marina laughed when she heard your question about babies born at home or in hospitals. Of course, almost everyone here has their babies in the hospital."

January 2, 1962

"DEAR MOTHER;

"Well, I have pretty good news. We *shall* receive our visas about the middle of February, which means we may arrive in the U. S. about the first of March, give or take a month or two. [In his enthusiasm Lee forgot that the baby would be born in March, which would make immediate travel unlikely.]

"I would like you to do something important for us. Get in touch with the Red Cross in Vernon and then to contact an organization called 'International Rescue Commission,' or any organization which aids persons from abroad get settled.

"We need $800 for tickets from Moscow to New York and from New York to Texas.

"You show them the enclosed letter from the Embassy. You can tell the Red Cross that at time of writing my wife has been granted non-quota immigration status for entrance into the United States, and that both of us have now received Soviet visas to leave the Soviet Union.

"Tell them all outstanding documentation has already been resolved. We only need the money for the tickets now.

"Ask them to contact the American Embassy, Moscow for information and if they send money, to send it: c/o US Embassy, Moscow USSR.

"I want you to try to get the money through some organization and not try to collect it yourself, alone.

"Do not, of course, take any loan—only a gift. And don't send your own money.

"A lot of organizations exist which help people in our case, so it won't do any harm to take a try. . . ."

Here was the old, more familiar Lee Oswald talking. A great change? "A lot of organizations exist to help people in our case"! In his case, indeed! How could he conceive that any organization existed to rescue a defector who was still basically a Communist, who had denounced his own country and who now wanted to bring a Russian wife whose background was unknown with him to the United States? What Lee was obviously saying was "There are a lot of organizations that can be made suckers of; take their money if you can get it, but for heaven's sakes don't assume responsibility in my name or yours for paying it back." Lee did not understand, nor did he care to, a whit more about principle or ethics now than he had before when he lied to get out of the Marine Corps.

Lee did not ask his brother to do these little tasks. He asked his mother. He was sure of her reaction. Marguerite went all out in contacting the Vernon Red Cross. She worked for weeks trying to contact the International Rescue Commission and was indignant when the local Red Cross worker implied that she had no intention of helping a Communist defector. That was a motherly reaction, and it must be remembered that Marguerite never did believe that Lee was a simple defector. She clung to the notion that he was somehow an agent of the U.S. Government.

Three weeks later Lee had another favor to ask of his mother, and again she went to work on the problem:

"Go to the nearest office of the 'Immigration and Naturalization Offices' and fill out and file an 'affidavit of support' on behalf of my wife. This is a technical point in regards to permission to enter the U. S. for Marina and must be made in the U. S. You simply fill out a blank (there may be a charge of a few dollars) and that's all.

"Please do this now as they are actually waiting for this document in Moscow."

Although it is common practice for Americans to sign such affidavits guaranteeing the support of immigrants in the event they are unable to find work, certainly Marguerite was in no position to offer such help. Lee, however, did not hesitate to ask her to make this commitment. As it turned out, Marguerite either decided she was not in a position to sign the affidavit or she may have been advised by the Immigration Service that she was not qualified. Therefore, she prevailed on one of her employers to sign the paper.

Lee's gratitude was so remarkable for this kindness that he limited his comments to "Today I received the affidavits from Mr. Phillips." He then abruptly changed the subject, and it was a month later that it occurred to him to ask his mother, "Who is Mr. Phillips? Since you work at a new place now do you still have contact with him?" But still not a word of appreciation. It was just one more thing that Lee took for granted.

In her efforts to find a way of raising some money for Lee, the thought occurred to Marguerite that perhaps the newspapers might be of help, either from the point of view of paying for Lee's story on his return to the United States or perhaps enlisting their sympathy now that Lee had come to see the light. She wrote suggesting this idea. His reaction was negative:

"As to your questions about the money problem I don't know if giving the story to the newspapers is too good. Maybe you'd better hold off for a while about that. I'll tell you when."

To her suggestion that she plan to come and meet him in New York, he replied coldly:

"The baby is due around March 1. We will probably fly into the U.S. on an airplane and I see no reason for you to come to New York to meet us. . . ."

And then a further rebuff:

"I want you to understand that although you can aid in certain small ways, this business about our coming to the U. S. is relatively simple. Don't make it more complicated than it is."

This was hardly the tone of voice that indicated Lee was about to alter his attitude toward his mother and take her to his bosom. It must have been a keen disappointment to her when he said in March:

"You asked whether I'll be staying at your place or Robert's in Fort Worth. I don't think I'll be staying at either but I will be visiting both. In any event, I'll want to live on my own and probably will finally live in Fort Worth or New Orleans."

When testifying before the Investigating Commission, Robert's comment on his relationships with Marguerite seemed to have been the general feeling of all three children toward their mother: "She is rather persistent, and this is not new to me—we have never really gotten along. She tries to dominate me and my wife, and I might say that applied to John and his family and also to the extent that it applied to Lee and his wife, and there is just generally the picture as far as I and my mother are concerned."

On February 15 an event happened that might have had a maturing influence on anyone less self-centered than Lee Oswald:

"Dawn. Marina wakes me. It's her time. At 9:00 we arrive at the hospital. I leave her in care of nurses and leave to go to work. 10:00, Marina has a baby girl. When I visit the hospital at 5:00 after work I am given news. We both wanted a boy. Marina feels well. Baby girl, O.K."

The style of Lee's "Historic Diary" is usually terse, but his reaction to the birth of a daughter rather than a son is remarkable for its lack of elaboration.

He reported on February 23: "Marina leaves hospital. I see June for first time."

Somehow the entries that follow in his diary are typical of Lee Harvey Oswald. He did not have time to comment on the appearance of the baby, Marina's reactions at becoming a mother or his own feelings, but he went into considerable detail about a relatively petty matter that represented his personal battle with bureaucracy. He had to record his defiance of authority:

"I go to register (as prescribed by law) the baby. I want her name to be June Marina Oswald. But those bureaucrats say that her middle name must be the same as my first—a Russian custom supported by law. I refuse to have her name written as 'June Lee.' They promise to call the City Hall and find out in this case since I do have a U.S. passport."

The next day he was told that none of the officials knew exactly what to do, but everyone agreed it should be done according to the usual form. Lee admitted he lost that struggle. The child was named "June Lee" according to protocol.

Lee had learned from his correspondence with his mother that the Marine Corps had given him a discharge that was other than honorable. He did not seem to be certain that it was a "dishonorable discharge," as he sometimes referred to it, when in reality it was an "undesirable discharge." This action had been taken after his denunciation of the United States and his declaration that he intended to spend the rest of his life in the USSR.

Although much was made of this after the fateful events in Dallas, and although he had written a letter of protest to Texas Governor John Connally, who had served as Secretary of the Navy, it would appear that Lee's reaction to this action has been generally misunderstood. In searching for a motive for Lee's murder of President Kennedy and his wounding of Governor Connally, speculation naturally developed that he was seeking revenge for a grievous personal injury. Nowhere do his reactions appear to have been violent to his Marine Corps discharge. His comments on this subject to his mother and brother are calm, collected, even in some respects indifferent.

Having been informed by his mother of the Marine Corps action, he wrote, "If you don't have that letter from the Marine Corps telling about the discharge, how about getting a copy? I would like to have some material on which to start before going into the discharge matter with the Marines." This is not like Lee's language when he was indignant. And then in a letter to Robert he explained why he was not too upset by the action. "Mother wrote me a letter the other day in which she informed me that the Marine Corps had given me a dishonorable discharge in November 1959. Did you know this?" In light of Lee's character, his next sentence was not surprising: "Of course, this is not too bad. It relieves me of reserve duty, but still I should take this into account."

In a matter-of-fact tone of voice he continued, "I wrote to John B. Connally, Secretary of the Navy who lives in Fort Worth asking about my dishonorable discharge. Maybe you could ask him to look into the case since I don't know whether the Russians will let the letter through."

Even after Lee had returned to the United States he did little or nothing to argue his military status. A routine review turned down his appeal for reconsideration, but he did not seem to brood about it. To be relieved of reserve duty and any sense of responsibility for future military service appeared to be a fair settlement to him. Certainly this so-called "grievance" had nothing to do with the shooting in Dallas. The Commission's ballistic research indicates there was "persuasive evidence" that the bullet which struck Governor Connally was a total accident. Had a Secret Service man or Vice President Johnson been riding in that "jumper" seat he might have been the one to be hit.

One thing, however, that did interest Lee now was finding out what the Texas newspapers had said about his defection in 1959. After reminding his mother of the need of the affidavit for Marina's support, he asked:

"Also you can see about sending me some clippings or columns from the Fort Worth papers for the month of November 1959. I want to know just what was said about me in the Fort Worth newspapers so I can be forewarned. If you don't have the clippings yourself, you can always get back issues of newspapers by applying at their offices or the public library."

Now again, as the time of his return to the United States drew near, he quizzed Robert:

"You once said that you asked around about whether or not the U. S. Government had any charges against me. You said at that time, 'no.' Maybe you should ask around again. It's possible now that the government knows I'm coming, they'll have something waiting.

"If you find out any information about me, please let me know. I'd like to be ready on the draw, so to speak."

A few days after Lee asked his mother for clippings he repeated the request to Robert:

"You wouldn't have any clippings from the November 1959 newspapers of Fort Worth, would you?

"I am beginning to get interested in just what they did say about me and my trip here.

"The information might come in handy when I get back. I would hate to come back completely unprepared."

In late February or early March Lee commented on an event of widespread international interest. He seems to have been keeping up with the news. He told Robert:

"I heard over the Voice of America that they released Powers, the U-2 spy plane fellow. That's big news where you are, I suppose. He seems to be a nice, bright American-type fellow when I saw him in Moscow."

Whatever Lee's worries about the Russians whom he "distrusted," the Fort Worth newspapers and what they may have said about his defection, and the charges which he imagined might be brought against him in the United States, the State Department had decided that he deserved the help of the Government in returning to the United States. The propaganda value of a defector redefecting was probably a consideration, although officials testified before the President's Investigating Commission that on technical grounds they had no basis to deny Oswald's citizenship. They also cited the chronic problem in Moscow of "psychotic" individuals who later prove an embarrassment, having made public denunciations similar to that interview of Oswald with Miss Mosby and the basic department policy to be liberal with defectors.

In the same letter to Robert in which he again asked about "charges," he reported, "The Embassy (U. S.) said they will see about a loan for us when we leave so it seems our money problem will not be too great."

However, two months later, after June was born, there was still some delay with the loan. Lee gave his mother typical advice:

"Well as you see, we still have not gotten off yet. The holdup is from the Embassy which is apparently trying to get us money from other sources than itself for our tickets to the U. S. Probably they'll approach you for money again. Don't pay any attention to them."

Lee felt confident now that he had the full support of the Embassy and the State Department. He looked at the delays in granting him a loan as mere bargaining on the part of the U.S. Government. He had received the clippings from the Fort Worth papers and was "ready to draw." He had assured his mother, "We are in constant touch with the Embassy so all is well."

Just before his departure he cautioned Robert:

"In case you hear about our coming or the newspapers hear about it (which I hope they won't) I want to warn you not to make any statement whatsoever about us. None at all!! I know what was said about me when I left the U. S. as mother sent me some clippings. However, I realize that it was just the shock of the news which made you say all those things. However, I'll just remind you again not to make any statements or comments if you are approached by the newspapers, between now and the time we actually arrive in the U. S."

The returning defector had no qualms about laying the law down to his brother now—and reproaching him indirectly for things Robert had said. Lee had received a $435.71 loan from the Embassy, and, together with the cash he had saved up himself, his and his family's transportation back to America was assured. On May 30 he advised Marguerite, "Well, here we are in Moscow getting ready to leave for the USA. I'll be sending a telegram or otherwise informing you as to where we shall embark and so forth. Everything is O.K. so don't worry about us."

On June 13, Lee, Marina and June arrived by boat in New York. The next day they flew to Fort Worth, Texas.

CHAPTER 8

A DEFECTOR COMES HOME

Robert Oswald met Lee at the Dallas airport. For Robert, who had trained himself never to be too outwardly emotional (he had long since learned that emotions can wound), it was a choked-up moment. When Robert had joined the Marines and left home Lee must have been twelve or thirteen. Before that—well, there had been periods when they had lived together, but very short periods at that. Robert and his half-brother, John Pic, had lived in an orphanage a long time and then gone to a military school in Mississippi. Hearing Lee spout directions to Marina now in that outlandish language made him suddenly realize he didn't know Lee Oswald, the grown-up man, at all.

Lee looked as if he was expecting someone else to meet him. He had a slightly disappointed expression.

"What, no photographers or anything?"

"No, I have been able to keep it quiet," Robert explained. For an instant he thought he saw annoyance in Lee's eyes. Robert wondered what he could have done wrong.

"Have you had any calls at the house from the press?" Lee persisted.

Robert explained that, yes, he had had several calls, but he had been vague in his answers. He had not told them that Lee was arriving at Love Field.

Lee was curt in his instructions to Marina. Robert couldn't understand a word, but his brother's tone of voice was cutting. "Mother couldn't come," he explained. "She's on her nursing job at Crowell."

A typical trait of Lee's was that he acted as if he couldn't care less. Absent-mindedly he heard only what he wanted to hear, and he was thinking of something else now. Robert had no idea what he was thinking about. Could it have been the interview he had so carefully planned, with the answers worked out in advance?

There could be no question about it. Lee had the temperament of a man who thought of himself in dramatic sweeps. Certainly when he had gone to Russia he had imagined that he would be met with a good deal more fanfare when he told Rimma, his Intourist guide, that he wanted to give up his own country and become a Soviet citizen. He had not been prepared for the indifference he encountered. In fact, the frustration of it all, of being rejected and told he would have to leave the country like any American tourist whose visa had expired, depressed him so deeply that he had tried to kill himself. He was nearly three years older now, but was he really any more mature? Had Robert known some of the truths about Lee's character he would have been dismayed. Despite Lee's admonishments to Robert about the press, hadn't he really expected to be met by an army of photographers and reporters, and hadn't he really expected to be treated like a "real patriot" with headlines and praises in the Fort Worth papers? **"American returns.** Declares Russia is no place for him. Praises freedom of press, religion and opinion in USA."

They drove directly from the airport to Robert's house in Fort Worth. On the way Lee pointed out a few landmarks to Marina and explained things Robert couldn't understand. Lee then seemed to shake off his preoccupation and asked questions about the family, about how things were going with Robert, even asked about the Governor's race and mentioned some old times when they were at the farm and went hunting together. Lee had never been much of a marksman, but he did like to get out in the woods and look for game. Some of the best memories he and Robert shared were when Marguerite had made a home for them in a rural Texas community and they had roamed the fields together carrying their .22s.

It occurred to Robert that it was awkward not having Marina speak English. This was not going to be easy, having a foreigner in the house. How would Vada communicate with her when Lee wasn't around? Certainly Lee would want her to learn English just as quickly as possible. As long as Marina didn't speak English everywhere they went eyebrows would be lifted. Everyone they met would be reminded that she was a Russian and that Lee Oswald was that defector who had been quoted in the Fort Worth papers as denouncing his country. If Lee was going to settle down and forget his oat-sowing past, it would be important for him to help Marina learn English. It probably wouldn't be easy for Lee to find a job as matters stood. In Texas there was a strong feeling against radicals and a deep suspicion of "Reds." Whether Lee liked it or not, he would have to do everything he could to cover his past. Robert had had some embarrassing moments when the publicity of Lee's defection connected him with the name Oswald. He was not ashamed of it—not ashamed of his brother now that Lee had come to recognize the error of his ways—but the sooner he stopped speaking Russian in public with Marina the better. Certainly this would be obvious to Lee. Robert was not the kind of person to make unsolicited suggestions to anyone.

Something of the relationship between Lee and Robert—and the quality of minding his own business that characterized the older Oswald—was reflected in Robert's testimony before the Commission. He was asked about Lee, "At the time he resided in your home those six or eight weeks, were your relations with him cordial or friendly?"

"It was cordial, yes, more or less like he had not been to Russia. We were just together again."

"Did you have any political discussions with him at any time?"

"No, sir, I did not."

"He never discussed political matters with you?"

"No, sir, he did not. I would say we had a tacit agreement it was never brought up."

"By tacit do you mean that—"

"An unspoken agreement that we never would discuss it."

"Had you arrived at this agreement because on previous occasions you had disagreed about political matters?"

"No, sir, that was not the reason. We just never discussed politics."

"Did you have any interest in political affairs? I mean—"

"A little bit, sir."

"I mean from a philosophical point of view?"

"My own interest in politics from a philosophical point of view would be that I considered myself a conservative, a born conservative. Certainly agreed one hundred per cent with the U.S. Constitution and the laws that are set forth, and it is my upbringing, and it is what I always believed in and I will always believe in it."

"Did you say that was your mother's philosophy too?"

"Would I say that?"

"Yes."

"I would say—I will tell you, at this present time I feel like perhaps she has been hurt a great deal and perhaps her thinking is being changed at this very moment and at the present time since November [1963]. But prior to that time my opinion would be that she would be of the same opinion that I was."

"That is why you said your attitude was based on your 'upbringing'?"

"Yes, sir."

Robert Oswald was the third witness the Commission called to Washington. Many of the questions which had to be followed up carefully by the members bore on the loyalty and truthfulness of other witnesses. The general feeling of the American public was that a possibility might well exist that Lee had accomplices in his plans to shoot the President. His personal background was so unusual—and his way of living after he returned to the United States so seemingly erratic, as reported in the press—that, following the policy adopted by the Commission in its early administrative sessions, every aspect of the crime had to be probed.

Lee's brother Robert proved over the course of the investigation to be a fine citizen with no taint of unreliability of any kind. Lee Oswald was his brother. He had helped him to return to Fort Worth, as would be expected of any brother. Beyond that he had absolutely no connections with his brother's crime. He had no idea until the moment of the shooting that his brother was even capable of a criminal act.

My initial impression of Robert was quite favorable as he walked into the Commission hearing room accompanied by his attorney, William MacKenzie, a prominent member of the Dallas bar. Robert was trim in appearance, more handsome, in a clean-cut way, than his brother Lee. As he testified before the President's Commission I had the distinct feeling that he was wiser and had better judgment than his formal education might have justified. Here was a young man, conservatively dressed, soft-spoken, conscientiously trying to recall incidents of his family's history of many years ago. As probing questions were put to him about his youth and his relationships with Lee, I often wondered whether I could have been as precise if asked similar questions concerning my own family and three younger brothers. Quite honestly, like most individuals, I would have had tremendous difficulty reconstructing family problems and time sequences.

He was asked at the time of his appearance before the Commission whether he had any opinion as to his brother's guilt in the matter of the Dallas assassination. He replied, "Based on the circumstantial evidence that has been reported in newspapers and over the radio and television, I would have to say that it appears that he did kill President Kennedy."

"Would you, having reached that conclusion, and having known him all his life, would you give us any reason why he may have done this?"

"No, sir, I could not."

"It came as, I would think, a great shock to you?"

"Yes, sir, it certainly did, and I might add that the Lee Harvey Oswald I knew would not have killed anybody."

Robert's opinion in this matter agreed with the majority of witnesses who came before the Commission. Many regarded Lee Oswald as an eccentric; some called him a "screwball" and a "misfit," but few claimed to have had the impression that he could commit such a frightful crime. No single person knew Lee Oswald that well, with the possible exception of Marina, who gradually learned how dangerous he could be but who was caught in one of the most merciless and tragic traps a human being has ever been caught in.

The first few days after Lee's return to Fort Worth, staying with his brother Robert, his wife Vada and the children, were full of those pleasant moments that come to hours of reunion. For the moment all the harsh thoughts of the past were forgotten. Lee and Robert had some things in common—memories of youth and stories of adventures in the Marine Corps. They did what brothers will do when they meet after a long absence, and, carefully avoiding any critical comments, Robert did his part to make Lee feel at home. Between Vada and Marina the business of making friends was not quite so easy. Marina's English was limited to such simple phrases as "like" or "no like," and, even among young women with lots of things to talk about, such as the care and upbringing of children, this was not easy. Brothers can sometimes forget how hard it must be for wives who are utter strangers to adjust to the closeness they are expected to accept. The conversations veer off on some reminiscence which pleases those brought up together but would certainly leave a gap between a Russian girl and a native Texan, conversations blocked even further by a language barrier. But everyone was cheerful and tried to be helpful to one another. It was obviously a temporary situation. The house was only a two-bedroom bungalow, which, with three children and four adults, must have become cluttered.

But it was lots of fun to watch Marina's reactions to the normal things in American life. The experience of entertaining a foreigner always helps Americans to see their environment in a fresh light. Robert described the experience he had in taking Marina to a huge supermarket:

"I remember the occasion quite vividly. If you have ever had the opportunity, sir, to take a person of that nature into a supermarket and watch the expression on their face as to the magnitude of the food and the variety of the food that was in her presence—and I believe for the first time to any extent—it was quite a pleasant observation, I might add, sir. She was quite overwhelmed."

"Surprised or overwhelmed?"

"Surprised."

"There is nothing like it in Minsk?"

"I feel certain, sir, there is not."

Members of the Commission were asking these questions not out of idle curiosity. Commentators had raised the earnest question as to whether it was possible that Marina herself could be a trained agent and perhaps had even been in this country before, preparatory to a deliberate attempt to have her marry an American and plant her as an agent in the United States. No possibility, no matter how seemingly farfetched, could be ignored.

"Did you get the impression that her reaction was such to indicate that at least she had never seen anything of this nature?"

"Yes, sir, I was of the exact opinion she had not seen anything anywhere comparable to that in the nature of a food store."

"Now, did you get the reaction that was a spontaneous reaction on her part?"

"Most certainly it was, sir."

"She was not putting on an act to impress you and Lee and anyone accompanying you?"

119

"No, sir."

Marina testified that the first week or two Lee did what any normal person would do on having come back from a long trip. He sat around and talked about his experiences, entertained a good listening audience and relaxed a bit. Marguerite, on the other hand, stated that he immediately went out to look for work and that she felt bad that it was necessary for him to find employment so soon. However, Marina's recollection is probably more accurate, because it was several days before Marguerite could get away from her nursing job to visit Lee and Marina. Marguerite's version of her first encounter with Marina and her reunion with Lee reflects some of her personal feelings and temperament:

"I received a speedletter from the State Department stating that Lee would leave Moscow, and how he would leave and arrive in New York—on June 13, 1962. I was on a case at Crowell, Texas. I am a practical nurse. And I was taking care of a very elderly woman whose daughter lived in Fort Worth, Texas, so I was not able to leave and meet Lee.

"Robert, his brother, met him, and Lee went to Robert's home.

"Approximately about a week later, I could not stand it any more. I called the daughter—the patient's daughter—and had her come to take care of her mother, and took three days off and went to Fort Worth to see Lee and Marina.

"Marina is a beautiful girl. And I said to Lee, 'Marina, she doesn't look Russian. She is beautiful.'

"I asked him where he had met her, and he said he met her at a social function, a community function.

"I said, 'You know, Lee, I am getting ready—I was getting ready to write a book on your so-called defection.'

"I had researched it and come to Washington in 1961, and, by the way, asked to see President Kennedy because I had a lot of extenuating circumstances at the time because of the defection.

"He said, 'Mother, you are not going to write a book.'

"I said, 'Lee, don't tell me what to do. I cannot write the book now, because, Honey, you are alive and back.' But at the time I had no way of knowing whether my son was living or dead, and I planned to write the book.

"But don't tell me what to do. It has nothing to do with you and Marina. It is my life because of your defection.

"He said, 'Mother, I tell you, you are not to write a book. They could kill her and her family.' "

It seemed to this member of the Commission that Lee's dictating what his mother should or shouldn't do and Marguerite's equally blunt reply revealed the stony impasse their personalities brought about. After nearly three years of separation neither temperament had softened to the other. Lee could be as firm in his attitudes as his mother was positive. The fact that Marguerite recalled this incident of tension between them as one of the first incidents of their reunion foretold other conflicts.

Marguerite continued: "So I stayed in Fort Worth two or three days. I did not live at Robert's home. I rented a motel. In fact, the lady of the mother I was taking care of paid my motel expenses while I was in Forth Worth. But I went there every day."

After the assassination Marguerite, following her theory that even Marina might be involved in a plot, made a good deal of her suspicion that Lee's Russian wife really spoke English all the while, although careful investigation by the Commission indicates that Marina's knowledge of English was about what one would expect of a newcomer to America who had never studied the language.

"While I was there, Marina is a pharmacist. I have a medical book, and Lee was saying that he was losing his hair and how he had become bald because of the cold weather.

"So I got the medical book, looking up baldness, and the treatment for baldness, and Marina came by and read the prescriptions.

"So I said, 'Lee, she reads English,' and he said, 'Mother, that is Latin, of course, that is universal.' "

Lee's explanation was most certainly reasonable, and the Commission was persuaded that Marina's knowledge of English was rudimentary.

"And this is the time that Lee had gone to the public stenographer, made the statement that he was writing a book.

"You probably have that information. It was highly publicized.

"I myself gave him the ten dollars that he gave the public stenographer."

Lee's proposed book that Marguerite mentioned was found among his papers. It was a descriptive account of the political, social and economic life in Minsk and the Soviet Union. In the hands of a more skillful writer it might have appealed to a publisher. But Lee no more had the training and background to write an interesting book than he had to do a lot of other things he thought himself capable of.

"I bought Marina clothes, and brought clothes to her while at my daughter-in-law's house, bought diapers for the baby. And Marina had more clothes when she arrived in the States than I now have."

Marguerite's testimony before the Commission was colored by her bewilderment at being cut off from Marina after the assassination—which was Marina's own choice. On the one hand she was complimentary to Marina and, on the other, critical.

"So what I am trying to state is as we go further into the story, it had been stated that my son neglected Marina and that she didn't have any clothes. The Russian people have stated that all throughout Texas in the papers. And that is not true. I happen to know, because I myself bought Marina three dresses. And my daughter-in-law bought dresses, and my daughter-in-law's sister.

"So then I went back to Crowell, Texas, and I was not satisfied in my mind because the way they lived. They only had a two-bedroom house [Robert and Vada]. As you know, Robert has two children. And there was another couple [Lee and Marina] with another child.

"So I decided I would quit this job and help the children all I could. So I did. I gave notice. And I came to Fort Worth and I rented an apartment at the Rotary Apartments, which is on West Seventh and Summit."

Lee, Marina and June had now been living with Robert for two or three weeks since their arrival in Fort Worth. The house was indeed crowded. It was Marguerite's own decision to leave her job in Crowell and use her savings to rent an apartment. She invited Lee and Marina to come and live with her. Marina found nothing objectionable about her mother-in-law. She seemed happy to have someone who liked to help her with the baby. Lee may have had reservations about getting under the wing of his mother. But the decision was made: they would go and live with Marguerite. She had a car and was willing to show Marina around and help Lee get to job interviews. It was not long, however, before Marguerite got on Lee's nerves. Marina and Lee got into sharp arguments about his intolerance toward his mother. Although she seldom had fifty cents in her pocket of her own, Marina was finding American life very much to her liking. She would be happy now if Lee would settle down, get a job, pay their debt to the State Department, and then start building toward a life like Robert and Vada enjoyed. It wasn't sumptuous but it was pleasant. Marina could see that there were many opportunities in a country like this. And there was no reason that Marina could see why Marguerite couldn't be a part of their household. It might even be helpful in getting established. But Lee was just plain belligerent. Already he was finding fault with everything around him. He was making fun of Robert's life, saying he was just a typical little capitalist with a small horizon. He criticized everything about the way Americans lived—their interest in cars and refrigerators, homes and other possessions. What was wrong with those things? Marina asked herself. Lee just couldn't seem to agree with anything normal, not even the sensible things his own mother suggested. Sometimes she sided with her mother-in-law and then there was real trouble. They would have arguments that would end with Lee in a fury. What was wrong with him anyway? She had never known Lee as a man like this in Russia. He had wanted to come to America just as much as she. She found it to her liking and he seemed to resent that she did.

It was as if Lee didn't belong to his own country. He had boasted once that for years he had trained himself not to make any friends, not to form any attachments. Marina thought it peculiar that he had lived in Fort Worth when he was younger and yet he didn't have a single school friend; he didn't seem to know a person in the entire area except his brother and his mother. At least in Russia he had had his friends at the factory. Here he didn't know a soul and didn't seem to care to know anyone. That just wasn't natural.

This was a matter of considerable interest to the Commission. Because of the mystery of Lee Oswald's motivation in shooting a President, the public and press found it hard to believe that he was a "loner." Many of the problems of the investigation could be solved only by meticulous inquiry into every last acquaintance and associate Lee ever had. The Commission staff compiled a list of hundreds of names of persons mentioned in one way or another in connection with Lee Oswald, and in turn checked acquaintances of acquaintances. One of the astounding conclusions was that, aside from his immediate family and a few relatives, Lee Oswald had no friends or acquaintances when he returned from Russia. There is no record in thousands of pages of testimony of his contacting a single person, other than his family, whom he had ever known before. If the important links in belonging to a place, a community or a nation are the personal ties and associations, the love of one's heritage, the faith in one's society and history, Lee Oswald in truth did not belong to this country. His family meant little or nothing to him; his mother eventually became anathema. In his writing he made it perfectly clear that he did not believe in his country's history or its institutions. Marina was right if she got the impression that he was a stranger in his own homeland. No wonder he soon appeared to be unhappy and irascible to an unusual degree. Who then were the people whose names appeared in the papers after the assassination? Who were the people he associated with in the eighteen months from the time he came back from Russia until his death? How did he come to know them and why were there so many with Russian names and peculiar backgrounds?

There is a saying in the Dallas–Fort Worth area that if a person is just passing through town and stops a stranger on the street to ask directions, the chances are ten to one that the answer will be "Sorry, sir, I just arrived here yesterday myself from the East." Or "You'd better ask a native if you can find one. I've been here two months and haven't met a person yet who was born here." In its way the Dallas–Fort Worth area is one of the most heterogeneous complexes in America. The economic pace and the role it plays as a commercial and distributing center of the great Southwest gives it that character. Add the exploring spirit of oil speculators, the restless wanderings of the people associated with drilling and wildcatting, and the new influx of workers, engineers and executives connected with the aviation business, and the area is cosmopolitan to say the least. A small but cohesive group is the Russian families of Fort Worth and Dallas. Through their common language tie and origin they are well acquainted with one another although they may live many miles apart. Distance in Texas is measured in driving time rather than mileage.

These friendly and generous people were apt to take a new Russian arrival into their circle quickly—that is, if he was the right kind of Russian—conservative, anti-Communist and interested in the Orthodox Church. Most of them had come to America as refugees, either because of the persecutions of Lenin and Trotsky in the old days or Stalin more recently. One of the less conventional in the group—namely George de Mohrenschildt, an acquaintance of Lee

Harvey Oswald after his return from Russia—testified about the "Russian colony" in the Dallas–Fort Worth area. He was asked how the group would react to the arrival of a new Russian in the area.

"They would be exceedingly interested, naturally."

"Curious?"

"Exceedingly curious."

"Now, would that include you?"

"Yes."

"And your wife?"

"Yes.

"Well, aside from us, the most curious would be George Bouhe, because he actually met us first—the first in Dallas—he told us about Oswald, as far as I remember. Because he is curious by nature. He wants to know what is going on. He wants to convert them to the Greek Orthodox Church and so on."

"Would there be any effort to help these people become acquainted throughout the community?"

"If they—if that couple came from Soviet Russia, from the Soviet Union, you mean?"

"Well, let's assume that."

"Well, the old guard would not do anything. They would be curious—they might meet them and very soon afterwards they would get disgusted with them, because what they would say to them would not fit with their beliefs. And we know that Soviet Russia is a going concern. To them it is not, it does not exist. It just isn't there."

In referring to the "old guard," George de Mohrenschildt meant the Russians who had left their homeland many years ago. They left because they couldn't live with communism, and they had now become more American than Russian. Politically they were entirely out of sympathy with the Government of the USSR and would be classified in most respects as political conservatives. Many were successful private businessmen in the Fort Worth–Dallas area. Their interest in modern Russia was purely a matter of inherited cultural traditions, common language bonds and religion. Such a person was Peter Gregory, the first Russian in the area that the Oswalds were to meet. Since Lee did not have a single friend to contact on his return from Russia, the meeting with Gregory was significant for both of them. Through Gregory the Oswalds met George Bouhe and, in turn through Bouhe, George de Mohrenschildt, and thus each character in the drama is linked to this original contact with the Russian colony. Neither Marina nor Lee had any other acquaintances. Lee did not make friends with workers on his jobs. They were never in his home—only the Russian group and those introduced by them.

Peter Gregory, a successful petroleum engineer, consultant for a group supervising activities in the very important Yates Oil Field in Pecos County, Texas, testified voluntarily. I felt that he was a proud gentleman, scholarly, who spoke and acted with dignity. He was obviously earnest in his concern to help the Commission. He convincingly told how he met Oswald, who was then seeking his first employment after returning from Russia.

"It was in the middle of June 1962 [perhaps within a week or two of Oswald's return; he was still living with Robert]. On that particular morning I was in the office. My telephone rang, and the voice on the other end told me that my name was given to him by the Fort Worth Public Library. He knew I was teaching at the library [this was a civic enterprise Gregory was engaged in, teaching once a week during the winter months people interested in learning Russian], that he was looking for a job as a translator or interpreter, and that he would like for me to give him a letter testifying to that effect [as to his qualifications].

"He spoke to me in English, so I suggested to him, not knowing who that was, that he might drop by my office, and I would be glad to give him a test. He did. He came by the office, long about eleven o'clock that morning, and I gave him a short test simply opening a book at random and asking him to read a paragraph or two and then translate it.

"He did it very well. So I gave him a letter addressed to whom it may concern that in my opinion he was capable of being an interpreter or translator.

"After that, I asked him—I noticed that he spoke with what I thought to be a Polish accent, so I asked him if he were of Polish origin and he stated that he was not, that he was raised in Fort Worth, Texas, but that he learned Russian in the Soviet Union, where he lived for two and a half or three years.

"He told me that he married a Russian girl and that he brought his wife with him, and they also had a baby.

"I told him that I knew of no openings at the time—I didn't know of any—for services of a translator or interpreter, but that if he would leave his address I would be glad to get in touch with him if and when I learned of any such openings."

Thus Lee Oswald made his first acquaintance in the Fort Worth–Dallas Russian group. There was nothing political about it. There was no sinister meaning or any more significance to it than a friendly gesture by an upstanding local businessman. Thorough investigations of Peter Gregory's background indicate that he is a fine community-minded individual. He was naturally interested in the oddity of a Fort Worth boy who had gone to Russia to live but even more interested in the fact that Marina Oswald was a native-born girl, supposedly of good education, who would speak contemporary Russian, which Gregory did not.

Peter Gregory had a son, Paul, at the University of Oklahoma who was majoring in economics and also studying Russian. Paul expressed a wish to take lessons from Marina. Here was an opportunity to do the Oswalds a good turn by hiring Marina to help teach Paul, and Paul in turn would get a fresh, firsthand insight into Russian as it was now spoken and a knowledge of current conditions in the USSR. Paul was home for his summer vacation, and this would work out fine to keep him on his toes during those weeks. Consequently a week or two later he and Paul called on the Oswalds at Robert's home. They made arrangements for Marina to teach Paul conversational Russian in an informal way.

"Did you discuss politics with Mr. Oswald?"

"No, sir, we did not."

"Did you get the impression from just talking to the Oswalds at this time that Oswald was treated pretty much as other Russians were in Russia or did you think he had a special situation there in any way?"

"My personal impression was that he was treated there as the rest of the Russians."

Paul Gregory took lessons from Marina from about the middle of August to mid-September, when he went back to the University of Oklahoma. Meantime, through the Gregorys, Lee and Marina became acquainted with a number of other Russians in the area who tried to help them, having once been refugees themselves and appreciating the hardships involved in re-establishing themselves in the area.

"Did your son tell you whether he had discussions with Oswald concerning politics and economics and things like that?"

"He mentioned once, I believe, that there were political discussions."

"What did he tell you about that?"

"He told me he thought Lee Oswald was pretty silly in his views."

"Did he express any other—"

"He also mentioned that he saw some book on Marxism, whether it was *Das Kapital* or some other book I don't recall now."

"Did he say that he thought Oswald was a half-baked Communist?"

"I think that is the expression he used, yes."

Robert's hope that Lee would settle down to a normal American life was not to be. He was constantly at war with his surroundings and the people who befriended him or employed him. And the friendship of the Russians who felt sorry for Marina he came to resent the most. They were teaching her to be an American, giving her a taste for comforts and luxuries. Why, now she was even smoking cigarettes and occasionally having a drink! Their quarrels were more frequent and increasingly bitter.

Living with Marguerite soon became unbearable for Lee. Through the Texas Employment Office he obtained his first job at the Leslie Welding Company. It was only common labor, but it brought in a pay check. Marguerite's dream that Lee's return would give her something to work for and eventually family living, which she had not had in many years, was not working out. Lee's touchiness on the subject of accepting any help aggravated the tension. He told his mother bluntly, "Now, Mother, I want you to understand right here and now—I want you to stop giving all these gifts to me and my wife. I want to give Marina whatever is necessary, the best I can do. I want you to keep your money and take care of yourself, because today or tomorrow you take sick, and you spend all your money on us, I will have to take care of you."

"What did you say to that?" Marguerite was asked.

"I agreed with him. And I said—the shock of it—I realize what a mother-in-law I was in interfering. And, of course, that is part of what we mothers-in-law do unconsciously. We try to help out our children, and in a way we are interfering in their life. They would rather have their own way of doing things.

"And I realized that I had interfered, and the boy wanted to take care of his wife. So no more was said about it.

"I go into many homes, being a nurse, and I see the problem also where the mothers and mother-in-laws bring things, and the men strongly object to it—they would rather do without, and have their wife do without, and they themselves be master of the home.

"So then I realized I was being a foolish mother-in-law and that he was perfectly right.

"I should save my money and take care of myself. He had a wife and a baby to take care of. If I didn't have any money he might have to take care of me. So I agreed with that."

"Did Marina say anything about that?"

"Well, no, Marina didn't know—unless she understood the English part. I have no way of knowing, you see."

On this occasion Marguerite realized how she had made trouble. She stated coherently what the root of the trouble had always been between her and her sons. But if she realized it, and if she was capable of correcting her fault, it was too late as far as her last son was concerned. With his second pay check from the Leslie Welding Company, Lee rented an apartment at 2703 Mercedes Street in Fort Worth and moved out, leaving Marguerite flat. He didn't even tell her where he was going, and he forbade Marina to open the door to his mother if she was able to discover where they had gone. He intended to sever all relationships with his mother, as he had when he went to Russia.

Marina thought this was a cruel way to treat Mrs. Oswald. She had been able to get along reasonably well with Marguerite, although there were times when Marguerite could be meddlesome. But Marina felt that a mother was a mother and she knew that Marguerite meant well. Marina hadn't known a mother in years.

A few days later Marguerite, with her persistent manner, found the number of the apartment and, while Lee was away at work, paid Marina a visit.

That night Lee was furious when he found out Marina had let his mother in. He raved and he threatened her. His anger was simply irrational and the hate in his eyes fearsome. Marina reported to an American friend that Lee had told her once that he didn't love her. Even in Russia he had gotten angry one night and said that, but now his brutality was getting beyond reason. Nothing was to Lee's liking —not the food she served, not the friends she made, not the way she dressed. But it wasn't just her; it was as if he was coming to hate the whole world and everyone in it. There was simply nothing he liked.

CHAPTER 9

LIFE ON MERCEDES STREET

LEE'S AND MARINA'S first Russian acquaintances in Fort Worth were Peter Gregory and his son Paul, to whom Marina gave conversational Russian lessons. Paul would pick Marina up in his car, take her shopping or just sight-seeing and get the advantage of hearing her expressions and accent. This was diverting for Marina, a great relief from the tensions and isolation of the apartment on Mercedes Street. And it brought in a little money—money Lee direly needed, because he was very anxious to pay back the State Department loan. Peter Gregory gave this description of the frugality of the Oswalds' living on Mercedes Street:

"It was practically a bare room. There was no furniture to speak of. There were the bare necessities; there was no playpen or crib for the baby. The baby was playing in the middle of the floor in the living room as I remember. It was an extremely primitively furnished room, and the rest of the house was the same way."

The Commission found that rumors that Lee Oswald lived in comparative luxury and had money from outside activities proved groundless. On Mercedes Street Lee and Marina lived a meager existence, although their furnishings gradually improved through the generosity of friends.

It was on Mercedes Street that their acquaintanceships among the Russian group broadened. Through the Gregorys they met George Bouhe, the leader of the so-called "Russian colony," and Anna Meller. They in turn introduced them to a number of others or told their friends about the Oswalds, so the word went around among the group that here was a new couple worth knowing. One of the most friendly was George de Mohrenschildt, a colorful person himself—about the only one of the group who appreciated Lee Oswald's nonconformity, because George de Mohrenschildt too was of an uncommon breed. Forthright and outspoken, George had many friends in many countries. By strange coincidence he had been a friend of Jacqueline Kennedy's mother, Mrs. Hugh Auchincloss. He was a free-lance petroleum engineer who had his flush days and lean ones. He liked people who were different, and he found Lee Oswald unusual. After the assassination some of the Dallas Russian group wondered if George de Mohrenschildt wasn't some kind of a radical himself. Investigation proved, however, that de Mohrenschildt had no connections of a dubious nature. He was just a man who always said what popped into his mind, and occasionally he shocked people by taking an unpopular stand. George de Mohrenschildt's sworn testimony of how he met the Oswalds and his first encounter with them provides a picture of their life on Mercedes Street. He was asked how he came to know the Oswalds.

"As far as I remember, George Bouhe, who is a close friend of mine, and a very curious individual, told me that there is an interesting couple in Fort Worth and that the Clarks know them already—Max Clark and Gali—they know them already. Somebody read about them in the paper—I don't know exactly, I don't remember the exact wording any more—that somebody read about them in the paper, maybe Mr. Gregory, and discovered them, made a discovery. But we heard from George Bouhe the first time."

"At this time were you aware that there had been an American who had gone to the Soviet Union, any story about his attempt to defect to the Soviet Union?"

"Yes."

"And that he had returned to the United States?"

"That is what I heard from George Bouhe."

"That was the first you ever knew anything at all about—"

"I never heard about them, never heard anything about them before."

"Now is that true of Mrs. de Mohrenschildt?"

"Same thing. I think we were both together when this conversation took place."

"When did it take place?"

"I could not tell you the date. I think in the summer of 1962."

"Now give your best recollection of what George Bouhe said to you about the Oswalds on that occasion."

"He said rather a complimentary account of them—I don't think he met them yet. I think he just heard about them."

"When George Bouhe spoke to you then—have you exhausted your recollections as to the conversation right at that point?"

"I am trying to think about it. I just remember that I got curious, what kind of a fellow he is, and what kind of a woman she is."

"Were you particularly interested when you heard she was pretty?"

"No, no, not particularly, no, because—but it is nice to know a good-looking girl rather than to know some monster."

"You have—"

"I am always curious to find somebody better-looking than horrible. We are talking about serious things."

"Well, it is part of the atmosphere, Mr. de Mohrenschildt. You have always had an interest in pretty women, have you not?"

"Sure, sure, naturally."

"And you have pursued and courted them?"

"I still do, I hope. Until the day I die.

"But anyway it was not really so. It was just an interesting couple who were—it pleased us to know that here is a pretty girl from Soviet Russia that had arrived, because we all picture Soviet Russian women like a commando—big, fat women, working in a brick factory."

"You were curious to find out more about them, were you not?"
"Yes."

"What did you do?"

"Again now my recollections are a little bit vague on that."

De Mohrenschildt's uncertainty about dates and specific incidents was understandable. He had known the Oswalds only a few months —from summer of 1962 until the spring of 1963, when he moved to Haiti with his wife to follow up petroleum explorations he had contracted for on that island. The shooting had come to him as a great surprise.

"I tried, both my wife and I, hundreds of times to recall how exactly we met the Oswalds. But they were out of our mind completely because so many things happened in the meantime. So please do not take it for sure how I first met them."

"We want your best recollection."

"My best recollection—I even cannot recall who gave me their address in Fort Worth. I don't recall that. Either George Bouhe or the Clarks.

"And I think a few days later somebody told me they live in dire poverty, somewhere in the slums of Fort Worth.

"I had to go on business to Fort Worth with my very close friend, Colonel Orlov. And to the best of my recollection Lawrence and I were on some business in Fort Worth and I told him, 'Let's go and meet those people,' and the two of us drove to this slum area in Fort Worth and knocked on the door, and here was Marina and the baby. Oswald was not there."

"This was during the daytime?"

"Late in the afternoon, after business hours, five o'clock."

"You identified yourself?"

"Yes, I said a few words in Russian. I said we were friends of George Bouhe. I think he was already helping them a little bit, giving them something for the baby or something. I think he had already been in—he helps everybody. He has been helping her especially. And so the introduction was fine.

"And I found her not particularly pretty, but a lost soul living in the slums, not knowing one single word of English, with this rather unhealthy-looking baby, horrible surroundings."

"Now we are interested in a couple of things. You found that she knew substantially no English?"

"No English at all at that time. I think she knew maybe—I remember that I asked her, 'How do you buy things in the store?' and she said, 'I point with my finger and I can say yes and no. That is all.'"

"Did you go into the home—was it a house or apartment?"

"It was a shack, near Sears, Roebuck, as far as I remember—near that area. I don't know if you went down there. A little shack which had only two rooms, sort of clapboard type building. Very poorly furnished, decrepit, on a dusty road. The road even was not paved."

"What did you talk to her about?"

"Just asked her how she likes it here and how she was getting along. Does she get enough food? Something like that—completely meaningless conversation.

"I think Lawrence was there, you know, but he did not understand what I was saying—he doesn't know Russian." [De Mohrenschildt speaks several languages fluently, including Russian, his native tongue.]

"Did you ask about her husband?"

"I said, 'Well, I would like to meet your husband.' "

"She said he would be back from work soon. She asked me to sit down, offered me something to drink. I think she had some sherry or something in the house. This is the best of my recollection.

"And Lawrence sat down, and found her very nice. And then after a little while Oswald, Lee, appeared."

"You had never seen him before?"

"Never seen him before."

"What happened and what was said?"

"Well, he loved to speak Russian."

"Did you introduce yourself? And explain why you were there?"

"Yes, I said, 'I'm a friend of George Bouhe. I want to see how you are getting along.' "

"Did you speak in Russian or English?"

"In English at first and then he switched to Russian."

"What was your impression of his command of Russian?"

"Well, he spoke fluent Russian, but with a foreign accent, and made mistakes, grammatical mistakes, but he had remarkable fluency in Russian."

"It was remarkable?"

"Remarkable—for a fellow of his background and education, it is remarkable how fast he learned it. But he loved the language. He loved to speak it. He preferred to speak Russian than English any time. He always would switch from English to Russian."

"Did you discuss life in Russia, how he got there?"

"I don't think the first time. I don't think the first time I said anything at all, you know. Possibly he told me that he had been in Minsk, and that got me curious because I had lived in Minsk as a child, and my father was the so-called Nobility Marshal of Minsk. He got me curious, you know.

"But I do not recall for sure whether it was the first time I met him or the second time or third time. I don't remember. I think it was a very short meeting the first time because Lawrence Orlov was there, and he wanted to get back home, so we just said, 'Well, we will see you,' and possibly Marina had mentioned that her baby needed—that she needed some medical attention with her teeth, and that the baby had not been inoculated. Possibly that was that time. But I am not sure."

"At least there was a time when that did arise?"

135

"Yes, yes."

"Her need for dental care, some attention needed to be given to the child?"

"Yes."

"Your impression was the child looked rather on the sickly side?"

"Yes, very much so. It was kind of a big head, bald big head, looked like Khrushchev, the child—looked like an undergrown Khrushchev. I always teased her about the fact that the baby looked like Khrushchev."

"Now you had this visit and returned home?"

"I think the first visit was very short, and we drove back with Lawrence and I remember on the way we discussed that couple and both had a lot of sympathy for her especially. But he also struck me as a very sympathetic fellow."

"Give me your impression of him at that time—your first impression."

"The first impression and the last impression remain more or less the same. I could never get mad at the fellow."

"Why?"

"Sometimes he was obnoxious. I don't know. I had a liking for him. I always had a liking for him. There was something charming about him; there was some—I don't know. I just liked the guy—that is all."

Of all the witnesses who came in contact with Lee Oswald, George de Mohrenschildt was virtually the only one who said he had taken a liking to him. Oswald didn't intimidate George de Mohrenschildt, and he knew in George's presence that here was an educated man whom he could not upstage, intellectually or otherwise. Oswald could pride himself about being well traveled. De Mohrenschildt had traveled more than he. Lee might preen himself on being well read. George could twist him in circles on this. And as to political philosophy, Lee might never admit that George knew anything about this, but if anyone could make him doubt his theories in this area, de Mohrenschildt would be the man to do it. In short, Lee respected de Mohrenschildt—a feeling he seldom had toward anyone or anything.

"When you reached home, you reported on this—"

"You know he was very humble with me—he was very humble. If somebody expressed an interest in him, he blossomed, absolutely blossomed. If you asked him some question about himself, he was just out of this world."

Marina testified that Lee Oswald considered de Mohrenschildt his only "friend." In some ways de Mohrenschildt understood Lee Oswald better than anyone aside from Marina.

At the time George de Mohrenschildt met the Oswalds, Lee was still working at the Leslie Welding Company, the job he had found just before he moved out on his mother. He walked from the apartment on Mercedes Street to the shop, which was not far. His work was common labor and he loathed it. Altogether he was finding life back in the United States unpleasant, and he resented these Russians —particularly George Bouhe—intruding on his life.

But what irked Lee the most was the way these new acquaintances were influencing Marina. Now she was wanting to be like the rest of them. Lee found it more and more difficult to avoid fights with her. She was obsessed with wanting to dress like an American. She thought it was smart to smoke because that's what the sophisticated women did. She was less and less sympathetic to his political ideas. He sometimes felt very much alone in his world. His surroundings irked him; Marina irked him. He had gotten so he couldn't even express his feelings toward her, or did he really have any feelings? He just felt cold and indifferent. And sometimes she would ride him unmercifully—get on a subject she knew he would be needled by and then run it into the ground until he lost his temper. She just didn't understand how he felt about things.

From Marina's viewpoint she blamed Lee:

"Sometimes, apparently without reason—at least I did not know reasons, if any existed—he became quite a stranger. At such times it was impossible to ask him anything. He simply kept to himself. He was irritated by trifles."

"Do you recall any of the trifles that irritated him, so as to help us know the picture?"

"It is hard to remember any trifling occurrences, sometimes such a small thing as, for example, dinner being five minutes late, and I do mean five minutes—it is not that I am exaggerating—he would be very angry. Or if there was no butter on the table, because I hadn't brought it from the icebox, he would with great indignation say, 'Why is there no butter?' And at the same time if I had put the butter on the table, he wouldn't have touched it.

"This is foolishness, of course; a normal person doesn't get irritated by things like that."

"Could you tell us a little about when he did beat you, because we have reports that at times neighbors saw signs of his having beat you, so that we might know the occasions and why he did such things."

"The neighbors simply say that because I have a very sensitive skin, and even a very light blow would show marks. Sometimes it was my fault. Sometimes it was really necessary to just leave him alone. But I wanted more attention. He was jealous. He had no reason to be. But he was jealous of even some of my old friends, old in the sense of age."

"When he became jealous, did he discuss that with you?"

"Yes, of course."

"What did he say?"

"I don't remember. Basically that I prefer others to him. That I want many things which he cannot give me. But that was not so."

Marina was not expansive before the Commission. I felt that her replies were brief, perhaps too much so before investigators who were seeking the maximum of information. Some of her Russian-colony acquaintances saw the facts differently.

On their first acquaintanceship when George Bouhe took Marina to Elena Hall, another Russian-speaking Fort Worth American, Elena saw bruises on Marina's face. Elena was a dental technician and Bouhe hoped to help Marina by arranging for care. At this time Lee and Marina had been back from Russia only two or three months. Later Elena Hall, who was divorced from her husband, came to know Marina well. Asked about Marina's part in the Oswalds' domestic difficulties, she explained to the Commission, "Well, I think she was stubborn and he was just cruel to her, and they would argue for nothing, just nothing, and he would beat her all the time."

"Beat her?"

"Oh, yes. In fact the first time she came to my house with George Bouhe, she had black-and-blue over half of her face and I didn't ask at that time."

Later, Elena Hall had occasion to question Marina, and Marina confessed that Lee beat her.

Did Marina discuss her marital relations with Mrs. Hall?

"Yes. Well, she is, I think, she is a very nice girl. And I told her, 'Marina, you are in such a difficult financial situation, and you'd better not have children for quite a while, and when you have a better financial situation, you can have them.' And she said, 'Well, I don't know.'

"And I told her, 'If you want to, I have a lady doctor, Dr. Taylor. If you want me to, I will take you there. She will give you some things.'

"And she said, 'No, I don't think so.'

"She said, 'Our married life is so strange that I don't think I ever will have any children any more,' because he was very cold to her."

"Did Marina indicate at that time that she and Oswald did not have normal sexual relations?"

"Very seldom. The thing that she told me, 'Very seldom.'"

"Tell me everything that you can remember about that subject that Marina told you."

"That was the only thing that was worrying me, her to not have children, because they are in such bad shape, and that is the only thing she told me.

"And I said, 'If you think you want any more.' So it is none of my business, you know."

"Is that all Marina said about that subject?"

"We didn't talk any more, because it was my suggestion to her to not have children, and she told me that, and that was all."

"Did she ever tell you that Oswald would—was not very much of a man in that sense?"

"Yes, that is what she told me."

"They very seldom had sexual relations?"

"Yes, sir."

"Did you ever discuss that question with her any other time?"

"No."

"Did you form any impression as to how Lee and Marina were getting along with each other?"

"No. Couple of times I told her, 'Why do you argue with him about little things?' and she said, 'Oh, because he is not a man.' That is what she told me. For instance, I like hot peppers and he didn't like it. Well, is nothing wrong with a man who doesn't like peppers. John [Elena's former husband] doesn't like it at all. And at the table they were eating, and I ate the peppers, and he wouldn't touch, and she said, 'He is afraid of everything, hot peppers.'

"And he said he doesn't like it, and they had an argument about that. And after he left I said, 'Marina, you shouldn't do that because, well, some people like them and some don't.'

"Well, things like that, she would start with him and they had an argument. Probably if I would be there, they would have a fight or something."

"Did you ever have the feeling that Marina was a good wife to Oswald, or did you have the feeling that she was not particularly a good wife?"

"Well, she is a little bit the lazy one, and she can sleep forty-eight hours a day. That is the only thing. And maybe they had trouble because of this and little things, like I said, about the peppers and so on."

"Did you ever see or hear of Marina making fun of Oswald in front of other people?"

"Who?"

"Marina making fun of Lee?"

"Oh yes, she would do it."

"Can you think of any specific examples?"

"She always was complaining about him. He was not a man. He is afraid. I don't know, not complete, I guess, or something like that. Not a complete man."

"You had the feeling, I gather from what you said, that if there were difficulties in the Oswald marriage, they were not entirely Lee Oswald's fault? It also would be some of the fault of Marina?"

"Yes."

Both Jeanne and George de Mohrenschildt had similar impressions of Marina's contribution to the strife that went on between Lee and Marina. George was very outspoken on the subject of Marina's laziness, although it must be remembered that the de Mohrenschildts are extraordinarily energetic people. At one time they hiked all the way from the Texas border to the Panama Canal—adequate proof of their physical reserves.

Jeanne de Mohrenschildt, an unusually dynamic person, said, "She is lazy. You see, there are people that they actually are no good, but still they have something very nice about them, that you cannot really be furious with them or mad, you really can't. She is lazy and I know it, because she stayed once overnight."

"Where? At your home?"

"Yes, with the baby. And I tell you—if I stay with somebody overnight, I will jump up the first thing in the morning, see what I can do to help, knowing I will be doing everything.

"She didn't. She slept. I actually had to waken her up. She did the same thing—she stayed in our daughter's home overnight. Because when her teeth were pulled, she was not in condition to go back. She was the same way—very lazy. And I just couldn't understand it, a young person. Maybe she was ill. We talked about it—maybe we have just too much energy. For a young girl to sleep late and not be active . . .

"The proof of her laziness is that she didn't do much about learning English, in spite I gave her the records, and we gave her one of our little phonographs. I had beautiful records to learn English—I bought them in New York when I arrived."

"Is it that she was lazy that she didn't pursue learning English, or did Oswald object to her learning English?"

"According to her, Oswald objected, and he also told us himself that he wants to speak with her in Russian, because he doesn't want to forget Russian.

"But then we got onto Oswald. He didn't want to forget his Russian. That was the reason, not to let his wife learn English—because she was the only person he could speak Russian to."

"He could still speak Russian to her, even though she learned English, couldn't he?"

"Of course—that is what we told him. We said, 'You are crippling her, she has to learn English. She cannot live in this country without the language, she cannot do anything.'

"He was strange in many, many ways.

"But he never appeared to be violent or anything."

For some reason Lee would get especially upset with Marina's desire to smoke. Likewise it annoyed him when she had a drink. Although his Russian diary indicated he often drank in Russia, and prior to that in the Marine Corps, not a single witness testified that he drank to any extent when he returned to the United States.

When asked about Marina's smoking, George de Mohrenschildt volunteered, "Oh boy, this is an interesting question. She loved to smoke and would smoke as many cigarettes as she could lay her hands on. And you know, Oswald did not smoke and forbade her to

smoke. This is the reason—one of the reasons they fought so bitterly
—because he would take the cigarette away from her and slap her."

"In your presence?"

"In my presence, would take the cigarette away from her and
push her: 'You are not going to do that,' in a dictatorial way. So I
would say, 'Now stop it. Let her smoke,' and then he would relax.
But that is the type of person he was. But not in our presence—when
we were away, Marina said he would not let her smoke nor drink, I
think. He refused to let her drink either. And she liked to have a
drink. With all her defects she is more or less a normal person, and
rather happy-go-lucky, a very happy-go-lucky girl."

I can confirm at least in part George de Mohrenschildt's observations regarding Marina's smoking habits. As she answered one question after another from the witness end of the Commission's working table she smoked a lot, particularly after the tension of the first
few hours wore off. Her mannerisms were those of a person who
smoked self-consciously.

The Commission continued to question de Mohrenschildt:

"What about his drinking?"

"I never saw him drink. Maybe he would take a very little, but I
never saw him drink more than half a glass—as far as I remember. I
didn't pay too much attention. Maybe that is why he was tense, because he did not drink enough. He was always tense. That guy was
always under some kind of pressure."

"You have that impression?"

"Yes, always some kind of pressure."

"And this was an inner pressure, you thought?"

"Yes, some inward pressure."

In her testimony Marina conveyed the impression that she did
nothing to complain about the standard of living she and Lee were
forced to live on. She made a point of saying that she had never had
much and therefore a few dollars a day satisfied her wants. If this
were literally true, why would Oswald seem to resent the better
things the Russian group enjoyed?

George de Mohrenschildt had a different impression. In the matter
of whether Lee was able to drive a car, he testified, "I have the impression he said he didn't know how to drive, but I couldn't swear to
that. And naturally Marina was needling him all the time to buy an
automobile."

Although Marguerite Oswald said that she had made up her mind not to interfere in Lee's and Marina's affairs, she was still living in the Fort Worth area and was visiting the Mercedes Street house. She testified, "It has been stated in the papers that my son was giving Marina black eyes and possibly he had beat her. And this is by the Russian people.

"Now, living at this home in Fort Worth, I had gone by several times I had a day off, and Marina was not at home.

"I said to her, 'Marina, Mama come to see you yesterday. You no home.'

"She didn't answer.

"I said, 'Marina, Mama come see you, you no home, Marina.'

" 'No. I go to lady's home to take English lessons.' "

"Do you know who she was speaking of?"

"I do not know for a fact. But my son Robert will know. And that is why it is important to call him. That is what I am trying to say, Chief Justice Warren. These others will know this part of my story, give you the facts.

"I am assuming it is Mr. Peter Gregory's wife that started these lessons. But Marina was taking English lessons.

"Now, they lived at a corner house [on Mercedes Street], and there is Carol Street, and opposite Carol Street is a parking lot for Montgomery Ward. They live approximately two blocks from Montgomery Ward. So I had gone by, as I am stating several times. You have to understand—this is just six or seven weeks they have been in this home.

"Then Marina was not home. I could not understand where so fast that they could have so many friends, that this Russian girl didn't speak English and know her way about, could be gone all day long. That worried me. [It appeared these were times when Marina was with Paul Gregory giving him Russian lessons rather than her learning English.]

"So I sat in the car on Montgomery Ward's parking lot, where I could see the house, because I want to see who Marina was going to come home with.

"The door was open. I went in the house and no one was there.

"By this time I was wondering how she could be gone all the time, being a stranger in town.

"I sat in the car all day long. She didn't show up.

"Finally I went home, had my supper, left my apartment, and on the way going back to the house Lee was leaving Montgomery Ward.

"Now, they did not have a phone. I am just assuming—this is not a fact—that Lee went to a telephone trying to locate his wife because I was coming from Montgomery Ward. He got in the car with me, and we had about a block to go. I entered the home with Lee, and I said, 'Lee, where is Marina?' Of course I knew that she was not at home because I had stayed in the car all day.

"He said, 'Oh, I guess she is out with some friends.'

" 'Would you like me to fix some supper?'

" 'No, she will probably be home in time to fix my supper.'

"So I left. I am not going to interfere in their married life. But I did offer to fix him supper. And I went back to make sure Marina still wasn't home.

"I walked in the home with my son.

"So approximately two days later—not approximately, but two days later I went to the home and my son was reading—he read continuously—in the living room, and Marina was in the bedroom, which I could not see Marina. And I said to Lee, 'Tell Marina I am here.' "

Whereupon Marguerite—the mother-in-law who knew the faults of other mothers-in-law—went into the bedroom and found Marina with a black eye.

"Did you ask Marina how she got the black eye or anything about it?"

"Yes, in the bedroom. I was shocked.

" 'Mama, Lee.' Just like that.

"So I went into the living room and said, 'Lee, what do you mean by striking Marina?'

"He said, 'Mother, that is our affair.'

"And so that ended. I wasn't going to interfere any further.

"Now this has been publicly stated by the Russian friends, that he beat his wife; I don't know if he did beat his wife. I happened to see the black eye. I know that he hit her and gave her a black eye. Marina said so, and my son said so. But how many times this happened, I don't know.

"But I am trying to point out that I don't approve of it. But I am trying to point out that everything is not according to Hoyle, as we say, in our American way of life."

What was not according to Hoyle was that Lee and Marina were on the verge of a separation. They were simply unable to live together peacefully, a fact which their newfound Russian acquaintances were more aware of than Lee's mother or brother. The problems were acute—the beatings, Lee's irritability, the jealousy Lee felt particularly toward George Bouhe, who in all earnestness had tried to help Marina. Marguerite's occasional intrusion into their affairs could not be blamed for the situation, although Lee wanted to escape Marguerite again. In his testimony George de Mohrenschildt was inclined to defend Lee more than other witnesses, but it was a two-sided incompatibility.

"Were there occasions when you knew them in which Marina would correct his grammar and there would be an altercation between them or something?"

"Oh yes. There was bickering all the time. I don't remember whether it was especially on the point of grammar, but there was bickering between them all the time.

"But as I said, the bickering was mainly because Marina smoked and he didn't approve of it, that she liked to drink and he did not approve of it. I think she liked to put the makeup on and he didn't let her use the makeup.

"My wife will explain a little more in detail what was going on between them, you see, because she was a confidante of Marina's, you see. I was not."

"Would you elaborate, please?"

"Well, my wife, being a woman, was interested in a woman's problems—you see, Marina's—in the baby and in her makeup, in the way she dressed and the way she behaved, you see."

"You made a comment that you just said your wife had confidence in Marina, but you didn't. What did you mean by that?"

"Confidence from what point of view?"

"I don't know."

"Yes, I mentioned that because I don't like a woman who bitches at her husband all the time, and she did, you know. She brought the worst out in him. And she told us after they would get into a fight, you know, that he was fighting also. She would scratch him also.

"She would scratch him?"

"She would scratch him also."

The Russians, who had observed the extent of the friction between Lee and Marina—particularly George Bouhe—had concluded that something must be done about the situation. Perhaps in a way they really had meddled too much in the Oswalds' affairs, but they all felt a great sympathy for Marina, this poor Russian girl who was caught in a situation she was not qualified to cope with, particularly the handicap she had in not being able to speak English. In ordinary circumstances a woman who was treated like this could get out and leave the house; she could find employment and make her own way. But Marina? How could she find work? There was talk among the group that she might find employment in a home as a maid or housekeeper, but even this was totally impractical. What would she do with the baby, and how could she communicate with her employers? From my observations of Marina in her voluminous testimony before the Commission I could not visualize her employed in someone's home as a domestic.

From the evidence it would appear that Lee was not unaware that a temporary separation might be a healthy thing. He seems to have wanted to get out from under the pressure, if not of Marina's bickering, as de Mohrenschildt described it, at least away from the whole Fort Worth atmosphere that seemed to be goading him—his mother, his loathsome job, a sense of always being trapped and humiliated. This was not a life for him. He had begun to think he had been better off in Russia. Did it plague him that he had made a mistake in marrying Marina just to spite Ella? She certainly wasn't the kind of girl he had hoped for—one who would understand his role in life; one who would be a helpmate. She took no interest in those things that seemed so important—his dream of a better political system, of himself as being a leader of a new movement. She had even gotten so that she was inclined to ridicule his ideas.

Lee Oswald was dreaming of a day of greater glory. Like Marx, he could foresee a new revolution—and sometimes he thought of himself as the man who might well lead the way. But here he was drudging in a sheet-metal shop, laboring at the lowliest tasks, bringing home a few dollars to keep body and soul alive. And there would be Marina to throw cold water on his dreams. There was nothing Spartan or heroic about her. She just wanted her comforts and to be like any other American. She had no interest in politics or political ideals at all. In fact she was uninspired intellectually. But he . . . de Mohrenschildt commented on a conversation he once had with Lee:

"One conversation I had with him—I asked him, 'Would you like to be Commissar in the United States?' just teasing him. And he said—he sort of smiled—you could see that it was a delightful idea. To me it was a ridiculous question to ask. But he took me seriously. I laughed with the guy. Sometimes I would laugh, I would tease him, and it was amusing. But I tried not to offend him, because, after all, he was a human being."

On the other hand, de Mohrenschildt observed, "Marina was definitely more appreciative of life in the United States."

"Was she inclined to discuss politics?"

"Not too much, no. That was Lee's main point, you see, to discuss politics."

"What was her attitude toward Lee's view in that respect?"

"She more or less considered him a crackpot, as far as I remember, you see. A few times, 'Oh, that crazy lunatic. Again he is talking about politics.'

"This is one of the reasons we liked her, because that was a very intelligent attitude, you see, but it was very annoying to Lee."

"That was another source of annoyance between them?"

"Yes. There were so many sources of annoyance, as you know, that it was just an unhappy marriage."

George Bouhe had inquired of his friends if there wasn't some way that Marina could get away from Lee for a while. He wanted to find someone she could live with peacefully, and Marina must have been agreeable to the idea. Contrary to the general impression that Lee was a chronically unemployed drifter who could not keep a job, he had been doing satisfactory work at the Leslie Welding Company. However, he was not happy with the work and he thought there was no future in it. Perhaps he should go to Dallas and look for work. It was said there were better opportunities there. Lee lent encouragement to the idea by leading the Russian group to believe that he was about to lose his job in Fort Worth. He told them the company was going broke and his future was therefore uncertain. Witnesses claimed George Bouhe was convinced he should get Marina away from the vicious influence of Oswald, and consequently he was doing everything he could to put out feelers for a job Lee might take in Dallas.

On Saturday, October 6, 1962, a number of Oswald's Russian acquaintances went to the Mercedes Street house. Lee told them he had lost his job at Leslie Welding, which was not true. They all became concerned and discussed his chances of finding work in Dallas. Those present included Anna Meller, Elena Hall, George Bouhe, Lee and Marina. Over the weekend some of the other Russian friends became involved in the problem of finding Lee a job in Dallas. Inasmuch as Elena Hall was divorced and living alone, she offered to take Marina in while Lee looked for suitable work. It would appear at least some of them—without actually saying so at the time—were glad to have Lee get out of Fort Worth so that Marina would not have to continue taking the brunt of his fits of brutality. Could this have been a prearranged "trial separation," which both Lee and Marina were agreeable to? Lee lied about losing his job, which gave him an excuse to go to Dallas. Marina agreed to go to live at Elena Hall's. Everyone cooperated in the move, which Marguerite—according to her own account—found mystifying:

"Now, this Sunday I went—this is very important, Gentlemen—I went to this home [Mercedes Street] and I was there—I asked to get off an hour or two to see the children, from this O.B. case at Rosenthals'. I went to see my son and daughter-in-law and they were nicely dressed. And while there, about ten minutes, a young couple came into the home, approximately the same age as Marina and Lee [probably George de Mohrenschildt's daughter and son-in-law, Alexandra and Gary Taylor], and they had a little boy who I would say was about six or eight months older than June. The woman put the little boy in the playpen with June, and June went to touch him and Marina got up and said, 'Oh, no, hurt baby.' She spoke English. So I said, 'Do you speak Russian?' to this couple. And they said, 'No, we don't. We are Americans but my father'—and I will have to say this or grandfather, I do not know which—'is a Russian from Siberia and that is how we know Marina and Lee.'"

Knowing nothing about the acquaintanceships of Lee and Marina with the Russian group, Marguerite thought perhaps this incident implied a plot of some kind.

"So the conversation was general. And in the general conversation

148

—now this couple was from Dallas, visiting my family in Fort Worth. The conversation was general.

"And she said, 'Lee, my father has this place of business in Dallas and will offer you a job in Dallas.'

"I said, 'Lee, I didn't know you wanted to give up your job and work in Dallas, because the Rosenthals that I am working for, her father owns the meat-packing house in Dallas, and she has told me that he employs hundreds of people, and if ever any time you are in need, to go see her father, that she would be sure he would give you a job.'

"So, gentlemen, this was on a Sunday.

"I made coffee and the house was in order. There was nothing packed.

"Lee got paid on a Friday from the Leslie sheet-metal works.

"Monday Lee and Marina packed their belongings and went to Dallas.

"Now, I understand that my son Robert helped him to move. And the way I know this—I went there on Tuesday, and the children had gone because they had left on a Monday. So I was all upset. They didn't tell me they were leaving.

"I said to Vada, 'Marina and Lee are no longer there, the house is vacant.'

"She said, 'Robert helped them to move, and they gave us the food in the refrigerator.'

"It came all of a sudden.

"They did not tell me they had left.

"So I accepted the fact that my son Lee did not want me to know that he was in Dallas.

"Now, Gentlemen, this may seem hard that I accept these things. But it is not. I am self-supporting. I have a life of my own. And if Lee decides that that is the way he wants it, I am not going to grieve or worry about it. I have to get my sleep in order to work. I have the ability of accepting things, the ability granted me by the grace of God, because of my difficulty in life. I have been a widow. I have had many, many obstacles and I have had to face them. And my faith gets stronger. I do accept things."

From that day Marguerite saw neither Lee nor Marina until the day of the assassination thirteen months later. Lee Oswald's mother actually knew less about the events immediately prior to November

22, 1963, than almost any other witness who appeared before the Commission. Lee went to Dallas and found a promising job with the Jaggars-Chiles-Stovall Company. Marina stayed with Elena Hall, her first separation from Lee, and she seemed happy, according to at least one observer, Max Clark. He testified, "We had formed the impression that he and Marina had separated."

CHAPTER 10

MARINA CHANGES HER MIND

WHILE RECONSTRUCTING the events of Lee Oswald's life in the first four months of his return from Russia, the Commission, its experts and cooperating agencies probed every possible detail of his day-to-day activities.

A careful tabulation was made of every cent of income either he or Marina had received. Each witness was asked, "Did you ever give the Oswalds cash, or what did you give them that might be construed as income?" The amounts were small, or, in the case of George Bouhe, gifts like a baby crib and help in getting Marina's teeth taken care of. Oswald resented these gifts. Marina accepted them freely. She received a record player from de Mohrenschildt and from others a few relatively small household items. At one point Lee bought a television set on credit with his brother's endorsement of the note, but he decided he did not want it and sent it back. There were no unusual expenditures. On the contrary, the Oswalds lived frugally.

In cash layouts, George Bouhe spent more than anyone else. De Mohrenschildt described Bouhe's interest in Marina:

"Bouhe is an elderly man. He wanted—almost like a daughter, you see. To him she was a poor girl whose father was an ex-officer, and she needed help. He would give her thirty, forty dollars, I think all at once."

"Did he ever collect money from you and others to contribute?"

"I don't think so."

"Did you ever give Lee Oswald money?"

"No."

"Did you ever give Marina any money?"

"Not as far as I remember. Maybe a dollar, maybe fifty cents, something like that for a bus. But never any money. I was in very difficult financial condition myself at that time. I don't think I gave her even fifty cents."

As to other gifts, de Mohrenschildt recalled, "Toys for the baby, definitely. And I am sure that my wife had given some dresses. But she will remember better than I do. But we never gave them one cent of money. This I recall—never—and Lee would not take money, you see. I might have given him a little bit if he had asked. But he was very proud about it. He resented when people gave something to Marina. Marina would take anything, you see—she would take anything from five cents up to anything. He had a very proud attitude. This is one of the reasons I sort of liked him, because of that. He was not a beggar, not a sponger."

Lee's take-home pay had been small at Leslie Welding. Because he had brought only the barest of necessities from Russia, getting a household established was a strain on his limited finances. He was repaying Robert's loan. Furthermore, he was conscientiously saving money and making payments to the State Department on his loan. As long as his debt was outstanding, the Government would not issue him another passport. This is standard practice. Whether at this time it occurred to Lee that he might some day want to leave the United States again is not clear. He was not happy and this was a possibility.

The only contacts he had with an agency at this time—other than his payments to the State Department—were with the FBI. Upon his return to the United States they took an interest in him, as his brother Robert reported in his testimony. He was asked, "Your mother, in her testimony before the Commission, gave the impression, and later in press stories, that she thought that maybe your brother was an agent of the CIA. Did you ever have any reason to think that?"

"No, sir, and the only time the thought ever entered my mind as to him being an agent of the CIA, or any other United States Government bureau, was on his return from Russia while residing at my residence in Fort Worth. The FBI had called and requested that he come down for an interview there in Fort Worth. On completion of his interview when I came home from work that night, he discussed it briefly, and I asked him how did they treat him, and so forth. He said just fine, and he says, 'They asked me was I a secret agent,' or some type of agent for the U.S. Government, and he laughed and said, 'Well, don't you know?'

"I remember that. That was just crossed out of my mind."

As I look back, it seems incredible to me that the FBI would ask Lee Oswald such a question. Why wouldn't they know, and what would prompt them to ask Lee—of all people—whether he was an agent of any U. S. Government service? If the FBI didn't know, who would know? Furthermore, hadn't some branch of the State Department checked him out carefully before he was permitted back in this country? It struck Lee Oswald as comical that he would be questioned in this fashion by the very agency responsible for the security of our nation. Indeed, if it weren't for the tragic consequences of the failure of all U.S. agencies to realize that they were dealing with a future assassin, the incident would stand as *the* classic boner in the annals of crime detection. It is understandable, however, that an individual agent, with only a partial file on the entire Oswald case, would ask this question. Marguerite had insisted when she went to the White House in 1961 that her son was a patriot and an agent of the CIA. She had been told, "No, he is not." But from her viewpoint why should she believe this? Hadn't the Government at first piously declared that Powers was not an agent when his plane was shot down and then later admitted he was on the CIA payroll? Aggressive as she was, Marguerite had not been able to get the answers she believed from anyone in Washington. Now, even the FBI was confused in turn by Marguerite's assertions.

Step by step the Commission traced the chain of statements and rumors that gave rise to the notion that Oswald might have been an agent of some branch of the U. S. Government. Patiently they also checked out his day-to-day activities after returning to America to ascertain whether he had any contacts with suspicious individuals or groups. Only by reconstructing a complete biography—actually more than a biography—in the form of a meticulous chronology of his daily life could the answers to such questions be rooted out. All of his landlords, both when he was living with Marina and when they were separated, were interviewed. The post-office records, YMCA registers where he lived alone, rental records and bank accounts were gone over by independent experts. Never has a man's life been so closely scrutinized by so many investigators in such a short period of time. During the weeks of Marina and Lee's first separation, he lived part of the time at the YMCA in Dallas. Marina lived with Elena Hall in Fort Worth. How long the separation was intended to last varies with the opinion of the witness. Marina passed the matter over casually, as if she simply intended to live with Mrs. Hall a few weeks while Lee was seeking a new job in Dallas and getting organized. George Bouhe may have hoped that it meant a permanent separation through which Marina would be freed of the tyranny of Oswald.

Max Clark, a close friend of Elena Hall's, recalled the circumstances of this separation.

"Approximately when was it that Marina moved in with Elena Hall—do you remember?"

"Sometime in October of 1962; the exact date I don't know. I know that she had been over there a few days when Elena Hall had an automobile wreck late one night. We received a phone call from the hospital to pick up this Marina and the baby and take them to the hospital because Elena was under the impression that she had killed the baby or Marina in the car wreck. She thought that they were involved."

"Were they in the car at all?"

"No, they were not in the car, but she was injured pretty badly, apparently during this car wreck. So we went by to this Elena Hall's house about ten that night and took her to the hospital, and then of course she had been given sedatives and—Elena Hall—and I don't know whether she knew any more about it. I did not see her that night."

"Did Marina see Elena Hall that night?"

"I think so but I am not sure. I know we took them to the hospital and then we took Marina and the baby back to her home, to this Elena Hall's home, and, of course, during—from that period while Elena was in the hospital my wife had to take food or pick up this Marina and buy her groceries or milk for the baby and look after her because she could not speak English and had no transportation or any way to get food. So usually every day my wife would go over and either take her to the grocery or take her food."

"One of the things the Commission is doing, in an attempt to learn as much as we can about Oswald, is we are trying to put together a schedule of income and outgo of funds throughout the entire time he lived in this country after he returned from Russia. I would like to have you, if you could recollect as best you can, the exact amount of food, groceries or money or other things that your wife provided for Marina Oswald while she lived at Elena Hall's house. Do you have knowledge of those things?"

"Actually, it was probably very small because Elena was in the hospital, to my recollection, not more than a week, and during that time apparently there was—she bought her some groceries, and I do recall she said she bought her a carton of cigarettes. I doubt if it would exceed ten or fifteen dollars."

"As far as you know the only things that your wife did provide to Marina were these things you described?"

"Yes."

"Do you know whether she gave Marina any money?"

"I am sure she did not give her any cash. No."

"Would you go on with your story now, please."

"So upon—when this Elena Hall was in the hospital, my wife would see Marina about every day, and I think that one evening during that week I took her and the baby and my wife to a restaurant for dinner one night, and then on the Sunday following this hospital treatment, and while Elena was still in the hospital, Marina asked my wife if we would come over on Sunday afternoon and have some Russian dinner that she would prepare for us, and this Elena's ex-husband was coming into town from Odessa, and if we would come over there, three or four o'clock Sunday afternoon, she would prepare this dinner. So we planned on going over there and we did, and when we got there Oswald was there. That was the first time either my wife or myself had met Oswald, so we were there, oh, I would say approximately two hours. Sometime after we arrived, then John Hall, as I recall, came in from the hospital. He had been over seeing his wife, and then we sat around and talked and we ate later on, and then we left rather early in the evening. Well, probably, I don't recall the time, but it must have been seven or eight o'clock."

"Did you know whether Oswald ever stayed at Elena Hall's home while Elena was in the hospital?"

"I have no way of knowing. I did not think he did. It was my impression he was in Dallas at the time. In fact, we were quite surprised to see him that Sunday afternoon because we had formed the impression that Marina and he had separated. I don't know definitely because I couldn't talk with Marina. She only spoke Russian at the time."

"Did your wife have the impression that there had been marital difficulties between the Oswalds at that time?"

"Yes."

"Can you tell us any specific reasons why your wife thought that?"

"None other than the conversations and the fact that Marina seemed quite happy with him gone, more than the fact that she did not seem to miss him, and the fact that he wasn't there."

The plan to have Marina stay with Mrs. Hall—if it was for any permanent stay—was now altered by two circumstances. First, the automobile accident had left Marina alone in Mrs. Hall's house a week so that her friends had to step in and take care of her, and second, John Hall and Elena Hall's divorce was being reconsidered by them. A few days after Elena's return from the hospital, she went to New York to see friends.

As Elena described the situation, "When I got out from the hospital—I think it was in the end of October, after my accident—I stayed home I think three or four days."

"Was Marina there at the time?"

"Yes, she was there. Then I went to New York on the thirty-first of October. I went to New York, and when I came back on the fifteenth [November], they were gone."

"You don't know exactly when they moved out?"

"No, no."

The Halls would not have been too concerned about this at the moment. They were remarried on November 17, 1962. Having Marina live with them in these changed circumstances would not have been practical anyway, particularly if she slept "forty-eight hours a day," as Elena had characterized Marina's habits.

The Oswalds were gone. Elena Hall did not know where or when. To live in an acquaintance's home, to enjoy the generosity of friends' friends, even to the extent of accepting food and cigarettes, and to depart without so much as a Thank-you note or an explanation of where one is going constitutes a peculiar outlook on one's relationships with other human beings. It might be argued that Marina knew the Halls were going to be remarried and removed herself from their private affairs so as not to trouble them. Without leaving a farewell note? It may be reasoned that Lee had again persuaded Marina that her Russian friends were interfering with their personal domestic relations and therefore to depart without leaving a trail would protect them from these intrusions in the future. The records show that Lee Oswald felt an unusual sense of obligation to repay fully any debts he incurred—but Marina? George de Mohrenschildt testified, "She would take anything she could get."

It was Tuesday, October 9, 1962, that Lee did not show up for work at his old job with the Leslie Welding Company. That weekend Marina had gone to live with Elena Hall. On October 12, Friday, through the Texas Employment Office, Lee began working at the Jaggars-Chiles-Stovall Company in Dallas as a trainee photographer. He took a room at the YMCA and, as Max Clark testified, visited Marina at least on one weekend occasion when she made bortsch for the Clarks and John Hall. Recovering from her accident, Elena Hall got out of the hospital about the "end of October" and then on the thirty-first went to New York for two weeks, where she joined her former husband. Sometime during that period Marina decided to go back with Lee, and they took up residence at 604 Elsbeth Street, Dallas.

Interrogating the landlady on Elsbeth Street, Mrs. Mahlon F. Tobias, the Commission obtained a mixed impression of the success of this reunion.

"Now were you in the office when that apartment was rented? Did you have the first contact with him?"

"Yes, he came in our house."

"Why don't you tell me about that?"

"Well, the night he came over to rent the place—"

"It was at night?"

"In the evening, yes, and then he didn't take it, but he wanted to look around. He asked my husband if he might look around."

"Was anybody accompanying him?"

"No. Just Oswald, my husband and I."

"How was he dressed?"

"Well, he always seemed to wear slacks and just a T-shirt. So it was a week later before he came back to rent it."

"He waited a week?"

"Yes."

"You told him what the cost was?"

"Yes, my husband told him that."

"Did he say anything about money at that time? Did you make any inquiry as to whether or not he was working, where he worked?"

"No, Mr. Oswald was very qiuet. He had very little to say, so when he came back he told my husband he had a wife and a child."

"Were you there when he made this statement that he had a wife and a child?"

"Yes, and when they came in—I didn't see anyone for quite some time, perhaps ten days or two weeks, and I said to my husband, 'I thought he told us he had a wife and a child.' He said, 'Well, he did.'

"We don't know when he moved in because he could have used that driveway to the back door—you understand what I mean?"

"Yes."

Although Mrs. Tobias did not know the precise day Lee moved in, it was the third of November, just after Elena Hall had left for New York, that he made a five-dollar key deposit and paid sixty-eight dollars for the first month's rent. It was a week or ten days after that that Mrs. Tobias saw Marina for the first time and realized she didn't speak much English. She asked Lee, "What nationality are you folks?"

"Oh, we are Czech."

For the first time it appears that Lee wanted to disguise the fact that Marina was Russian.

Lee and Marina were now reunited at 604 Elsbeth Street. Marina testified that whenever she left Lee he would come to her, beg her to return and promise to mend his ways. On the surface there was no reason now they couldn't settle down like other couples and make a reasonable success of living together. Lee's job at Jaggars-Chiles-Stovall had promise. In a sense he was serving an apprenticeship, learning to photograph and do mock-ups for printing mats—a well-paid profession when one acquires journeyman status. Lee stated that he enjoyed this work, but his supercilious attitude toward other people remained unchanged.

George Bouhe tried to counsel him. "Lee, you've got a job, a lithographic job at a dollar forty-five an hour as an apprentice. If you apply yourself, in a couple of years you'll have a skill that can be salable any place."

"You think so?" was Lee's sardonic answer.

He didn't thank George Bouhe for his help in getting the job through one of Bouhe's acquaintances at the employment office.

"Well, I'd like to hear how you get along."

And for two or three days thereafter Lee would taunt Bouhe by calling him on the phone at 6:00 P.M. after his work. "I'm doing fine," he would say. "Bye." And then, without saying anything else, he would hang up.

Lee Oswald just couldn't accept an ordinary pattern of life. Within a few weeks he was digressing from his job. Instead of concentrating on his work at the plant, he was writing letters to leftist periodicals, offering to do free photographic reproduction work for them. His mind was on "the cause," not on the business of establishing himself in a worthwhile profession. Somehow he was determined to get recognition on a higher level of world affairs. He had what some psychologists would call the "political disease," and his disposition was to quarrel with anything or anyone who got in his way. According to witnesses, Marina got in his way by belittling his dedication to dreams of leadership in a vaguely defined revolutionary movement. He made no lasting connections with existing organizations because immediately he found fault with the way they were being run. At least he expected Marina to agree with him, to submit to his discipline. He once told her when they disagreed, "I am the commander." Every man likes to feel he is the leader of his own family and that his wife believes in him and his cause. But with Marina and Lee Oswald the gap between their ambitions was too great. Immediately upon being reunited on Elsbeth Street, despite Lee's promises to change, they were battling again.

Innocently, Mrs. Tobias said to Marina the first occasion they met, "Your husband says you are Czech."

Marina shook her head no. She made it clear to her landlady that she was Russian. Why would he lie about that? Mrs. Tobias wanted to know.

Marina got it across to her. "My husband said it was bad, and my husband told me if I said I was Russian, people would be mean to me."

When Lee found out that Marina had contradicted him and let

Mrs. Tobias know she was Russian, he forgot his promises of reform and beat her up. The reunion was off to a bad start.

Other tenants in the apartment building were soon aware that this couple did not get along. Mrs. Tobias reported the complaints of neighbors. "Yes, they seemed to disagree, and they didn't get along so good, and the tenants would come and tell my husband they kept them awake and the baby cried so much and that he could hear them falling down as if Mrs. Oswald was hitting the floor, so my husband went over and he said he was sorry but there was nothing going on and that everything was okay, and we had one tenant over him and she came over and she said, 'Mrs. Tobias, I think he has made a new opening down there.' She said, 'I think he's put her right through there.' And he did break a window—my husband had to fix that."

Mrs. Tobias was asked what kind of a housekeeper Marina was.

"Well, I was never in there but once, and I'll tell you why I was in there then. This fellow came over and he said to my husband, 'I think he's really hurt her this time.' "

"Now was this another tenant?"

"A tenant, yes, and we didn't hear her out at the clothesline, and my husband said, 'Why don't you and I go over and rap on the door and see if she will come to the door and see if she's okay.' He said, 'We can tell her that the sweeper is over here—she hasn't found the sweeper—she doesn't know anything about it.' "

"That would be the sweeper to use in the apartments?"

"A vacuum sweeper."

Mrs. Tobias testified that when Marina came to the door she had a housecoat on and she had marks on her face.

Jeanne de Mohrenschildt testified that at least during one period of her life Marina had run with what we in America would consider a very fast crowd. Jeanne de Mohrenschildt did not entertain a high opinion of Marina's energy, her qualifications as a mother, her training or her morality.

"She had no idea how to feed that baby. The baby was raised on sugar, water and sugar, no food. It is just terrible, like prehistoric times she was raising that baby. That is why I insisted immediately she register the baby in the clinic. The baby was nine months old, didn't have diphtheria, whooping cough, polio injection—didn't have anything.

"I don't think the baby was ever at the doctor. The way she was feeding him, every time the baby cried she gave him sugar water, put sugar in the milk, everywhere, you know. Children have to have a proper diet, a balanced diet.

"I told her, 'You are living in a civilized country now. You have to raise the baby correctly.'

"Constantly pacifier in the mouth, dropping it on the floor, putting it in her mouth, infected teeth and putting it in the baby's mouth. It is fantastic the baby wasn't sick all the time.

"Seeing all that, I couldn't stand it. I insisted on her taking the baby to the clinic helping her, extract all those teeth."

"Marina's teeth?"

"Yes, Marina's teeth that were infected because they weren't doing her any good anyway. It was too dangerous for the baby to be close to the mother with all this infection. In fact, I was trying to make arrangements to make some bridges for her later on that could be paid gradually, you know, and that is what I was trying to do for her. This was logical and natural. Anybody would do the same thing."

"Yes, of course."

"She just didn't know any better, you know. That was shocking to me because I had the impression—in fact Marina doesn't fit at all my ideal, not ideal—but how to say it, my feeling about Soviet youth. I pictured them entirely different. I pictured them all sportsmen, very tough, you know, just thinking of their work, sportsmen or something, you know. Some field that they are interested in and that is it. She seems to be exactly opposite to everything. She wasn't a sports girl at all. She didn't have any particular desire for anything, you know. She didn't have determination and goal or anything like that in her life. She was just living, you know, absolutely opposite, and when she told us how they behave in Russia, that was absolutely too—I never thought that. I thought they were very, very proper and very—"

"What did she say about how they behaved?"

"Well, these sort of orgies, you know, wild parties and things like that that I would never think youth would be busy with that because we saw some youngsters in Yugoslavian companies in camps— maybe we saw the healthier ones and the bad ones stayed in the city probably—but they were all just like Scouts, you know, just like we were brought up, all interested in sports or collections or something, you know. They had wonderful healthy interests.

"And Marina was exactly opposite all these things. In fact in spite of that, she was a pharmacologist—that means she had a good head. But somehow she was not at all what I would picture as a Soviet girl.

"It was entirely opposite, and maybe she is an exception, or maybe they all are—I don't know."

"And she related to you these wild parties and orgies in Minsk. Was that in the presence of Lee?"

"No, I don't think so. Lee was there very little, because he was always working or something. One evening I talked with her very long when she came over to go to the dentist, and the baby was asleep and George was asleep, and she wanted to talk, and we sat down and had some wine and she could smoke all she wanted. So she told me quite a lot of things. I was really sorry for her.

"I gave her a nightgown and a little nylon coat that went on and she was sitting and touching it. 'Can you imagine me wearing that?' you know. It was something out of this world to have such things on her. That was sort of touching, you know. She really is pleasant. You cannot be very angry with her."

"You have testified quite a while. Now, tell me, what kind of person was she? What is your definite impression now? You have told me she told you about these wild orgies. When you use that expression I assume they were parties of—"

"Sexual orgies. I mean things that would never occur to us."

"In this country?"

"In this country. I would say China too. I was brought up in China and never heard of such things, you know. Youth never acted like that at all.

"So it definitely looks like a degeneration, you know. Definitely degeneration."

"You found her, while you knew she was a pharmacist—"

"Yes."

"You immediately noticed that she was ignorant, let me say."

"In bringing up the child."

"In bringing up this child?"

"Absolutely."

"That she fed her sugar and water?"

"Milk and sugar."

"Milk and sugar and was inattentive as to cleanliness with the child?"

"The child was more or less clean, but with this pacifier thing."

"The pacifier would fall on the floor, she would pick it up and stick it in the baby's mouth."

"No, first she would put it in her infected mouth and then in the baby's mouth—it was even worse. That is what I objected. Pick it off the floor. The floor was less germs than her infected tooth, but she was not aware of it. That is what didn't make sense, didn't make sense at all. After all, a pharmacist—it also didn't make any sense to me how could she, came from the country where all the medical help is supposed to be absolutely free."

Like her husband, Jeanne de Mohrenschildt has exceptional background and talents. Her judgments of Marina have to be considered in the light of a person who exacted extreme proficiency and discipline of herself. Born of an outstanding Russian family (her father was manager of the Trans-Siberian Railway in Harbin, China, before the revolution), she had made her way to America, virtually taught herself English and became a highly successful dancer. Then, when this profession ceased to support her, she took up dress designing with such artistic success that she earned large fees for consulting with leading dress manufacturers. She had joined a firm in Dallas, currently a style center in America, and made her way by virtue of talent and hard work to the top of the business ladder. Some of Jeanne de Mohrenschildt's opinions may seem harsh, but except for a matter of degree they do not differ substantially from other witnesses.

How much Lee knew about this aspect of Marina's past there is no way of determining. Certainly he was aware of untidy habits, such as those Jeanne de Mohrenschildt cited in the matter of feeding the baby and the pacifier. He was jealous of Marina when others paid her special attention, but whether this had anything to do with a feeling that she might become involved with another man is impossible to say. However, he did discover that Marina had written an old boy friend in Russia, which resulted in a beating for Marina she admitted she deserved.

One day Lee went to his post-office box in Dallas. There he found a letter in Marina's handwriting returned for insufficient postage. She had forgotten the new increase in postal rates. He opened the letter and confronted Marina with it. She told this old boy friend what a miserable life she was leading with Lee Oswald. She bluntly stated that she wished she had not married Lee but had married the boy friend instead and remained in the Soviet Union.

Because of Lee's sensitivity to the reproaches of strangers, to be told in writing that his wife respected him so little that she would write a letter like that to an old boy friend, that obviously he was not even the master of his own family, let alone the great world leader he dreamed of becoming, was provocative to the point of producing uncontrolled fury.

Was this the occasion on Elsbeth Street when the window was broken and the neighbors complained to Mrs. Tobias? Was this the incident that brought on the comment by a tenant that "I think he has made a new opening down there"?

Lee had once proudly confided to his diary that Marina was madly in love with him. Considering that his relationships with most everyone else he came in touch with were a failure, it was intolerable that his wife would not accept his views. In her testimony Marina so carefully played down the extent of Lee's brutality toward her—saying in one instance, "Oh, of course there are always small things that come between husband and wife"—that there is no way of judging how ferociously he beat her on this occasion. Hadn't Marina actually come to fear for her life when Lee would go into these rages? In any case it was not more than two weeks after they had agreed to try to live together again that a second separation took place. This time Marina fled at night to the home of another Russian acquaintance, Mrs. Anna Meller, who affirmed the incident in her typical Russian-accented English.

"It vas in November, I think on certain Monday about ten in the evening, she vill call me and say that her husband beat her and she came out from the apartment and reached the filling station and said the man—she did not have a penny—and the good soul helped her to dial the number and she's talking to me if she can come over my house. I vas speechless because to this time I even didn't know they were in Dallas. To understand, sir, vee vent to Fort Worth two or three times to help Marina and then vas for certain period quiet and then I do not know how long, maybe six weeks, maybe month, maybe three weeks and then I had this call. 'Vhere are you?' She said in Dallas. Certainly, there my husband vas at home; I came to my husband I asked him if ve can take Marina. He did not vant to. Vee have one-bedroom apartment and he said, 'Do not have very much space.' I like maniac voman started to beg and said, 'Vee have to help poor voman; she's on the street vith baby. Vee could not leave her like that; vee had our trouble and somebody helped us. My husband said, 'Okay, let her come.' She said to me she did not have a penny of money. I said, 'Take a taxi and come here and vee vill pay the vay. So about eleven or ten-forty she came over our house so like she vas staying in light blouse and skirt vith baby on her hand, couple diapers and that vas all—no coat, no money, notting."

"Did she appear to have been beaten up at that time? Did she have bruises?"

"She vas very nervous—did not try to cry very much but you can see she vas shaking.

"I vill not say exactly but she vas out of herself."

"Did she tell you what she and Oswald had been arguing about?"

"I do not remember. She said he beat her and I do not remember asking really for vhat or something. I did not ask for arguments, really because it vas so shocking and so unagreeable. I do not think I vent into detail."

Mrs. Meller considered that Marina was in poor physical condition at this time. "She vas so skinny to this time and so undernourished—look as skinny as she could be and she did not feel good. She had pain everywhere in her body and, looking at her, I decided to take her to doctor and let check her health a little bit."

I had a similar impression of Marina's physical makeup even during her appearances in the witness chair. She was thin and slight of build. On the other hand I had the distinct feeling that within this seemingly frail woman there was a certain sturdiness of body and spirit which belied her appearance.

Knowing that she could not keep Marina long in her small apartment, Mrs. Meller turned to George Bouhe for a solution to this problem. Bouhe felt strongly that Marina could not go back to Lee. Bouhe in turn contacted a number of the other members of the Russian colony—Mrs. Declan Ford, Mrs. Anna Ray and George de Mohrenschildt.

Mrs. Ford testified, "I think it must have been at—in late October or the first part of November when Mr. Bouhe called me and said that Marina made a call to Anna Meller and told her she is leaving her husband because of she can't stand the beating and treatment any longer from Lee Oswald."

"When Mr. Bouhe called you and told you about this, did he tell you anything about why Marina was leaving Lee Oswald?"

"Yes, he said because of mistreatment and she decided she is not going to return to him any longer, and Mr. Bouhe said, told her, if she made a promise to him she is not going to return to that man he would help her all he could to find a place to stay permanently, such as maybe as help at home at somebody's house until she learns enough English to start going on her own whatever she could do."

Marina arrived at the Mellers' in the middle of the night with only the clothes on her back. If this was to be a permanent separation, someone had to help her move things from the apartment. George de Mohrenschildt told the Commission how he helped Marina move and about Lee's reactions. Mrs. Tobias, the landlady, recalled that a man with a convertible came to 604 Elsbeth Street and said he was taking Marina away from Lee for a while.

De Mohrenschildt remembers, "I do not recall whether she called us in and asked us to take her away from him, or George Bouhe suggested it. I just don't recall how it happened. But it was because of his brutality to her."

"And when you entered that apartment you observed she had a black eye?"

"A black eye and a scratched face."

"Did you inquire about it?"

"She said, 'He has been beating me,' as if it was normal—not particularly appalled by this fact but 'He has been beating me,' but she said, 'I fight him back.'

"So I said, 'You cannot stand for that. You shouldn't let him beat you.'

"And she said, 'Well, I guess I should get away from him.' "

When Lee appeared, de Mohrenschildt told him he was taking Marina away as well as the baby.

"And Lee said, 'By God, you are not going to do it. I will tear all her dresses and I will break all the baby things."

"And I got very mad this time. But Jeanne, my wife, started explaining to him patiently that it is not going to help him any. 'Do you love your wife?' He said, 'Yes.' And she said, 'If you want your wife back some time, you better behave.'

"I said, 'If you don't behave, I will call the police.'

"I felt very nervous about the whole situation—interfering in other people's affairs, after all.

" 'Well,' he said, 'I will get even with you!'

"I said, 'You will get even with me?'

"I got a little bit more mad, and I said, 'I'm going to take Marina away.'

"So after a little while he started—and I started carrying the things out of the house. And Lee did not interfere with me. Of course, he was small, you know, and he was a very puny individual.

"After a while he helped me to carry the things out. He completely changed his mind."

"He submitted to the inevitable?"

"He submitted to the inevitable, and helped me to carry things. And we cleaned the house completely.

"We have a big convertible car, and it was loaded—everything was taken out of that house. And we drove very slowly to the other part of the town, Lakeside, where the Mellers lived, and left her there."

"Did Lee accompany you?"

"No, that was it. The next day or a few days later—I don't remember exactly when—George Bouhe called me and said, 'George, you should not give Lee the address of where Marina is'—I think he came to see me about that—'because he is a dangerous character, and he has been threatening me, and he had been threatening Marina on the telephone.' "

"He knew where Marina was?"

"Maybe I am confused a little bit. He knew George Bouhe's telephone number, and wanted to know the telephone number and address where Marina was. And this time my wife and I said we do not have the right not to tell him where she is, because she is his wife, and we should tell him where Marina is.

"Now, I don't recall how it happened—maybe Lee came over to our apartment in the evening. Anyway we gave him the address of the Mellers, you see, and told him that the best way for him to do is to call ahead of time if he wants to see Marina, talk to her on the telephone, and if she wants to see him, she will see him. And he was very happy about that—because I thought it was a fair thing for the fellow to do.

"I repeat again, I liked the fellow, and I pitied him all the time. And this is—if somebody did that to me, a lousy trick like that, to take my wife away, and all the furniture, I would be mad as hell too. I am surprised he didn't do something worse.

"I would not do it to anybody else. I just didn't consider him a dangerous person. I would not do it to somebody else.

"Well, anyway, later on—this is from hearsay again, now—Marina moved to Declan Ford's house, because I think the Mellers got tired of her, and then she moved eventually to somebody else's house —the name you mentioned here before—a Russian girl who married an American—Thomas something."

"Ray?"

De Mohrenschildt's opinion of what had brought this second separation was blunt: "The difficulties were this: she was—just incompatibility. They were annoying each other, and she was all the time annoying him. Having had many wives, I could see his point of view. She was annoying him all the time—'Why don't you make some money?' Why don't they have a car? Why don't they have more dresses? Look at everybody else living so well, and they are just miserable flunky! She was annoying him all the time. Poor guy was going out of his mind."

"And you and your wife were aware of all this, were you?"

"Yes."

"And had discussed it?"

"We told her she should not annoy him—poor guy, he is doing his best, 'Don't annoy him so much.' And I think I mentioned before one annoying thing. She openly said he didn't see her physically— right in front of him. She said, 'He sleeps with me just once a month, and I never get any satisfaction out of it.' A rather crude and completely straightforward thing to say in front of relative strangers, as we were."

"Yes."

"I didn't blame Lee for giving her a good whack in the eye. Once it was all right. But he also exaggerated. I think the discussions were purely on that basis—purely on a material basis and on a sexual basis, those two things—which are pretty important."

"Yes, they are."

Marina stayed with the Mellers in their crowded little apartment a week, and then through arrangements made by George Bouhe she moved to the Declan Fords'. Here Lee contacted her and began to beseech her to return home.

Mrs. Ford testified:

"Did Lee Oswald come to see Marina while Marina was at your house?"

"No, he did not, but he did talk to her on the telephone. I think approximately after three days after she stayed with me he called her up every night. I think he did call every evening."

"Did Marina talk to him on the telephone?"

"She was hesitating at first, but he wouldn't leave the telephone until she came to the telephone and she was talking to him. I didn't hear what she was saying, but she was telling him not to call her again, and not to bother, she was not going to return to him."

"Now, did Marina pay you anything for the privilege of staying at your home at that time?"

"No, I did not expect it."

"Was there any arrangement she would work in the house?"

"No, there was no arrangement, no."

"Did she mention that Lee Oswald was jealous of the Russian friends that Marina had?"

"Yes, she did. She told me that—that he was."

"Did they argue about that?"

"Well, I didn't know if they were arguing about that. I know she said that he was very jealous of them helping Marina and jealous for the reason that he wasn't able to provide her at the time with any of the things that they were giving Marina, clothes, and baby clothes, and I think that he was—it was making him rather mad because he said he was unable to buy the things for her at the time, and I know that he was not accepting things people were giving him. He was telling her not to take them, but she was taking them because she needed them. I suppose they were arguing about that, but I don't remember the particulars."

"Did you form an impression at the time that Marina lived with you for that week as to what the cause of their difficulties might be?"

"She mentioned one time that soon after marriage he told her that he didn't love her any more in any way. So I don't know what is the difficulty."

"Did you think Marina might have been partially responsible for it?"

"My own opinion was that Marina was responsible for it. I think Marina was and I think now she is a rather immature girl."

"She is what?"

"I think she is rather immature in thinking. And a lot of times she agreed herself about provoking him in a way by arguing about his mother or things of some sort."

"What did she tell you about arguments concerning his mother?"

"Well, I don't know really. She would say something that he was badly brought up, or something like that."

"He was what?"

"Badly brought up, some sort of thing, and he would get mad and slam her for that or something and then he was telling her not to let Mother in, and when Mother comes to the apartment she would let her in and then they would argue over that."

George Bouhe hoped to keep Marina away from Lee, but Lee was persistent. The paradoxical alternating of moods, the sudden changes from not seeming to love Marina to not being able to live without her, kept their relationship in constant turmoil. And Marina had similar inconsistencies. She would think she couldn't tolerate him another day, she would provoke him in a dozen contemptuous ways, and next give in to him and submit to another round of abuse. Perhaps George Bouhe, an elderly bachelor, couldn't fathom this. If he thought it was going to be easy to solve Marina's problem simply by separating them, he did not understand that although two people cannot live together, they cannot live apart either. In addition, he had undertaken a difficult problem in trying to find a semipermanent home for Marina. Mrs. Ford's house was larger than the Mellers', but she had her own family and obligations. If Marina had been the kind to make herself unusually helpful, if she had been in a position to be helpful rather than a responsibility, Bouhe might have had an easier time.

Mrs. Ray explained, "Mrs. Ford called me up and said could I please see if I could keep her at my house a little while since she was going to have company. I said certainly she was welcome. She was alone and with the baby at the time. She came to my house on a Saturday. I am not sure about the date—all I know is the day—spent one day with me and since I have no baby bed she went back to Mrs. Ford's house. Sunday I moved her completely over to my house with baby clothes and crib."

The effect of three moves in two weeks must have been to give Marina a less sure sense of the practicality of Bouhe's plan. It impressed her that to leave Lee permanently involved realities she wasn't prepared to deal with. People were trying to be nice to her, but how long could she go on moving from house to house? Bouhe thought perhaps he could find a home where she could help out as a domestic. Was this really practical with a small child of her own? George Bouhe was a dear old man. He meant well. He really wanted to help her, as he did all other friends in trouble, but did his scheme really make sense? None at all, and she had to face the facts. Now— and many other times in the coming months—she found she was trapped by circumstances. She knew she must learn English if she was ever to escape, but a new language was not something Marina could learn in a few days, weeks or even months. Mrs. Ray was wonderful to take her in, but what next? It was a frightening outlook.

Night after night at the Fords', Lee had called and implored her to come back to Elsbeth Street. He had promised in a breaking voice that he would never strike her again, that he knew he was wrong and that if she would forgive him he would settle down and act like other normal husbands. Perhaps this time he really meant it. Marina knew that she was not without fault. Three weeks away from him and she could see things more objectively. For example, that letter she had written—it wasn't the right thing to have done and she knew it.

Mrs. Ray did not get to know Marina well enough to have an opinion. Continuing with the events of that Sunday afternoon when she moved Marina to her house, Mrs. Ray testified, "Lee called about four in the afternoon and he asked me if he could come see his baby and wife, and I said certainly he can come out. He asked me 'How I could get?' I told him what bus to take and my husband picked him up at the corner filling station on Preston and Forest.

"He came out and they went in the bedroom to talk. They talked about an hour in the room by themselves, and by that time it was getting to be suppertime so I invited them to stay and have something to eat with us. He ate and she decided to go back with him, so my husband packed everything back up in the car and took them to Elsbeth Street."

As Marina told her version, "He telephoned me several times begging me to return and he came to Anna Ray's and he cried and you know a woman's heart—I went back to him. He said he didn't care to live if I did not return to him."

Marina had made a fateful decision. However she may deserve to be criticized in other respects, in this instance she really had no choice.

George Bouhe was furious with her. He felt she had broken a promise. But it was her life and not Bouhe's. Most of the Russian group, however, shared one opinion with Bouhe. They had all tried to help. They had failed. They did not like Lee Oswald, and if Marina insisted on living with him they just didn't care to put up with his disagreeable ways. From that day on the contacts between the Oswalds and members of the Russian colony became less and less frequent. During the Christmas holidays George de Mohrenschildt picked the Oswalds up and took them to a party. They were not truly welcome.

CHAPTER 11

LEE AND MARINA—REUNITED

L EE AND MARINA had now been in the United States six months.
Their marriage had been through a series of crises. Marguerite's
hopes that the return of her youngest son from Russia might give
her an opportunity to establish a family relationship with at least one
of her children had been shattered. Lee and Marina had moved away
from her twice. The first time she had discovered their apartment in
Fort Worth on Mercedes Street, and Lee had beaten Marina for letting her in. The second time they had simply disappeared from
Fort Worth and she had returned to her lonely life as a practical
nurse living in other people's homes.

   Robert, however, had at least kept track of Lee's moves. Lee had
advised him of his post-office box number in Dallas. Just before
Thanksgiving he dropped Lee a note and invited him and his wife to
dinner on the holiday. He did not know that Lee and Marina were
separated at the time. The day before Marina decided to return to
Lee, Lee wrote his brother:

November 17, 1962

DEAR ROBERT:
   In answer to your kind invitation for Thanksgiving, we'd love to come
and we'll be in Fort Worth Thanksgiving morning. We shall come by
bus, and I'll give you a ring on the phone from the bus station (about
9:00-10:00). See you soon.

LEE

   Lee may have used this invitation as a lever in persuading Marina
to at least join him for Thanksgiving. Family holidays have a way of
rejoining people who are otherwise alienated. As Lee promised, he
and Marina arrived in Fort Worth together for Thanksgiving dinner. Not a suggestion of their troubles was mentioned to Robert or
Vada.

The absence of any warm family relationship as far as Marguerite was concerned is apparent, considering she was not invited to this dinner. The cruel fact is that neither Lee nor Robert wanted her interfering with their lives.

The two brothers, Robert and Lee, had a pleasant day together. Marina enjoyed the family atmosphere. She could not help telling herself again that Robert was a sensible person. He enjoyed the ordinary things of life, and if Lee could only be like this . . .

But Lee was not like Robert. As much as he liked his brother, as close to a true friend as he ever had, he silently criticized him. Robert was working for the Acme Brick Company, putting in long hours and giving his whole life to what? No doubt he was making profits for the owner of that business, profits for someone else. That was wrong, and Robert wasn't perceptive enough to realize it. He was being exploited just like all other employees. The whole system was wrong. Again and again Lee pondered the injustice of this system. Why should others profit from the efforts of the workers? In the years he had spent in Russia it had become clear to him that the Russian Communist system was not right either. Karl Marx had been right, not Stalin or Khrushchev. Lee's vision of a system better than either communism or capitalism seemed clear to him. In the end both systems would fail because they would destroy each other in an atomic war. They were imperialistic, greedy, devoid of ideals. Basically the Marxist ideal of a state without a profit motive was perfect, but the leaders of the USSR had corrupted that principle. Lee foresaw the war to the extermination of two evil powers. Someday, out of world chaos, would come his opportunity to prove himself the great leader he knew he was. But it was tedious waiting. Wasn't there some way he could precipitate the chaos? His thoughts dwelled on the subject. During his working hours at Jaggars-Chiles-Stovall he would dream about the future—Lee Oswald, the great leader. George de Mohrenschildt had mocked his ambitions; Marina was continuously making fun of him. In the Marine Corps he had been nicknamed "Ozzie Rabbit," after Harvey, the rabbit in the moving pictures. Marina didn't know this, but she frequently made the unfortunate mistake of saying, "Oh, you're a brave rabbit!"—a Russian expression that goaded him to fury. They were reunited at Elsbeth Street, but they were no closer than before. She belittled him and antagonized him at every turn. Again there were fights.

Again there were complaints to the landlord from other tenants.

It was now nearing Christmas, and although in Russia this was a holiday celebrated only in a few churches, Marina couldn't help catch the excitement of all the activities Americans become involved in at this season. The music in every store—some of it very lovely music, moody like Russian songs and sentimental—and all the beautiful store-window displays appealed to Marina's sense of festivity. She had always liked holidays and the gaiety of people in a happy spirit. It was fun, and as de Mohrenschildt had said, "She was a fun-loving person."

And what was Lee's reaction? He said Christmas was a crass commercial fraud. He said the only reason it was celebrated was to make a better profit for the capitalists and give the merchants a chance to exploit the people. Religion, he said, was a joke—a "racket" to further the exploitation of the masses by the rich people.

On Elsbeth Street they did not have a Christmas tree. Lee did not believe in such nonsense. The day would have passed without notice from him had it not been for the thoughtfulness of John and Elena Hall, who stopped by Christmas Day to bring June a present. It was the first time Marina had seen them since their remarriage and her first separation from Lee. She envied their seeming happiness. She only wished her going back to Lee had been such a success. It hadn't been, and they both knew it.

Aside from the Halls, none of the Russians felt inclined to invite Lee and Marina to their holiday festivities. On the other hand, George de Mohrenschildt felt sorry for them, and when a party was planned at the Fords' for the weekend after Christmas, he asked permission to bring them. Some of the Russians felt this was an intrusion; they definitely didn't want the Oswalds, especially Lee, who had insulted almost every one of them. George de Mohrenschildt all but insisted, however, and the Fords agreed. George picked them up and brought them along. Their reception was not especially cordial.

On this occasion, however, Lee aroused Marina's jealousy. From the moment he arrived at the party and met an attractive Japanese girl who was a guest, he completely ignored Marina and sat in the corner talking to this girl. It was the only time Lee had paid any attention to another woman, and Marina resented it.

Sometime during this period Marina's feelings reached a point of desperation. The trap she found herself in was insidious. From her two attempts to escape—first, when she went to live with Elena Hall, and then when she had made her frantic call to Anna Meller from the gasoline station, clutching June and a few diapers—she had learned that she was not prepared to cut herself off from Lee. She had no way of making a living, and, despite Bouhe's good intentions, she could not expect others to solve her problem. Now the situation was even more hopeless. She had alienated her mentor, Bouhe, as well as a number of other Russians, and was thus cut off even from that unsatisfactory line of escape. She was so desperate that she confessed she thought of suicide as a way out. By nature she was not a morose person who would brood herself into this frame of mind. She loved life, and she loved good times. She couldn't help thinking of happier days when she had lived in Minsk, making good wages, living with her uncle, with little or no responsibility, and going to dances when she felt like it. Although she had no illusions that life in Minsk was as good as it might be in America in different circumstances, her existence on Elsbeth Street was unbearable. During the day she became terribly lonely and depressed. When Lee would come home at night there was nothing but bickering and beatings. He might kill her sometime. Wouldn't it be better if she would take her own life?

But then what about June? What would become of her? Strangely enough Lee loved June. He made a big fuss over her; in fact, she seldom could do anything wrong as far as he was concerned. He lavished all the kindness and tenderness he did not have for his wife on his daughter. He would sometimes play with her by the hour, as if June was the only human being in the world he loved. Marina thought about suicide, but she could not bear the thought of leaving June alone. She knew it was something she couldn't do; it was just a thought that haunted her and made her desperation greater. There was one other possibility. Like a caged animal, she had frantically tried every known exit.

Just before New Year's she sent the Russian Embassy a very warm greeting in Washington. The card said,

November 30, 1962

To: All Russian employees of the Soviet Embassy

* * *

DEAR COMRADE REZNICHENKO!

We wish you and through you, to all employees of the Soviet Embassy,

176

a happy New Year. We wish you much health, success and all of the best. Best wishes to all your family.

Sincerely,
MARINA
AND LEE OSWALD

Was the warmth of this greeting in anticipation of the letter she wrote February 17? She had come to the one final route of escape; she testified that Lee forced her to write it, but other evidence indicates that although she might not want to go back to Russia, she had to get away from Lee, and this was the only escape left to her.

February 17, 1962
Dallas

DEAR COMRADE REZNICHENKO!

I beg your assistance to help me to return to Homeland in the USSR where I will again feel myself as full-fledged citizen. Please let me know what I should do for this, i.e., perhaps it will be necessary to fill out a special application form. Since I am not working at present (because of my lack of knowledge of the English language and a small child), I am requesting you to extend to me a possible material aid for the trip. My husband remains here, since he is an American by nationality. I beg you once more not to refuse my request.

Respectfully,
MARINA OSWALD

The Embassy answered her request three weeks later:

EMBASSY OF THE
UNION OF SOVIET SOCIALIST REPUBLICS
Consular Division
1609 Decatur Street, N.W.
Washington, D. C.

Mrs. Marina Oswald
Box 2915 Dallas,
Texas, USA

March 8, 1963

DEAR MARINA NICOLAEVNA!

In reply to your letter we inform you that for purpose of examining your request concerning your return to the homeland it is necessary for you:

177

To fill out an application in 3 copies,

Furnish 3 copies of your detailed biography,

Write a request in the name of our Ambassador to USSR in 3 copies.

About your voluntary wishes to return to your homeland with indication of your profession in which you would wish to work and also of the place of residence:

Furnish 3 photos of passport size signed on the face of the photograph and also photographs of your child. Furnish one or two letters from your relatives residing in the USSR who are inviting you to live with them.

After receiving from you above-mentioned documents we will forward your request for processing to the local Soviet authorities. Time of processing requires 5 to 6 months.

In event of any questions or difficulties please write to us or call us on the telephone. Our address is 1609 Decatur Street, N.W., Washington, D.C.

The reply from the Russian Embassy, although friendly and personal, did not hold out the hope of speedy action on Marina's appeal for a return to the USSR. There were forms to be filled out, questions to be answered and the likelihood of months of delay. She and Lee now had another issue to quarrel about. Marina insisted that if she was going back to Russia with June she wanted a divorce from Lee. After all, what sense did it make for them to be permanently separated and still married? Perhaps Marina was thinking of her old boy friend and the possibility of starting marriage again with a man of her own background. Lee would not hear of this. He didn't want her, but he wouldn't let her be free either.

Then why go back to Russia? Marina wanted to know.

Lee insisted that she would be better off, that she could get her old job back, and, living again with her uncle, she would find things easier.

To Marina all this made little sense. She was willing to go back to Russia—anything to get away from the tyranny of Lee Harvey Oswald. On the other hand, it would be senseless to go back there and still be legally tied to a marriage that wouldn't work. Did he intend to go back to Russia sometime himself? He refused to say.

Marina's dilemma became more depressing. She had written her letter to the Soviet Embassy on February 17, 1963. Within a few days she knew she was again pregnant! And then, to add vexation to her problems, Mr. Tobias, the landlord, ordered them to quit the apartment. The other tenants wouldn't stand for any more noise.

Marina's memories of these events appear to have been faulty when she testified before the Commission. When asked why she and Lee moved from Elsbeth Street to Neely Street, she replied that she simply liked the Neely Street apartment better. The Tobiases had a different recollection of the circumstances, however. After one of the incidents which had brought complaints from the neighbors, Mrs. Tobias testified, "So my husband told them if they didn't straighten up, or, you know, they were so annoying that the other people had to rest too, that he was sorry but they would have to find another place."

"And it was shortly after that that they left?"

"Yes, shortly after that they moved in over on Neely Street."

How could matters become more complicated for Marina? Her Russian friends had lost all interest in her problems. Lee was insisting that she go back to Russia for "her own good" and yet refused to consider a divorce, and now she was pregnant. How long would it be before they would be asked to move from the Neely Street apartment?

In the worst way Marina Oswald needed a friend to whom she could turn. She needed someone she could talk to—but the possibilities were limited to the Russian-speaking colony, all of whom had lost interest, and the de Mohrenschildts were busy with their plans to move to Haiti and his efforts in behalf of the National Foundation for Cystic Fibrosis, of which he was one of the originators. By a previous wife de Mohrenschildt had had two children, both of whom were born with this frequently fatal disease. Together they had founded the national society. He was in the midst of a money-raising campaign for that worthy cause.

On February 22, however, a friend of the de Mohrenschildts gave a party to which Lee and Marina were invited. De Mohrenschildt showed movies of the walking trip he and Jeanne had taken through Mexico. Lee Oswald was bored, but Marina made a new acquaintance who inadvertently became so deeply involved in the events of the next few months that she was even unjustly suspected by some to have been an accomplice in Oswald's assassination of the President. Thus the Oswalds entered the life of Mrs. Ruth Paine. She met

Marina at this party at Everett Glover's. She was not a Russian like most of the others. She was an American studying the Russian language and she took a liking to Marina.

They both needed a friend. She and her husband, Michael, were separated, although on a friendly basis, and she was living alone in their home at Irving, Texas, near Dallas. Knowing Marina would give her an opportunity to improve her speaking knowledge of Russian. Knowing Ruth Paine, on the other hand, would give Marina a friend to cling to during many a desperate hour to follow.

Before the party broke up Ruth Paine asked Marina for her address. She would contact her sometime soon. As it happened, events developed rapidly to bring their lives closely together—and, for Ruth Paine, closer to a more tragic destiny than she could have imagined.

On March 3, just after the Oswalds had moved, she wrote Marina, who answered promptly:

"Hello Ruth! Yesterday I received your letter and was very happy that you had not forgotten us. Come and see us, certainly. Anytime from morning on, whatever is convenient for you. I think Tuesday a possibility, as we have moved to a new apartment and I must clean up the house. Please don't be offended at putting off our get together that long. I will be happy to see you and your children. Meantime I wait. Until then, thanks again for not forgetting us.

Sincerely,
MARINA OSWALD"

A few days later Ruth Paine visited Marina and they quickly became intimates, sharing views on their common problems. Because of the importance of her knowledge of Lee Oswald's activities in the next few months, the Commission made a detailed study of her life and associations. What kind of a woman was Ruth Paine? Members of the Commission came to have a high regard for her honesty, generosity and earnestness of purpose. She was an exceptional young woman whose background bespoke a fine American tradition of idealism and aspiration. She was well educated, and prior to her marriage she had spent her time in many worthy projects—trying to help people, trying to learn more about the problems of the world and trying to improve herself.

Mrs. Paine in her personal appearance before the Commission gave me the strong feeling that she was a thoroughly wholesome lady desperately trying to be cooperative and constructive. On occasion during her several days of testimony she would leave the witness chair for one reason or another, and I noted that she was taller than average, a little thin, attractive but not sophisticated, well but not glamorously dressed.

But there was one sorrowful thing in her life. Her marriage had been only a partial success. The man she married she greatly admired because he too was a forthright, honest man. But apparently, for him, there had been something lacking. He had recently come to the conclusion that he did not really love her, and, being a straightforward and candid man, he had told her as much. Putting reason above uncontrolled emotions, they had both tried to find an answer to this age-old dilemma of a one-sided love. They had agreed to separate and let each person try to find himself. They parted without rancor, and not necessarily on a permanent basis. They just rationally agreed to live apart and try to find out what the solution was to their marital confusion. Neither was really happy living alone, but they had not been happy living together. And so according to an agreed arrangement, they lived apart.

Ruth Paine worked hard to fill the void in her life created by the absence of Michael. She was not a weak person, and she wasn't going to let this get her down. Furthermore, Michael had been supporting her and the children conscientiously. He would visit the house frequently, and he was just sincerely trying to get his own bearings.

On the morning in March when Michael Paine was introduced to the members of the Commission, which was the usual custom in the hearing room before a witness took the oath to tell the truth, the whole truth and nothing but the truth, I felt uneasy in his presence. However, as he testified and as I observed him more closely under the stress of interrogation I came to the conclusion that he was able, conscientious, well educated, a philosophical type when it came to society's problems and government. At the end of his appearance I was completely satisfied with his reliability.

For many years Ruth Paine had been interested in foreign languages. In her early work with clubs and organizations she had had to deal with immigrants who spoke various languages. She was accustomed to the accents of German and Yiddish; she had studied other languages, and recently she had decided that Russian would be a worthwhile tongue. There would be a demand in schools for some-one who could teach Russian. If Michael eventually decided on di-vorce and remarriage, she would have to face up to it; she couldn't depend on him financially forever, nor did she want to be that de-pendent. If she could qualify herself to teach Russian, that would not only be remunerative but stimulating as well. Furthermore, she was a Quaker by faith, a pacifist by conviction, and at one time she had been part of a movement to bring young Russian people to the USA with the hope that, through cultural exchange, some basis of understanding could be created. She was simply an idealist who could not accept the theory that the only way to deal with a potential enemy was with rockets and atom bombs. Surely, if there was ever a time to call on the rationality of men, this was it. In whatever she did, she tried to practice the Quaker ideal of Christian benevolence. She and Michael had practiced it. Why couldn't nations?

Although Ruth Paine was older than Marina, here were two young mothers in trouble. Their bond then was two-fold: they could communicate to some degree in Russian, and their domestic affairs gave them a certain emotional affinity. Almost exactly the same day that Ruth Paine visited Marina's new apartment on Neely Street, Lee Harvey Oswald, under the alias of A. Hidell, was dis-patching a form order to Klein's Sporting Goods Company in Chi-cago for a Mannlicher-Carcano rifle with a telescopic sight.

Ruth Paine's careful testimony and her habit of making memos of things that happened in the ordinary routine of her life were a great help to the Commission. I was impressed that she had carefully main-tained, unlike many busy housewives, a daily memo pad. During her testimony and on many critical occasions she referred to these nota-tions to refresh her memory when Commission questions were asked. I thought to myself how fortunate someone, innocently in-volved in this drama, had written such comments, which by happen-stance would be invaluable in reconstructing critical events related to the assassination.

"I recall walking to the park, and I think this was the first visit," Ruth Paine related, "and we sat and talked. It was warm weather, March in Dallas. And the children played on the park equipment, and we talked, and she told me she was expecting a baby and asked me not to talk about it among the Russian community."

Marina appears to have felt she could confide in Ruth Paine from the outset—at least in womanly matters of this sort.

Mrs. Paine continued, "I just said I wouldn't talk about it, that it was up to her to make such an announcement when she felt like it."

At this meeting with Marina, Lee Oswald was not present. Ruth Paine had deliberately arranged to meet at a time of day when Marina would be alone. She wasn't really interested in Lee, and she hadn't warmed up to him much at Glover's party.

Had she taken an active dislike to him? "Not an active dislike, but I didn't like him. I think we can say that."

Elaborating on that first meeting with Marina in the park, Ruth Paine went on, "I recall that we talked, and as I said, it may be the first visit, and the second melded in my mind. She said she was expecting a baby. She said that Lee didn't want her to learn English, or to help her with it, that he spoke only Russian to her and to their baby, June. And she told me—now let me say that my calendar does show a notation of the twentieth of March. It says, 'Marina,' and I judge I went to see her at her home on that day, or brought her to my house. I am not certain."

She was asked to try to stick with the occasion at the park first.

"Well, I was impressed talking with her in the park with what I felt to be her need to have a friend. This was virtually our first meeting, but she confided to me something she did not want generally known among the Russian segment.

"She inquired of me, a young woman, about birth-control methods, and she said she felt—well, clearly the pregnancy had surprised her, but she said she didn't believe in abortion and didn't want to consider such a course."

"Did you think it was curious that her husband was averse to her acquiring some facility with the English language?"

"I thought it was distinctly thoughtless on his part, even cruel."

"Did she express an interest then in acquiring some facility?"

"Not against his wishes, no. She didn't express an interest in learning English through me, for instance."

This is an interesting sidelight on Marina. George de Mohrenschildt said he thought Marina was plain lazy about learning English. George Bouhe was not too impressed with the efforts she had made on her own behalf, and we find a curious contradiction between those who seem to think all of this was Lee's fault and those who can't give Marina very much credit for being ambitious to find a way out of her plight. That he had her intimidated is probably true, but there are energetic people who wouldn't have let that stand in their way.

As the Commission listened to the testimony of many witnesses, the complexity of Marina's character became more apparent. She was not the simple, straightforward and helpless figure she appeared to be in newspaper pictures and somewhat calculated press releases. We shall see that she too knew how to keep her secrets well, whether for self-preservation or other reasons.

On the next visit Ruth Paine could recall, Marina told her that Lee wanted her to go back to the Soviet Union. Marina said she did not want to go.

"The Commission is interested in that. Will you please relate it?"

"She said she did not want to go back, that he asked her to go back."

"Alone?"

"To the Soviet Union. As she described it, I judged that meant a divorce."

Ruth Paine was particularly moved by the belief that Lee Oswald was forcing an innocent young mother into a decision she hated—namely, being forced to go back to the USSR against her will. She had no idea of the magnitude of the domestic troubles that previously had developed between them, of what long-standing duration these conflicts had been and of what part Marina may have contributed to the antagonism of the situation. She knew nothing of the letter Marina had written to her old boy friend in the USSR telling the mistake she had made in marrying Lee and how she wished she had married the Russian instead. She did not know, as George de Mohrenschildt and his wife did, that she had nagged Lee, belittled him and run him down mercilessly in public. Ruth Paine was as innocent of the other side of Marina as was the Commission when Marina first came to Washington to testify.

Less than a month after her first private conversations with Marina, Ruth Paine composed a letter as a sympathetic reaction to Lee's pressuring of Marina to go back to Russia. Mrs. Paine by now had become so emotionally involved in the matter that she felt impelled.

to do something about the situation. In her own words, this is how it happened:

"I wrote a letter to her in the effort to gather my words. I couldn't just discuss it with her. My language was not that good.

"What I wanted to do was to offer her an alternative to being sent back, an economic alternative, and I thought for some time, and thought over a week, about inviting her to live with me—I was alone with my two children at the time—as an alternative to being sent back. If he thought he couldn't support her, or didn't care to, or whatever reason he had, I simply wanted to say she could stay and live with me if she wanted to.

"I wrote such a letter, really, to gather—"

"Do you have it?"

"Yes, I do. This letter was never sent."

"And this letter is dated the seventh of April?"

Three days after Mrs. Paine prepared her generous offer, Lee Oswald stealthily left his apartment on Neely Street carrying a rifle into the darkness. He made his way to the neighborhood in which Major General Edwin A. Walker resided, put the rifle in working order, cocked the bolt and sighted through the telescopic lens, which brought the head of his intended victim into close range, and fired.

CHAPTER 12

THE WALKER INCIDENT

O N JANUARY 29, 1963, Lee Oswald finished making his repayment of the State Department loan that brought him back to the United States. Besides having now relieved himself of a debt that had kept him scrimping for money, another event took place about this time that might have cheered an ordinary person and given him some optimism. Particularly in the case of Lee Harvey Oswald it would have seemed a source of enthusiasm. He liked children; everyone who knew him attested that he was a most loving father, the one thing that seemed totally normal about him. Now in February Marina knew that she was going to have another baby, and to be at all consistent it would seem that this news would have cheered him and given him motivation to work harder at his apprenticeship, because he told friends he liked his work. He saw some dignity and sense of importance in being a qualified photo-printer and learning all the processes that go to reproduce pictures in newspapers and advertisements. But Lee Harvey Oswald's reactions were not that logical. His mind was working along other lines. Shortly after he had left Fort Worth to seek work in Dallas, he had rented a post-office box, number 2915. Since he had made every effort in Fort Worth to avoid his mother, this practice of renting post-office boxes rather than using his home address had become a fetish. It was part of his pleasure in being secretive. Now a new element of deliberate deception entered his mind. He had invented an "alias" for himself and was sending out letters marked A. Hidell, PO Box Number 2915, Dallas, Texas.

On March 12, 1963, Lee Oswald ordered a rifle with a telescopic sight from Klein's Sporting Goods Company in Chicago. The same day he apparently ordered a revolver from another mail-order firm in Los Angeles. But both were ordered shipped not to Lee Oswald, Box 2915, Dallas, Texas, but to A. Hidell. Who was A. Hidell? How had this name been invented? Marina believes he invented it because it sounded like "Fidel," and later he became an active exponent of the Fair Play for Cuba and Castro. None of his friends or acquaintances had heard him express admiration for Castro at this point. If Marina is right about how he happened to pick this alias, his mind—as usual—was working far ahead of any plans that were obvious.

The rifle was shipped from Chicago on March 20, 1963, just twenty-one days before a bullet was to crash through the window of General Walker's home at night while the general sat at his desk working on his income taxes.

Marina told Jeanne de Mohrenschildt a few days after the incident, "We are so short of money, and this crazy lunatic buys a rifle." The things Marina did not tell Mrs. de Mohrenschildt, however, would have made her hair curl.

Lee Oswald picked up the rifle addressed to A. Hidell. This was about fifteen days before the Walker incident. Marina told Jeanne de Mohrenschildt when she later asked what he was doing with a rifle, "Oh, he goes in the park and shoots at leaves and things like that." She commented, "Oh, he just loves to shoot."

And so one day Lee called to Marina and told her he wanted her to take some pictures in back of the house. She said she was surprised to find him all dressed up, with a revolver in a holster, the rifle in his hands and a copy of one of the militant periodicals he had also had sent to PO Box 2915.

She demanded what he wanted a picture like that taken for. He replied he wanted her to keep a copy of it for June.

On April 6 Lee lost his job at Jaggars-Chiles-Stovall. It would be convenient to connect his despair over this loss of a position he had apparently liked with the incidents to follow. His desperate plan to eliminate General Walker actually preceded his being fired by some weeks, long enough to have ordered a rifle from Chicago and to have practiced with it. Those who question how much Oswald might have practiced with this weapon have to shrug away the testimony by Marina which was repeated by Jeanne de Mohrenschildt and appears to be firmly established. He had trained himself for this sniper's job, and he didn't intend to miss. Marina stated that he said he previously had made visits at night to the area of Walker's home. To practice dry-sighting? To wait for the chance for a shot that could not fail?

In Marina's words, the story takes on a chilling matter-of-factness:

April 10, 1963: "That evening he went out, I thought that he had gone to his classes, or perhaps that he just walked out, or went out on his own business. It got to be about ten or ten-thirty, he wasn't home yet, and I began to be worried. Perhaps even later.

"Then I went into his room. Somehow I was drawn into it—you know, I was pacing around. Then I saw a note there."

1. This is the key to the mail box which is located in the main post office in the city on Ervay Street. This is the same street where the drug store, in which you always waited is located. You will find the mail box in the post office which is located 4 blocks from the drug store on that street. I paid for the box last month so don't worry about it.

2. Send the information as to what has happened to me to the Embassy and include newspaper clippings (should there be anything about me in the newspapers). I believe that the Embassy will come quickly to your assistance on learning everything.

3. I paid the house rent on the 2nd so don't worry about it.

4. Recently I also paid for water and gas.

5. The money from work will possibly be coming. The money will be sent to our post office box. Go to the bank and cash the check.

6. You can either throw out or give my clothing etc. away. Do not keep these. However, I prefer that you hold on to my personal papers (military, civil etc.).

7. Certain of my documents are in the small blue valise.

8. The address book can be found on my table in the study should you need same.

9. We have friends here. The Red Cross also will help you. [Red Cross in English.]

10. I left you as much money as I could, $60.00 on the second of the month. You and the baby [apparently] can live for another 2 months using $10.00 per week.

11. If I am alive and taken prisoner, the city jail is located at the end of the bridge through which we always passed on going to the city (right in the beginning of the city after crossing the bridge).

Marina's eye raced to reread the note that sounded so crazy. There was no opening "Dear Marina" and no closing "Goodbye" or "Love" or anything else. What in heaven's name did he mean, "Send the information as to what has happened to me to the Embassy and include newspaper clippings (should there be anything about me in the newspapers)"?

It dawned on Marina now why Lee had urged her to go back to Russia. He had hoped to get her out of the country before he committed some desperate act of this sort. He had been contemplating this for months apparently, and perhaps in the back of his mind was the hope that after he had done his work—whatever his motives—he would be able to make an escape back to the USSR and there again he would be a "hero" for having eliminated someone he considered an enemy. Oh, this hero obsession that plagued Lee. He just couldn't settle for being an ordinary, decent human being.

Time passed, and then there were footsteps on the porch. Suddenly the door opened, and there was Lee, tense and pale.

For a moment she couldn't get out a word as she stared at him. Finally she blurted, "What's happened?"

He told her he had shot at General Walker. He didn't know whether he had killed him, but he had shot at him.

"And he told me not to ask any questions."

And then as I well recall Marina told the Commission—with a restraint that undoubtedly seemed exaggerated, because every word had to be passed through the translator painfully—"Of course, I couldn't sleep all night. I thought that any minute now the police will come. Of course, I wanted to ask him a great deal. But in his state, I had best leave him alone—it would be purposeless to question him."

Purposeless indeed! As a matter of fact, with what Marina knew of Lee's violent temper, the physical beatings she had taken, she more likely thought for once to keep her mouth shut or be killed. After all, she had just heard a professed would-be murderer admit that he had shot at a man with the intent to kill.

The Commission asked, "Did he say any more than that about the shooting?"

Marina replied, "Of course in the morning I told him that I was worried, and that we can have a lot of trouble, and I asked him, 'Where is the rifle? What did you do with it?'

"He said that he had left it somewhere, that he had buried it, it seems to me, somewhere far from that place, because he said dogs could find it by smell.

"I don't know—I am not a criminologist."

"Did he tell you why he shot at General Walker?"

"I told him he had no right to kill people in peacetime, he had no right to take their life because not everybody has the same idea he had. People cannot all be alike.

"He said that this was a very bad man, that he was a fascist, that he was the leader of the fascist organization, and when I said that even though all of that might be true, just the same he had no right to take his life, he said if someone had killed Hitler in time it would have saved many lives. I told him that this is no method to prove your ideas by means of a rifle."

"Did you ask him how long he had been planning to do this?"

"Yes. He said he had been planning for two months. Yes—perhaps he had planned to do so even earlier, but according to his conduct I could tell he was planning—he had been planning this for two months, or perhaps a little even earlier."

"Did he show you a picture of the Walker house then?"

"Yes."

"That was after the shooting?"

"Yes. He had a book—he had a notebook in which he noted down quite a few details. It was all in English. I didn't read it. But I noticed the photograph. Sometimes he would lock himself in his room and write in the book. I thought that he was writing some other kind of memoirs, as he had written about his life in the Soviet Union."

"Do you know anything else he had in it besides the Walker house picture?"

"No. Photographs and notes, and I think there was a map in there."

"There was a map of the area where the Walker house was?"

"It was a map of Dallas, but I don't know where Walker lived. Sometimes evenings he would be busy with this. Perhaps he was calculating something, but I don't know. He had a bus schedule and computed something."

"Did he explain to you about his being able to use a bus just as well as other people could use a car—something of that kind?"

"No. Simply as a passenger. He told me that even before that time he had gone also to shoot, but he had returned. I don't know why. Because on the day that he did fire, there was a church across the street, and there were many people there, and it was easier to merge in the crowd and not be noticed."

Here one might start notes for a "Handbook for Assassination" by Lee Harvey Oswald. Amateur killer? Hardly. Principle 1—obtain a high-powered telescopic rifle. Principle 2—study the area of intended assassination scene carefully with the aid of maps. Principle 3—make several dry runs to be sure of all the conditions likely to arise. Principle 4—choose exact time for act according to best opportunity for escape: "easier to merge in the crowd and not be noticed." Principle 5—escape by bus in large city easier than escape by automobile. Killer less suspected. To those who believe that Lee Harvey Oswald had neither the wit nor the knowledge to execute a blueprint for assassination, let them consider that the police of Dallas, with all their intensive efforts, never turned up a clue leading to Lee Harvey Oswald as the man who shot at General Walker. He even remembered to bury the rifle so that "dogs couldn't smell" it out, according to Marina.

And to those who want to believe that it would require plain madness for a man to shoot from the Texas School Book Depository Building and calmly walk away from it after buying a Coca-Cola in the lunchroom, let them consider the coolness with which Lee Oswald before shooting at General Walker wrote a "farewell note" to Marina, knowing that she was two or three months' pregnant, knowing that she couldn't communicate with more than a few words of English, knowing that she had sixty dollars between herself and the end of nowhere.

The layman may care to leave to the psychiatrists what specific kind of insanity this must be, but with hindsight the entire story of Oswald's attempt to shoot Walker reads like the preview of a more horrible tragedy that was to occur some months later. And we shall see that by the narrowest twist of fate, his part in the affair went undetected. Marina knew for certain about it. She was the only one, other than Lee Oswald himself, who did. How well she knew is underlined by her testimony:

"When he fired he did not know whether he had hit Walker or not. He didn't take the bus from there. He ran several kilometers and then took the bus. And he turned on the radio and listened, but there were no reports."

"The next day he bought a paper, and there he read it was only chance that saved Walker's life. If he had not moved, he might have been killed."

"Did he comment on that at all?"

"He said only that he had taken very good aim, that it was just chance that caused him to miss. He was very sorry that he did not hit him.

"I asked him to give me his word that he would not repeat anything like that. I said this chance shows that he must live and that he should not be shot at again. I told him that I would save the note, and if something like that should be repeated again, I would go to the police and I would have the proof in the form of that note.

"He said he would not repeat anything like that again."

Destiny had written another of its tragic turns. Marina had made the decision. She made up her mind that she would do nothing to divulge Lee's part in the Walker affair, but she would hold the note over his head to keep him from doing anything like that again. Although she would tell the de Mohrenschildts that Oswald was a "lunatic" for buying a rifle when they were so badly off, she apparently did not really think he was a dangerous lunatic. He had beaten her, he had lied to her, he had taken money they needed to purchase an assassination weapon; but it was her decision—either from fear or from a strange sense of loyalty, or love turned inside out—not to do anything just now. But when would she do anything? Her hand was nearly forced a few days later.

The attempt on General Walker's life was made on April 10, 1963. Easter that year came four days later. What a bitter irony that certain seasons and dates seem to repeat as critical days in the lives of Lee and Marina Oswald. It was on Easter Day 1961 when she had gone to visit Lee Oswald in the hospital at Minsk and had taken him a colored egg, which so surprised and pleased him that he began to think of marrying her to spite Ella. And now this same holiday nearly proved his own undoing and but for a smallest trick of fate might have averted all the terrible events which were ultimately to follow.

Fun-loving, and sometimes inordinately sentimental in a reverse sort of way, the de Mohrenschildts happened to think of June Oswald on this Easter holiday. Perhaps they knew that Lee wouldn't think to provide a little Easter cheer for June because he didn't believe in such baubles—not even Christmas trees. But the de Mohren-schildts did think of such things, and they decided they must do something to make June's Easter more exciting. To the toughest cynic—and sometimes George de Mohrenschildt appeared to be that way—what is youth without some of the pleasures and symbols of holiday seasons? So George and his wife Jeanne decided that it would be fun if June had a toy rabbit on the night before Easter, and they drove to the Oswalds' home after dark.

By then the gun had been dug up and brought back to the house.

The de Mohrenschildts found no lights on. It was Saturday night, just seventy-two hours after Lee Oswald had unsuccessfully carried out his blueprint for Walker's murder. Tonight he was home, per-haps tamed a little by fear and Marina's threat. Never a man to be worried by formalities, George de Mohrenschildt pounded on the door until he had aroused the Oswalds. They were greeted at the door by a call from the Easter Bunny—a pink bunny. The Oswalds turned on the lights and invited them in.

That the incident of the Walker shooting actually happened as Marina told it cannot be doubted, with or without ballistics, because of the coincidence that Jeanne and George de Mohrenschildt will never forget. Irony deepened on irony.

Jeanne de Mohrenschildt recalled the incidents that then happened as follows:

First she told how they banged on the door and awakened the Oswalds. She did not remember who came to the door—Lee or Ma-rina—but they were welcomed and entered the house. It was the new apartment on Neely Street, and they had never been there be-fore. Marina was proud to show it off to the de Mohrenschildts.

"And I believe from what I remember George sat down on the sofa and started talking to Lee, and Marina was showing me the house.

"Then we went to another room and she opens the closet, and I see the gun standing there.

"I said, 'What is the gun doing over there?'

"She said, 'Oh, he just loves to shoot.'

" 'Where on earth does he shoot?' Where can he shoot when they lived in a little house?"

"Oh, he goes in the park and shoots at leaves and things like that," Marina replied calmly.

How did it strike Jeanne de Mohrenschildt?

"Personally I love skeet shooting. I never kill anything, but I adore to shoot a target, target shooting."

"Skeet?"

"I just love it."

"Didn't you think it strange to have someone say he is going in a public park and shooting leaves?"

Mrs. de Mohrenschildt recorded her reaction—which presumably might be the reaction of anyone in the circumstances who liked shooting and guns.

"But he was taking the baby out. He goes with her and that was his amusement."

"Had anything been said up to this point in your acquaintance with the Oswalds of his having had a rifle or shotgun in Russia?"

"No."

"No discussion of hunting in Russia?"

"In fact we never even knew he was a sharpshooter or something. We never knew about it."

"No, then, what did you do? Go into some other part of the house?"

"I came back to the room where George and Lee were sitting and talking. I said, 'Do you know what they have in their closet? A rifle,' and started to laugh about it."

This comment, and the one that followed, must have cut across Lee Oswald's consciousness like a searing blade. In a moment when he was being his most congenial, feeling quite enthusiastic to have George de Mohrenschildt drop in, because he really liked George, he could almost anticipate what was coming next. Before he could utter a word, George looked at him with that look of mockery and said point-blank, "Did you take a pot shot at Walker by any chance?"

For an instant there was stark silence. George recalled in his testimony that he remembered that Lee "sort of shriveled, became tense and made a peculiar face." Jeanne de Mohrenschildt failed to notice any particular change in Lee's expression, but she sensed that George was being, as usual, bold in his humor, and she started to laugh. The tension momentarily must have stabbed at Lee and Marina. How could anyone accidentally hit exactly upon the truth? What did George de Mohrenschildt really know? Had he actually found out in some roundabout way that Lee was really the man who shot at Walker? Marina had a sinking feeling that what the police hadn't found out that night she had lain awake George had discovered. The joy and relief she had felt when the pounding at the door a few minutes earlier had turned out to be the de Mohrenschildts rather than agents of the police, as it would certainly happen in Russia, plunged. This would certainly be the end now.

But, instead, George de Mohrenschildt had had his little joke. Along with the others he burst into peals of laughter. When they had all had their good laugh, they exchanged a few pleasantries, the de Mohrenschildts were thanked for their thoughtfulness in bringing June a pink bunny, and everyone moved toward the door.

Perhaps to relieve her nervousness, Marina got Jeanne some roses. There was a large rosebush right by the outside staircase. It was a natural gesture in response to the gesture of the pink rabbit, and it was sure to close the subject of General Walker and the shooting. It did. The de Mohrenschildts never thought of the incident again until months later when the newspaper revealed that Lee Oswald actually had taken a shot at General Walker. Incredible!

Like so many things in this biography of an assassin, it just couldn't have happened that way, but it did! Because the de Mohrenschildts could confirm Marina's own story, it cannot be an invention, and the fact that it occurred gives us a clear insight into the dangerous personality of Lee Harvey Oswald. Unfortunately, it did not occur to George de Mohrenschildt that Oswald actually might have been the would-be assassin of Walker—it was such a good joke!

As for Marina—well, like all the other dramatis personae, accidental or deliberate, in this awful tragedy, only history can judge the mistakes she may have made. After all, she was the wife of this "lunatic," and under our law a wife is not required to stand witness against a husband, no matter how bad he may be. In one sense, it is a simple proposition: put yourself in her shoes. To those who would judge harshly, let them answer first how they would have acted in similar circumstances. Should she have gone to the FBI or the Dallas police and told the whole story? If she had, she would have had to inform against her own husband and would be the only witness who could have convicted him. She would send her own husband to prison. If, on the other hand, she had been thoroughly convinced he was insane and had decided to have him committed, how could she have done this without revealing his criminal actions? How could she have got him declared incompetent without informing on him? There was a middle path, perhaps—to have talked it over with someone she trusted; but whom could she trust? She was trapped by her own inability to speak English. She could only confide in someone who spoke Russian, and who would this be? She had acquaintances, yes, among the Russian-speaking people of Dallas, but they were people she had known less than a year. Where to turn? She was alone with her dreadful secret—alone with a madman. The "farewell" note she had—the only concrete evidence that Lee Oswald was connected with the Walker shooting—she hid away in the leaves of a book she had. It was a Russian *Book of Useful Advice* for cooking and housekeeping.

CHAPTER 13

FLIGHT TO NEW ORLEANS

THOUGH LEE HARVEY OSWALD had not committed a murder, nevertheless he had proven he was capable of murder. He was sorry he had missed General Walker. He ridiculed the police and the FBI for not being able to identify the bullet as having been fired from his Mannlicher-Carcano rifle. It gave him a sense of secret power to know he had outwitted the authorities—thus far at least. In his own mind he had proven once again what fools government officials could be, as well as all the rest of the public. The newspapers had written ridiculous speculations about the attempt on Walker's life. They were chasing false leads and blaming civil-rights leaders.

Still, it might be wise to get out of Dallas for a while. Marina was practically hysterical with fear that the police would find him out. And it was still possible. The papers had reported that ballistics tests indicated that the shot had been fired by a different caliber rifle—reasonable assurance they wouldn't pick up his trail. But as long as he had to seek a new job it might be sensible to go somewhere else. Marina wanted him to go to New Orleans, where he had lived as a child. Well, he would take a few days to think about it. There might be an outside chance that if he left Dallas immediately someone would think it suspicious and link him with the shooting. Unlikely, but possible. He would wait a few days more.

Ten days after the shooting, Marina and Ruth Paine arranged a picnic with the children. Ruth Paine had made up her mind that if Lee was still insisting on Marina's going back to Russia, she would offer the poor girl a chance to remain in America with her. She had even gone to the trouble of having a dinner to which she invited her husband, Michael, so that he might meet the Oswalds and give his approval or disapproval of the plan. However, she had not actually made the offer. She never mailed the letter.

She was asked by the Commission, "Didn't you think that was a little presumptuous on your part to invite a man's wife to come live with you?"

"Well, toward Lee it was presumptuous. I will have to refer again to the letter of April 7, where I said I didn't want to hurt Lee by such an invitation, but if they were unhappy, if their marital situation was similar to mine—and this is not specifically in the letter— but if he just did not want to live with her, that I would have offered this as an alternative, really to both of them. I didn't want to get into a position of competition with Lee for his wife. I thought about that and thought he might be very offended."

"It is possible he might very well be."

"Yes, it is possible he might even have been violent, but I didn't think anything about that."

"Did you have any impression of him up to this moment on this score?"

"No."

"As a man of temper?"

"No."

Ruth Paine's description of how Lee behaved at the picnic a few days after he had tried to commit murder sheds an interesting light on his self-composed temperament.

"He spent most of his time fishing. We saw almost nothing of him and heard virtually nothing from him. I was impressed with his unwillingness to be sociable really in this situation. He came to eat when it was time and complained about the food."

What was Lee thinking of while he waited for the fish to bite at his line? Was he thinking how famous he would be by now if he had managed to shoot that "fascist," General Walker?

"Was your husband present at this picnic?"

"No, he was not."

"Did you supply the food?"

"No, Marina had cooked it. He complained about it. He caught a fish, as I recall, and took it home to be cleaned. I hardly know who would clean it."

"Did you have any conversation with him other than some pleasantries?"

"I don't think so. I can't even think of the pleasantry."

At the end of the picnic Ruth Paine had a poor impression of the civility of Lee Oswald, and her sympathy for Marina was more intense than ever. They made arrangements that Ruth would call on Marina, as she had been doing in the morning, four days later.

At no time did Marina Oswald breathe a word to Ruth Paine of her husband's attempt to shoot Walker, nor was there any talk at the picnic of plans to leave Dallas. On April 24 Mrs. Paine arrived to make her agreed call on Marina. She was dumfounded to find Lee Oswald packed and about to leave town.

"Was this a surprise to you?"

"This was a distinct surprise."

"What time of the day did you arrive, or night?"

"Midmorning. Perhaps around ten."

"And then you found him packed, or packing to leave?"

"He was fully packed. I was evidently expected. I and my car, because he asked if I could take these bags and duffel bags, suitcases, to the bus station for him."

"Yes."

"Where he would buy a ticket to go to New Orleans, and he said he had not been able to—"

"This is what he said to you is what I am interested in."

"That he said—"

"Yes."

"He said he had not been able to find work in Dallas, around Dallas, and Marina suggested going to New Orleans, which is where he had been born."

"He said she had suggested—?"

"Yes. That is my best recollection."

"Was Marina present now while he is relating this?"

"Yes, I think so."

"You arrived at the home and this man was all packed to go to New Orleans?"

"Yes."

"Had you had any discussion with Marina about her coming to live with you of which she was aware prior to this occasion of April 24?"

"I had discussed with her the possibility of her coming at the time the baby was expected."

"When was the baby expected?"

"Mid-October."

"But there had been no discussion up to April 24 to your recollection, even about your inviting Marina to come to live with you?"

"You mean on a more permanent basis, other than to say when the baby was due?"

"Yes, which would be in the fall of the year."

"That is right. There was none. I remember feeling when I arrived that they were, and probably appropriately, making their own plans, and wondering whether I should have already made this invitation, but I had not."

"You say they were already making their own plans. Are you seeking to imply that they had some notion she might join you?"

"No, I don't think there was any notion. I am trying to say I recall that I hadn't made that invitation at that time."

"What did you say, Mrs. Paine—excuse me. First have you exhausted your recollection of everything that Lee Oswald said on that occasion when you arrived there?"

"Yes."

"What did you say?"

"I said yes, I would take his bags to the station if he wanted me to."

"All right."

"And we then did."

"You just left?"

"Take them to the bus station to be checked."

"Did Marina accompany you?"

"Marina went, and he checked the baggage. It was rather more than he could have carried on the city bus, and I am sure he preferred me to a taxi because I don't cost as much."

"You didn't cost anything?"

"That is right."

Mrs. Paine described how at the bus station Lee went in and bought two tickets—one for himself to be used later that day and another for Marina. However, it became clear in the conversation that Marina did not intend to go with Lee at the moment. He would go ahead to New Orleans, try to find a job, and at some later date when he called she would follow on the bus. Thus he intended to leave one ticket for Marina to use in the future. She would stay at the Neely Street apartment until he advised her he was settled.

With typical generosity two thoughts went through Mrs. Paine's mind. Marina was pregnant. A thirteen-hour bus ride to New Orleans would certainly be a hardship on the girl. How would this girl who spoke practically no English get along by herself in Dallas living alone on Neely Street?

Immediately she made the suggestion to Lee and Marina that Marina stay with her in Irving while waiting to hear from Lee. She would be happy to take a little trip to New Orleans with the station wagon when the time came; it would save Marina a strenuous bus journey. Meantime, Marina could live with her in Irving. There was no need to keep paying rent for an apartment.

Lee and Marina accepted the offer with alacrity. He returned to the ticket office, cashed in the extra ticket and gave Marina some money.

"Did he get on the bus then and depart?"

"No, the bus left in the evening. We all drove back to the apartment after he had checked the baggage, and he helped load the baby things and things that Marina would need during the next few days into my car, and we emptied what was left there of the things that were in the apartment, and which belonged to them. I drove with Marina and June and my two children back to my house, and he stayed at the apartment. He was scheduled to leave by bus, city bus, and an interstate bus that evening."

"How long did Marina remain in your home on that occasion?"

"She stayed then until May ninth—well, excuse me, she stayed until the tenth of May."

"You have an entry, do you not, in your diary as to May ninth or tenth?"

"Yes."

"Read it."

"It says now going over to the eleventh, 'New Orleans.' "

"And you have written across then 'May tenth and May eleventh,' is that right?"

"Yes."

"What does the 'New Orleans' signify, please?"

"Lee called on the evening of the ninth to say he had work."

"You recall that?"

"I recall that definitely. Marina says, '*Papa nas lyubit*, Father loves us, Daddy loves us, he got work and he wanted us to come.' She was very elated."

"This is Marina talking to you?"

"I could see as she talked on the phone."

"You overheard this conversation?"

"Afterward. She said over and over, '*Papa nas lyubit*, Daddy loves us, Daddy loves us.'"

"She was elated?"

"She was elated and, let's see, we tried to think when we could leave, and first said over the phone that we would leave on the morning of the eleventh. But I thought it would be too long to do all this one day, and we accelerated our preparations and left midday on the tenth, which got us to Shreveport."

"Before we get into this, and I would like to cover this interim period. There was a sixteen-day period now, approximately, maybe we will limit it to fifteen days, that Marina stayed with you in your home."

"That is right."

"Did you have conversations with her about her husband?"

"Yes."

"About their life in Russia?"

"Well, even going so far as to wonder—"

"During this fifteen-day period?"

"Yes. We had such conversations."

"Would you please relate to us your discussions with Marina with respect to her husband, Lee Harvey Oswald?"

"Well, she wondered if he did, in fact, love her."

"What did she say?"

"She said she supposed most couples had at some time wondered about this. She wondered herself whether she loved him truly."

"Was there any discussion about his having struck her?"

"No, none. No, none. She never mentioned to me ever that Lee had struck her."

"And during all the visits you ever had with her, all the *tête-à-têtes*, her living with you on this occasion we now described as fifteen and a half days, and in the fall, was there any occasion when Marina Oswald related to you any abuse, physical abuse, by her husband, Lee Harvey Oswald, with respect to her?"

"There was never any such occasion."

"Up to this time, that is, the time she came to you on the twenty-fourth, you had never seen any bruises—"

"No, I never saw her—"

"—on her person?"

"No, I never saw her bruised."

"Was there any discussion during these fifteen days of any occasion when Marina had gone off to live with someone else?"

"No, I think she told me that in the fall."

"I see. As long as I have raised that, would you please give us the time and the occasion, and tell us what occurred?"

"What she told me?"

"What she said. When was this?"

"This probably was in October. She told me that the previous year she had—"

"Nineteen sixty-two?"

"Yes. She had in the fall, she had gone to a friend's home, left Lee. She described his face as she left as shocked and dismayed and unbelieving."

"Unbelieving?"

"In a sense that she was truly walking out on him."

"Excuse me. Did she put it in those terms, that she was leaving?"

"She was leaving, yes."

"She left him?"

"Yes, and went to stay with a friend. Then moved to the home—"

"Did she name the friend?"

"She did not name the friend, no. The friend's name came up in another connection, but I had no way of making the connection until after I learned about this to whom she referred."

"Do you now recall the name?"

"She went to Katya Ford's."

"To the Fords'?"

"To Katya, being the friend, Mrs. Ford."

"Mrs. Ford."

"And then moved. She did not tell me this. She had moved on the weekend to a different home. Then Lee came there, pleaded for her to come back, promised that everything would be different. She went back and she reported—as she reported it to me—things were no different."

"Were not different?"

"Were not different."

"Did you undertake a discussion with her as to what the things were that were disturbing her?"

"That offended her that much? No. I did not."

"That led her to leave her husband?"

"No."

"There was no discussion of that?"

"No."

"Did you ever witness any altercations?"

"Indeed I saw them argue a good deal."

"Sharp arguments?"

"Yes."

"But no violence of any kind?"

"No physical violence."

"Any profanity?"

"I am not sure I know Russian profanity. He was very curt and told her to shut up quite a great deal."

"In your presence?"

"Yes."

"In the presence of others?"

"Particularly in New Orleans the first time when we went down, when I took her to New Orleans in May, he was very discourteous to her, and they argued most of that weekend. I was very uncomfortable in that situation, and he would tell her to shut up, tell her, 'I said it, and that is all the discussion on the subject.'"

"What were the kinds of discussions that prompted this?"

"I recall feeling that the immediate things they were talking about were insufficient reason for that much feeling being passed back and forth, and I wondered if I wasn't adding to the strain in the situation, and did my best to get back to Texas directly. But the—well, I do recall one thing, yes. We arrived with a big load of blackberries that we bought from a vendor along the street."

"On the way down?"

"On the way down, on the road, and ate them, and then he, one morning, started to make blackberry wine, and she bawled him out for it, what a waste of good blackberries, and she said, 'What do you think you are doing? Ruining all this.' And he proceeded, and argued about it, but thought he should, you know, defend himself. On this occasion she was making the attack in a sense and didn't think he should do it this way, and so, under fire and attack, he continued.

But then the next day she observed that he had tossed it all out and lost heart over the argument and decided it wasn't—"

"He tossed out the wine?"

"He tossed it out, yes."

"You detected, then, irritability as between them. Is that a fair statement?"

"That is accurate."

"And anger rose to the surface pretty easily?"

"Very easily."

"What was your impression? Of course he hadn't seen her then for a couple of weeks."

"That is right."

"Tell us about it—when she came in. Did they embrace?"

"Yes. We arrived at his uncle's in one section of New Orleans and had a very friendly half hour or so."

"Was he there?"

"Yes, he was there. He introduced her and little June, and played with June, on his shoulders, perhaps. At any rate he was very glad to see the baby and was congenial and outgoing. We talked with the relatives for a short time.

"Then the uncle drove them to the apartment—I was following with my children in my car—drove to the apartment he had rented, which was in a different section of the city. And Lee showed her, of course, all the virtues of the apartment that he had rented. He was pleased that there was room enough. It was large enough that he could invite me to stay, the children to spend the night there. And he pointed out this little courtyard with grass, and fresh strawberries ready to pick, where June could play. And a screened-porch entryway. And quite a large living room. And he was pleased with the furniture, and how the landlady had said this was early New Orleans style. And Marina was definitely not as pleased as he had hoped. I think he felt—he wanted to please her. This showed in him."

"Tell us what she said. What led you to that conclusion?"

"She said it is dark, and it is not very clean. She thought the courtyard was nice, a grass spot where June could play, fenced in. But there was very little ventilation. We immediately were aware there were a lot of cockroaches."

"Was she aware of this, and did she comment on that?"

"I don't know as anything was said. He was pretty busy explaining. He was doing his best to get rid of them. But they didn't subside. I remember noticing that he was tender and vulnerable at that point, when she arrived."

"He was tender?"

"Hoping for—particularly vulnerable, hoping for approval from her, which she didn't give. It wasn't a terribly nice apartment. And she had been disappointed, because when we first arrived she thought that the home we were going to was the apartment."

"She thought the Murrets' home?"

"Yes. So when we came up to the Murrets' home, she said, 'This is lovely, how pleased I am.' So that she was in—disappointed by contrast with the apartment that she really had to live in."

"She expressed this?"

"She expressed her disappointment, yes, and didn't meet his hopes to be pleased with it."

"As compared with their previous place of residence, how was the New Orleans apartment? It was bigger, I gather."

"It was larger. It was darker, less well ventilated. It was on the first floor, the other was upstairs. I would say they were comparable in cost and in attractiveness."

"What about vermin?"

"I didn't see any vermin at the first place. But then I didn't spend the night there."

"So the welcoming was cordial?"

"The welcoming was cordial."

"They seemed to have a fine relationship at that moment?"

"Yes."

"But as the weekend progressed, and she saw the new apartment, all the time you were there, you were aware of friction and irritability?"

"Yes."

As a result of the immediate revival of tension between Lee and Marina, Ruth Paine made up her mind to cut her visit short. There was nothing more she could do but hope that if she removed herself the strain would pass and somehow the marriage might be patched up. She had already, however, suggested to Marina that when the baby was due it might be easier for her to have the baby in Texas, where Lee—as a former employee of the area—would be entitled to medical assistance. Ruth Paine offered to take Marina in again, if they decided that was the thing to do. She could take care of June while Marina was in the hospital. The subject was left open for future discussion, as Marina promised to write her friend.

Ruth Paine packed up and drove back to Irving with her children. She had her own marital problems to worry about.

The next report she had from Marina, however, was not encouraging.

25 May 1963
New Orleans

DEAR RUTH! Hello!

Here it is already a week since I received your letter. I can't produce any excuses as there are no valid reasons. I'm ashamed to confess that I am a person of moods. And my mood currently is such that I don't feel much like anything! As soon as you left all "love" stopped, and I am very hurt that Lee's attitude toward me is such that I feel each minute that I bind him. He insists that I leave America, which I don't want to do at all. I like America very much and think that even without Lee I would not be lost here. What do you think.

This is the basic question which doesn't leave me day or night. And again Lee has said to me that he doesn't love me, so you see we came to mistaken conclusions. It is hard for you and me to live without a return of our love—interesting, how will it all end?

CHAPTER 14

RUTH PAINE CORRESPONDS
WITH MARINA

How will it all end?" The question raised by Marina had much more significance to her than to Ruth Paine. No person could live with the hidden knowledge that one's husband was a potential murderer of black moods and not be apprehensive of the future. No one who had taken the brunt of the rages Lee Oswald was capable of could ignore the precariousness of an existence fraught with his humors. And there was the matter of that rifle. Marina knew that somehow Lee had taken it with him to New Orleans. It was not a toy, not a plaything in his hands, and she knew it. She also knew he owned a revolver. While in New Orleans she knew he sat on the screened porch in the darkness practicing the bolt action of the rifle. She could hear the click of the operating lever, the metallic slam of the bolt as he rammed it forward with angry determination. And then at times he would become almost hysterical with despair. His sense of frustration seemed to smash him. From swagger and bravado he would collapse into tears.

"You have stated in some of your interviews that your husband would get on his knees and cry and say that he was lost. Do you recall when this happened?"

"That was in New Orleans."

"Was it more than one occasion?"

"When he said that. That was only once."

"And do you know what caused him to say that?"

"I don't know."

"You don't know whether there was some occasion or some happening that caused it?"

"No."

Could it have been when Marina had belittled him, perhaps called him a "brave rabbit" or said, "You're a big hero"? Or was it when she ridiculed his simple impulse to make blackberry wine? He had been proud of the apartment he had chosen for her in New Orleans. She had found fault with it. Couldn't he do anything to please her? What Marina did may have had nothing to do with his unhappiness. In her correspondence with Ruth Paine during the period the Oswalds lived in New Orleans it would not appear she saw it that way. The give and take between the two women whose personal lives were so unhappy gives insight into the paradox of their feelings. All of these letters are translations from Russian.

June 1, 1963

DEAR MARINA,

Congratulate me! The director of St. Mark's School asked me to teach both this summer and the coming year. So I intend to stay home in Texas in June, July and from the first of September.

In August the children and I will be on the island in Paoli—a small town near Philadelphia.

Thank you for your good letter. Everything you do and think is interesting to me. A pity there were no crabs the first time. There will be next time, likely.

I asked Michael to live with me again, but he doesn't want to. I think now that it is time to consider divorce. On Thursday I will be at the office of a lawyer in Dallas. I don't intend to hurry, I just want to talk with her now. (The lawyer is a woman.) Michael and I don't fight, it's just he doesn't want me.

Sincerely,
RUTH

June 5, 1963

DEAR RUTH, (you prefer to spell it that way) Hello!

Not only do I congratulate you, but I am also very happy for you that you can have work according to your liking. How fine that everything has come out well in this regard at least. But it is very sad news about your relations with Michael. Very, very sad. And I understand you doubly, as it is the same story with Lee, who has made it plain that he doesn't want to live with me. But he doesn't give me a divorce, rather insists that I go away to the Soviet Union, which I certainly don't want to do. I can only console you with this: that you are not the only rejected one in this world. In many ways you and I are friends in misfortune. But surely a person can carry on through all the most heavy losses, trials and misfortunes. I think we will not perish, but that something will smile brightly on us too. Don't you think so? Soon you will set out on your vacation, and I wish you and the children a good trip.

With us everything is as it used to be. A gloomy spirit rules the house. The only joy for me and for Lee (I think) is June. It seems to me the baby has moved, but very weakly, and this time I worry. It's high time to go to the doctor.

Today I received a letter from a girl friend (from Russia). Her mother has died—it is such a pity both for her and her mother. Cancer is a frightful thing, and to lose one's mother is also frightful. I love this friend of mine very much and grieve for her terribly. They have written me nothing from home for a long time. I don't know their news. It is good you write me, otherwise I would have no one to talk to. You know that Lee either yells at me or is silent, but never talks. It is oppressive. But no doubt it is tiresome for you to read my melancholy letters—they cast a gloom, not cheer. But for the time being there is nothing cheery about me. Please write me your news when you have time and inclination. Thank you again for everything and for your letter. Greetings from Lee. I kiss and embrace you and the children.

Sincerely,
MARINA

Then, written on Mrs. Paine's letter to her, which she corrected and sent back, was the answer to a question Mrs. Paine asked: "Have you and Lee found any Russians in New Orleans yet?" Her answer: "Not yet, and Lee doesn't want me to make contact with them."

Evening
July 11

DEAR MARINA,

If Lee doesn't wish to live with you any more, and prefers that you go to the Soviet Union, think about the possibility of living with me. It would be necessary, of course, to live dependent upon me for a year or two, while the babies are small, but please do not be embarrassed. You are an able girl. Later, after a year or two, you could find work in America. I think that after a year or two I will live in Philadelphia. My sister lives in Washington. There will be work for you somewhere.

You know, I have long received from my parents. I lived "dependent" a long time; I would be happy to be as an aunt to you. And I can. We have sufficient money. Michael would be glad. This I know. He just gave me $500.00 extra for the vacation or something necessary. With this money it is possible to pay the doctor and hospital in October when the baby is born. Believe God. All will be well for you and the children. I confess that I think that the opportunity for me to know you came from God. Perhaps it is not so, but I think and believe so.

210

It disturbs me a great deal that I explain my thoughts so badly. But it disturbs me more not to hear news from you and not to know what you are thinking and doing.

Marina, come to my home the last part of September without fail. Either for two months or two years. And don't be worried about money.

I don't want to hurt Lee with this invitation to you. Only I think that it would be better that you and he do not live together if you do not receive happiness. I understand how Michael feels—he doesn't love me, and wants the chance to look for another life and another wife. He must do this, it seems, and so it is better for us not to live together. I don't know how Lee feels. I would like to know. Surely things are hard for him now, too. I hope that he would be glad to see you with me where he can know that you and the children will receive everything that is necessary, and he would not need to worry about it. Thus he could start life again.

Write please,
Sincerely,
RUTH

DEAR, DEAR RUTH!

Here I have already received 4 letters from you. Every day one, four days in a row. There are no words to thank you and Michael for the thoughtfulness you show me. Now, each thing in turn. First, thanks for the calcium which I guessed only you could have sent, as I found no return address or name on it. I drink the yeast and calcium regularly. And besides that Aunt Lillian gave me many vitamins. As you see I am surrounded by much attention. Dear Ruth, now regarding your invitation to come and live with you for rather a long time. For me, of course, it is very tempting, since besides all the conveniences I could also learn English. Lee and I have not talked about it. I am afraid to talk to him, as I know he will be very hurt. While I was at your house, I wrote him about Philadelphia—that I could go there with you. Many times he has recalled this matter to me and said that I am just waiting for an opportunity to hurt him. It has been the cause of many of our arguments. And as we have enough such, I don't care for any new ones. I am very happy now, that for a considerable period he has been good to me. He talks a lot about the coming baby and is impatient to have a son. Such an attitude on his part pleases me, even if it is only because of the baby. He has become much more attentive and we hardly quarrel. True, I have to give in a great deal, it could not be otherwise. But if one wants peace, then it is necessary to give in. We went to the doctor. My condition is normal. I judge that the baby is due (by the book) about October 22nd. But it seems to me (by my calculations) it will be about the 8th of October, since it seemed to me I first felt the baby move on the 21st of May—plus 140 days equals Oct. 8th. But we will see when it will be.

Dear Ruth, a huge thank-you to you and Michael for the invitation to live with you. I will try to take advantage of it if things really become worse—if Lee becomes coarse with me again, and treats me badly. Sweet Ruth, I am so thankful to you for your good and sympathetic heart. And wherever I am I will always say that plain Americans are good, peaceful and intelligent, that they are talented and sensitive people, as no doubt all plain people are everywhere. All the people (Americans) who have surrounded me here at all times showed me much consideration and good will. And I believe the impression this has created in me about Americans is correct. I love your people and your country and I thank you, and all, that you are such good people. God grant there would always be peacetime and that people would treat each other only so. You see what emotions your invitation and attitude towards me have evoked! It's all your fault. Ha-ha!

Dear Ruth, now another question. If, as is possible, it becomes necessary for me to come to live with you, in order to say that I am a dependent of Michael's, surely it would be necessary to have an official divorce. Isn't that so? But I think Lee would not agree to a divorce. And to go from him simply to become a burden to you—that I don't wish. Surely Michael would need to have a paper showing that I am living at his expense. But no one would just take his word for it. Right?

There. For the time that is all I will write about myself. Lee sends greetings, but he doesn't know about the content of your letters. I am telling him that I wrote you about how he is treating me.

P.S. Lee has found out that right next to us there is a large hospital where maternity care costs $75.00 upon entry, and then $50. to $55.00. That comes to $125.00 to $130.00. Not terribly expensive, right? I hope that everything will be fine and the baby and I will come then just for one to two months for a visit.

I kiss and embrace you, dear Ruth, and also Lynn and Christopher, that is, little Chris. I wish you all the very best.

Sincerely,
MARINA

P.S. A huge greeting and thanks to Michael. Have you got the photographs which you took in New Orleans? June feels fine, runs about, eats poorly. I feel normal, only it has been very hot here and I fainted once. But all is well.

July 21

DEAR MARINA,

I was so happy to receive your fine letter. Happy too that you have been to the doctor, and everything is normal. Once you said to me that June was born two weeks early, is that right? Likely you are right that the day of birth will be around October 8th.

I am now planning to leave here on Saturday, the 27th of July. We are driving to the ocean. After 5 days I hope to be at my mother-in-law's on the island "Naushon." The island is not too far from Boston. We will be there from July 31 to August 11 (I think). My address there:

Ruth Paine
c/o Young—(this is not necessary to write)
Harbor House
Naushon Island
Woods Hole, Mass.

Then we will drive to Paoli, a small town near Philadelphia. My address there until the 10th of September will be:

Ruth Paine
c/o Arthur Young—(important here)
Paoli, Penna.

Then we go to Columbus, Ohio, where my mother and my father live.

How would it be if we come to you in New Orleans then? We can arrive in the evening of the 18th and spend a day or two with you. You can tell me then if you want to come to me for the birth of the baby. Of course, I want you to come very much. I would be happy to have company at home, and glad to look after June while you are in the hospital and later while you are weak after the birth. June would be fine here with the children, in the yard, etc. Our home, of course, is accustomed to children.

If you want to come to my home, then we can travel together to Dallas. (About the 20th of September, or whenever.) But perhaps Lee will not let you go. It will be painful for him without his wife, his children. True, also that here it costs more than at the hospital about which you wrote me in your letter. Earlier I looked for a hospital where it cost less—but we don't have such. All together, for the doctor and the hospital here will be $225.00. I'm very sorry. Well, we can talk about it in person, right?

Please write me using the familiar thou. Try. Nothing is so difficult for you in Russian as it is for me. And tell please—is it correct to write thou with a capital letter in letters like you?

I wrote Ruth Kloepfer about you. She is like a secretary for the New Orleans Quaker church. I asked her if she knows any Russians in New Orleans. I also wrote Mrs. Paul Blanchard, the secretary at the Unitarian church in New Orleans, and asked her if she knows Russians there. Perhaps one or the other will find a Russian friend for you there.

Write without fail. Greetings to Lee, please. Kiss June.

Sincerely,
RUTH

DEAR RUTH, Hello!

I've not written for a long time. Forgive such a long silence, but it was for this reason. We had a small vacation, that is, we had an opportunity to go visit Lee's brother. We drove with his aunt, uncle and sister and her husband and children (she arrived from Texas) to the town of Mobile (Alabama) to see a son of Aunt Lillian. He is a priest, or more properly he is studying at a Catholic institute—or however it is called. I don't know. We spent several fine days there. I was able to see more States in America, Mississippi and Alabama. True, it is just a little. I liked that green town, there was much, much green. We drove along the coast of the Gulf of Mexico, which I have long hoped to see. While such a trip is pleasant, all the same we became tired. Recently I have not been feeling entirely well because of the oppressive heat in New Orleans. It is very hot here, and the air humid. For me this is rather hard to take. Especially before thunder storms, when the atmospheric pressure changes. But, thank goodness, there is not much time left to wait. I hope for a speedy and fortunate delivery.

Dear Ruth, I thank you so much for your thoughtfulness, and that you were so kind as to write those women. Mrs. Ruth Kloepfer called; [for] that I am very thankful to her, for having taken out time to stop by and see us. I liked her very much. Don't you think her a fine woman? And such a pleasant and winsome face. She explained that her daughter is studying Russian, but is presently traveling and is not in America. It was pleasant to meet her and we are thankful to you for it.

Dear Ruth, of course, certainly come to see us. We will look for you about September 20th, as you wrote. We will be happy (especially I) to see you and also I want just to talk. Dear Ruth, don't be angry with me for such a long silence, all right?

Still a little about our life. June runs about, grows and is a great joy for us. Lee doesn't have work now, already for 3 weeks. But we hope that everything will clear up, right? For the time being it is difficult to find work, but possibly at the end of summer there will be more openings, when some go to study. But we are not downcast and are hoping for better times.

Now about how to write thou. It is always written with a small letter, while you, when it has reference to a person, is always written with a capital letter.

The verb—to try
I will try, thou wilt try—future tense
I tried—past tense
I am trying—present tense. From the verb to try

I don't know if I have explained it well. Finally let me wish you a good vacation and fortunate trip. We are looking forward to your being here. I kiss and embrace you and the children. I hope everything is going well with them. Greetings from Lee.

Until we meet in New Orleans.

Sincerely,
MARINA

P.S. Thanks for your good letter!

CHAPTER 15

NEW ORLEANS EPISODE

W HEN LEE OSWALD TELEPHONED Marina from New Orleans and urged her to join him, he had found a job at the William B. Reily Company, Inc., working with coffee-processing machines. Marina was overjoyed at the prospect of the family being together again, and hastened, with the help of Ruth Paine, to New Orleans. It was just a month after Lee had attempted to murder General Walker, and he had succeeded thus far in eluding any suspicion. He had calmly taken a public bus from Dallas and quickly found employment. As far as the Russian group was concerned, he had dropped out of sight. Since Marina had found a mentor in Ruth Paine, she had not bothered to contact her old friends. George de Mohrenschildt had gone on a trip with his wife and later moved to Haiti. Lee's mother, Marguerite, had no idea where they were, and on this occasion Lee did not even bother to notify his brother of his move.

In one of his writings during his defection to Russia he had explained how for a number of years he had avoided forming any personal attachments. He deliberately avoided making any personal friends or associations. His isolation had become a habit. Even at work he avoided striking up any acquaintanceships. His foreman at the Reily Company found his behavior aggravating.

"Did Oswald have any other associates or people that worked with him closely in the plant, or would you say that you probably worked with him as closely as anybody else?"

Charles Le Blanc, Oswald's superior, testified, "Well, I imagine I was about the closest, myself and the other maintenance man."

"Did Oswald ever talk about his family?"

"No, that was something he very seldom talked about, and myself and the engineer, Emmett Barbe, we always were talking about our families. Oswald, he never would bring in his family and it was a good while after he was employed with us that I actually found out he was married, because I didn't think he was married because he never did talk about his wife and kids or nobody."

"Did Oswald eat lunch with anybody?"

"Not that I know of. He had never eaten with me, I know."

"There weren't any of the men there that, as far as you knew, he ever really talked to—"

"No."

"Or anyone he ever opened up to in any way?"

"No. I tell you he was a boy of very few words. He would walk past you and wouldn't even ask you how you are doing, or come and talk, like a lot of us, we would stop and maybe pass a few jokes or just talk a little with each other, but him—I think it was three months that he was with us—still I think if he said a hundred words to me, it was plenty, because even when I was breaking him in he wasn't the type boy that would ask you different things about the machines. I was doing all the talking and he was just looking."

"Did you ever form any opinion of Oswald—just generally what did you think of this guy?"

"I just—I used to always think—I didn't know whether he was right or whether he had troubles on his mind or what. I mean, I couldn't actually figure what was actually wrong with him, because, I mean, we would go on break and sit on the driveway on the bench, and he looked like he would be staring into space, and sometimes you would think he was looking right at you, and if you would happen to go to say something, he wouldn't answer you. Looked like that is how far his mind was."

"He seemed to be thinking of something else?"

"Yes, and looked like his mind was far away at all times."

Almost immediately upon his arrival in New Orleans, Lee neglected his job and dreamed of other things. He made no effort to satisfy his employer.

Mr. Le Blanc recalled, "When they first hired him—well, they brought him up to me, because I was to break him in on his job, so I started the procedure of going—start from the fifth floor on down, work a floor each day with him to take and get him broke in on the job and start showing him the routine, how to go about greasing, and the first day, I mean when I was showing him, it looked like if he caught on to it, all right, and if he didn't, it was still all right. He looked like he was just one of those guys that just didn't care whether he learned it or he didn't learn it. And then after I took and—we usually go by the week, because usually after a week anybody with mechanical knowledge, there is nothing to it, because all it is is finding the grease and oil fittings and we put him on his own. I put him on the fifth floor and told him to take care of everything on the fifth floor and I would be back shortly to check. I would take and put him up there, and about a half hour or forty-five minutes or so, I would go back up and check how he is doing. I would go up there and I wouldn't find him. So I asked the fellows that would be working on the floor had they seen him, and they said yes, he squirted the oil can a couple of times around different things and they don't know where he went. So I would start hunting all over the building. There is five stories on one side and four on the other. I would cover from the roof on down and I wouldn't locate him, and I asked him, I said, 'Well, where have you been?' And all he would give me was that he was around. I asked him, 'Around where?' He says, 'Just around,' and he would turn around and walk off."

Lee's attitude toward his job was one of complete indifference. It seemed to his fellow employees that he was in a stupor. However, on one occasion he did give Charles Le Blanc a glimpse of his true thoughts. The conversation was brief but to the point. Lee came into the shop and stood watching Le Blanc doing his work. Le Blanc asked him, "Are you finished with your greasing?"

"He said yes. So he asked me, said, 'Well, can I help you?' I said, 'No, what I am doing I don't need help.' So he stood there a few minutes and all of a sudden he said, 'You like it here?' I said, 'What do you mean?' He says, 'Do you like it here?' I says, 'Well, sure I like it here. I have been here a long time, about eight and a half years or so.' He says, 'Oh, hell, I don't mean this place.' I said, 'Well, what do you mean?' He says, 'This damn country.' He turned around and walked off. He didn't say any more. And then after that a lot of times I would be looking for him and the engineer would be looking for him, and on quite a number of occasions when it would get to be a coffee-break time—we usually go next door to the Crescent City Garage to get a Coke—and there he would be sitting in there drinking a Coke and looking at these magazines."

The magazines that Lee Oswald read in the Crescent City Garage when he was not to be found on his job were about guns. The proprietor of the garage was a sports-gun enthusiast, a member of the

National Rifle Association, and in his spare time worked on sporterizing his collection of weapons. Lee spent many hours when he should have been doing his job sitting around Adrian Alba's garage discussing the qualities of various rifles.

"Did these absences of his occur pretty much all the time, or did it get worse as he stayed there?"

"Well, towards the last it begin to get pretty regular, and that is when I think they decided to let him go. And another thing I recall: He had this habit, every time he would walk past you he would just [demonstrating]—just like a kid playing cowboys or something—you know, he used his finger like a gun. He would go, 'Pow!' and I used to look at him, and I said, 'Boy, what a crackpot this guy is!' "

"That is what you thought?"

"Yes. Right off the bat I said, 'This is a crackpot,' right off."

"Did he seem to just use his fingers like that, as a gun, as a joke, you mean, or—"

"Well, I didn't know what to think of it, you know, because he— on quite a number of times he would do that, you know. If you would walk past him, he would do that."

"Did he smile or laugh, or what?"

"No. When he would do it, he wouldn't even crack a smile. That is what used to get me. If somebody would be doing something in a joking manner, at least they would smile, but he was one that very seldom would talk or would smile either, and that is why I could never figure him out."

The degree to which Lee's erratic behavior on his job at the Reily Company could be considered technically psychotic is impossible to determine. He scribbled illegibly in the log book and misspelled obvious words. Le Blanc explained, "On a couple of occasions I told him if he could write plainer it would be a lot better for me to check, because a lot of times if something would go wrong with a machine we would go to that greasing log and check when is the last time it was greased, and when you would look at his writing it would be like Greek—you couldn't hardly understand it."

"What did he say about that?"

"Well, he would look at you and turn around and walk off."

"He wouldn't say anything?"

"Wouldn't say nothing. That is what used to get me. I used to—if

I bawled him out about not greasing something, ordinarily a man would tell you, well, I will try to do better, or that is the best I could do, or something like that, but that is what used to get me so mad when he would give me no answer whatsoever, and that is when I told him one day, I said, 'You are going to end up driving me crazy if I am going to have to keep up with this guy, because he don't give me an answer whatsoever if I bawl him out about his job or anything.' "

"Who did you tell that to—Mr. Barbe?"

"Well, I think it was Barbe I told that to."

"He is a sort of a—what?—engineer, plant engineer?"

"Yes, he is the plant engineer."

The Crescent City Garage where Lee Oswald was spending much time at his employer's expense was just next door to the Reily Company. In the office the proprietor had a coffeepot, a coffee table, chairs and a large magazine rack. He also had a Coke machine. He had no objection if the men from the Reily Company stopped in for a Coke or to swap conversation. Lee was one of his most frequent visitors.

"He pursued the issue of ordering guns," Adrian Alba testified, "and how many guns had I ever ordered, and how long did it take to get them, and where had I ordered guns from."

"What did you tell him? And just tell us the conversations that you had with him."

"I told him that I had a gun on order at the present time, a U.S. thirty-caliber carbine, and he asked had I received the gun, on several occasions, after that. I told him no, that I hadn't. And he asked me would I consider selling him the gun if and when I got it. I told him no."

"Was there anything peculiar about this particular rifle that made Oswald want it? Or why did he want you to sell this rifle? Do you know?"

"He told me he had a couple of guns, and he would like to have the carbine. He was familiar with the carbine from the service, I believe."

"And this was the regular M-1 carbine?"

"Regular M-1 carbine, yes."

"And from whom had you ordered that carbine? Do you recall?"

"Through the National Rifle Association."

"Did Oswald indicate to you what other kind of rifle or weapons that he had?"

"No, he didn't.

"He did make a remark that he had—I think he said he had several rifles and several pistols, but he did not go into the nature of the arms, or how much, or what they were."

"Did he ever express any interest in any rifle that you indicated that you had, other than this M-1 carbine that you told him you had ordered?"

"One 30.06 Springfield rifle that I had."

"Did you have that?"

"I was in the process of sporterizing that at the garage at the time—"

"What did he say about that particular weapon?"

"He said what was it worth to me, and I told him it was worth over one hundred dollars to me. There was no follow-up on that."

"Was this particular rifle that you have referred to a Japanese rifle?"

"No, it wasn't.

"I had a Japanese rifle down there that was not for sale, and he was more partial to the Japanese rifle than the Springfield and the carbine put together."

"He was really interested—"

"He was more interested in the Japanese rifle."

"Had you already sporterized that?"

"That was completely sporterized."

"What do you do to a rifle when you sporterize it?"

"Alter the stock, eliminate some of the weight and the length of the stock, because it is a military piece to start with, and you glass-bead the stock."

"And what does that mean?"

"To accurize the stock, and you put this where you have all metal to wood contact in the stock. It is referred to as accurizing and sporterizing and customizing a piece."

"Now, what did Oswald say about this particular Japanese rifle?"

"Nothing other than his desire to possess the gun, or to purchase the gun from me."

To Adrian Alba there was nothing unusual about Lee Oswald's interest in all these matters. It was a normal line of conversation for any gun enthusiast.

Marina Oswald was asked, "When did you first notice the rifle at New Orleans?"

"As soon as I arrived in New Orleans."

"Where was it kept there?"

"He again had a closetlike room with his things in it. He had his clothes hanging there, all his other belongings."

"Was the rifle in a cover there?"

"No."

"Did you notice him take it away from your home there in New Orleans at any time?"

"No. I know for sure that he didn't. But I know that we had a kind of a porch with a—a screened-in porch, and I know that sometimes evenings after dark he would sit there with his rifle. I don't know what he did with it. I came there by chance once and saw him just sitting there with his rifle. I thought he is merely sitting there and resting. Of course I didn't like these kind of little jokes."

"Can you give us an idea of how often this happened that you recall?"

"It began to happen quite frequently after he was arrested there in connection with some demonstration and handing out of leaflets."

"Was that the Fair Play for Cuba demonstration?"

"Yes."

"From what you observed about his having the rifle on the back porch, in the dark, could you tell whether or not he was trying to practice with the telescopic lens?"

"Yes, I asked him why. But this time he was preparing to go to Cuba."

"That was his explanation for practicing with the rifle?"

"Yes. He said that he would go to Cuba. I told him I was not going with him, that I would stay here."

"On these occasions when he was practicing with the rifle would they be three or four times a week in the evening, after the Fair Play for Cuba incident?"

"Almost every evening."

In view of later events, a conversation Oswald had at the Crescent Street Garage has a macabre implication. Alba remembered that he and Lee had discussed the striking and killing characteristics of different caliber rifles. Lee was very interested in that subject.

"We discussed the wounding effects of combat guns of the small caliber versus the large caliber, yes."

"What was that discussion?"

"Well, the small caliber in the field would tend to disable a man and require two men to cart him off, versus the larger caliber, which would knock out a man permanently. Having been left with a wounding effect, you would survive a larger caliber wound; your chances of survival from a larger or large-caliber wound would be greater than the smaller caliber. We went into the discussion of basing the thing on the ice pick versus the bread knife—I don't think I mentioned this part to the FBI—reflecting on the whole picture that you would be better off receiving a wound from a ten-inch bread knife than you would be being gigged once with a two- or three-inch ice pick, and that reflecting the difference between the large-caliber wound and the small-caliber wound."

"What led you and Oswald to agree that you would be better off being hit with a bread knife than with the ice pick?"

"Internal bleeding."

"There would be more internal bleeding from the ice pick?"

"Small caliber or the ice pick, yes."

"So that you both agreed that the small-caliber bullet would be more deadly than the larger one?"

"Being left with a wounded effect; in other words, if it was my intention to destroy an animal, I would prefer the large caliber, but if an animal was wounded with a large-caliber or a small-caliber bullet, I would say that the smaller caliber bullet would be more deadly in the end than the large-caliber wound, and he might survive the large caliber with an open wound."

"During the course of this conversation, did Oswald indicate in any way whether the rifles that he had were large-caliber or small-caliber weapons?"

"None other than the weapons were of the military, and I don't know—that part is an assumption on my part or whether he actually said it.

"He went to no length at all in discussing his firearms. In fact, it was my experience with Lee Oswald that you had to ask Lee Oswald questions. Either Lee Oswald was talking to you, or he wasn't talking at all. And I may have asked him what he had in the way of firearms."

"Did he mention that he had a pistol, or pistols?"

"If I remember correctly, I think he said he had a few, or a couple, or two. I am not definite."

"Do you remember whether Oswald seemed more interested or was disposed more in favor of rifles than pistols? Or did he seem—"

"Very definitely toward the rifle side."

"He was more interested in rifles?"

"Very little interested in the pistols. I had as many as three or I think at one time four pistols down there, and Lee Oswald was very, very keen towards the rifles that were among my sporterizing projects, and so on; other than the pistols, he had very, very little interest in the pistols."

"How did this fellow impress you?"

"He certainly didn't impress me as anyone capable or anyone burdened with a charge of assassinating the President of the United States, let alone any individual, for that matter. Our conversations were purely the gun magazines, the firearms themselves, and little of anything else, unless, of course, he was pretty much leading the conversation or doing the talking himself, on the same conversation level all the time—about the firearms."

"Did he strike you as being peculiar in any way?"

"Yes, he did. He was quiet."

"He was quiet?"

"He was quiet. You could ask Lee Oswald two or three questions, and if Lee Oswald wasn't apparently interested in the course of the conversation, he would just remain paging through the book and look up and say, 'Did you say something to me?'

"I hesitate putting the conversation back to Lee Oswald pursuing it first, but all you had to do was mention guns and gun magazines and Lee Oswald was very free with the conversation."

"Did he seem to have an interest in firearms that was abnormal or extremely great, or anything like that?"

"None."

"Other than the fact that he was quiet, was there anything about him that struck you as being odd or peculiar?"

"No."

"You didn't suspect he was a violent kind of person, or anything like that, the time that you knew him, did you?"

"I would answer that indeed not. I had never gotten the impression from Lee Oswald that he was capable of any plot or assassination, or what have you, of that nature."

"And were you surprised when you heard he had been arrested in connection with the assassination?"

"I was very much surprised."

"After you heard he had been charged with the assassination, did it seem to you then that he could have been capable of such a thing? Or did you hold to your former opinion?"

"I think I held to my former opinion. My formal opinion, things I have seen on television, of course, and read in the newspapers, and so forth, has laid out some suggestive pattern that Lee Oswald was a subversive, et cetera, toward the country, and maybe even the President, or something; but prior to that assassination he gave me no indication at any time that he was burdened with such a charge, or that he was concerned or involved with anything of that nature.

"He had never at any time spoken against the President or the country. He had never at any time, prior to the assassination, of course, mentioned Communist to me, or anything suggestive or leading to it, or otherwise."

"Do you remember whether he mentioned the President at all, one way or another?"

"I think I might answer that with a definite answer. I can't remember any time that Lee Oswald had ever mentioned the President, the country, foreign countries, et cetera."

"Is it customary or the usual sort of thing for people in this area to discuss politics, or discuss the President? People that come into your garage or—"

"Well, the usual trend of conversation in the garage, other than the garage business or the personal customers' cars or neighbors that walk in the garage that want change for the Coke machine, et cetera, would be either politics—I would say mostly politics more than anything else."

"What was the attitude of most of the men towards President Kennedy? Was he well liked down here, or was he not highly thought of?"

"He was very highly thought of for his convictions, for his stand on his convictions, but he wasn't too well thought of for his stand on the integration program to the South."

"Was it common for the people to complain about that sort of thing?"

"That is correct."

"And you never heard Oswald discuss that?"

"Not once."

"Was he ever present when the subject was discussed by others, as far as you can recall?"

"I really wouldn't know, or be able to comment whether he was or not. It's very possible that he was, and maybe on several occasions, but not to my recollection."

"He never responded in any way?"

"No."

Thomas Alba's impressions of Lee Harvey Oswald agreed with dozens of other witnesses in most every respect. They never dreamed he might be capable of violence. They found him unusually taciturn and solitary. He was never known to have said a critical word about President Kennedy. In New Orleans he seldom discussed his political leanings with anyone else. The last thing in the world they could have believed him to be was a potential assassin. To everyone but Marina he kept his secrets well hidden. He was studiously mum. No one had an over-all knowledge of his history and temperament, and no one suspected he was dangerous.

His bosses at the Reily Company had no reason to be interested. They simply fired him on July 19, 1963, because he deserved to be fired.

CHAPTER 16

FAIR PLAY FOR CUBA

ALTHOUGH HIS FELLOW WORKER, Charles Le Blanc, and the garage proprietor, Adrian Alba, couldn't fathom what was going on
in Lee Oswald's mind, Marina knew exactly. In her letters to Ruth
Paine she was frank about her domestic problems and Lee's insistence that she go back to Russia. However, she did not say anything
about Lee's other unusual activities. Lee had made it clear to Le
Blanc that he hated "this damned country." As far as Alba was concerned he could get a response out of Lee only when he talked about
guns. Lee stared out into space and ignored direct questions. He had
no interest in his job and courted dismissal. Although the expression
on his face was blank and unreadable, his mind was not idle. Lee, as
usual, was contemplating great historical achievements. Now his
mind had fixed on Cuba and Fidel Castro. There was a revolution
that offered opportunities for a young, bold leader! As the days of
boredom at the Reily Company had dragged on, more and more
Lee's mind became obsessed with the notion that if he could get to
Cuba, there would be the place for him. He had no intention of
spending a lifetime in a factory squirting grease into alemite fittings,
or, like his brother Robert, peddling bricks for some capitalist profit-
eer. He was destined to be a great revolutionary leader.

Marina was aware that Lee had these grandiose ideas about himself. She described them to the Commission:

"At least his imagination, his fantasy, which was quite unfounded,
was to the fact that he was an outstanding man. And then the fact
that he was very much interested, exceedingly so, in autobiographical works of outstanding statesmen of the United States and others."

"Was there anything else of that kind that caused you to think
that he was different?"

"I think that he compared himself to these people whose autobiog-
raphies he read. That seems strange to me, because it is necessary to

227

have an education in order to achieve success of that kind. After he became busy with his pro-Cuban activity, he received a letter from somebody in New York, some Communist—probably from New York; I am not sure from where—from some Communist leader and he was very happy. He felt that this was a great man that he had received the letter from.

"You see, when I would make fun of him, of his activity to some extent, in the sense that it didn't help anyone really, he said that I didn't understand him, and here, you see, was proof that someone else did, that there were people who understood his activity.

"I would say that to Lee—that Lee could not really do much for Cuba, that Cuba would get along well without him, if they had to."

"You would tell that to him?"

"Yes."

"And what would he say in return?"

"He shrugged his shoulders and kept his own opinion."

Lee knew that Marina would never appreciate his dreams or the important place he would some day occupy in history. It was maddening to have her continually belittling his schemes. She wanted to get away from him? Well, he could live without her too—or could he?

"At this time in New Orleans did he discuss with you his views?"

"Yes."

"What did he say about that?"

"Mostly—most of the conversations were on the subject of Cuba."

"Was there anything said about the United States—not liking the United States?"

"No. I can't say—he liked some things in Russia, he liked some other things here, didn't like some things there, and didn't like some things here.

"And I am convinced that as much as he knew about Cuba, all he knew was from books and so on. He wanted to convince himself. But I am sure that if he had gone there he would not have liked it there, either. Only on the moon, perhaps."

"Did he tell you what he didn't like about the United States?"

"First of all, he didn't like the fact that there are fascist organizations here. That was one thing. The second thing, that it was hard to get an education and hard to find work. And that medical expenses were very high."

"Did he say who he blamed for this?"

"He didn't blame anyone."

"Did he ever say anything about President Kennedy?"

"No. At least—I was always interested in President Kennedy and had asked him many times to translate articles in a newspaper or magazine for me, and he always had something good to say. He translated it but never did comment on it. At least in Lee's behavior —from Lee's behavior I cannot conclude that he was against the President, and therefore the thing is incomprehensible to me. Perhaps he hid it from me. I don't know. He said that after twenty years he would be Prime Minister. I think that he had a sick imagination—at least at that time I already considered him to be not quite normal—not always but at times. I always tried to point out to him that he was a man like any others who were around us. But he simply could not understand that.

"I tried to tell him that it would be better to direct his energies to some more practical matters and not something like that."

Marina's advice to Lee that he would be better off concentrating his efforts on the normal accomplishments of life fell on deaf ears. His ambition was inflamed with the belief that "after twenty years he would be Prime Minister." Did he mean Prime Minister of Cuba?

It is surprising that Lee said twenty years and not a much shorter period of time. His impatience to achieve glory and recognition had driven him on other occasions to seek the shortest way to his objectives. He had never learned forbearance or an adult appreciation that even small accomplishments require self-discipline. He never seemed to understand that the price of modest success exacts from most human beings long years of toil and perseverance. He expected success at once. He would lash out at society when he did not get what he wanted immediately.

Perhaps I should point out that today the Fair Play for Cuba Committee name does not have quite the provocative impact it had in 1962 and 1963. Prior to and after the Cuban missile crisis these words were a call to arms to both sides. The Commission hearings relating to Oswald's activities in New Orleans must be read in this context. As the witnesses—Marina, Ruth Paine, Carlos Bringuier and the others—testified a member of the Commission had to look back a few months to appreciate the intensity of feelings Lee Oswald's activities in behalf of the Fair Play for Cuba Committee evoked.

Lee's first plan for getting to Cuba was typically melodramatic and rash. He would hijack an airplane and force the pilot to fly him to Havana.

"Did he describe that idea to you?" the Commission asked Marina.

"Yes."

"And when he told you of it, did he indicate that he wanted to be the one who would kidnap the airplane himself?"

The Commission probed to find out if Lee had any accomplices in this scheme, but extensive investigation indicated that his Cuban ventures were planned and executed alone.

"Yes, he wanted to do that. And he asked me that I should help him with that. But I told him I would not touch that rifle.

"That sounds very merry, but I am much ashamed of it."

Marina testified that Lee studied the airplane schedules from New Orleans. At that time there had been a number of incidents where pro-Castro partisans had hijacked planes, held the pilot at gun point and headed for Havana. The idea was not original, but that mattered little to Lee Oswald. It was a direct and dramatic way of accomplishing his purpose. He could use his pistol to make the men in the cockpit submit, but he needed an accomplice to hold the passengers in their seats. It would be a simple matter if she would cooperate. In the eyes of Castro he imagined he would cover himself with glory. He would come to the leader's attention immediately; it might catapult him to the top echelon of military command in Cuba. Here was a way to escape the humdrum existence he loathed.

But Marina refused to have any part of the crazy scheme.

"Did you tell him that using the rifle in this way, talking about it, was not in accordance with his agreement with you?"

The farewell note he had written the night he went out to shoot General Walker was still between the pages of the *Book of Useful Advice*, tucked away where Marina could use it as evidence against him. She could take it to the police.

Marina claimed she talked Lee out of this plan for getting to Cuba. He concocted another plan, however. His mind was now entirely concentrated on a defection to Cuba. When he had defected to Russia he had become lost in the massive bureaucracy of the Soviet

230

system. He hated that bureaucracy as much as he hated the American way of life. The Russians had been indifferent to his talents. They had stuck him away in a radio factory in Minsk. His personal obscurity was as ignominious as in Dallas or New Orleans. But in Cuba he knew it would be different. There he would rise to leadership. There he would show Marina how great he could be, and she would live to regret her belittling of his talents. If she refused to cooperate with him in hijacking a plane, he would prove he didn't need her. There was another way he could get to Cuba, not as direct, but it would get him there all the same.

Ruth Paine had finally made her offer by letter in which she invited Marina to live with her in Irving, Texas. Marina now had a definite alternative to going back to Russia. The first step in Lee's plan, therefore, was to identify himself publicly with the pro-Castro movement in America so as to prepare a reputation for himself. He had taken an interest in the Castro cause earlier. He knew better than to make the mistake of arriving in a foreign country obscure and unwelcomed. He remembered those black days in Moscow only too well—the balding bureaucrat who told him to go back to the United States, his discouragement at being turned away, leading to his attempted suicide. If Marina had been willing to cooperate with him in hijacking a plane, the notoriety he would receive would ingratiate him to Castro, but under the second plan he would have to accomplish this in another way. First, he would establish a Fair Play for Cuba Committee in New Orleans; he would found a chapter and stir up local activity. Then he would undertake some action that would give him newspaper publicity. Finally, when he was well known as a friend of Castro, he would go to the nearest Cuban Embassy (which would be Mexico City) and ask for permission to enter that country. This was not as dramatic a plan as hijacking a plane, but it was entirely logical to Lee Oswald. Once inside Cuba, he would find ways of advancing himself. Lee Oswald knew well the story of an obscure lieutenant who made his way from the island of Corsica to the throne of France. To compare himself and Napoleon Bonaparte would not have seemed farfetched. He renewed an earlier correspondence with the head office of the Fair Play for Cuba Committee in New York and received instructions on how to proceed in organizing a chapter in New Orleans. Further investigation by the Commission did not reveal a shred of evidence that he had any collaborators in this venture beyond the formal instructions he thus received from New York. It was another of Lee Harvey Oswald's lone adventures, although he did force Marina to forge bogus signatures for him. This was something Marina failed to mention on her first appearance in Washington. Commission handwriting experts suspected the forgeries by Marina and confronted her with their suspicions when she was called back a second time.

"Mrs. Oswald, I will hand you Commission's Exhibit 819 and ask you particularly about the signature at the bottom."

"That is Lee's handwriting, and this is mine."

"Where the words 'A. J. Hidell, Chapter President' on Commission Exhibit 819 are in your handwriting?"

"Yes."

"Would you tell the Commission how you happened to sign that?"

"Lee wrote this down on a piece of paper and told me to sign it on this card, and said that he would beat me if I didn't sign that name on the card."

"Did you have any other discussion about your signing that name?"

"Yes."

"What discussion did you have?"

"I said that this sounded like Fidel. I said, 'You have selected this name because it sounds like Fidel,' and he blushed and said, 'Shut up, it is none of your business.'"

"Was there any discussion about who Hidell, as signed on the bottom of that card, was?"

"He said that it was his own name and that there is no Hidell in existence, and I asked him, 'You just have two names,' and he said, 'Yes.'"

"Was anything else said about that matter at any time?"

"I taunted him about this and teased about this and said how shameful it is that a person who has his own perfectly good name should take another name, and he said, 'It is none of your business. I would have to do it this way, people will think I have a big organization,' and so forth."

"Did you ask him why he needed to have the other name in your handwriting rather than his own?"

"I did ask him that and he would answer that in order that people will think it is two people involved and not just one."

"Did you ever sign any more such cards with the name 'Hidell'?"

"Only this one."

"And you never signed the name 'Hidell' on any other paper at any time?"

"Only once."

"Where did this actual signing take place, Mrs. Oswald?"

"In New Orleans."

"Where in New Orleans?"

"In what is the name of the street where we lived."

"Had you ever heard the name 'Hidell' before?"

"I don't remember whether this was before or after Lee spoke to the radio. I think it was after."

"Did he use the name Hidell on the radio?"

"I think that he might have when he was talking on the radio said that Hidell is the president of his organization but, of course, I don't understand English well and I don't know. He spoke on the radio using his own name, but might have mentioned the name 'Hidell.'

"This is what he told me when I tried to find out what he said on the radio."

"This might have been on television also?"

"He told me that someone had taken movies of him for to be shown later on television, but I don't know if they ever were."

"Did you ever sign the name 'Hidell' at any subsequent time to any document?"

"I only remember this one occasion."

Marina testified she did not know Lee had used the name "A. J. Hidell" before, in ordering the rifle to shoot General Walker.

When pressed harder by a member of the Commission, Marina admitted that she probably had signed more than one membership card—two or three perhaps—but she stuck to her story that this was the only occasion she falsified Hidell's signature.

"When did his Fair Play for Cuba activity occur—before or after he lost his job?"

"After he lost his job. I told him it would be much better if he were working because when he didn't work he was busy with such foolishness."

"What did he say about that?"

"Nothing."

Lee Oswald's Fair Play for Cuba activity was foolishness to Marina, but to him it was part of a well-thought-out plan. He wanted to impress the national leaders in New York that he had a real organization, and he wrote letters detailing elaborate activities that never took place. The very fact that he was attempting to make his achievements look important momentarily confused investigators— and particularly confused the public through news reports. How deeply was he involved in a well-organized intrigue on the part of pro-Castro supporters? The Commission investigated every possible lead. Aside from two youths he hired to help distribute leaflets, no other person could be found who had had any connection with Lee Oswald or the dummy Fair Play chapter he claimed to have flourishing. But Lee Oswald knew how to make propaganda. His purpose was to get himself well advertised as a friend of Cuba. He did this by making a direct approach to the anti-Castro patriots in New Orleans. He deliberately provoked a street brawl that gave him headlines in the newspapers and a chance to espouse his ideas over radio and television.

Marina confirmed that she believed Lee's main purpose in all this activity was to obtain publicity.

"Do you think he wanted to be advertised and known as being in support of Cuba before he went to Cuba?"

"Yes."

"Do you think he thought that would help him when he got to Cuba?"

"Yes."

"Did he tell you anything about that, or is that just what you guess?"

"He would collect the newspaper clippings about his—when the newspapers wrote about him, and he took these clippings with him when he went to Mexico."

In New Orleans, the anti-Castro forces were headed by a young Cuban whose name was Carlos Bringuier. In Cuba he had been an attorney and Assistant Secretary for the Criminal Court in Havana. Being firmly anti-Communist, he had fled Cuba in May 1960, and after a temporary sojourn with his family in Guatemala and Argentina he came to the United States on February 8, 1961. He came as an immigrant, as a resident, not as a refugee. When he arrived in New Orleans he founded a news letter for Cubans named *Crusada*. He became active in anti-Castro groups. At the moment he encountered Lee Oswald for the first time he carried the title "New Orleans Delegate of the Cuban Student Directorate," and he conducted limited anti-Castro propaganda activities as time off from his work would permit.

On August 5, 1963—two and a half weeks after he had been discharged from the Reily Company—Oswald showed up at Bringuier's place of work. Although he was now the fictitious chapter president and only member of the pro-Castro New Orleans chapter of the Fair Play for Cuba Committee, he chose to acquaint himself with his opponent's activities by pretending to want to join Bringuier in his work.

Bringuier recalled the incident for the Commission.

"I was talking in the store with one young American—the name of him is Phillip Geraci—and five minutes later Mr. Oswald came inside the store. He start to look around, several articles, and he show interest in my conversation with Geraci. I was explaining to Geraci that our fight is a fight of Cubans and that he was too young, that if he want to distribute literature against Castro, I would give him the literature, but not admit him to the fight.

"At that moment also he start to agree with I, Oswald start to agree with my point of view and he show real interest in the fight against Castro. He told me that he was against Castro and that he was against communism. He told me—he asked me first for some English literature against Castro, and I gave him some copies of the Cuban report printed by the Cuban Student Directorate.

"After that, Oswald told me that he had been in the Marine Corps and that he had training in guerrilla warfare and that he was willing to train Cubans to fight against Castro. Even more, he told me that he was willing to go himself to fight against Castro. That was on August 5.

"I turned down his offer. I told him that I don't have nothing to do with military activities, that my only duties here in New Orleans are propaganda and information and not military activities. That was my answer to him.

"He insisted, and he told me that he will bring to me next day one book as a present, as a gift to me, to train Cubans to fight against Castro."

"Did Oswald mention during this conversation that he could easily derail a train, for example, by securing and fastening a chain around the railroad track? Do you remember him mentioning something like that?"

"Well, you see, I do not exactly remember all the details, because we were talking for about—I believe about one hour. He could have mentioned that, because he was talking about the experience that he had in guerrilla warfare in the Marine Corps. Before he left the store, he put his hand in the pocket and he offered me money."

"Oswald did?"

"Yes."

"How much did he offer you?"

"Well, I don't know. As soon as he put the hand in the pocket and he told me, 'Well, at least let me contribute to your group with some money,' at that moment I didn't have the permit from the City Hall here in New Orleans to collect money in the city, and I told him that I could not accept his money, and I told him that if he want to contribute to our group, he could send the money directly to the headquarters in Miami, because they had the authorization over there in Miami, and I gave him the number of the post-office box of the organization in Miami.

"And after that, I left the store, because I had to go to the bank to make the deposit, and Oswald was in the store talking to my brother-in-law—that is my partner in the store—Rolando Paez."

"Is that P-a-e-z?"

"That is right. Oswald was talking to him for about half an hour, and later on when I came back from the bank I asked to my brother-in-law, 'Well, what do you think about this guy who was here?' "

"Did he tell you his name was Lee Oswald?"

"Yes, he told me that his name was Lee Oswald, and he told me one address in Magazine Street, but I didn't remember at that moment the number, and when I asked to my brother-in-law that, he told me that Oswald looked like really a smart person and really interested in the fight against communism, and he gave to my brother a good impression, and I told my brother that I could not trust him, because—I didn't know what was inside of me, but I had

236

some feeling that I could not trust him. I told that to my brother that day. Next day, on August 6, Oswald came back to the store, but I was not in the store at that moment, and he left with my brother-in-law a guidebook for Marines for me with the name 'L. H. Oswald' in the top of the first page. When I came back to the store, my brother-in-law gave to me the guidebook for Marines. I was look in the guidebook for Marines. I found interest in it and I keep it, and later-—I forgot about that just for three days more—on August 9, I was coming back to the store at two o'clock in the afternoon, and one friend of mine with the name of Celso Hernandez came to me and told me that in Canal Street there was a young man carrying a sign telling 'Viva Fidel' in Spanish, and some other thing about Cuba, but my friend don't speak nothing in English, and the only thing that he understood was the 'Viva Fidel' in Spanish. He told me that he was blaming the person in Spanish, but that the person maybe didn't understood what he was telling to him and he came to me to let me know what was going on over there.

"At that moment was in the store another Cuban with the name of Miguel Cruz, and we went all three with a big sign that I have in the store in color. The sign is the Statue of Liberty with a knife in the back, and the hand, the initials of the Soviet Union, and it said, 'Danger. Only Ninety Miles from the United States Cuba Lies in Chains.' We pick up the sign and we went to Canal Street to find the guy.

"We were walking all Canal Street from Rampart Street, but we could not find him. We were asking to different people in the street, but nobody saw him, nobody told us, Yes, I saw him, or, He went to this side. I decided to get a Canal streetcar until about the 2700 block of Canal Street, and we came back in the Canal streetcar, but we could not find him at that moment.

"I went back to the store, but just three or four minutes later one of my two friends, Miguel Cruz, came back running and told me that the guy was another time in Canal Street and that Celso was watching him over there.

"I went over there with the sign another time, and I was surprised when I recognized that the guy with the sign hanging on the chest, said, 'Viva Fidel in the Land of Cuba,' was Lee Harvey Oswald. Until that moment I only knew Oswald as a guy who was offering his service to train Cubans, and when I saw that he was with a sign defending Fidel Castro and praising Fidel Castro, I became angry.

That was in the 700 block of Canal Street just in front of the store where I was working my first year here in New Orleans.

"When I saw that was Oswald and he recognized me, he was also surprised, but just for a few seconds. Immediately he smiled to me and he offered the hand to shake with me. I became more angry and I start to tell him that he don't have any face to do that, with what face he was doing that, because he had just came to me four days ago offering me his service and that he was a Castro agent, and I start to blame him in the street.

"That was a Friday around three o'clock at this moment, and many people start to gather around us to see what was going on over there. I start to explain to the people what Oswald did to me, because I wanted to move the American people to fight him, and I told them that that was a Castro agent, that he was a pro-Communist, and that he was trying to do to them exactly what he did to us in Cuba, kill them and send their children to the execution ward. Those were my phrases at the moment.

"The people in the street became angry and they started to shout to him, 'Traitor! Communist! Go to Cuba! Kill him!' and some other phrases that I do not know if I could tell in the record."

"You mean they cursed at him, they swore at him?"

"That is right, some bad phrases, bad words."

"Yes."

"And at that moment one of the Americans push him by one arm. One policeman came. When policeman came to me and asked me to keep walking and to let Oswald distribute his literature that he was handing out—he was handing out yellow leaflets of the Fair Play for Cuba Committee, New Orleans chapter—and I told to the policeman that I was Cuban, I explained to him what Oswald did to me, and I told him that I don't know if he was against the law or if was enforcing the law, but that I will not leave that place until Oswald left and that I will make some trouble.

"The policeman left, I believe going to some place to call the headquarters, and at one moment my friend Celso took the literature from Oswald, the yellow sheets, and broke it and threw it on the air. There were a lot of yellow sheets flying. And I was more angry, and I went near Oswald to hit him. I took my glasses off and I went near to him to hit him, but when he sensed my intention, he put his arm down as an X, like this here [demonstrating]."

"He crossed his arms in front of him?"

"That is right, put his face and told me, 'O.K., Carlos, if you want to hit me, hit me.'

"At that moment, that made me to reaction that he was trying to appear as a martyr if I will hit him, and I decide not to hit him, and just a few seconds later arrive two police cars, and one of the policeman over there was Lieutenant Gaillot, G-a-i-l-l-o-t. They put Oswald and my two friends in one of the police cars, and I went with Lieutenant Gaillot in the other police car to the First District of Police here in New Orleans.

"When we were in the First District of Police, we were in the same room, one small room over there, and some of the policemen start to question Oswald if he was a Communist, what he was doing that, and all those things, and Oswald at that moment—that was in front of myself—was really cold blood. He was answering the questions that he would like to answer, and he was not nervous, he was not out of control, he was confident in himself at that moment over there.

"One of the questions that they asked to him was about his organization, the Fair Play for Cuba, and I saw him showing some papers that—I believe they were the credentials of the Fair Play for Cuba Committee, that the Fair Play for Cuba Committee is a national organization, and when he told that, he was so kind of proud that it was not a small group but a national group all over the United States, and they asked of him the name of the members. No. Excuse me. Before they asked him if he has any office. He told them no, that there were—they were holding the meetings in different house, different homes, different members of the organization, one night in one house, another night in another house, but in front of me he didn't told nothing about any office. When they asked him about the name of the members, he answered that he could not tell the name of the members in front of myself, because he will not like to let me know who were the ones who were helping him here in the city, and at that moment the police came out of the room and that was the last time that I saw him that day."

"Did the police keep you in jail too?"

"Well, yes. I had to put—they took my fingerprints and my picture, and I have to put twenty-five-dollar bond that night with my two friends too, and I don't know, but after the assassination I heard that Oswald didn't put the twenty-five-dollar bond, that somebody went to the First District and make—I believe you call that an affidavit or something like that, and he will appear in court and he will put the twenty-five dollars. He didn't put the twenty-five-dollar bond. That is what I heard. I didn't saw that. I am not sure of that. Next time that I saw him—"

"Did you appear in court later?"

"Yes, sir. Later. That was August twelfth."

"Yes, on Monday."

"Monday."

"And you pleaded not guilty to the offense that you were charged with?"

"That is right, that is right, and he pleaded guilty."

"Oswald was there in court?"

"Yes, sir.

"In August twelfth, we appear in the Second Municipal Court in New Orleans. I came first with my friends, and there were some other Cubans over there, and I saw when Oswald came inside the court. I saw him. He went directly to sit down in the middle of the seat of the colored people. See, here in the court you have two sides, one for the white people and one for the colored people and he sat directly among them in the middle, and that made me to be angry too, because I saw that he was trying to win the colored people for his side. When he will appear in the court, he will defend Fidel Castro, he will defend the Fair Play for Cuba, and the colored people will feel good for him, and that is a tremendous work of propaganda for his cause. That is one of the things that made me to think that he was really smart guy and not a nut.

"When the judge call us, he plead guilty, I plead not guilty, and my friends plead not guilty. I brought the Marines' guidebook, the guidebook for Marines, and I explain to the judge that the incident was originated when Oswald tried to infiltrate the organization and that if he will not do that, I will not have any fight with him in the street, and I showed to him the guidebook for Marines with the name of Oswald on the front of the first page, and the judge dismisses the charges against us and fined him ten dollars."

"Fined Oswald ten dollars?"

"Ten dollars—that is right. In the court was at that moment one cameraman from WDSU, and he make—he did an interview to Oswald after the trial and he took some movies of ourselves, and later I receive one phone call from Bill Stuckey [Stuckey was a local radio news commentator]. I had talk to Stuckey the day of the trial in the morning. I met him in the bank and I explained to him what was going on in the Second Municipal Court, and he was the one who send the reporter over there to the trial. I am not sure if was the same day or next day of the trial Stuckey called me asking for Oswald's address. I get the affidavit from the court dissertation, and I give to him the address in dissertation, and I asked him why he was looking for that. He told me that he was going to make an interview to Oswald. I disagreed with him that moment. I told him that I was thinking that it was not good to let a Communist go to radio station and tell all his lies, because there are many people who do not know exactly what is happening in Cuba. Stuckey offered me to make another interview to me next Saturday in his program, but I didn't agree with that neither, and I asked him to arrange a radio debate, because in that way we could tell our point of view at the same moment in the same place."

Stuckey, the radio commentator, agreed to a debate between Oswald and Carlos Bringuier.

"August twenty-first, the day of the debate, I went to WDSU radio about five-thirty, thirty minutes before the time of the debate. When I went to the lobby, there were already there Bill Stuckey and Lee Harvey Oswald. I shake hands with Stuckey. Stuckey indicate to me that Oswald was there. Oswald stand up and came to me and shake hands with me. I was talking to Stuckey for a few minutes, and after that Stuckey left the lobby and went inside the WDSU radio station to check—I believe that was to check in what room we will have the debate. I was talking to Oswald that day before the debate started. I was trying to be as friendly to him as I could. I really believe that the best thing that I could do is to get one Communist out of the Communist Party and put him to work against communism, because he know what communism mean, and I told to Oswald that I don't have nothing against him in the personal way, just in the ideologic way. I told him that for me it was impossible to see one American being a Communist, because communism is trying to destroy the United States, and that if any moment when he will be at bed he will start to think that he can do something good for his country, for his family, and for himself, he could come to me, because I would receive him, because I repeat to him I didn't have nothing against him in the personal way. He smiled to me. He told me—he answered me that he was in the right side, the correct side, and that I was in the wrong side, and that he was doing his best. That were his words at that moment.

"Before we went inside the room of the debate he saw my guide-book for Marines that I was carrying with me, because I did not know what will happen in the debate and I will have to have that weapon with me to destroy him personally as a traitor if he doing something wrong in the debate. When he saw the guidebook for Marines he smiled to me, and he told me, 'Well, listen, Carlos, don't try to do an invasion with that guidebook for Marines, because that is an old one and that will be a failure.' That was his joke in that moment.

"After that we went to the debate, and I think that you have the whole history of the debate, you have the transcription and every-thing, [so] that I don't have to go inside that, because that is subjec-tive, not objective, you have the objective, and that is the debate."

The debate gave Lee the additional publicity he was seeking. Ob-viously it did not change his Communist convictions or plans to go to Cuba.

The Commission members had an opportunity to hear a replay of the New Orleans debate in which Oswald was a principal figure. I was surprised by his better-than-average vocabulary and fluency, considering the limitations of his formal education. As I listened to the give and take, Oswald had a potential, although maybe minor league, to qualify as a rabble-rousing demagogue.

CHAPTER 17

LEE HEADS FOR CUBA

THE STREET BRAWL with Carlos Bringuier, his subsequent arrest, the television films and radio debate gave Lee the newspaper headlines he wanted. He now had printed proof to show the Cuban Embassy in Mexico City that he was a friend and worthy of joining the revolutionary patriots in Havana. To make the matter even more official, at his own request he was interviewed by the FBI; he wanted to appear persecuted by them to make his pro-Castro pose more convincing. Lee was well aware that obtaining entry into Cuba, especially with status, would not be easy. Castro's agents would be impressed that he had let the FBI know where he stood. He hoped he could strengthen his appearance of dedication by later implying that the FBI was watching him. He had deliberately pleaded guilty before the judge. He had tried to infiltrate Bringuier's anti-Castro organization. He had set the stage for a hero's welcome when he reached Havana, and yet he seemed to have an anxiety that gaining entrance might still be difficult. He prepared a second string to his bow.

During the summer he had applied for a new passport. This had been issued to him as a routine matter. He had repaid his loan to the State Department and technically was in good standing. Marina testified that in one of his fits of depression he had told her he thought he would go back to Russia too; there was nothing in America to hold him. However, Marina did not know that when he wrote the Russian Embassy in Washington asking them to consider readmitting both him and Marina, he had included a note asking that his application be processed separately from hers, implying that he might want to do something different. The Commission was unable to determine positively the significance of this request, but from subsequent events it would appear that he wanted to be in a position to go to Russia only if his Cuban adventure failed. He did not want to be tied to Marina in every move.

He would send Marina back to Russia, where she would be safe. He would then set out on his own ventures. If the Cuban officials denied him admission, he could tell them he was en route to Moscow and simply wanted to stop over in Havana. Once in Havana, he would find a means of staying there. A few years earlier, his attempted suicide had persuaded Russian officials to let him stay in the USSR. A repeat of this strategy would not be likely in Cuba, but Lee was a man who knew how to manipulate officials. Hadn't he outwitted most of them in his career? The Dallas police were still baffled by the Walker affair, and yet five months later Lee had no hesitation in requesting an FBI interview at the police station in New Orleans. He thought government officials were idiots.

The bureaucratic delay at the Russian Embassy in Washington was troublesome. There had been months of correspondence over Marina's request. And at times Marina had been emphatic that she would not go back. Now Ruth Paine was persistent in her requests that Marina come to live with her. She had written a dozen letters during the summer. Again and again she had suggested that Marina return to Dallas to have the new baby. It was getting close to that time now, and she had recently written that she planned to visit New Orleans around the twentieth of September, when the matter could be discussed in more detail. Marina did not show Lee all of Ruth Paine's letters, but he had a good idea of their contents. If the Russian Embassy was so slow about making a decision, why wouldn't it fit his plans well to let Ruth Paine take Marina to Irving?

Lee was a master at decoying people. He completely misled Ruth Paine into believing that he was hunting hard for a job. He made up a story for Adrian Alba at the garage next to Reily's that had no basis in fact. Lee had learned long ago that deceit is a powerful tool when used to outwit honest people. With barefaced duplicity he told Alba a lie.

"The last time I saw Lee Oswald was when he told me that he was leaving for Michoud. He had put in an application at Michoud, where he was going to make the big money, in this town here. He mentioned that prior or about three weeks prior to leaving.

"When he did leave, he came in the office and he says, 'Well'—this was approximately ten o'clock in the morning—he said, 'Well, I will be seeing you.' I said, 'Where are you headed?' He said, 'Out there, where the gold is.' I said, 'Where is that?' He said, 'I told you I was going out to Michoud and that I had an application out there.' He said, 'Well, I have heard from them, and I have just wound up things next door at the coffee company, and I am on my way out there now.'

"That, again, was approximately—I may stand to be corrected on my timing—but that was approximately some weeks before the assassination."

"What is this 'Michoud' that he mentioned to you? How do you spell it?"

"That's the national air space program, the rockets, out in Gentilly. That's NASA."

"What kind of an operation do they have there? Is it a manufacturing operation?"

"It is the rocket, the Atlas rocket, I believe."

"They construct them there, is that correct?"

"That is correct."

"Did he tell you what kind of work he was going to do for the organization?"

"No, he didn't."

"You mentioned 'Michoud,' and is that the name of a city there?"

"Michoud, that's this particular section of Gentilly, Gentilly section, where the plant is located."

Lee may have gone through the motions of looking for a job after he was fired from the Reily Company, but his energies were being spent on Fair Play for Cuba activities. Ruth Paine had given a definite date when she would arrive, and he was waiting for her to help solve his problem of what to do with Marina.

Did Lee and Marina openly discuss the plan to take advantage of Ruth Paine's hospitality? The way events fell in place after Mrs. Paine's arrival, one can only conclude that they had reached an understanding. At one time shortly after the assassination Marina told the FBI she didn't know anything about Lee's trip to Mexico en route to Cuba. She later confessed she knew all about it, and it was implicit that she knew he did not intend to come back. One may interpret her excuse for this dishonesty in a number of ways, but in any event her falsifications were a far cry from the truthfulness her Quaker friend, Mrs. Paine, would think proper.

When Marina appeared before the Commission, she was quizzed on this matter.

"When you were asked before about the trip to Mexico, you did not say you knew anything about it. Do you want to explain to the Commission how that happened?"

"Most of these questions were put to me by the FBI. I do not like them too much. I didn't want to be too sincere with them, though I was quite sincere and answered most of their questions. They questioned me a great deal, and I was very tired of them, and I thought that, well, whether I knew about it or didn't know about it didn't change matters at all, it didn't help anything, because the fact that Lee had been there was already known, and whether or not I knew about it didn't make any difference."

To the average American mind, Marina's explanation of her lies to the FBI is an incredible twisting of logic. It is almost an Oriental kind of rationalization, perhaps not as cold-blooded as some of Lee's reasoning, but similar. If Marina had said forthrightly that the reason she lied was fear of being implicated in Lee's crime, that would be understandable. Her convenient way of failing to tell facts—as, for example, her forgery of the A. J. Hidell signature—until confronted with cold proof made the Commission's work much more difficult.

"Was that the only reason that you did not tell about what you knew of the Mexico City trip before?"

"Yes, because the first time that they asked me I said no, I didn't know anything about it. And in all succeeding discussions I couldn't very well have said I did. There is nothing special in that. It wasn't because this was connected with some sort of secret."

Marina didn't see anything special in the fact that the FBI was trying to find out the truth about one of the most heinous crimes in history and that she was hindering their work. This was not the first or last time her concept of truth muddied the waters.

The degree to which she and Lee had planned Ruth Paine's role in their departure from New Orleans prior to September 20 was not clear. However, she told the Commission about writing Ruth Paine after Lee had lost his job.

"And it is at that time I wrote a letter to Mrs. Paine telling her that Lee was out of work, and they invited me to come and stay with her. And when I left here [New Orleans] I knew that Lee would go to Mexico City. But, of course, I didn't tell Mrs. Paine about it."

How completely Ruth Paine was misled into thinking that Lee was simply going elsewhere to look for work while Marina had her baby stands out in Mrs. Paine's own account of what transpired when she reached New Orleans.

"I arrived midafternoon, as I remember."

"And you went directly to their home, did you?"

"Yes."

"What did you find when you reached the home?"

"I was expected. They had groceries bought."

"Who was home?"

"Marina and Lee and the baby, June. I spent the night there that night and the succeeding two nights. Lee bought the groceries while there, was host. At one point, Mrs. Ruth Kloepfer [an acquaintance of Ruth Paine's] came and visited with her sister—excuse me, with her two daughters. That was after I had made a telephone call to her."

"These daughters were adults, or were they children?"

"The daughters were grown daughters.

"He seemed in good spirits that weekend. I found him—he made a much better impression on me, I will say, that weekend than the last weekend I had seen him, which was in May.

"I could see, and it was the first time that I felt that he was concerned about his wife's physical welfare and about where she could go to have the baby, and he seemed distinctly relieved to consider the possibility of her going to Dallas County and getting care through Parkland Hospital and clearly pleased that I wanted to offer this, and pleased to have her go, which relieved my mind a good deal.

"I hadn't wanted to have such an arrangement come about without his being interested in having it that way."

Indeed, Lee was very interested in having it that way. Just as Mrs. Paine's appearance in Dallas that day had made his flight to New Orleans more convenient, so now his exit for Havana was assured by Mrs. Paine's hospitality. Her station wagon had room enough for a rifle he could hardly take on the bus to Mexico City.

"During the course of this, did you say three days you were there?"

"Three nights, two days."

"Two days and three nights there was then a discussion between yourself and Marina, yourself on the one hand, Marina and Lee on the other, in which it was determined that Marina would return with you to Irving, Texas, for the purpose of having the birth of her child in Irving?"

"That is right."

"And Lee did participate in those discussions?"

"Yes."

"Now, during the course of the time you were there, was there any discussion of the fact that Lee was at that time jobless and would be seeking a position?"

"I knew from Marina's letters that he was out of work."

"Yes."

"We did have one short conversation, and this was in English. I began it. He was willing to proceed in English."

"This is one of the few occasions in which he permitted himself to speak with you in English?"

"That is correct. I asked him if he thought his application [Mrs. Paine assumed Lee would tell the truth in his job applications about having lived in Russia] was any impediment to his getting and keeping a job. He said he didn't know, and went on to say that he had already lost his job when he was arrested for passing out literature pro-Cuba here in New Orleans. And he said he spent the night in jail, and I said, 'Did Marina know that?'

" 'Yes, she knew it.' This was as much of a revelation, accurate revelation of what he had done as I ever got from him."

"Had you up to this moment heard of Lee Harvey Oswald's activities, if any, of any character and to any extent, with respect to the Fair Play for Cuba Committee?"

"I had not heard of any such activities. The name of the committee was not mentioned. I did not know the name of the committee until it appeared in the newspapers after the assassination."

"Now, how did Lee Harvey Oswald describe that? What did he say?"

"He said that he was passing out pro-Castro or pro-Cuba literature and that there were some anti-Castro people also caused some disturbance, and that he had spent the night in jail."

"And did I understand you correctly to say that he assigned that as a possible—"

"No, on the contrary."

"As possibly having had some effect on his loss of position?"

"On the contrary, he made the point that he had already lost his job before this happened."

"That he had lost his position before the Fair Play for Cuba incident?"

"So that he did not know, he could not cite an instance where his application had made difficulty for him in his work."

As to whether there was any uncertainty in Marina's mind about Lee's plans, or her submission to them, she was asked, "Did he tell you why he wanted to go to Mexico City?"

"From Mexico City he wanted to go to Cuba—perhaps through the Russian Embassy in Mexico somehow be able to get to Cuba."

"Did he say anything about going to Russia by way of Cuba?"

"I know that he said that in the Embassy. But he only said so. I know that he had no intention of going to Russia then."

"How do you know that?"

"He told me. I know Lee fairly well—well enough from that point of view."

"Did he tell you that he was going to Cuba and send you on to Russia?"

"No, he proposed that after he got to Cuba that I would go there too somehow.

"But he also said that after he was in Cuba, and if he might go to Russia, he would let me know in any case."

Lee was blithefully taking off on an adventure that could well have meant a permanent separation from Marina. A child would be born in his absence. He was leaving Marina with a relative stranger to shift for herself.

Marina commented, "And I told him, if he doesn't accomplish anything to at least take a good rest. I was hoping that the climate, if nothing else, would be beneficial to him."

If the Commission members were nonplussed by Marina's casual way of commenting on Lee's departure, they did not know at the time of her first appearance the chaos of Lee's and Marina's domestic life. One might be led to believe that she was happy to see him go, and he was happy with the prospect of getting away from her.

Ruth Paine continued, "I was impressed during these two days with his willingness to help with the packing. He did virtually all the packing and all the loading of the things into the car. I simply thought that gentlemanly of him at the time. I have wondered since whether he wasn't doing it by preference to having me handle it."

"I was about to ask you your impression in that direction. Did he seem eager to do the packing?"

"He did, distinctly."

"Distinctly eager?"

"I recall he began as early, you see, as Saturday night and we left Tuesday morning."

"And did you have the feeling it was just a touch out of the ordinary? But at the time it didn't arouse enough interest on your part to have a question in your mind?"

"No, I would have expected it of other men, but this was the first I saw him taking that much interest."

"It did arrest your attention on that score, in any event?"

"Yes."

"Now, you were there for two full days and three evenings. Would you tell us, what did you do during these two days and three nights? When I say 'you,' I am including all three of you."

"Of course, afternoons we usually spent in rest for the children, having all small children, all of us having small children."

"Whenever this doesn't include Lee Harvey Oswald, would you be good enough to tell us?"

"When he was not present?"

"That is right."

"My recollection is that he was present most of the weekend. He went out to buy groceries, came in with a cheery call to his two girls, saying, '*Yabutchski*,' which means 'girls,' a Russian word for girls, as he came in the door. We went out to wash diapers at the local washateria, and stayed while they were done and went back."

"You and Lee?"

"I don't think that he went. My recollection is that Marina and I went."

"He remained home?"

"Yes."

"Did you visit with any of their in-laws?"

"No."

"Did they visit while you were there?"

"No."

"Did they come there?"

"No. I have already referred to a visit from Mrs. Kloepfer with her two girls, which must have been the day before we left, on Monday.

"No, Sunday—it must have been Sunday. It wasn't much time altogether, because Sunday was the day before we left."

"Is Mrs. Kloepfer a native American?"

"I have no idea. She speaks natively."

"But she does have a command of the Russian language?"

"Oh, no, no. Her daughter has had one year of Russian in college and was much too shy to begin to say anything, thoroughly overwhelmed by meeting someone who really spoke."

"Have you described for us generally the course of events in the two days and three nights you were there?"

"Well, much of the last portion, some of the last portion of Sunday was spent packing up. It was a very well-loaded automobile by then, because I already had a great many of my own, including a boat on the top of the car to which we attached the playpen, stroller and other things on top.

"We left on Monday morning, yes, Monday morning early, the twenty-third, and it seemed to me he was very sorry to see her go. They kissed goodbye, and we got in the car and I started down, intending really to go no farther than the first gas station because I had a soft rear tire, and I wasn't going to have a flat with this great pile of goods on top of not only my car but my spare, so I went down to the first gas station that was open a couple of blocks down and prepared to buy a tire.

"Lee, having watched us, walked down to the gas station and talked and visited while I arranged to have the tire changed, bought a new one and had it changed. I felt he wished or thought he should be offering something toward the cost of the tire.

"He said, 'That sure is going to cost a lot, isn't it?'

"And I said, 'Yes, but car owners have to expect that.'

"That is as close as he came to offering financial help. But it was at least a gesture."

"There was no financial help given you?"

"There was no financial help."

"Mrs. Paine, did he ever, during all of the period of your acquaintance with the Oswalds, ever offer any reimbursement financially or anything at all to you?"

"No, he never offered anything to me."

"Was there any discussion between you and him on the subject?"

"No. As close as we came to such discussion was saying that when they had enough money and perhaps after Christmas, they would get an apartment again, and I judged, felt that he was saving money towards renting a furnished apartment for his family."

"Did you have any feeling that he, in turn, felt that he might not be seeing Marina any more?"

"I had no feeling of that whatever."

"None whatsoever."

"He told me that he was going to try to look for work in Houston, and possibly in Philadelphia, were the two names he mentioned."

"We are interested in that, in this particular phase of the investigation. Did he make that statement in your presence, in the presence of Marina?"

"I don't recall."

"I take it that this was elicited by a discussion of the subject of his going to look for work after you girls had left, is that correct?"

"About what he would do after we left?"

"Yes."

"Yes."

"Now, would you repeat just what he said on that subject?"

"He told me that he was going to go to Houston to look for work, or possibly to Philadelphia."

"Did he say anything about having any acquaintances or friends in either of those towns?"

"He did. You recalled to my mind he said he had friends in Houston."

"Did he mention other towns he might undertake to visit?"

"No, he didn't, or any other friends."

"Was there any inference, or did you infer from anything he said, or might have been said in your presence, that after you girls left he intended to leave New Orleans? To look—"

"He was definitely planning to leave New Orleans after we left."

"Promptly?"

"Yes."

"You had that definite impression?"

"Yes."

"And he put it in terms of leaving New Orleans to go to Houston, or what was the other town?"

"Possibly Philadelphia."

"Possibly Philadelphia. Now, during all that weekend, was there any discussion of anybody going to Mexico?"

"No."

"Was the subject of Mexico discussed at any time, and in any respect?"

"Not at any time, nor any respect."

"On the trip back to Irving, Texas, did Marina say anything on the subject of Mexico?"

"No."

"Did you girls discuss what Lee was going to do during this interim period?"

"Only to the extent that he was looking for a job, but I think that discussion, my memory of it, comes from a discussion with Lee rather than a discussion with her.

"I may say that we never talked about any particular time he would see Marina again."

"You did not?"

"He kissed her a very fond goodbye, both at home and then again at the gas station, and I felt he cared and he would certainly see her. And this I recalled the other night. It should be put in here. As he was giving me this material I have already mentioned, that indicated his claim to one-year residence in Texas—I can't remember just what I said that elicited it from him—but some reference to, shall I say that you have gone? He said, 'Oh, no, that might appear that I had abandoned her.'

"And I was glad to hear him say that he didn't at all want it to appear, or to feel of himself, that he had abandoned her."

CHAPTER 18

THE PACKAGE IN THE GARAGE

Marina's emotions as she and Ruth Paine left New Orleans in the heavily loaded station wagon must have been mixed. Lee had told Ruth Paine that he was not abandoning Marina. He had mentioned to Marina the possibility that after he was established in Cuba he would send for her, and yet she never really knew what to think of his conduct. The night he went out to shoot General Walker he had, in effect, abandoned her. His farewell note indicated he knew there was a good chance he would be apprehended, perhaps even killed in a gun fight with the police, or executed for his crime. Then again and again he wanted to send her back to Russia with no promise of ever rejoining her. The prospect of being abandoned was nothing new to her. She had lived with the threat for months. Three times she had gone to live with others. She did not know whether he loved her or not. In her first appearance before the Commission she was very mild in her criticisms of Lee. She pictured him as an attentive and helpful husband. However, as the investigation proceeded and the magnitude of their domestic difficulties became obvious to investigators, she shifted her story. In her final appearance, one of the Commission members explored this question, perhaps with a touch of irony.

"I gather from your evidence, Mrs. Oswald, that Lee was a very devoted husband, unusually so for an American husband, even though you had little spats at times. Do you think that he advised you [to go back to the Soviet Union] because he thought something was going to happen that would involve the family in difficulties?"

On this occasion Marina told the truth.

"No."

"You don't think so."

"No, he was not a good husband. I may have said so in my deposition, but if I did, it was when I was in a state of shock."

"You not only said so in your deposition, Mrs. Oswald, but you testified in your testimony before the Commission several times that he was a very good husband, and he was very devoted to you, and that when he was at home and not employed that he did a great deal of the housework and in looking after the children."

"Well, I also testified to the fact that he beat me on many occasions, so some of the statements I made regarding him were good and some were bad."

"In other words, some of them were not true that you made?"

"No, everything was true."

"Everything was true?"

"Yes. I made statements in the record that he was good when he did housework and washed the floors and was good to the baby, and again he was not good when he beat me and was insolent."

"Did he beat you on many occasions?"

"Rather—many."

"Well, you only testified to one, did you not, before the Commission?"

"I was rather embarrassed to discuss this before the Commission, but he beat me on more than one occasion."

"And you stated at that time that you bruise very readily, and that's the reason you had such a bad black eye? Did you not testify to that?"

"Yes."

"Was that true or not true?"

"It is true—it is—whatever I said."

"It is true that you bruise easily, but that was just one of many occasions he had beat you?"

"On one occasion—yes."

"But you didn't testify to the others, did you?"

"I think I testified only about one particular occasion that I was asked about, whether he beat me or not, and I replied that he did, but he beat me on more than one occasion."

"Did he ever fail to provide for you and the children?"

"No. While he never earned too much, but when he had the job and earned, say, around two hundred dollars a month, we never had any particular need of anything. However, Lee was so frugal, not only frugal but he kept part of the money in his own possession all the time that was not available for the family."

"You always had plenty to eat and the children had plenty to wear?"

"Not really. We were never hungry, but we didn't have much. We were never too hungry, but we never had any plentitude. We never had too much, and I wanted—I always wanted this and that, but that was not available."

"But he never made a great deal of money, did he?"

"I marvel now how we managed to live on what he earned at that time. In comparison with what I have now. We spent twelve or fifteen dollars a week at that time—you know, we can live—that was for milk and so on."

"He didn't spend any money on himself, did he? He wasn't extravagant in his own habits? He didn't spend his money on clothes or whisky or women or things of that kind, did he?"

"Oh, no."

"Well, I mean just extravagance in his own habits. He was frugal in his own eating habits, he didn't eat much when he was away from home, did he?"

"No."

"Now, going back to your personal relations, Mrs. Oswald, with Lee. Do you think he wanted to send you back to Russia just to get rid of you?"

"This is the questions that I am puzzled about, and I am wondering about it myself, whether he wanted to get rid of me."

"Do you think he was really devoted to the children, or was he just putting on a show about liking the children?"

"Yes, he loved the children. I believe he loved the children, but at times—one side of his life was such that I wondered whether he did or not. Some of the things that he did certainly were not good for his children—some of the acts he was engaged in."

"He knew you would take the children back to Russia with you if you wanted, did he not?"

"Of course I would have taken the children with me to the Soviet Union."

"It seems to me that I recall once or twice in this testimony when you had had some little domestic trouble, as all married couples have, that he had cried, which is most unusual for a man in this country— men don't cry very often—and do you think that he cried despite

256

the fact that he wasn't very devoted to you and loved you a great deal?"

"That fact that he cried, and on one occasion he begged me to come back to him—he stood on his knees and begged me to come back to him—whether that meant that he loved me—perhaps he did. On the other hand, the acts that he committed showed to me that he didn't particularly care for me."

"You think then that his acts that he committed outside your domestic life within the family, within the realm of the family, was an indication that he did not love you?"

"The fact that he made attempts on the lives of other people showed to me that he did not treasure his family life and his children, also the fact that he beat me and wanted to send me to the Soviet Union."

"And you think that the fact that he promised you after the Walker incident that he would never do anything like that again, but did, is an indication that he didn't love you?"

"Logically—yes. That shows to me that he did not love me. At times he cried and did all sorts of helpful things around the house. At other times he was mean. Frankly, I am lost as to what to think about him. And I did not have any choice, because he was the only person that I knew and I could count on—the only person in the United States."

"Did he beat you very often, Mrs. Oswald, strike you hard blows with his fists? Did he hit you with his fists?"

"When he beat me, sometimes he would beat me hard and sometimes not too hard. Sometimes he would leave a black eye and sometimes he wouldn't, depending on which part of me he would strike me. When we lived in New Orleans he never beat me up."

"Did he ever beat you in Russia before you came to this country?"

"No."

"Did he ever beat you badly enough, Mrs. Oswald, for you to require the services of a doctor, a physician?"

"No."

"Did he ever strike you during your pregnancy, when you were pregnant?"

"Yes."

Translator: "She said, 'I think.' She said, 'I think.' "

"Yes, he did strike me."

"What reason did he give for striking you, usually?"

"Well, the reasons were if—they were very petty—I can't even remember what the reasons were after this quarrel was over. Sometimes he would tell me to shut up, and I don't take that from him. I'm not a very quiet woman myself."

"I'm not—what?"

"I'm not a quiet woman myself, and sometimes it gets on your nerves and you'll just tell him he's an idiot and he will become more angry with you.

"When I would call him an idiot, he would say, 'Well, I'll show you what kind of an idiot I am,' so he would beat me up."

"Did you ever strike him?"

"I would give him some in return."

"Did you ever strike him with anything other than your hand?"

"Well, I think at one time I told him that if he would beat me again I will hurl a radio, a transistor radio, and when he did strike me I threw the radio at him."

"You missed him?"

"No—it broke. I missed him."

"You missed him?"

"I tried not to hit him."

"Mrs. Oswald, during the course of your testimony, you testified that Lee often called you twice a day while he was working away from home. Why do you think he called you if he was not in love with you?"

"When he was away from me, he told me that he missed me."

"You don't think that's an indication that he loved you?"

"This shows—this would show that he loved me. He was a two—double—dual personality."

"Split personality."

"Dual personality."

"Split personality—that's it."

Although the Commission had been investigating the circumstances surrounding Lee Oswald's life for nearly ten months and Marina had testified twice before, it was not until three weeks before the final report was published that she spoke out in this fashion. The facts she then revealed were strong confirmation of statements made by other witnesses—namely, that their domestic life was chaos; that she wanted many things that Lee could not afford to give her; that she was perfectly capable of resorting to physical violence herself; and that, most of all, she frequently belittled him by calling him an idiot or some other stinging epithet.

With the revelation of these facts, beyond question the picture of Marina Oswald as a serene, demure young lady was bound to change, and the Commission gained deeper insight into the emotional stresses that beleaguered Lee Oswald. It is not difficult to see that in addition to his sense of personal failure, his inability to obtain prominent recognition he felt he had the genius to deserve, his marriage was likewise a failure. Although he might not have loved Marina in the unswerving fashion of a storybook romance, she was the only one who could partially console him for his failures. He wanted her admiration—and it may be that some of his audacious acts were partly motivated by a desire to prove to her that he really was important, strong and forceful. Even if Marina had been able to give him all her admiration, it would not have been enough. She was only a small consolation for his overwhelming desire for power and recognition. Perhaps it humiliated him even more deeply to think that Marina was not even his first choice. He had married her on the rebound from Ella. He had said proudly in his diary in the early days of their marriage, "She is madly in love with me from the very start." Well, it did not prove to be the kind of blind adoration he apparently expected. And it did not include respect when she ridiculed him in front of others. According to two witnesses, she even belittled his manliness.

The significance of the failure of his Cuban venture, therefore, becomes more instructive. Marina was not certain she would ever see Lee Oswald again as the station wagon lumbered through the outskirts of New Orleans, headed toward Irving, Texas. With the background of beatings and brawls she had experienced with Lee, it is possible she never wanted to see him again.

There could be no doubt in Marina's mind that Lee was a desperate man. He was capable of dreaming up most any "crazy" scheme. It was possible that he might still try to hijack a Mexican airplane or something equally as outlandish. If an adventure like that failed, as it probably would, he would be killed, along with perhaps a dozen other passengers in the plane. Or he might join some adventurous group and attempt to smuggle himself into Cuba and be shot by a firing squad. Marina said nothing of her apprehensions to Mrs. Paine. Mrs. Paine was under the impression that Lee was going to seek work in Philadelphia or Houston. But Marina knew that in the next two or three days Lee would be on his way to Mexico City. Would she ever hear from him again? Considering the terrible fifteen months she had been through since they had come to the United States, no one could be critical of her if she hoped not. Whatever contribution she had made to the failure of their marriage, she could not correct the imbalance of his ambitions. And how could she cope with his crazy obsession about guns?

In her final appearance before the Commission, her fears in regard to Lee's future conduct were explained.

"You stated that you first learned that he had the rifle early in 1963."

"In the year that he bought it, I learned it."

"You had seen him clean it, you had watched him sight the rifle in New Orleans and work the bolt?"

"In New Orleans?"

"Yes, in your testimony you said you saw him sitting on the little back porch—"

"On the little back porch—yes."

"And sight the rifle?"

"I'm sorry, I might be mixed up."

"When you testified that you believed he did some target practice at least a few times?"

"In New Orleans?"

"I don't know where."

"In Dallas or New Orleans? Yes—when we lived on Neely Street."

"He had told you that he had used this rifle to fire at General Walker?"

"Yes."

"Now, was it your opinion throughout these months that he was keeping this rifle for his purpose of using it again, firing at some individual, perhaps an official of the United States Government?"

"He never expressed himself.

"When the assassination of President Kennedy took place, I was asking people whether—people in general—whether General

Walker was with President Kennedy. It perhaps was a silly question, but I thought that he—"

"Listen to my question: During this time, didn't you have the opinion that he was keeping possession of this rifle and practicing with it for the purpose of using it to shoot at some individual, and perhaps an official of the United States Government?"

"I never thought—I was afraid to think that he would do anything like that until the shooting of General Walker occurred."

"But now my question: After that, the continued possession—"

"After the attempting of the killing of General Walker, I thought he might do it, but I didn't visualize that he could do anything like that."

"When you testified before the Commission you said—generally —you didn't think Lee would repeat anything like that—'Generally, I knew that the rifle was very tempting for him.' 'Very tempting for him'—what did you mean by that, about the rifle being very tempting for him? Did you believe he might be tempted to shoot at someone else?"

"Yes, I was afraid that he did have temptation to kill someone else."

"Mrs. Oswald, you testified that when you talked to Lee after he had shot at General Walker, or told you he had shot at General Walker, he said that it would have been well if someone had killed Hitler because many lives would be saved, is that correct?"

"Yes."

"After that, you testified that many times or a number of times he read you articles about President Kennedy?"

"Yes."

"And said at one time, discussing President Kennedy's father, that he had made his money through wine and he had a great deal of money, and that enabled him to educate his sons and to give them a start.

"I want you to remember and tell the Commission if he did ever express any hatred or dislike for President Kennedy. You have several times not changed but you have told the Commission things you did not tell them when first asked.

"Now, if he did speak to you about President Kennedy, we think you should tell the Commission."

"I don't think he ever expressed hatred toward President Kennedy, but perhaps he expressed jealousy, not only jealousy but—"

"Envy."

"Envy, but perhaps he envied, because he said, 'Whoever has money has it easy.' That was his general attitude. It was not a direct quotation."

"Pursuing this, I asked you that very question in Washington back in February, and the answer was 'No.' I asked you whether or not your husband ever expressed hostility toward President Kennedy. Is your answer still 'No'?"

"My answer is 'No.' "

"He never expressed himself anything against President Kennedy, anything detrimental toward him. What I told them generally before I am repeating now too."

"Did he ever indicate to you, except in the Walker situation where he said he'd shot at General Walker, that he would kill anyone?"

"No."

According to their testimony, neither Mrs. Paine nor Marina Oswald saw Lee load the rifle into the station wagon when he was so busily engaged in the packing. In view of her continued fears about Lee's use of the rifle, Marina may have been concerned whether he intended to take it with him to Mexico City or whether he had disposed of it. She knew he had kept it in a closet at their apartment in New Orleans on Magazine Street. She testified she did not see him load it, although there were a number of duffel bags and other packages into which it would have fitted.

Michael Paine, Ruth's estranged husband, came to the house in Irving, however, to help unload the station wagon. He recalled, "I don't remember whether the date was September. I remember that was the date they came back from New Orleans, and I do remember that my wife asked me to unpack some of their heavy things from their car."

"You must have moved the duffel bags from the station wagon into the garage."

"That is right. I unpacked whatever was remaining in the station wagon to the garage.

"So sometime later I do remember moving about this package which, let's say, was a rifle—anyway it was a package wrapped in a blanket. The garage was kind of crowded, and I did have my tools in there, and I had to move this package several times in order to make space to work, and the final time I put it on the floor underneath the saw where the bandsaw would be casting dust on it, and I was a little embarrassed to be putting his goods on the floor, but I didn't suppose, the first time I picked it up I thought it was camping equipment. I said to myself they don't make camping equipment of iron pipes any more."

"Why did you say that to yourself when you picked up the package?"

"I had, my experience had been, my earliest camping equipment had been a tent of iron pipes. This somehow reminded me of that. I felt a pipe with my right hand, and it was iron—that is to say it was not aluminum."

"How did you make that distinction?"

"By the weight of it, and by the I suppose the moment of inertia, you could have an aluminum tube with a total weight massed in the center somehow, but that would not have had the inertia this way."

"You were just feeling this through the blanket though?"

"I was also aware as I was moving his goods around of his rights to privacy. So I did not feel—I had to move this object. I wasn't thinking very much about it, but it happens that I did think a little bit about it, or before I got on to the working with my tools I thought, an image came to mind."

Michael Paine did not identify the object rolled in the blanket as a rifle; he thought of metal tent poles.

Although she had not seen it loaded, Marina was most definite in her belief that the rifle was transported back in the station wagon. She must have been relieved to know that Lee had not taken it with him to Mexico. Without it, a hijacking scheme, or the temptation to use the gun in some other violent action, was less likely to get him in trouble. She was asked about the rifle.

"Do you know whether or not the rifle was carried in the station wagon?"

"Yes, it was."

"Did you have anything to do with loading it in there?"

"No. Lee was loading everything on because I was pregnant at the time. But I know that Lee loaded the rifle on."

"Was the rifle carried in some kind of a case when you went back with Mrs. Paine?"

"After we arrived, I tried to put the bed, the child's crib together, the metallic parts, and I looked for a certain part, and I came upon something wrapped in a blanket. I thought that was part of the bed, but it turned out to be the rifle."

"Do you remember whether the pistol was carried back in Mrs. Paine's car, too?"

"I don't know where the pistol was."

Arriving back in Irving, Ruth Paine and Marina settled down to normal living. Although Marina knew the rifle was in the garage, she had no reason to dread the thing. It was the first time since the shooting of Walker that she could sleep soundly, safe in the knowledge that Lee wouldn't be using it. No doubt she still had some restless nights wondering if the police or the FBI wouldn't yet identify Lee as the would-be assassin of Walker. Only five and a half months had elapsed. An efficient police department would still be searching for clues. The thought often plagued her that Lee might again become obsessed with what he called Walker's "fascism." It was comforting to know he was far away from Dallas and the rifle well hidden in the garage. And it was a great relief not to be under the pressure of Lee's bad humors and carping. With a woman's sense of well-being at the prospect of bringing another child into the world, she was happy in Irving.

Why was Ruth Paine so kind to Marina? Everyone had been kind in Fort Worth and Dallas. It just seemed to be the American disposition. Ruth Paine would rush about the house being very energetic. They would converse back and forth in Russian, and actually Ruth's fluency was improving every day. Marina felt that the arrangement of her living with Ruth was going to work very well. She didn't feel entirely a charity ward because she was helping Ruth master Russian, and it would be costly for her to hire a tutor. It was a pleasant life—no violent arguments with anyone, no anxieties when the doorbell rang. And every day she was more and more aware of the new life stirring within her. Ten days or more and the baby would be born!

The morning of October 4 Ruth Paine went to the hospital and gave her blood. She came home feeling fine but a little weak.

Shortly after lunch the phone rang. It was Lee Oswald, and he was not in Mexico or Cuba. He was in Dallas!

CHAPTER 19

THE FRUSTRATED DEFECTOR

THE PROSPECT OF a quiet and untroubled future for Marina was dashed by the jangle of a telephone. Lee had left New Orleans on September 25. He arrived by bus in Mexico City two days later. Now it was October 4, and he was back again.

The chanting chorus of a Greek tragedy foretells the events which will envelop the heroes of a play. In the assassination of President Kennedy there were no prophets or seers who could warn the audience that a web of circumstances was evolving which would lead him to a rendezvous with death in Dallas. In retrospect, the unbelievable coincidences that took place just couldn't happen—and yet they did, with an inexorability that no playwright could expect an audience to believe. A hundred small events in the next fifty days could have happened differently, any one of which would have averted the killing. A split-second difference in the timing could have changed everything. But events moved relentlessly to their tragic culmination. As the Commission pieced together the events and scrutinized each scrap of evidence, every member had a feeling that somehow the story could be rewritten. Couldn't someone have shouted a warning? Couldn't someone have foreseen that this man was warped and twisted and that he was on the parade route aiming a high-powered rifle at the President? It was like living an experience backward. Why had fate been so cruel as not to have unmasked this man sooner as the would-be killer of General Walker? How could such a coincidence happen that he would get a job in a building whose sixth-floor window would make a perfect vantage point for murder? Why weren't there other people on that floor at the moment who would have thwarted his plan? Why, why, why! At each turn in the investigation Commission members hoped they could find some new fact that would turn the clock back, or at least make the sorrowful events meaningful. But there was no meaning beyond the will of the killer to pull a trigger. To be able to find evidence of a plot would have at least let people say, "Well, now I understand." It would take away some of the terrible sense of futility and bafflement. But after ten months of hard labor, it was not to be. There was no way of explaining the crime, except to spread the record out before the public and let it judge. Ruth Paine and Marina provided a large part of the information that led up to the moment of the shooting. Their testimony was checked in every conceivable way. Such coincidences simply could not happen. But they did.

Ruth Paine would not have been as surprised or troubled by Lee's return as Marina was. She knew nothing about the rifle in the garage; she knew little of Lee's erratic history; she had no idea he had gone to Mexico City in an effort to defect to Cuba. Houston, where Lee was supposed to be looking for work, is not so far from Dallas that Lee's reappearance would cause her any great surprise.

"Now, you and Marina arrived home on the twenty-fourth of September, with the packages and contents of the station wagon, and, save the duffel bags, they were moved into your home, and everybody settled down?"

"Yes."

"When next was there—did you hear from Lee Harvey Oswald at any time thereafter?"

"Not until the afternoon of the fourth, which I have already referred to."

"No word whatsoever from him from the twenty-fourth of September?"

"Twenty-third we left him in New Orleans."

"Twenty-third of September until the fourth of October?"

"That is correct—no word."

"Did you and Marina have discussions in that ten-day period about where Lee was or might be?"

"No."

"None whatsoever? Did you have any discussion about the fact that you hadn't heard from Lee Harvey Oswald in fourteen days or ten days?"

"No, we didn't."

"No discussion on that at all. What did you and Marina discuss during that ten-day period?"

"I can't recall which was during that period or which was after—general conversation."

"Was it generally small talk, ladies' talk about the house?"

"It was generally what my vocabulary permitted, and then she would reminisce, her vocabulary being much larger, about her life in Russia, about the movies she had seen. We talked about the children and their health, we talked about washing, about cooking."

"She expressed no concern during this ten-day period that no word had been heard from Lee?"

"No."

"Did she do or say anything during that period to indicate she did not expect to hear from him during that ten-day period?"

"No, she did not."

"Did it come to your mind that it was curious you hadn't heard from Lee Harvey Oswald for ten whole days?"

"No, it didn't seem curious. I know he had spent at least two weeks looking for work on previous occasions in different cities and I thought he wanted to find something before he communicated."

"But in view of the affection that had been evidenced on the day of departure on the twenty-fourth, you were not bothered by the fact that not even a telephone call had been received in ten days?"

"If he was not in town I wouldn't have at all expected a telephone call because that would have cost him dearly."

"He might have made it collect."

"I didn't expect that either."

"Was there any reference or discussion between you and Marina during that period of the possibility that he was off in Houston looking for work?"

"No, there was not."

"You are sure there was just no discussion of the subject at all during that whole ten-day period with Marina?"

"I don't recall any discussion of it."

"She expressed no concern and you none?"

"That is right."

From Marina's testimony it would appear she did not particularly expect to hear from Lee. In addition to what she told the Commission, the FBI reported that after the assassination, when she finally admitted to them she knew that Lee had gone to Mexico, she confessed she understood he planned to defect to Cuba. There might be months without hearing from him. One does not defect without a certain risk. He was determined to go there, and he might have to detour in some other fashion. And did she really care?

Ruth Paine continued her comments.

"You heard from him on the fourth of October?"

"Yes."

"Would you give the Commission the circumstances, the time of day and how it came about?"

"He telephoned in early afternoon, something after lunchtime."

"The phone rang. Did you answer it?"

"Yes."

"And did you recognize the voice?"

"He asked to speak to Marina."

"Whose voice was it?"

"Well, after he asked to speak to Marina, I was certain it was Lee's."

"What did you say?"

"I said 'Here' and gave her the phone."

"You didn't say 'Where are you?' or 'I am glad to hear from you, where have you been?'"

"No. I thought that was hers to ask. If he wished to speak to her and I gave her the phone and, of course, that is what was then asked. I heard her say to him—"

"You heard her side of the conversation, did you?"

"Yes."

"All right. What did you hear her say?"

"I heard her say 'No, Mrs. Paine, she can't come and pick you up.'"

"Was she speaking in Russian?"

"Yes."

"Throughout?"

"Yes."

"When Lee asked for Marina, did he speak in English or Russian?"

"I don't recall. And Marina went on to say, 'Ruth has just been to Parkland Hospital this morning to donate blood. She shouldn't be going driving now to pick you up.'"

"You are giving the conversation now of it that you heard?"

"Yes. Then I heard Marina say, 'Why didn't you call?' "

"You did hear her say that?"

"I believe so. I certainly remember her saying it afterward. She hung up and she explained the conversation to me."

"What did she say to you?"

"That he had asked for me to come in to downtown Dallas to pick him up and she said no, he should find his own way.

"Then she said that he had said that he was at the Y, staying at the Y, and had been in town a couple of days, to which she said, 'Why didn't you call right away?'

"Then he also asked whether he could come out—this was, of course, during the conversation—and she referred the question to me—could he come out for the weekend—and I said yes, he could."

"This was while she was still talking on the telephone?"

"Yes. Prior to his asking for a ride. So then they hung up and I went grocery shopping."

Ruth Paine did not indicate that Marina showed any elation in knowing Lee had returned from Mexico. She was blunt in telling him Ruth Paine would not come and chauffeur him to Irving. She told him to get out the best way he could. She let him know she was not happy he had been in Dallas a day or two without letting her know. Her reactions must have been deeply troubled. The past two weeks had been so free from worry. Now Lee was back again, and she would have to listen to all his troubles. Here was one more frustration, one more change of plans, one more rebuff Lee would undoubtedly blame someone else for. Now whose fault would this be? She had told him that if he succeeded in getting to Cuba she might join him after he was settled down. But now? Ruth Paine had made all the arrangements at the hospital. Everything was going fine. Well, Lee could just stay at the YMCA in Dallas or a rooming house. Marina intended to remain in Irving and have her baby as scheduled. The future would have to take care of itself.

Lee was now most anxious to see Marina. It was as Marina said: when he was with her, he didn't seem to care about her, but when he was away he needed her more than he realized. He hitchhiked his way to Irving in about an hour. Inasmuch as Ruth had already gone to the grocery store, we have no way of knowing how the first moments of reunion were.

Lee told Marina about the frustrations of his trip. He had been refused permission to enter Cuba by the authorities. He had taken all his clippings, membership cards and other evidence so laboriously created for the purpose in New Orleans to the Cuban Consulate and had been denied a visa.

Silvia Tirado de Duran—the Mexican employee at the Consulate—had tried to explain the regulations. Oswald could not be given permission to enter Cuba en route to Russia (which had been his strategy) until he had a Russian visa. He would have to go to the Russian Embassy first, and then when he had his authorization from them, they would consider a Cuban visa.

He was furious. He brandished his clippings from the New Orleans papers, shouted how he was a friend of Cuba, that he was former secretary of the Fair Play for Cuba Committee and deserved better treatment than this for his troubles. Hadn't he spent a night in jail in behalf of the cause? Hadn't he distributed handbills at his own expense? Here—here was the proof! What kind of treatment was this?

He became so agitated and red-faced that the female clerk felt it necessary to call the Consul himself. The Consul was obdurate. He repeated the regulations and told Oswald to go to the Russian Embassy. Oswald gave him a piece of his mind. They had strong words.

Oswald left in a fit of fury. Impossible idiots! Why were the true purposes of revolution always bogged down in bureaucratic red tape?

Oh, these words, words, words! They were so tedious to Marina. Hadn't she heard them a million times? How many hours had she listened to Lee rant and rave like this on other occasions? And everything had been so peaceful until that phone had rung.

Lee went on to tell her how he had gone to the Russian Embassy and asked for the visa he had applied for previously. He had made that application to Washington, but certainly they could clear it in Mexico City. It had been several months in process.

The Russian Embassy was polite but, like all bureaucracy, slow. They would make inquiries in Washington. Would he call back? Perhaps they would have an answer in a day or two.

At the end of the first day in Mexico City, Lee had accomplished nothing other than to antagonize the Cuban Consulate staff. He must have seen his dreams of joining the great Cuban Socialist experiment ebbing. Premier in twenty years? This was an unsatisfying start.

Blocked by bureaucracy—would this forever be his frustration?

The second day Oswald had no better luck. Permission had not come from Washington. He called the Russian Embassy again and again. No word.

Every day he called, and every day he got the same answer. Now he was told it might take three to four months to get the Russian visa. Four months! That was impossible. He had money enough for only a few more days, and since he could not speak more than ten words of Spanish, his chances of finding a job were nil. His tourist card was good for only fifteen days.

Marina testified that there were times when Lee Oswald's bravado would suddenly seem to collapse. He had broken down on at least one occasion and wept, saying he was lost. Whether these moods could be classified as "psychotic" and as a result of sudden conflict with reality in a world which was otherwise dreamlike to him, no one can say. He was not in his adult life observed by experts, and we have only the pattern of his erratic behavior from which to judge. Because we know, however, that Lee Oswald was inclined to resort to violent acts when he was thwarted, it is hard to believe that he accepted the fiasco of his Mexican trip without great inner turmoil. His was a grandiose dream. His hour of greatness was to have come when he had covered himself with glory in Cuba. He no doubt harbored visions of proving to Marina that he was indeed a great man. He had been cheerful and jovial as he helped Ruth Paine pack the station wagon—in an ebullient humor at the prospect of moving quickly to success. Didn't he see far ahead to the day when Cuba would survive a war of extinction between the two giant imperialistic powers, the USA and the USSR, and *he* somehow in the turmoil would gain leadership?

We have only Marina's meager testimony as to how he reacted to the collapse of this grand vision. She was not one to live in a world of speculations.

"Did you notice any change in your husband after this trip to Mexico?"

"In my opinion he was disappointed in not being able to get to Cuba, and he didn't have any great desire to do so any more because he had run into, as he himself said, into bureaucracy and red tape. And he changed for the better. He began to treat me better."

"Will you tell us how he treated you better?"

"He helped me more—although he always did help. Perhaps he was more attentive. Perhaps this was because he didn't live together with me, but stayed in Dallas. Perhaps also because we expected a child, and he was in a somewhat elated mood."

This was Marina's testimony when she made her first demure appearance before the Commission in Washington. The third time she appeared, and told more frank details of Oswald's brutality, she was not quizzed on this particular question. He couldn't have treated her better for long, because he visited her on only a few weekends before the assassination. The last visit was the night before the shooting.

In dealing with Lee Oswald on his return from Mexico, Marina was in the most secure position she had been in since coming to America. The magnanimity of both Ruth and Michael Paine was not likely to change, because it was a sincerely felt tenet of their Quaker faith. Marina was a person in need and they were glad to give generously. If she chose to keep Lee at arm's length, she could do so. She testified that she made it clear to Lee on his return from Mexico that he may as well stop pressuring her about going back to Russia. She was not going back.

This casually stated bit of testimony, plus her statement that she did not care to live with Lee at that time because of the coming of the baby, would seem to indicate that for the first time she was in a position to tell him a few things if she wanted to and make them stick.

Despite the fact that Marina said she had hoped the climate in Mexico would be beneficial to Lee's health, she could scarcely have felt pleased with the spending of money on a venture that proved a fiasco. Lee had left her no money—none, at least, that Ruth Paine knew about.

"Was there any discussion about the expense of making that trip?"

"Yes, but we always lived very modestly, and Lee always had some savings. Therefore, he had the money for it."

"Did he say how much it would cost?"

"He had a little over a hundred dollars, and he said that that would be sufficient."

It is hard to imagine an American girl being faced with the possibility of never seeing a husband again quietly accepting his departure without leaving a cent of cash, and at the same time knowing he had $100 or more. But as Peter Gregory observed later, "She had no choice."

Now she had a choice. She felt sure of Ruth Paine's friendship and protection.

"Did he talk about getting you a silver bracelet or any presents before he went?"

"It is perhaps more truth to say that he asked me what I would like, and I told him that I would like Mexican silver bracelets. But what he did buy me I didn't like at all. When he returned to Irving from Mexico City and I saw the bracelet, I was fairly sure that he had bought it in New Orleans and not in Mexico City, because I had seen bracelets like that for sale there. That is why I am not sure that the bracelet was purchased in Mexico.

"Lee had an identical bracelet which he had bought in either Dallas or New Orleans. It was a man's bracelet."

"The silver bracelet he gave you when he got back had your name on it, did it not?"

"Yes."

"Was it too small?"

"Yes, I was offended because it was too small, and he promised to exchange it. But, of course, I didn't want to hurt him, and I said, 'Thank you. The important thing is the thought, the attention.'"

"Did your husband stay with you at the Paines' after that first night when he returned from Mexico?"

"Yes, he stayed overnight there. And in the morning we took him to Dallas."

"And by 'we' who do you mean?"

"Ruth Paine, I and her children."

"Do you know what he did in Dallas then?"

"He intended to rent an apartment in the area of Oak Cliff and to look for work."

"Do you know whether he did that?"

"Yes, I know that he always tried to get some work. He was not lazy."

"Did he rent the apartment?"

"On the same day he rented a room, not an apartment, and he

telephoned me and told me about it."

"Did you discuss the plans for this room before you took him to Dallas?"

"No, I asked him where he would live, and he said it would be best if he rented a room. It would not be as expensive as an apartment."

"Do you know where your husband looked for work in Dallas at that time?"

"No. He tried to get any kind of work. He answered ads, newspaper ads."

"Did he have trouble finding work again?"

"Yes."

"How long after his return was it before he found a job?"

"Two to three weeks."

The job that this frustrated defector found was in the Texas School Book Depository. The date he began work was October 16, 1963.

CHAPTER 20

A JOB AT THE TEXAS SCHOOL BOOK DEPOSITORY

F EW QUESTIONS THE COMMISSION had to deal with in its ten months of investigation required more thorough inquiry than "How did Lee Oswald get his job at the Texas School Book Depository?" No schemer could have chosen a better place from which to commit the crime. If there was an assassination plot thought out by master minds, it was a place they might well have chosen for their trigger-man. Just at a point in the parade route where the motorcade would have to slow; just high enough above the street to make a perfect shot through a telescopic sight; even the sixth floor itself, piled high with cartons of books, made an ideal ambuscade for a gunman, and Lee Harvey Oswald was there at the right moment, rifle in hand. No writer of a TV suspense drama could have conceived a better setting. Creaking elevators, ceilings covered with grit and cobwebs, dusty windows that would screen the killer—it was simply too pat. It seemed as if there just *had* to be more to this story than had yet been revealed. It was a classical setting for a crime of this nature. Certainly one man, who according to public information was not noted for his intelligence, could not have planned and carried out this killing by himself. It just didn't seem possible.

There were dozens of twists one could readily give to this situation. Lee Oswald was a Marxist. He had defected to Russia and had lived there many months. Hadn't he been carefully trained for this purpose as part of a scheme to overthrow the Government? There must have been some sinister significance behind this act. It was also soon publicized that Oswald was active in a New Orleans movement of Fair Play for Cuba. Fidel Castro certainly had no love for Jack Kennedy. He had even given long harangues loaded with the threat that there were ways and means of dealing with the President of the United States. Then there was the theory that if there wasn't a plot from the Left there must have been a plot from the Right. Scarcely a day went by for a member of the Commission without finding a new theory in his mail. There were theories by detective-story writers, theories by amateur sleuths, theories from crackpots writing from asylums, theories from well-meaning housewives, theories from college professors and psychologists. The speculations on plots of all kinds would comprise a literature of itself that would have strained the combined imaginations of Wilkie Collins, A. Conan Doyle and Edgar Allan Poe. And why not? This was the most baffling real-life crime in history. No one of these theories could be taken lightly by the Commission, nor was it. But most of the speculations had to begin with the basic theory that Lee Oswald was a "plant" in the Texas School Book Depository.

One of the purposes this member of the Commission has had in writing this story has been to let the reader feel first hand the experiences that brought the Commissioners to their conclusions. It was not surprising to read that Europeans in particular discounted the conclusions of the Report and continued to believe in plot theories. This will probably go on through the ages, as it has in the case of other assassinations. But in the months the Commission spent endless hours listening to witnesses, reading depositions of hundreds of other witnesses, each member came to know the key witnesses—perhaps better in a sense than he would know a member of his own family. He came to know their strengths and foibles. He became a good judge of their accuracy and honesty. He learned detailed circumstances—some relevant, some irrelevant—about their lives and, through assessment of their characters, could give the proper weight to their testimony. The reader is now familiar with a number of the chief figures in the life of Lee Oswald. He has heard them speak, just as the Commissioners did. He has shared their experiences as revealed in the record. How did Lee Oswald really happen to be in that sixth-floor window the noon of November 22, 1963?

Mrs. Ruth Paine gave this simple and straightforward account. Ruth Paine was not only a reliable witness; she was a person with the kind of mind for details that proved a boon to the work of the Commission. Her memory was supplemented by a calendar pad she happened to keep, a date book she could not have falsified if she had wanted to. She knew details with a precision that no witness could have established.

Returning to Dallas after the reunion weekend in Irving, Lee Oswald rented a room at 621 Marsalis Street. He told Marina this would be less expensive than a room at the YMCA or an apartment. With Ruth Paine's and Marina's assent he would look for a job during the week and visit on the weekend. The extent to which this arrangement was a "separation" from Marina is indeterminate. She explained why she did not want to be with Lee on the eve of the baby's coming.

The Commission asked Mrs. Paine, "What discussion went on between you and Marina—that is, the subject matter with respect to his weekend visits?"

"She wanted to be certain it was all right for him to come out—you know, that it wasn't too much of an imposition on me. We got into the discussing his efforts to find a job. Then Monday, the fourteenth, as best as I recall, was the first time we talked about him, more than to say it was too bad he didn't find something. This is the—"

"During the course of the week was there discussion between you and Marina respecting Lee Oswald's attempt at employment?"

"No."

"Now, there came an occasion, did there not, that weekend or the following weekend, at which there was a discussion, at least by you, with some neighbors with respect to efforts to obtain employment for Lee Harvey Oswald?"

"As best I can reconstruct it this was, while having coffee at my immediate neighbor's, Mrs. Ed Roberts', and a lady present was Mrs. Bill Randle, and Lee had said over the weekend that he had gotten the last of the unemployment compensation checks that were due him and that it had been smaller than the others had been and disappointing in its smallness, and he looked very discouraged when he went to look for work."

"Did he say anything about amount?"

"No, he didn't. Just less."

"All right."

"And the subject of his looking for work and that he hadn't found work for a week came up while we were having coffee, the four young mothers at Mrs. Roberts' house, and Mrs. Randle mentioned that her younger brother, Wesley Frazier, thought they needed another person at the Texas School Book Depository, where Wesley worked.

"Marina then asked me, after we had gone home, asked me if I would call—"

"Was Marina present during this discussion?"

"Yes, Marina was present, yes, indeed."

"Did she understand the conversation?"

"It was a running translation, running faulty translation going on."

"You were translating for her?"

"I was acting as her translator. And then after we came home she asked me if I would call the School Book Depository to see if indeed there was the possibility of an opening, and at her request, and I did telephone—"

"Excuse me, please."

"Yes."

"While you were still in the Roberts' home was there any discussion at all of the subject mentioned by you or by Mrs. Randle or Mrs. Roberts or anyone else of calls to be made or that might be made to the Texas School Book Depository in this connection?"

"I don't recall this discussion. As I recall it was a suggestion made by Marina to me after we got home, but I may be wrong."

"But that is your best recollection that you are now testifying to?"

"Yes."

"Is that correct?"

"Yes."

"You reached home and Marina suggested that 'Would you please call the Texas School Depository?' "

"Yes."

"What did you do?"

"I looked up the number in the book and dialed it, was told I would need to speak to Mr. Truly, who was at the warehouse, the phone was taken to Mr. Truly, and I talked with him and said—"

"You mean the call was transferred by the operator?"

"To Mr. Truly, and I said I know of a young man whose wife was staying in my house, the wife was expecting a child, they already had a little girl, and he had been out of work for a while and was very interested in getting any employment and his name, and was there a possibility of an opening there, and Mr. Truly said he didn't know whether he had an opening, that the young man should apply himself in person."

"Which made sense."

"Made very good sense for a personnel man to say."

"Did you make more than one call to this Texas School Book Depository?"

"No."

"Only the one?"

"Only the one."

"What was the date of this call?"

"Reconstructing it, I believe it was October fourteenth."

"What day of the week is October fourteenth?"

"It is a Monday."

"Following that call and your talking with Mr. Truly, what did you do?"

"Began to get dinner. Then Lee called to the house."

"In the evening?"

"In the early evening."

"Did you talk with him?"

"Marina talked with him, then asked—then Marina asked me to tell Lee in English what had transpired regarding the possible job opening, and then I did say that there might be an opening in the School Book Depository, that Mr. Truly was the man to apply to. Shall I go on?"

"Yes."

"The next day—"

"Excuse me, I meant go on as far as the conversation was concerned."

"That is all there was."

"Mrs. Paine, I would like to return just for a moment to the conversation in the Roberts' home. Was any possible place of employment in addition to the Texas School Depository mentioned?"

"No."

"You have no recollection of any other suggestions as to possible places of employment?"

"I have no recollection of that."

Although from thorough investigation of Ruth Paine's background, including her parents, her youth, her college career, her

279

outside activities, the Commission believed her to be a completely trustworthy witness, the importance of the question justified cross-checking and verifying to the smallest detail. Mrs. Paine's mother in Pennsylvania came upon a letter she had received from Ruth about this time telling of Lee's job efforts. Ruth Paine volunteered the letter as evidence after her mother recalled receiving it. She explained, "It may be significant here to say, my letter to which I have already referred—"

"Commission Exhibit No. —"

"Four-two-five, which says, 'Lee Oswald is looking for work in Dallas,' does not give a time of day."

"What is the date of that letter?"

"October fourteenth, Monday."

"This is the letter to your mother?"

"But I don't normally write letters any time except when the children are asleep. They sometimes nap, but usually this is in the evening.

"If it were in the evening it means that he had gotten the suggestion as to a place to apply, but I didn't mention that. I only mentioned that he was looking and was discouraged.

"I bring this out simply to say that I had no real hopes that he would get a job at the School Book Depository.

"I didn't think it too likely that he would, but it was worth a try."

"Did you hear from him then either on the fourteenth or fifteenth in respect to his effort to obtaining employment at the Texas School Depository?"

"He called immediately on Tuesday, the fifteenth, after he had been accepted, and said he would start work the next day."

"When you say immediately, what time of day was that?"

"Midmorning, I would say, which was contrary to his usual practice of calling in the early evening."

"By the way, is the call from Dallas, Texas, to Irving a toll call?"

"No."

"What is its cost—ten cents?"

"I expect so."

"Did you answer the phone on the occasion he called?"

"Yes."

"What happened?"

"He asked for Marina."

"He said nothing to you about his success?"

"No."

"As soon as you answered he asked for Marina?"

"Yes."

"Did he identify himself?"

"No, but I am certain he knew that I knew who he was."

"You recognized his voice, did you?"

"Yes."

"You called her to the phone. Did you hear her end of the conversation?"

"Yes."

"What took place by way of conversation?"

"She said, 'Hurray, he has got a job.' Immediately telling me as she still talked to the telephone that he has been accepted for work at the School Book Depository and thanks to me and she said, 'We must thank Mrs. Randle.' "

"Did you return to the telephone and speak with him?"

"No."

Ruth Paine's account of how she helped Lee get the position at the Texas School Book Depository was verified by the witnesses concerned—Mr. Roy S. Truly, Mrs. Bill Randle, with whom her brother Wesley Frazier lived, and the other woman present at the coffee, the hostess, Mrs. Dorothy Roberts. Each of these persons in turn was extensively investigated for any motives he or she might have for altering the truth or covering up anything. They all proved to be loyal Americans whose normal pattern of life was like a typical housewife or businessman in the United States. To doubt their word would be like doubting the word of your well-known neighbor. It just doesn't happen in Texas, or Michigan, or Indiana, that three neighborhood housewives could be engaged in a plot to assassinate a President. Before the subject came up in the coffee-klatch, neither Lee nor Marina Oswald could have had any knowledge of an opening at that building, nor is there any possibility Lee placed himself there with a foreknowledge that a Presidential motorcade would pass by there. The dates of the plans being made in Washington, of the public announcements of the parade route, just don't check out with that possibility.

But there was another strange coincidence recalled by Mr. Roy

Truly that gave deeper irony to the fatal results of Lee's employment. Roy Truly recalled that when Lee came in to ask him for a job, Roy Truly had two possibilities in mind. One position he needed to fill was in a warehouse used for storage by the Book Depository firm that was some distance away from what eventually became the motorcade route. While talking to Lee he was considering the man's qualifications. Should he send him to the other warehouse or use him in the Book Depository itself as an order filler?

He was impressed with Lee's apparent earnestness and alert manner. He thought here was a man who appeared bright enough not to make mistakes on the order blanks. Roy Truly made his decision. He would use him at the main building. As Mrs. Paine reported, the next day Lee went to work. He also decided to change roominghouses, and, after inspecting a home at 1026 North Beckley Avenue in the Oak Cliff area, he advised the landlady he would take it.

He calmly informed the landlady that his name was "O. H. Lee." He had adopted another alias, and for what reason? No one will ever know the murky reasoning of Lee Oswald when he decided to hide behind another false name. At the time he did this, he had no idea that the FBI had reopened their file on him. He himself had requested an interview with an agent in New Orleans two months earlier, but he had no reason to believe they might follow him back to Texas. If the use of this fictitious name indicates that Lee was planning some other act of desperation, the specific scheme could not have been the assassination of President Kennedy by making use of the Texas School Book Depository. He had no knowledge on which to base that kind of scheme. Marina's version of how Lee got the job at the Depository did not vary from Ruth Paine's.

"We were due to receive unemployment compensation, but it was getting close to the end of his entitlement period, and we received one more check."

"Did you discuss with him possible places of employment after his return from Mexico?"

"No, that was his business. I couldn't help him in that. But to some extent I did help him find a job, because I was visiting Mrs. Paine's neighbors. There was a woman there who told me where he might find some work."

"And when was this?"

"I don't remember. If that is important, I can try and ascertain the date. But I think you probably know."

"Was it shortly before he obtained work?"

"As soon as we got the information, the next day he went there and he did get the job."

"And who was it that you got the information from?"

"It was the neighbor whose brother was employed by the School Book Depository. He said it seemed to him there was a vacancy there."

"What was his name?"

"I don't know."

"Mrs. Oswald, you told us about your knowledge about the trip to Mexico and said that you were under oath and were going to tell us all about what you knew.

"Did your husband ever ask you not to disclose what you knew about the Mexican trip?"

"Yes."

"And when was that?"

"Before he left. I had remained and he was supposed to leave on the next day, and he warned me not to tell anyone about it."

"After he returned to Dallas from his Mexico trip, did he say anything to you then about not telling he had been to Mexico?"

"Yes, he asked me whether I had told Ruth about it or anyone else, and I told him no, and he said that I should keep quiet about it."

"You said before that you learned about the Depository job at some neighbor's home. Is that right?"

"Yes."

"In whose home was that?"

"I don't know her last name. When you walk out of the Paine house, it is the first house to the right. I am trying to remember. Perhaps later I will."

"Was it the lady of that house who told you, or someone that was a guest there?"

"Perhaps you know the name."

"Do you know a Mr. Frazier that had a job at the Depository?"

"I didn't know his name. I knew that it was a young man. I don't think he was eighteen yet."

"And was he the brother of this friend who was at the neighbor's house?"

"Yes."

"And he was the one that your husband rode from Irving into Dallas from time to time to go to work, did he?"

"Yes, after Lee was already working this boy would bring Lee and take him back with him to Dallas."

"And when did he take him, ordinarily?"

"Eight o'clock in the morning."

"And did he take him on Monday morning?"

"Yes."

"Usually each week he would take him on Monday morning?"

"When Lee came for a weekend, yes."

"And then when did he bring him back from Dallas?"

"At five-thirty on Friday."

"Did Mrs. Paine have anything to do with your husband getting this job at the Depository?"

"She had no direct connection with it, but an indirect connection, of course. I lived with her and she talked to a neighbor and mentioned that Lee was out of work."

"Was it Mrs. Paine that found out about the job?"

"Yes."

"On the weekend before your husband got his job at the Depository, did he spend that with you at the Paines'?"

"Yes."

"Did he come home Friday or Saturday?"

"On a Friday."

"When he returned to Dallas on Monday, the fourteenth of October, did he tell you he was going to change his room?"

"No."

"Do you remember what your husband's pay was at the Depository?"

"It seems to me that it was also a dollar and twenty-five cents."

"About how much a month did it run?"

"It seems to me it was two hundred ten to two hundred thirty dollars."

"Do you recall the hours that he worked?"

"It seems that—it seems to me that it was from eight-thirty A.M. to five P.M."

"And did he work the weekend or any overtime?"

"No. It does happen in that Depository that they work overtime. But he did not have to work any."

"During the week when he was in Dallas and you were at Irving, did he call you from time to time?"

"Daily, twice."

"Did he leave his telephone number in Dallas with you?"

"Yes. I don't have it; it was in Paines' notebook."

Lee left the phone number of the Beckley Avenue house with Mrs. Paine so she might call if Marina went into labor. He did not tell Ruth or Marina the address of this house, nor did he instruct them to ask for "O. H. Lee" if they called. This was not like Lee to overlook a detail which could cause him embarrassment. It seems a possibility that his mind was muddled at this time. Certainly his sense of values was no less mixed up than it had been for many years. Why did he need an alias, or had his secret world become reality?

The following weekend Lee had reason to celebrate. Any ordinary person would have found the events of that weekend enough to make the outlook happy. He returned to Irving, hitchhiking a ride with his fellow employee, Wesley Frazier, whose sister had suggested the job. He had found steady work, and it was not the kind of job he disliked—work that was relatively interesting and clean.

That night, on Friday, October 18, he was twenty-four years old. Marina and Ruth had prepared a cake with birthday candles, and Michael Paine was on hand to share in the celebration. It was a pleasant occasion, and again with reasonable application and effort he could make something out of the opportunity Roy Truly had given him. For a person who seemed to have a great interest in learning and education, working in a building crammed with textbooks might have stimulated an ambitious man. Wasn't Lee ambitious? Indeed he was ambitious, but he was a great believer in short cuts. To be famous—that was his dream. And here he was twenty-four, with the bitter taste of his recent Mexican fiasco still rankling. Sometimes he appeared to be plagued with a desperate sense that time was running out on him. To anyone whose sense of values was near normal, prospects were not so dismal. He had a job. He could look forward to saving money and renting an apartment so that he and Marina could be reunited.

That Sunday night—the twentieth—two days after a happy birthday celebration, Marina knew her time had come. Mrs. Paine recalled the circumstances.

"He was at the house in Irving when labor began, and stayed at the house to take care of June and my two children, who were sleeping, while I took Marina to the hospital, since I was one who could drive."

"All right. The twentieth—when did you take her to the hospital?"

"Around nine o'clock in the evening."

"What day?"

"Sunday, the twentieth of October."

"And Lee Harvey Oswald was out there on that weekend on one of his regular visits?"

"Yes. The first one since he had employment.

"I took her to the hospital and then I returned. I didn't feel I could stay. I thought I should get back to my children."

"That was Sunday night?"

"Sunday night. He went to bed, put Junie to bed. I stayed up and waited what I considered a proper time and then called the hospital to hear what news there was. They had implied I could come and visit too, but that would have been incorrect, and learned that he had a baby girl. I then went to bed and told him in the morning."

"You did not awaken him then?"

"I did not waken him. I thought about it and I decided if he was not interested in being awake I would tell him in the morning."

"And the morning was Monday?"

"Yes."

"Having learned that he was the father of a baby girl, I assume you told him that?"

"Yes."

"Did he go to work that day?"

"Yes."

"Did he return to Irving that evening?"

"Yes. It was agreed when he left that he would return that evening."

"Did he visit Marina at the hospital that evening?"

"When he arrived it was not decided whether he would go to the hospital or not. He thought not, and I thought he should, and encouraged him to go."

"Why did he think he ought not to go?"

"I am uncertain about this. This thought crossed my mind that perhaps he thought they would find out he was working, but I had already told them he was working since I had been asked at the hospital when she was admitted, and I mentioned this, and it may have changed his mind about going, but this is conjecture on my part."

"In any event he did go?"

"He did go. It was a good thing, as he was the only one admitted. I was not either a father or grandmother, so I was not permitted to get in."

"I see. And you waited until his visit was over and returned home with him?"

"That is right."

"Did he return to work the next morning?"

"Yes, he did."

CHAPTER 21

WHAT THE FBI DIDN'T KNOW
ABOUT OSWALD

A MONTH BEFORE Lee Harvey Oswald killed President John F. Kennedy he became a father for the second time. Both Marina and Ruth Paine testified that he was most attentive and affectionate toward his first daughter, June. True, he had hoped for a son in Minsk and in his diary expressed disappointment, but there is no evidence that having another daughter disturbed him. He hadn't stayed awake that night to find out, so he couldn't have been too concerned. He did not object to having Ruth Paine take over the traditional role of a father rushing his wife to the hospital. It was the practical thing. She could drive a car. He could not. Had he had any real concern, he never would have left Marina in his effort to defect to Cuba. Although affectionate to children, he apparently had as little sense of obligation to his offspring as he did to society as a whole. He liked to play with children, but he didn't regard them as his first responsibility. Dreams of fame and political leadership were more important. It would be surprising if in his new identity as "O. H. Lee" he intended to give up the visions of greatness that plagued him.

Most accounts of Lee Oswald picture him as a drifter—a sometimes employed misfit who could not get or hold a job. This is an incorrect portrayal. From the time he returned to the United States, Oswald was employed much of the time. In Fort Worth he voluntarily left the Leslie Welding Company and yet found work in Dallas immediately. He lost two jobs by dismissal, but in the first case he was preoccupied with the mission of ridding the world of General Walker, and later, in New Orleans, in preparing for his defection to Cuba. He complained to all who would listen that in America one could not get or hold a job. He insisted the economic system gave him no chance for a future. At age twenty-four Lee Oswald had never tried to make anything of his opportunities.

One of the few skills Lee mastered was the art of deception. He gloried in the sense of power it gave him to know that he was misleading people. In all the literature of crime, however, it would be difficult to find an example of a mind more deceitful than that of Lee Harvey Oswald. He deceived almost everyone he came in contact with. He had no other power, and so he gloated over this hidden reserve. It was the source of his arrogance, the wellspring of his conceit.

One witness to Oswald's flight from the scene of the Officer Tippit murder thought he heard Oswald muttering, "Poor, dumb cop!" He had just taken a man's life in cold blood. This was Lee Oswald. His contempt was universal.

Therefore, in deceiving Ruth Paine and seeking to throw the FBI off the track, he was playing a game he exulted in. When he did these things, he had a sense of power in the face of his other frustrations. In the few weeks just prior to the assassination he skirted dangerously close to being unmasked. With his perverted sense of personal power, he may even have wanted it this way. The thought appears to have gathered force in his mind that he would show not only Marina but the whole world who Lee Oswald was. On two occasions he tipped his hand to Ruth Paine, but she was so unbelieving she didn't know what to do about it. Given a slightly stronger prod, she might well have called the FBI, and they in turn might have detected what an unbalanced and dangerous person he was.

Why was Lee Oswald working in the Texas School Book Depository? Because a neighbor told a neighbor and Roy Truly hired him. Why didn't the FBI regard Lee Oswald as a dangerous character and warn the Secret Service?

Incredible as it may seem, the FBI knew that Lee Oswald was an employee of the Texas School Book Depository three weeks before the assassination! Unbelievable as it is, they interviewed Ruth Paine on two occasions and spoke to Marina once within the month President Kennedy was shot!

The Commission carefully reconstructed the sequence and character of all interviews the FBI had with Lee Oswald, Marina and Ruth Paine. They ransacked the files of every agent having anything to do with Oswald. They checked witness upon witness and approached the question raised by Attorney General Carr, Hudkins, Feldman and others with a thoroughness beyond question. Members of the Commission investigated the grave question of whether Lee could be an agent of any United States Government department with an intensity of purpose that left no stone unturned. They looked into the allegations that he received money by Western Union in small payments and found there was no basis for the rumor. They scrutinized his income from all sources to ascertain if he lived within his means. No lead was ignored, no assertion belittled. What contacts did Lee Oswald have with the FBI? On his return from Russia he was checked out twice.

It was while Lee and Marina were living with Robert in the first month of their residence in Forth Worth that Lee was called to the office of the local agent as his brother Robert reported. This is the occasion Lee made fun of the FBI for asking him if he was an agent of any U.S. department. Investigation indicated the agent asked this question for one reason. In January 1961, as we have read, Marguerite made her trip to Washington, at which time she asserted that her son Lee really wasn't a bad boy who had defected. He was, she suspected, an agent. By her own testimony, the basis for this allegation was nothing but her own assumptions. She had said, "I have no proof. If I had proof I wouldn't be here."

On a previous occasion Marguerite had been interviewed as to why her son had defected. At that earlier date she made no mention of the "agent" angle, as she did when she visited Washington.

Again about two months after Oswald's return, while he was living on Mercedes Street and had a job at Leslie Welding, the same FBI agent, John W. Fain, dropped by his apartment to find out how Lee was settling down. This was the occasion Marina mentioned when Lee sat with the agent in the car in front of the house and she became angry because the dinner was spoiled while Lee and the agent talked.

The purposes of both these interviews were to determine whether Lee was cured of his admiration for the Soviets; whether he was now going to behave himself and settle down to normal living; whether he had been recruited by the Soviets to act in any capacity hostile to the United States; and generally to evaluate his loyalty. This was not long after the date Lee had written in his own memos that he thought the Soviet system was wrong, that he loathed Russian bureaucracy; therefore, with his skill in duplicity, it was not difficult for him to convince the FBI agent that he was through sowing wild oats and intended to settle down to respectable living.

This particular agent was about to retire from government service, and he had to make the decision whether to close Lee Oswald's file or hand it on to his successor. He was persuaded Lee meant what he said. He decided to close the file. There were no more interviews of Lee Oswald in this phase of his Dallas–Fort Worth residence.

Had the FBI continued its surveillance of Lee Oswald during this period, what difference might it have made? They could have known all along that he continued to subscribe to Communist literature and that he took it to work with him at the Jaggars-Chiles-Stovall plant. Had they chosen from the start to recruit the confidence of his landlords they might well have found out much sooner that Lee behaved violently toward Marina. Only an intensive search would have revealed his use of an alias through his postal box, and the question of whether they would have been alerted to his purchase of a rifle and a revolver from mail-order houses is moot. An experienced investigator knows that these things can be found out, but he would also know the almost prohibitive cost in time and money. Raising these questions in hindsight is only productive of bringing to the attention of experts what they already know. Unless one has a police state with informants everywhere, there is a point where common sense has to govern. Did the agent in this case reach that point of common sense? This is for public opinion to decide. The Commission had mixed feelings on this question. It is certain that defectors in the future will be watched more closely.

The next interview Oswald had with the FBI was at his own request in New Orleans. Circumstances indicate he called the FBI in in an effort to dramatize his Fair Play for Cuba activity and to make it look official to Castro's agents that he was a bona-fide friend of Fidel's. Carlos Bringuier testified that Lee crossed his hands in front of himself, hoping Bringuier would strike him and help him appear as a martyr. It would seem that in the same sense Oswald sought to be persecuted by the FBI. However, at that time, Lee didn't care if he burned his bridges. He had made up his mind to leave America and the FBI behind. When he was balked in his attempts in Mexico City, however, he had no alternative but to come back to the United States. The FBI picked up his trail a few weeks later.

From the information they had now gathered through the New Orleans episode, and the CIA report of Oswald's contacts with the Soviet Embassy in Mexico City, the FBI renewed its interest in Lee

Oswald. How they contacted Mrs. Paine was described in her own words:

"The first visit [November 1] I understood to be a visit to convey to Marina that if any blackmail pressure was being put upon her because of relatives back home that she was invited, if she wished, to talk about this to the FBI."

"The first visit was a rather lengthy one?"

"It was, as Mr. Hosty described to me later, and I think the impression at the time, an informal opening for confidence. He presented himself. He talked. We conversed about the weather, about Texas, about the end of the last world war and changes in Germany at the time.

"He mentioned that the FBI is very careful in their investigations not to bring anyone they suspect in public light until they have evidence to convict him in a proper court of law, that they did not convict by hearsay or public accusation.

"He asked first of all if I knew did Lee live there, and I said 'No.' Did I know where he lived? No, I didn't, but that it was in Dallas.

"Did I know where he worked? Yes, I did.

"And I said I thought Lee was very worried about losing this job, and the agent said that, well, it wasn't their custom to approach the employer directly. I said that Lee would be there on the weekend, so far as I knew, that he could be seen then, if he was interested in talking to Lee.

"I should perhaps put in here that Lee told me, and I only reconstructed this a few weeks ago, that he went, after I gave him—from the first visit of the FBI agent I took down the agent's name and the number that is in the telephone book to call the FBI, and I gave this to Lee the weekend he came."

"You gave it to Lee?"

"I gave it to Lee."

"What weekend was that?"

"I am told that they came out on the first of November, so that would have been the weekend of the second, the next day. I don't recall anything Lee said. I will go on as to the recollections that came later. He told me that he had stopped at the downtown office of the FBI and tried to see the agents and left a note. And my impression of it is that this notice irritated."

"Irritating?"

"Irritated, that he left the note saying what he thought. This is reconstructing my impression of the fellow's bothering him and his family, and this is my impression then. I couldn't say this was specifically said to him later."

"You mean he was irritated?"

"He was irritated, and he said, 'They are trying to inhibit my activities,' and I said, 'You passed your pamphlets' and could well have gone on to say what I thought, but I don't believe I did go on to say that he could and should expect the FBI to be interested in him.

"He had gone to the Soviet Union, intended to become a citizen there, and come back. He had just better adjust himself to being of interest to them for years to come."

"What did he say to that?"

"Now as I say, this I didn't go on to say. This was my feeling. I didn't actually go on to say this. I did say, 'Don't be inhibited, do what you think you should.' But I was thinking in terms of passing pamphlets or expressing a belief in Fidel Castro, if that is why he had. I defend his right to express such a belief. I felt the FBI would too, that he had no reason to be irritated. But then that was my interpretation."

"Have you given all of what he said and what you said, however, on that occasion?"

"Yes. I will just go on to say that I learned only a few weeks ago that he never did go into the FBI office. Of course knowing, thinking that he had gone in, I thought that was sensible on his part. But it appears to have been another lie."

Marina's independent account of the FBI interviews was in substantial agreement with Ruth Paine's.

Note that neither Ruth Paine nor Marina knew Lee Oswald's roominghouse address in Dallas. They gave the agents his place of work as the Texas School Book Depository. Figuring prominently in all the "plot" theories is much speculation as to why Lee Oswald had FBI agent Hosty's phone number, office address and license number. Marina herself copied Hosty's license number at Oswald's request. There is no mystery about it. Although the FBI made these two calls, they did not contact Lee himself after his return from Mexico or just prior to the assassination. With his typical cunning he may have slowed them down by expressing indignation over his privacy being invaded.

Addressing Marina Oswald, the Commission asked, "Do you recall that you did have such an interview at Mrs. Paine's house when she acted as interpreter on November 1, 1963?"

"Yes."

"Were you present on November 5, 1963, when FBI agents Hosty and Wilson interviewed Mrs. Paine at her home?"

"I was in my room at that time busy with little Rachel, and I heard voices which I thought were voices of the FBI. I came out of the room and they were in a hurry to leave. They did not talk to me at that time, other than just a greeting."

"Do you know whether or not they had been talking to Mrs. Paine about you or your husband?"

"Yes. She told me about it, but I was not especially interested. She does not interpret quite exactly. She is hard to understand. But she told me that in general terms."

"You have told us about the fact that you got the telephone number of the FBI agent and gave it to your husband. Was that the November first interview when that happened?"

"Yes."

"I will hand you Exhibit eighteen and ask you if you can identify that for us, and tell us what it is."

"Lee's notebook."

"Is your handwriting in that Exhibit eighteen?"

"It must be, yes, I will find mine. There are many different handwritings in here. Different people have written in this notebook. Sometimes Russian friends in Russia would note their address in this notebook.

"This is mine."

"Will you tell us—is it a long notation by you?"

"No. That is my aunt's address when Lee would remain in Minsk while I went on vacation."

"Is much of that notebook, Exhibit eighteen, in your husband's handwriting?"

"The majority, mostly."

"Except for the page with your handwriting on it and the notations of other friends that you referred to, is it generally in your husband's handwriting?"

"I can tell exactly which is noted down by Lee and which is noted down by others."

294

"And it is a regular notebook that he kept for all types of notes?"

"This is from Russia."

"He started it in Russia?"

"Yes."

"And there are a number of notations that were made after you returned to this country, is that right?"

"Yes."

"I ask you if you recognize the handwriting there, where it refers to agent Hosty."

"Lee wrote that. And this is the license number."

"And the telephone number? The license number, the name and the telephone number are all in your husband's—"

"The date when he visited him, FBI agent, telephone, name, license number and probably the address."

"Are all in your husband's handwriting?"

"Yes."

"Do you know when they were entered in that notebook, Exhibit eighteen?"

"After the first visit."

"Did you note the notation 'November 1' on that page?"

"Yes."

"You think that is about the date of the first visit, then?"

"Yes."

"Now, did you report to your husband the fact of this visit November 1 with the FBI agent?"

"I didn't report it to him at once, but as soon as he came for a weekend I told him about it. By the way, on that day he was due to arrive."

"That is on November 1?"

"Yes. Lee comes off work at five-thirty—comes from work at five-thirty. They left at five o'clock, and we told them if they wanted to they could wait and Lee would be here soon. But they didn't want to wait."

"And by 'they' who do you mean? Do you recall the name of the other man beside agent Hosty?"

"There was only one man during the first visit. I don't remember his name. This was probably the date because there is his name and the date."

"Now, what did you tell your husband about this visit by the FBI agent and the interview?"

"I told him that they had come, that they were interested in where he was working and where he lived, and he was, again, upset.

"He said that he would telephone them—I don't know whether he called or not—or that he would visit them."

"Is that all you told him at that time about the interview?"

"No, I told him about the content of the interview, but now I don't remember."

"Do you remember anything else that happened in the interview that you could tell the Commission at this time?"

"I told you that I had told them that I didn't want them to visit us, because we wanted to live peacefully and that this was disturbing to us."

"Was there anything else?"

"There was more, but I don't remember now."

"Now, during this period of time—"

"Excuse me. He said that he knew that Lee had been engaged in passing out leaflets for the Committee for Cuba, and he asked whether Lee was doing that here."

"Did you answer that question?"

"Yes.

"I said that Lee does not engage in such activities here. This was not like an interview. It was simply a conversation. We talked about even some trifles that had no relationship to politics."

"Do you know whether or not your husband had any interviews or conversations with the FBI during this period?"

"I know of two visits to the home of Ruth Paine, and I saw them each time. But I don't know of any interviews with Lee. Lee had told me that supposedly he had visited their office or their building. But I didn't believe him. I thought that he was a brave rabbit."

The Commission investigated the supposed contacts the FBI were rumored to have had with Lee Oswald other than those reported by Ruth and Marina. There were none. FBI inquiries took the normal pace of field investigations in which no great need for urgency was involved. In looking back it is easy to say that the most pressing degree of speed was demanded. This is like saying to someone, "Jump!" after a lightning bolt has struck. The FBI's interest in Lee Oswald at this point was based primarily on his activities with the

Fair Play for Cuba Committee and his trip to Mexico. Anyone with a total knowledge of Lee's character might well have seen him as a potential assassin of President Kennedy, but the FBI did not have a total picture, nor did anyone else.

A puzzling thing happened to Ruth Paine a week after the FBI's last visit. As usual, Lee came to Irving, riding home with Wesley Frazier. This was the weekend of November 9-10. Ruth Paine, in her months of exposure to Lee Oswald, was not entirely unmindful that his conduct was erratic. The fact is, however, that until he returned to Dallas after his supposed job-hunting absence in Houston she had never seen a great deal of him. She thought she knew Marina well. They had lived together for three weeks prior to the departure for New Orleans and now seven weeks since the return. But Lee? It was really only a matter of a few days on visits and weekends that she had been in close contact with him. She had once or twice discussed with Michael whether Lee could be dangerous. They had both discounted it. On one occasion she testified that she had a distinctly uneasy feeling about Oswald. It was when he had said he had a "contact" in Houston who might help him find work.

"You wondered at the time?"

"I wondered to myself if there was one."

"What made you wonder?"

"I may say also I wondered, as I already have indicated for the Commission, I had wondered from time to time whether this was a man who was working as a spy, or in any way a threat to the nation, and I thought, 'This is the first I have heard anything about a contact. I am interested to know if this is a real thing or something unreal.' And waited to see really whether I would learn any more about it. But this thought crossed my mind."

On that occasion she learned nothing more, but less than two weeks before the assassination Lee gave her cause to be deeply concerned. Suddenly she discovered that Lee was either a preposterous liar or out of his mind. In her own words, this is what happened:

"This was on the morning of November ninth, Saturday. He asked to use my typewriter, and I said he might."

"Excuse me. Would you please state to the Commission why you are reasonably firm that it was the morning of November ninth? What arrests your attention to that particular date?"

"Because I remember the weekend that this note or rough draft remained on my secretary desk. He spent the weekend on it."

"All right, go ahead."

"He was using the typewriter. I came and put June in her high chair near him at the table where he was typing, and he moved something over what he was typing from, which aroused my curiosity."

"Why did that arouse your curiosity?"

"It appeared he didn't want me to see what he was writing or to whom he was writing. I didn't know why he had covered it. If I had peered around him, I could have looked at the typewriter and the page in it, but I didn't."

"But it did make you curious?"

"It did make me curious.

"Then later that day I noticed a scrawling handwriting on a piece of paper on the corner at the top of my secretary desk in the living room. It remained there.

"Sunday morning I was the first one up. I took a closer look at this, a sheet of paper folded at the middle. The first sentence arrested me because I knew it to be false. It said, 'The FBI is not now interested in my activities.' "

"Is that what arrested your attention?"

"Yes."

"What did you do?"

"I then proceeded to read the whole note, wondering, knowing this to be false, wondering why he was saying it. I was irritated to have him writing a falsehood on my typewriter, I may say, too. I felt I had some cause to look at it."

The rough draft of the letter which Mrs. Paine found was slightly different from the final version he mailed. However, in substance the draft Mrs. Paine found said the same things he wrote in the version received by the Soviet Embassy. It read:

"DEAR SIRS;

"This is to inform you of recent events since my meetings with comrade Kostin in the Embassy of the Soviet Union, Mexico City, Mexico.

"I was unable to remain in Mexico indefinitely because of my mexican visa restrictions which was for 15 days only. I could not take a chance on requesting a new visa unless I used my real name, so I returned to the United States.

"I had not planned to contact the Soviet embassy in Mexico so they were unprepared, had I been able to reach the Soviet Embassy in Havana as planned, the embassy there would have had time to complete our business.

"Of course the Soviet embassy was not at fault, they were, as I say unprepared, the Cuban consulate was guilty of a gross breach of regulations, I am glad he has since been replaced.

"The Federal Bureau of Investigation is not now interested in my activities in the progressive organization 'Fair Play for Cuba Committee', of which I was secretary in New Orleans (state Louisiana) since I no longer reside in that state. However, the F.B.I. has visited us here in Dallas, Texas, on November 1st. Agent James P. Hosty warned me that if I engaged in F.P.C.C. activities in Texas the F.B.I. will again take an 'interrest' in me.

"This agent also 'suggested' to Marina Nichilayeva that she could remain in the United States under F.B.I. 'protection', that is, she could defect from the Soviet Union, of course, I and my wife strongly protested these tactics by the notorious F.B.I.

"Please inform us of the arrival of our Soviet entrance visa's as soon as they come.

"Also, this is to inform you of the birth on October 20, 1963 of a DAUGHTER, AUDREY MARINA OSWALD in DALLAS, TEXAS, to my wife."

"Now I would like to ask you a few questions about your reaction to that. You have read that in the quiet of your living room on Sunday morning, the tenth of November."

"That is correct."

"And there were a number of things in that you thought were untrue."

"Several things I knew to be untrue."

"You knew to be untrue. Were there things in there that alarmed you?"

"Yes, I would say so."

"What were they?"

"To me this—well, I read it and decided to make a copy."

"Would having the document back before you help you?"

"No, no. I was just trying to think what to say first. I decided that I should have such copy to give to an FBI agent coming again, or to call. I was undecided what to do. Meantime I made a copy."

"But you did have the instinct to report this to the FBI?"

"Yes."

"And you made a copy of the document?"

"And I made a copy of the document. And after having made it, while the shower was running—I am not used to subterfuge in any way, but then I put it back where it had been and it lay the rest of Sunday on my desk top, and of course I observed that too."

"That is that Lee didn't put it away, just left it out in the room?"

"That he didn't put it away or didn't seem to care or notice or didn't recall that he had a rough draft lying around. I observed it was untrue that the FBI was no longer interested in him. I observed it was untrue that the FBI came—"

"Why did you observe that that was untrue?"

"Well, the FBI came and they asked me.

"I want to return now to the fact that I had seen these gross falsehoods and strong words, concluding with 'notorious FBI' in this letter, and go on to say I wondered whether any of it was true, including the reference to going to Mexico, including the reference to using a false name, and I still wonder if that was true or false that he used an assumed name, though I no longer wonder whether he had actually gone."

"There was a subsequent incident in which you did learn that he used an assumed name, was there not?"

"Yes, a week later."

"We will get to that in a moment. But was this—"

"But this was the first indication I had that this man was a good deal queerer than I thought, and it didn't tell me—perhaps it should have—but it didn't tell me just what sort of a queer he was. He addressed it 'Dear Sirs.' It looked to me like someone trying to make an impression, and choosing the words he thought were best to make that impression, even including an assumed name as a possible attempt to make an impression on someone that he was able to do espionage, but not to my mind necessarily a picture of someone who was doing espionage, though I left that open as a possibility, and thought 'Give it to the FBI and let them conclude or add it to what they know.'

"I regret, and I would like to put this on the record, particularly two things in my own actions prior to the time of the assassination.

"One, that I didn't make the connection between this phone number that I had of where he lived, and that of course this would produce for the FBI agent who was asking the address of where he lived."

"I will get to that, Mrs. Paine."

"Well, that is regret one. But then of course you see in light of the events that followed it is a pity that I didn't go directly instead of waiting for the next visit, because the next visit was the twenty-third of November."

"Now I am going to get to that. What did you do with your copy of the letter?"

"I put my copy of the letter away in an envelope in my desk. I then, Sunday evening, also took the original. I decided to do that Sunday evening."

"He had left?"

"No, he had not left."

"He had not left?"

"I asked the gentlemen present—it included Michael—to come in and help me move the furniture around. I walked in and saw the letter was still there and plunked it into my desk. We then moved all the furniture."

"When did you take it out of the desk?"

"I don't think he knew that I took it. Oh, that evening or the next morning, I don't recall."

"And this was the tenth of November?"

"Yes."

"Did you ever have any conversation with him about that?"

"No. I came close to it. I was disturbed about it. I didn't go to sleep right away. He was sitting up watching the late spy story, if you will, on the TV, and I got up and sat there on the sofa with him thinking, 'I can't speak,' wanting to confront him with this and say, 'What is this?' But on the other hand I was somewhat fearful, and I didn't know what to do."

"Fearful in what way?"

"Well, if he was an agent, I would rather just give it to the FBI, not to say 'Look, I am watching you' by saying, 'What is this I find on my desk?' "

"Were you fearful of any physical harm?"

"No, I was not."

"That is what I was concerned about."

"No, I was not, though I don't think I defined my fears. I laid down and said I couldn't sleep, and he said, 'I guess you are real upset about going to the lawyer tomorrow.'

"He knew I had an appointment with my lawyer to discuss the possibility of a divorce the next day, and that didn't happen to be what was keeping me up that night, but I was indeed upset about the idea, and it was thoughtful for him to think of it. But I let it rest there, and we watched the story which he was interested in watching. And then I excused myself and went to bed."

"What did you do ultimately with your draft of the letter and the original?"

"The first appearance of an FBI person on the twenty-third of November, I gave the original to them. The next day it probably was, I said I also had a copy and gave them that. I wanted to be shut of it."

"So I take it, Mrs. Paine, you did not deliver either the original or the copy, or call attention to the original or the copy with respect to the FBI."

"Prior."

"Prior to the twenty-third, did you say?"

"That is right."

"And what led you to hold onto this rather provocative document?"

"It is a rather provocative document. It provoked my doubts about this fellow's normalcy more than it provoked thoughts that this was the talk of an agent reporting in. But I wasn't sure.

"I of course made no—I didn't know him to be a violent person, had no thought that he had this trait, possibility in him, absolutely no connection with the President's coming. If I had, hindsight is so much better, I would certainly have called the FBI's attention to it. Supposing that I had."

"If the FBI had returned, Mrs. Paine, as you indicated during the course of your meeting with the FBI, November first, would you have disclosed this document to the FBI?"

"Oh, I certainly think so. This was not something I was at all comfortable in having even."

"Were you expecting the FBI to return?"

"I did expect them to come back."

CHAPTER 22

MR. O. H. LEE

Ruth Paine might have told the FBI about this strange letter. She didn't.

The FBI might have made another call on her in regard to Lee's address. They didn't.

Marina might have told Mrs. Paine the truth about Lee's trip to Mexico and many other alarming things she knew about her husband. She didn't.

On September 26, 1963, the Dallas *Morning News* had reported that President John F. Kennedy was planning to make a trip to Texas November 21 or 22. The day that report was published, Lee Oswald was traveling southward on a bus to Mexico City. He intended to defect to Cuba. Not until November 8, however, did the Dallas *Times Herald* confirm that Dallas was definitely to be included in the President's itinerary. Lee Oswald had been employed at the Texas School Book Depository since October 16. He wrote in his unusual letter November 9 that he hoped the Russian Embassy would forward both his and Marina's visas promptly. The motorcade route was announced in the local papers November 19, the earliest date Lee could have been sure the President's car would pass the Depository. But fate put him in the right place at the right time to play his black role.

And where were some of the other important figures who were so soon to be sucked into the vortex of events, their lives mercilessly caught up in a grievous destiny? Lee's brother, Robert Oswald, was plugging away at his job with the Acme Brick Company. He had not seen Lee in nearly a year since their Thanksgiving reunion of

1962. He knew nothing of his brother's strange conduct: his trip to Mexico, his Fair Play for Cuba activities, Lee's and Marina's domestic problems. He had only the impressions of Lee from their brief contacts more than a year ago and their companionship as children. Where was Lee's mother, Marguerite—out of the scene since Lee left Dallas? Trying to keep body and soul together working as a practical nurse: she struggled for survival and it was not an easy life.

By strange coincidence, when Thomas Wolfe wrote of Destiny he thought of Texas. He said, "Each of us is all the sums he has not counted: subtract us into nakedness and night again, and you shall see begin in Crete four thousand years ago the love that ended yesterday in Texas.

"The seed of our destruction will blossom in the desert, the alexin of our cure grows by a mountain rock . . . Each moment is the fruit of forty thousand years. The minute-winning days like flies buzz home to death, and every moment is a window on all time."

Prophetically, Thomas Wolfe might have written those lines for these impending moments.

"I wonder what would happen if somebody was to stand up and say he was utterly opposed not only to governments, but to the people, to the entire land and complete foundations of his society," Lee had once written.

Was it now that he was going to find out from first-hand experience?

The last full weekend Lee spent with Marina and Ruth Paine in Irving was the weekend of November 10. On Saturday, in addition to writing the letter to the Soviet Embassy, he went to the driver's-license bureau hoping to get a learner's permit. Ruth Paine had been encouraging him to learn to drive because she thought it was essential to his eventually getting a better job. She had given him several lessons since he returned from Mexico, and he was making good headway. It seems unusual that in view of the fact that Lee Oswald had a keen intelligence when he wanted to use it he had never learned the simple skill of driving a car. Perhaps that was one small thing in itself which had added to his sense of isolation. He had always been dependent on buses or hitching rides with others. As it turned out, however, Saturday was election day in Dallas and the license bureau was closed.

Monday, November 11, was Veterans Day and a holiday for Lee. He spent the day around the house and yard, apparently happy. He might have gone to the garage, where the rifle lay in the blanket. From time to time he went out there to check his possessions which were stored there while they were not needed. Despite rumors that Lee practiced at a shooting range that weekend, the Commission concluded that the circumstances were unlikely and that witnesses must have confused pictures of him they saw later with another person. There were a number of cases of mistaken identity that turned up in the course of the investigation. But Lee had practiced before, according to Marina—in a wooded area near Love Field and on the back porch in New Orleans. He had proven he was an adequate shot when he came within hairs of killing General Walker.

On Tuesday morning, November 12, Lee went back to his job and his roominghouse on Beckley Avenue in Dallas.

What were the relationships between Lee and Marina at this time? She testified they had improved. Hadn't they improved really because their affairs were in a state of suspension? Lee's letter would indicate he was still interested in Marina's visa to return to Russia although she had told him emphatically she would not go back. Ruth Paine was thinking of starting legal proceedings for a divorce so that she would be permanently living alone. She had told Marina more than once that she was welcome to live with her as long as it required for Marina to learn English and become self-sufficient. One gets the feeling that Lee was being held on a probation basis by Marina, which wouldn't be unreasonable on her part. Whatever other faults she might have had, she had been through some terrible experiences with this man. Although he denied to Ruth Paine he intended to desert her, he had on many occasions tried to drive her back to Russia. A renewed life with Lee, if it was going to involve more beatings, more threats, more lunatic escapades, wasn't something she would look forward to. During her pregnancy and early weeks of recovery (the baby was now three weeks old) she would naturally hold Lee at arm's length. Until he found his job he couldn't even provide for her, and Ruth was willing to help. Had he begun now to press her to rejoin him? Marina might logically have taken the position that she was happy being with Ruth just now, that in any case she meant to wait a while to see if Lee really intended to settle down. Why should she go back to his chaotic existence? If by his conduct he showed he had really given up all these crazy schemes and machinations—that would be one thing. But if he . . . She would just have to see.

The following weekend Marina specifically told Lee she did not want him to come to Irving. As Mrs. Paine understood it, "She felt he had overstayed his welcome the previous weekend, which had been three days, because he was off Veterans Day, the eleventh of November, and she felt it would be simpler and more comfortable if he didn't come out."

"Had you had a discussion with her prior to that time on that subject?"

"I had not suggested that to her."

"Did you overhear her tell him that?"

"I did tell her I was planning a birthday party for my little girl, and I heard her tell Lee not to come out because I was having a birthday party."

Marina explained that he didn't come the next weekend because she told him not to. "He had wanted to come. He had telephoned."

"What did you tell him about not coming?"

"That he shouldn't come every week, that perhaps it is not convenient for Ruth that the whole family be there, live there."

"Did he say anything about that?"

"He said, 'As you wish. If you don't want me to come, I won't.' "

Lee apparently spent the weekend before the assassination by himself. If he was premeditating his last desperate act, he had solitude in which to work out the details. Whether he had thought of this for some time and needed only an immediate provocation to crystallize his determination cannot be said. However, if he was looking for a fresh grievance to justify the blow against the world he was about to perpetrate, fate again seemed to provide it just at that moment.

Mrs. Paine narrated the incident as it took place.

"You had just finished relating that Marina had told him not to come that particular weekend?"

"Yes."

"Now, was there an occasion during the course of that weekend when a phone call was made to Lee Harvey Oswald? I direct your attention particularly to Sunday evening, the seventeenth of November."

"Looking back on it, I thought that there was a call made to him by me on Monday the eighteenth, but I may be wrong about when it was made."

"Did Marina call him this Sunday evening, November seventeenth?"

"No. There was only one call made at any one time to him, to my knowledge."

"Do you recall an occasion when a call was made to him and you girls were unable to reach him when that call was made?"

"Yes. I will describe the call, and there is a dispute over what night it was."

"I would like your best recollection first as to when it occurred.

"Was it during the weekend that he did not return to your home, the weekend immediately preceding the assassination day? Do you recall that Marina was lonesome and she wished you to make a call to Lee and you did so at her request?"

"I recall certainly we had talked with Lee on the telephone already that weekend because he called to say that he had been to attempt to get a driver's-license permit."

"Yes."

"Whether he called that Saturday or whether he had called Sunday, I am not certain. Indeed, I am not certain but what he had already called and talked with Marina the very day that I then, at her request, tried to reach him at the number he had given me, with his number in my telephone book.

"Junie was fooling with the telephone dial, and Marina said, 'Let's call Papa' and asked me—"

"Was this at night?"

"It was early evening, still light."

"Was it on a weekend?"

"I would have said it was Monday, but I am not certain of that."

"Was it—"

"That is my best recollection is that it was Monday."

"All we want is your best recollection. If it was a Monday, was it the Monday following the weekend that he did not come?"

"Yes, certainly it was."

"I see.

"That is, if it was a Monday, it was the Monday preceding the November twenty-second?"

"Yes."

"Was there any evidence that the hint you gave, or that was given to Lee Harvey not to come over this weekend, caused him any annoyance? Was he put out by this, and did he indicate it?"

"I made no such request of him. Marina talked with him on the phone."

"I realize that."

"And she made no mention of any irritation. Of course, I didn't hear what he said in response to her asking him not to come."

"But it is your definite recollection that his failure to come on the weekend preceding the assassination was not at his doing but at the request of Marina, under the circumstances you have related?"

"I am absolutely clear about that."

"Now, state—you began to state the circumstances of the telephone call. Would you in your own words and your own chronology proceed with that, please?"

"Marina had said, 'Let's call Papa,' in Russian and asked me to dial the number for her, knowing that I had a number that he had given us. I then dialed the number—"

"And that number is—?"

"WH 3-8993."

"When you dialed the number did someone answer?"

"Someone answered and I said, 'Is Lee Oswald there?' And the person replied, 'There is no Lee Oswald here,' or something to that effect."

"You dialed the telephone, someone answered, a male voice?"

"Yes."

"What did he say, and what did you say?"

"I said, 'Is Lee Oswald there?' He said, 'There is no Lee Oswald living here.' As best as I can recall. This is the substance of what he said. I said, 'Is this a roominghouse?' He said, 'Yes.' I said, 'Is this WH 3-8993?' And he said, 'Yes.' I thanked him and hung up."

"When you hung up then what did you next do or say."

"I said to Marina, 'They don't know of a Lee Oswald at that number.'"

"What did she say?"

"She didn't say anything."

"Just said nothing?"

"She looked surprised."

"You are quite sure you used the first name 'Lee,' did you? You did not say just 'Mr. Oswald' or something of that kind?"

"I would not say 'Mr. Oswald.' It is contrary to the Quaker practice, and I don't normally do it that way."

"Contrary to Quaker practice?"

"They seldom use 'Mister.' "

"I see."

"And you wouldn't have said 'Harvey Oswald,' would you?"

"I knew he had a middle name, but only because I filled out forms in Parkland Hospital. It was never used with him."

"You do recall definitely that you asked for Lee Oswald?"

"I cannot be that definite. But I believe I asked for him. Oh, yes, I recall definitely what I asked. I cannot be definite about the man's reply, whether he included the full name in his reply."

"But you did?"

"I asked for the full name, 'Is Lee Oswald there.' "

"Did you report this incident to the FBI?"

"I had no occasion to see them, and I did not think it important enough to call them after that until the twenty-third of November."

Twice then Ruth Paine had had a strong intimation that Lee Oswald was not a forthright and ordinary person. As Ruth Paine herself said, "I am not accustomed to subterfuge." With her very genuine live-and-let-live philosophy, it was not her temperament to be suspicious. If she believed Lee had really been in Mexico instead of Houston as he indicated in his letter, this too would have cast a suspicion over Marina, who had told her otherwise. She might believe that Lee was not telling the truth—but Marina? She could not bring herself to believe that.

"Did any event occur the following day with regard to this telephone call?"

"Yes. Lee called—"

"What was it?"

"Lee called at the house and asked for Marina. I was in the kitchen where the phone is while Marina talked with him. She clearly was upset, and angry, and when she hung up—"

"Excuse me, did you overhear this conversation?"

"I overheard the conversation, but I can't tell you the specific content."

"Please, Mrs. Paine, would you do your very best to recall what was said?"

"I can tell you what she said to me, which was immediately after."

"Thank you."

"She said immediately he didn't like her trying to reach him on the phone in his room at Dallas yesterday. That he was angry with her for having tried to reach him. That he said he was using a different name, and she said, 'This isn't the first time I felt twenty-two fires,' a Russian expression."

"Do you understand what she meant, or if not, did you ask for an explanation?"

"I did not ask for an explanation. I judge she meant she disagreed with his using a different name but didn't feel empowered to make him do otherwise, or even perhaps ask as a wife."

"How long a conversation was this? Was it—"

"Fairly short."

"Was she abrupt in her hanging up? Did she hang up on him?"

"No. She was angry, she was upset."

"And her explanation of her being upset was that he used the assumed name?"

"Well, she didn't explain it as such, but she said he had used it."

"He was angry with her because you had made the call?"

"Yes."

"Or she had made it through you?"

"Yes."

"Did any further discussion take place between you and Marina on that subject?"

"Yes. The following day he did not call at the usual time."

"That would be the following day, the twentieth?"

"I believe that was a Wednesday, and that is how I slipped a day."

"He didn't call at all on the succeeding day?"

"He didn't call at all, and she said to me as the time for normally calling passed, 'He thinks he is punishing me.' "

"For what?"

"For having been a bad wife, I would judge. For having done something he didn't want her to do, the objection."

If Lee was angry, Marina testified how intensely she felt about his latest deception. Would Lee ever be cured? How could she ever go back and live with him? His promises had again and again meant nothing.

"Were you quite angry with him about the use of the fictitious name?"

"Yes. And when he called me over the phone a second time, I hung up and would not talk to him."

"Did you tell him why you were so angry?"

"Yes, of course."

"What did you say?"

"I said, 'After all, when will all your foolishness come to an end? All of these comedies. First one thing, then another. And now this fictitious name.'

"I didn't understand why. After all, it was nothing terrible if people were to find out that he had been in Russia."

"What did he say when you said that?"

"That I didn't understand anything."

Lee was back to his favorite refrain. Marina did not understand him. Did anyone understand him? His life was plagued with the imbecility of his fellow men. Marina testified, "I am not ashamed of the fact that I am from Russia. I can even be proud of the fact that I am Russian. And there is no need for me to hide it. Every person should be proud of his nationality and not to be afraid or ashamed of it."

"What did he say in response to that?"

"Nothing."

"When he gave the fictitious name, did he use the name Hidell?"

"I don't know what name he had given. He said that he was under a fictitious name, but he didn't tell me which."

"Did he tell you he was coming Thursday?"

"No."

"Did you learn that he was using the assumed name of Lee as his last name?"

"I know it now, but I did not ever know it before."

On Thursday evening, November 21, Lee Oswald did an unusual thing. Uninvited and without permission from Marina or Ruth Paine, he came to Irving after work. Mrs. Paine was surprised to find Lee and Marina playing with June on the front lawn when she arrived home from some errands she had been doing. Both Ruth Paine and Marina thought at the time that he had come home to make amends for the quarrel over the phone, and Ruth agreed it was all right if he stayed.

"Thursday was the twenty-first. Do you recall that?"

"Yes."

"And the assassination was on the twenty-second."

"This is very hard to forget."

"Did your husband give any reason for coming home on Thursday?"

"He said that he was lonely because he hadn't come the preceding weekend, and he wanted to make his peace with me."

"Did you say anything to him then?"

"He tried to talk to me but I would not answer him, and he was very upset."

"Were you upset with him?"

"I was angry, of course. He was not angry—he was upset. I was angry. He tried very hard to please me. He spent quite a bit of time putting away diapers and played with the children on the street."

"How did you indicate to him that you were angry with him?"

"By not talking to him."

"And how did he show that he was upset?"

"He was upset over the fact that I would not answer him. He tried to start a conversation with me several times, but I would not answer. And he said that he didn't want me to be angry at him because this upsets him.

"On that day, he suggested that we rent an apartment in Dallas. He said that he was tired of living alone and perhaps the reason for my being so angry was the fact that we were not living together. That if I want to he would rent an apartment in Dallas tomorrow, that he didn't want me to remain with Ruth any longer but wanted me to live with him in Dallas.

"He repeated this not once but several times, but I refused. And he said that once again I was preferring my friends to him and that I didn't need him."

"What did you say to that?"

"I said it would be better if I remained with Ruth until the holidays. He would come and we would all meet together. That this was better because while he was living alone and I stayed with Ruth, we were spending less money. And I told him to buy me a washing machine, because two children it became too difficult to wash by hand."

"What did he say to that?"

"He said he would buy me a washing machine."

"What did you say to that?"

"Thank you. That it would be better if he bought something for himself, that I would manage."

"Did this seem to make him more upset, when you suggested that he wait about getting an apartment for you to live in?"

"Yes."

"Mrs. Oswald, why did the use of this false name by your husband make you so angry? Would you explain that a little bit?"

"It would be unpleasant and incomprehensible to any wife if her husband used a fictitious name. And then, of course, I thought that if he would see that I don't like it and that I explained to him that this is not the smart thing to do, that he would stop doing it."

"Did you feel that you were becoming more impatient with all of these things that your husband was doing, the Fair Play for Cuba and the Walker incident, and then this fictitious name business?"

"Yes, of course. I was tired of it.

"Every day I was waiting for some kind of a new surprise. I couldn't wait to find out what else would he think of."

"Did you discuss that with your husband at all?"

"Yes, of course."

"What did you say about that?"

"I said that no one needed anything like that, that for no reason at all he was thinking that he was not like other people, that he was more important."

"And what did he say?"

"He would seem to agree, but then would continue again in two or three days."

"Did you sense that he was not intending to carry out his agreement with you to not have another Walker incident or anything like that?"

"I generally didn't think that Lee would repeat anything like that. Generally, I knew that the rifle was very tempting for him.

"But I didn't believe that he would repeat it. It was hard to believe."

"How did your husband get along with Mrs. Paine?"

"He was polite to her, as an acquaintance would be, but he didn't like her. He told me that he detested her—a tall and stupid woman.

"She is, of course, not too smart, but most people aren't."

"Did he ever say anything to indicate he thought Mrs. Paine was coming between him and you?"

"No."

"Did the quarrel that you had at that time seem to cause him to be more disturbed than usual?"

"No, not particularly. At least he didn't talk about that quarrel when he came. Usually he would remember about what happened. This time he didn't blame me for anything, didn't ask me any questions, just wanted to make up."

"I understood that when you didn't make up he was quite disturbed and you were still angry, is that right?"

"I wasn't really very angry. I, of course, wanted to make up with him. But I gave the appearance of being very angry. I was smiling inside, but I had a serious expression on my face."

"And as a result of that, did he seem to be more disturbed than usual?"

"As always, as usual. Perhaps a little more. At least when he went to bed he was very upset."

"Do you think that had anything to do with the assassination the next day?"

"Perhaps he was thinking about all of that. I don't think that he was asleep. Because, in the morning when the alarm clock went off he hadn't woken up as usual before the alarm went off, and I thought that he probably had fallen asleep very late. At least then I didn't think about it. Now I think so."

CHAPTER 23

THURSDAY-NIGHT TRIP

Evidence indicates that prior to Thursday night Lee had made preparations to take his rifle to Dallas. Wesley Frazier was surprised when Lee asked if he could ride back to Irving with him that night. Frazier appeared before the Commission and recalled the details.

"I was standing there getting the orders in, and he said, 'Could I ride home with you this afternoon?'

"And I said, 'Sure. You know, like I told you you can go home with me any time you want to, like I say any time you want to go see your wife, that is all right with me.'

"So automatically I knew it wasn't Friday. I come to think it wasn't Friday, and I said, 'Why are you going home today?'

"And he said, 'I am going home to get some curtain rods.' He said, 'You know, put in an apartment.'

"He wanted to hang up some curtains, and I said, 'Very well.' And I never thought more about it, and I had some invoices in my hands for some orders and I walked on off and started filling the orders."

"That was on what floor?"

"This was on the first floor."

"About what time in the morning?"

"I would say sometime between eight and ten, because I go to work at eight and I would break at ten."

"It was before noon then?"

"Yes, sir."

"Did you see him at the noon hour?"

"I don't recall, to be frank with you. You know, I will just be frank with you. I say just like after a guy works there for a while and he comes by and he walks by you, you don't pay so much attention, but say like somebody else comes in there strange you automatically just look at them."

"Did you talk to him again until quitting time?"

"Well, to be frank with you, like I said, the only time—you know, like I say, he didn't talk very much and about the only time—other than like I told you about talking about them babies and about the weather, sometimes he would ask me some questions about a book because down there, I say, if you have ever been acquainted with books, a lot of times maybe just a little bit difference in a title or something like that would make the difference in what type of book they want, and sometimes maybe they will forget to put that on there and you look at the price.

"If you can tell the price, some editions we have a paperback and some we have hard bound and the price can automatically tell you which one they want, and sometimes he would ask me something like that, which book do they want, and I would tell him and that was about the only conversation we had."

"You didn't talk any more with him that day concerning the ride home?"

"Right."

"But you did go home with him?"

"That is he rode home with me."

"What time did you get off from work?"

"Four-forty."

"What time did you get to Irving?"

"Well, usually get there, if you make good time, get there maybe around five-twenty or five-twenty-five. But if you catch the traffic and catch the train crossing the tracks it is usually about five-thirty or five-thirty-five—it is just according to how bad the traffic is.

"If you get ahead of it before it starts coming out you can make pretty good headway."

"Did you make any stop out in the car before you got home?"

"No, sir, I don't believe we did."

"Did the two of you walk together down to the parking lot?"

"Yes, sir, we did."

"And you dropped him off at the place where his wife was staying, did you?"

"Yes, sir, I believe I did. I, to be frank with you, I say sometimes he rode home with me, but if I wasn't going to the store he would usually go on to the corner near the house and walk the rest of the way to the house up to where his wife was staying just about half a block from my house up to where he was, his wife was staying, so he would walk there just a little bit."

"Do you remember if you talked to him any on the walk down two or three blocks down to the parking lot, anything said that you can remember?"

"No, sir, I don't believe so."

"When you got in the car and went home do you remember if you said anything, if you said anything to him, or if he said anything to you?"

"No, sir, I don't believe he did. Like I said, he didn't talk very much. About the only time we would talk about the weather and babies, something like that."

"Do you remember this day whether or not you let him walk to the house where his wife was staying?"

"To be frank with you, I can't remember positively whether I let him off at the house or whether he got out there where I lived, just to be frank with you."

One of the mysteries never to be solved, unless Marina in years to come recalls something she has not yet related, is whether Lee had actually made up his mind to kill when he went out to Irving or whether the decision was still hanging fire, perhaps depending on whether Marina accepted what appeared to be his peace offers and agreed to come to Dallas to live with him. Wesely Frazier recalled that before the morning coffee break on Thursday, Lee came to him with his story about going to Irving to get "curtain rods." Thorough investigation by the Commission was persuasive that there was no intention on Oswald's part of seeking curtain rods but that he had devised this story to explain the package containing the rifle he carried into the Depository the next morning. He could have made up his mind to shoot at the President regardless of the outcome of his quarrel with Marina, or he could have left the rifle in the garage and simply told Frazier the next morning that he had discovered the curtain rods would not work in his room. That he was sensitive, however, to Marina's refusal to take an apartment with him there can be no question. The incident she related about her asking for a washing machine, and his agreeing, reminds one of the point de Mohrenschildt stressed to the effect that she was always demanding things he could not give. She admits she was toying with him. Her anger had

317

changed to "smiling inside." "I, of course, wanted to make up with him." Which was the real Marina Oswald—the one full of anger and indignation, or the one who wanted to make up? "And he said that he didn't want me to be angry at him because this upsets him." How much? Enough so that her rejection of his offer to come back would make the difference between the decision to kill or not to kill? In all likelihood history will never be able to judge.

The Commission delved carefully into every incident Marina and Ruth Paine related bearing on the night before the killing. They searched tirelessly for a clearer understanding of Lee Oswald's real motives. Many of these small events underlined the irony of what was to happen the next day.

Following the discussion about the washing machine and Marina's refusal to agree to an apartment in Dallas, she recalled, "He then stopped talking and sat down and watched television and then went to bed. I went to bed later. It was about nine o'clock when he went to sleep. I went to sleep about eleven-thirty. But it seemed to me that he was not really asleep. But I didn't talk to him."

"Why did you stay awake until eleven-thirty? Were you still angry with him?"

"No, not for that reason, but because I had to wash dishes and be otherwise busy with the household, take a bath."

"On this evening when you were angry with him, had he come home with the young Mr. Frazier that day?"

"Yes."

"When was the last time that you had noticed the rifle before that day?"

"I said that I saw—for the first and last time I saw the rifle about a week after I had come to Mrs. Paine."

"Did you ever see the rifle in a paper cover?"

"No."

"Could you describe for the Commission the place in the garage where the rifle was located?"

"When you enter the garage from the street, it was in the front part, the left."

"By the left you mean left of the door?"

"It is an overhead door and the rifle was to the left, on the floor. It was always in the same place."

"Was there anything else close to the rifle that you recall?"

"Next to it there were some—next to the rifle there were some suitcases and Ruth had some paper barrels in the garage where the kids used to play."

"The way the rifle was wrapped with a blanket, could you tell whether or not the rifle had been removed and the blanket just left there at any time?"

"It always had the appearance of having something inside of it. But I only looked at it really once, and I was always sure the rifle was in it."

"Before this incident about the fictitious name, were you and your husband getting along quite well?"

"Yes."

"Did he seem to like his job at the Depository?"

"Yes, because it was not dirty work."

"Had he talked about getting any other job?"

"Yes. When he went to answer some ads, he preferred to get some work connected with photography rather than this work. He liked this work relatively speaking—he liked it. But, of course, he wanted to get something better."

"Did you like the photographic work?"

"Yes. It was interesting for him. When he would see his work in the newspaper he would always point it out."

"When he said he would not be home that Friday evening, did you ask him why?"

"Yes."

"What did he say?"

"He said that since he was home on Thursday, that it wouldn't make any sense to come again on Friday, that he would come for the weekend."

"Did that cause you to think that he had any special plans to do anything?"

"No."

"Did you usually keep a wallet with money in it at the Paines'?"

"Yes, in my room at Ruth Paine's there was a black wallet in a wardrobe. Whenever Lee would come he would put money in there, but I never counted it."

"On the evening of November twenty-first, do you know how much was in the wallet?"

"No. One detail that I remember was that he had asked me

whether I had bought some shoes for myself, and I said no, that I hadn't had any time. He asked me whether June needed anything and told me to buy everything that I needed for myself and for June—and for the children.

"This was rather unusual for him, that he would mention that first."

"Did he take money from the wallet from time to time?"

"No, he generally kept the amount that he needed and put the rest in the wallet.

"I know that the money that was found there, that you think this was not Lee's money. But I know for sure that this was money that he had earned. He had some money left after his trip to Mexico. Then we received an unemployment-compensation check for thirty-three dollars. And then Lee paid only seven or eight dollars for his room. And I know how he eats—very little."

"On November twenty-first, the day before the assassination that you were describing, was there any discussion between you and your husband about President Kennedy's trip or proposed trip to Texas, Dallas and the Fort Worth area?"

"I asked Lee whether he knew where the President would speak and told him that I would very much like to hear him and to see him. I asked him how this could be done.

"But he said he didn't know how to do that and didn't enlarge any further on that subject."

"Had there ever been—"

"This was also somewhat unusual—his lack of desire to talk about that subject any further."

"Can you explain that to us?"

"I think about it more now. At that time I didn't pay any attention."

"How did you think it was unusual? Could you explain that?"

"The fact that he didn't talk a lot about it. He merely gave me—said something as an answer and did not have any further comments."

"Do you mean by that usually he would discuss a matter of that kind and show considerable interest?"

"Yes, of course, he would have told who would be there and where this would take place."

"Did you say anything about his showing a lack of interest at that time?"

"I merely shrugged my shoulders."

"Now, prior to that time, had there been any discussion between you concerning the proposed trip of President Kennedy to Texas?"

"No."

"While you were in New Orleans, was there any discussion or reference to President Kennedy's proposed trip to Texas?"

"No."

"Did your husband make any comments about President Kennedy on that evening, of the twenty-first?"

"No."

"Had your husband at any time that you can recall said anything against President Kennedy?"

"I don't remember any—ever having said that. I don't know. He never told me that."

"So apparently he didn't indicate any approval or disapproval, as far as he was concerned, of President Kennedy?"

"Yes, that is correct. The President is the President. In my opinion, he never wanted to overthrow him. At least he never showed me that. He never indicated that he didn't want that President."

"Did you observe that his acts on November twenty-first, the evening before the assassination, were anything like they were the evening before the Walker incident?"

"Absolutely nothing in common."

"Did he say anything at all that would indicate he was contemplating the assassination?"

"No."

"Did he discuss the television program he saw that evening with you?"

"He was looking at TV by himself. I was busy in the kitchen. At one time when we were—when I was together with him they showed some sort of war films, from World War II. And he watched them with interest."

"Do you recall films that he saw called *Suddenly* and *We Were Strangers* that involved assassinations?"

"I don't remember the names of these films. If you would remind me of the contents, perhaps I would know."

"Well, *Suddenly* was about the assassination of a President, and the other was about the assassination of a Cuban dictator."

"Yes, Lee saw those films."

"Did he tell you that he had seen them?"

"I was with him when he watched them."

"Do you recall about when this was with reference to the date of the assassination?"

"It seems that this was before Rachel's birth."

"Weeks or months? Can you recall that?"

"Several days. Some five days."

"Did you discuss the films after you had seen them with your husband?"

"One film about the assassination of the President in Cuba, which I had seen together with him, he said that this was a fictitious situation but that the content of the film was similar to the actual situation which existed in Cuba, meaning the revolution in Cuba."

"Did either of you comment on either film being like the attempt on Walker's life?"

"No. I didn't watch the other film."

"Was anything said by your husband about how easy an assassination could be committed like that?"

"No. I only know that he watched the film with interest, but I didn't like it."

"Do you recall anything else he said about either of these films?"

"Nothing else."

"Do you recall your husband saying at any time after he saw the film about the Cuban assassination that this was the old-fashioned way of assassination?"

"No."

"Do you recall anything being said by your husband at any time about Governor Connally?"

"Well, while we were still in Russia, and Connally at that time was Secretary of the Navy, Lee wrote him a letter in which he asked Connally to help him obtain a good-character reference, because at the end of his Army service he had a good characteristic—honorable discharge—but that it had been changed after it became known he had gone to Russia."

"Had it been changed to undesirable discharge, as you understand it?"

"Yes. Then we received a letter from Connally in which he said that he had turned the matter over to the responsible authorities.

"That was all in Russia.

"But here it seems he had written again to that organization with a request to review. But he said from time to time that these are bureaucrats, and he was dissatisfied."

"Do you know when he wrote again?"

"No."

"Was that letter written from New Orleans?"

"I don't know. I only know about the fact, but when and how, I don't know."

"Did your husband say anything to you to indicate he had a dislike for Governor Connally?"

"Here he didn't say anything.

"But while we were in Russia he spoke well of him. It seems to me that Connally was running for Governor and Lee said that when he would return to the United States he would vote for him."

CHAPTER 24

AN ORDINARY MORNING

NOVEMBER 22, 1963, began as an ordinary morning. Marina recalled, "In the morning he got up, said goodbye and left, and that I shouldn't get up—as always, I did not get up to prepare breakfast. This was quite usual.

"And then after I fed Rachel, I took a look to see whether Lee was here, but he had already gone."

Lee would be at work by now. It did not seem from the coffeepot that he had made any regular coffee. Well, perhaps he had just dashed off after a quick cup of instant. Lee was not a great breakfast eater.

Marina may well have had some reflective thoughts about the problems between herself and Lee the past few days. Her problems with this strange man were certainly not easy to solve. In a like position, what would any woman do? On the one hand she was driven to try to find a way of escaping from the terrors he would create. The frightening anxiety of never knowing what he would do next! The totally inconsistent way in which he would be sometimes solicitous, sometimes affectionate and then absolutely indifferent! Of course she had been upset to find he was living in Dallas under an assumed name. It was just the same sort of secretive disguise he had used when he got into trouble in New Orleans.

Marina testified she watched television all morning "even without having dressed."

For Ruth Paine, there was nothing really singular about that morning either.

"The evening of the twenty-first, did you sleep through the night?"

"Yes. I woke at seven-thirty."

"The children did not awaken you at any time during the night and nothing else awakened you?"

"I don't recall that anything woke me, no."

"Is your recollection sufficient that you were not awakened during the night, that is your definite impression at the moment?"

"I get up often in the night to change a diaper or cover a child, but this is a matter of habit and I don't recall whether this night contained such a getting up or not."

"You sleep with your children, do you not?"

"We are in the same bedroom."

"You awakened when in the morning?"

"At seven-thirty."

"And when you awakened, immediately after you awakened what did you do?"

"When I awoke I felt the house was extremely quiet and the thought occurred to me that Lee might have overslept. I wondered if he had gotten up in time to get off around seven o'clock, because I knew he had to go to meet Wesley Frazier to catch his ride. I looked about and found a plastic coffee cup in the sink that had clearly been used and judged he had had a cup of coffee and left."

"Did you see any other evidence of his having had breakfast?"

"That was all he normally had for breakfast."

"A plastic coffee cup with some remains in it of coffee?"

"Instant coffee, yes."

"What was his habit with respect to his breakfast when he made his visits?"

"It was very normal for him to take coffee."

"Was Marina up and about when you arose at seven-thirty?"

"No, she was not."

"Do you have a recollection of the garage area? Was the door to the garage, the entrance to the garage from the kitchen, closed or open?"

"It was closed. Would it help if I tried to narrate what happened?"

"Go ahead and narrate."

"I fixed breakfast for myself and my children, turned on the television set to hear President Kennedy speak in Fort Worth and had breakfast there. I left the house about nine with my little girl and boy, because she had a dentist appointment, the little girl. I left the television set on, feeling that Marina might not think to turn it on, but I knew that she would be interested to see President Kennedy.

"I then was gone until nearly noon, eleven-thirty or so, both to the dentist and on some errands following that, came back and there was coverage of the fact of the motorcade in Dallas, but there was no television cameras showing it, as you know, and Marina thanked me for having left the television set on. She said she woke up in kind of a bad mood, but she had seen the airport in Dallas and had been thrilled with this occasion and with the greeting he had received, and it had lifted her spirits."

At the very moment Marina was telling Ruth Paine how her spirits had been lifted by the TV scene of the President and Mrs. Kennedy being warmly greeted at the airport, an assassin—Lee Harvey Oswald—was probably maneuvering his way to the sixth floor of the Texas School Book Depository, breathlessly waiting for all the workmen to clear out of the area where they had been working so he could rearrange the book cartons of "Rolling Readers" to build his ambuscade and gun rest.

His plan could easily have been foiled at the last minute. At one of the nearby front windows sat a lone employee, munching away at his lunch. It was a fellow employee, "Bonnie Ray" Williams. Fate decreed that "Bonnie Ray" Williams would be sitting there, but fate also decreed that he would move just in time to give Lee Oswald his opportunity to shoot and flee.

Early reports of how "chicken bones" came to be at the window were dramatized erroneously. However, the true circumstances were no less spine-chilling. Again, but for the strange twist of circumstances that caused "Bonnie Ray" Williams to leave that window, President Kennedy might be alive today. Williams told his story:

"They called me up to help lay a floor on the fifth floor—they wanted more boards over it. As I say, business was slow, and they were trying to keep us on without laying us off at the time. So I was using the saw, helping cut wood and lay wood."

"You were laying a wood floor over the old floor?"

"Yes, sir."

"On the fifth floor?"

"Yes, sir."

"And when you finished on the fifth floor, what did you do?"

"After we finished on the fifth floor we started to move up to the

326

sixth floor. But at the time we didn't complete the sixth floor. We only completed just a little portion of it."

"By the time, you are talking about November twenty-second?"

"Yes, sir."

"And how long had you been on the sixth floor before—how long have you been working on the sixth floor before November twenty-second?"

"Let's see. Before November twenty-second, I think it might have been two days—it might have been two days."

"Did you know Lee Harvey Oswald?"

"I didn't know him personally, but I had seen him working. Never did say anything to anyone. He never did put himself in any position to say anything to anyone. He just went about his work. He never said anything to me. I never said anything to him."

"Did you ever have lunch with him?"

"No. The only time he would come into the lunchroom sometimes and eat a sandwich maybe, and then he would go for a walk, and he would go out. And I assume he would come back. But the only other time he would come in and read a paper or nothing, and laugh and leave again."

"But he would never say good morning or good evening?"

"He never would speak to anyone. He was just a funny fellow. I don't know what kind of a fellow he was."

"Did you notice what he read in the newspaper?"

"I believe one morning I noticed he was reading something about politics, and as he was reading this he acted like it was funny to him. He would read a paragraph or two, smile, or laugh, then throw the paper down and get up and walk out."

"Did you see Oswald on the sixth floor that morning?"

"I am not sure. I think I saw him once messing around with some cartons or something, back over the east side of the building. But he wasn't in the window that they said he shot the President from. He was more on the east side of the elevator, I think, messing around with cartons, because he always just messed around, kicking cartons around."

"What was his job?"

"His job was an order filler."

"What time did you knock off work for the lunch hour?"

"Well, approximately—between eleven-thirty to twelve, around in there. I wouldn't say the exact time, because I don't remember the exact time."

"What time do you usually quit for lunch?"

"We always quit about five minutes before time. During the rush season we quit about five minutes before time and wash up."

"Wash your hands and face before you eat lunch?"

"That is right."

"You say quit five minutes before time. What is the time?"

"Five before twelve."

"Did you quit earlier this day?"

"I believe this day we quit about maybe five or ten minutes, because all of us were so anxious to see the President—we quit a little ahead of time so that we could wash up and we wanted to be sure we would not miss anything."

"Now, did you go downstairs?"

"We took two elevators down. I mean, speaking as a group, we took two down."

"Was there some reason you took two down?"

"We always had a little-kids' game we played racing down with the elevators. And I think one fellow, Charles Givens, had the east elevator, and me and I think two or three more fellows had the west elevator. And we was racing down."

"Now, did something happen on the way down—did somebody yell out?"

"Yes, on the way down I heard Oswald—and I am not sure whether he was on the fifth or the sixth floor. But on the way down Oswald hollered, 'Guys, how about an elevator?' I don't know whether those are his exact words. But he said something about the elevator.

"And Charles said, 'Come on, boy,' just like that.

"And he said, 'Close the gate on the elevator and send the elevator back up.'

"I don't know what happened after that."

"You went down to the first floor. What did you do?"

"We went down to the first floor. I think the first thing I did I washed up, then I went into the domino room where I kept my lunch, and I got my lunch, came back out and went back up."

"Did you carry your lunch that day?"

"Yes, I did."

"Do you usually carry your lunch to work?"

"Yes, I do."

"And that day, on November twenty-second, how did you carry your lunch from home to work?"

"I carried my lunch from home to work in a brown paper bag. I believe it was size number six or maybe eight—paper bag."

"Number six or eight size paper bag?"

"Yes, sir."

"Small bag?"

"Yes, sir."

"Like you get in the grocery store?"

"Yes, sir."

"What did you have in your lunch?"

"I had a chicken sandwich."

"Describe the sandwich. What did it have in it besides chicken?"

"Well, it just had chicken in it. Chicken on the bone."

"Chicken on the bone?"

"Yes."

"The chicken was not boned?"

"It was just chicken on the bone. Just plain old chicken."

"Did it have bread around it?"

"Yes, it did."

"Before you went upstairs, did you get anything to drink?"

"I got a small bottle of Dr. Pepper from the Dr. Pepper machine."

"Did you have anything else in your lunch besides chicken?"

"I had a bag of Fritos, I believe it was."

"Anything else?"

"No, I believe that was all."

"You say you went back upstairs. Where did you go?"

"I went back up to the sixth floor."

"Why did you go to the sixth floor?"

"Well, at the time everybody was talking like they was going to watch from the sixth floor. I think Billy Lovelady said he wanted to watch from up there. And also my friend, this Spanish boy by the name of Danny Arce, we had agreed at first to come back up to the sixth floor. So I thought everybody was going to be on the sixth floor."

"Did anybody go back?"

"Nobody came back up."

"Where did you eat your lunch?"

"I ate my lunch—I am not sure about this, but the third or the fourth set of windows, I believe."

"Facing on what street?"

"Facing Elm Street."

"What floor?"

"Sixth floor."

"You ate your lunch on the sixth floor?"

"Yes, sir."

"And you were all alone?"

"Yes, sir."

"What did you sit on while you ate your lunch?"

"First of all, I remember there was some boxes behind me. I just kind of leaned back on the boxes first. Then I began to get a little impatient, because there wasn't anyone coming up. So I decided to move to a two-wheeler."

"A two-wheeler truck you mean?"

"Yes, sir. I remember sitting on this two-wheeler. By that time, I was through, and I got up and I just left then."

"Where did you go when you left there?"

"I went down to the fifth floor."

"How did you get down there?"

"I took an elevator down."

"You didn't go down the stairs?"

"No, sir."

"Bonnie Ray" Williams left the sixth floor just minutes before the Presidential motorcade reached the corner of Houston and Elm. He left just in time to leave Lee Oswald alone on the sixth floor. His reason for leaving? He was lonely. It was no fun to watch a parade by himself.

Now, to Wesley Frazier it was an ordinary morning too, except for the fact that he had a passenger he normally wouldn't have had on a Friday morning. His recollection of the events of the morning was a critical part of the Commission's evidence.

"I believe I got up around six-thirty—that is the time I usually get up, right around six-thirty there."

"Always eat your breakfast before you go to work?"

"Right."

"Do you remember the night before—that is, after you got home that night—that your sister asked you how it happened that Oswald came home with you?"

"Yes, I believe she did or something. We got to talking about something and said, I told her that he had rode home with me and told her he said he was going to come home and pick up some curtain rods or something. I usually don't talk too much to my sister. Sometimes she is not there when I am in because she is either at the store or something like that, and I am either—when she comes in, as I say—I am playing with the little nieces and we don't talk too much about work or something like that."

"This night, this evening, do you remember you did talk to her about the fact that Oswald had come home with you?"

"I believe I did."

"Did you tell her what he had told you?"

"Yes, sir. I believe she said why did he come home now and I said, well, he says he was going to get some curtain rods."

"The next morning you had breakfast about what time?"

"Between seven and seven-fifteen—that is the time I usually, I usually come to the breakfast table about seven."

"Breakfast table in the kitchen?"

"Yes, sir."

"And the kitchen windows look out on what street, West Brook or Fifth?"

"West Brook."

"They look onto West Brook?"

"Right."

"There is a back door, is there, to the kitchen?"

"Yes, there is. I say when we come in there we have a double carport more or less type of garage."

"Is that on West Brook?"

"Yes, sir, the entrance to the garage there, more or less carport, yes, the entrance is from West Brook."

"As you were having breakfast, did your mother say anything to you about—"

"I was sitting there eating my breakfast there, so sitting there I usually talk to my little nieces, you know—they have them cartoons on for a while and we usually talk a little bit back and forth while eating breakfast—and I was just finishing my coffee there and my sister, you know, was working over there around, you know the sink there, and she was fixing my lunch, so she was somewhere around there over on the cabinets fixing the cabinets, and Mother just happened to glance up and saw this man, you know, who was Lee looking in the window for me and she said, 'Who is that?'

"And I said, 'That is Lee,' and naturally he just walked around and so I thought he just walked around there on the carport right there close to the door, and so I told her I had to go, so I went in there and brushed my teeth right quick and come through there and I usually have my coat laying somewhere on the chair, and picked it up and put it on and by that time my sister had my lunch, you know, in a sack and sitting over there on the washer where I picked it up right there by the door, and I just walked on out and we got in the car."

"When he would go with you on Monday, on any Monday, was this the same procedure for getting to, getting in contact with you?"

"You mean coming in there and looking through the window?"

"Yes."

"No, sir, it wasn't. I say, that is the first time he had ever done that. I say, most times I would usually call him, you know, I was already out in the car fixing to go out the driveway there, and you know, around to pick him up if he hadn't come down, but most times, once in a while I picked him up at the house and another time he was already coming down the sidewalk to the house when I was fixing to pick him up and I usually picked him up around the corner there."

"Did this different method of him meeting you raise any questions in your mind?"

"No, sir, it didn't. I just thought maybe, you know, he just left a little bit earlier, but when I looked up and saw what the clock was, I knew I was the one who was running a little bit late because, as I say, I was talking sitting there eating breakfast and talking to the little nieces, it was later than I thought it was."

"Did you say usually you had to go by and pick him up?"

"Well, I said I had a couple of times. Most of the time, you know, he was usually walking down the sidewalk as I was driving out of the driveway, so therefore I didn't have to go up to the house there to pick him up. I just usually picked him up around the corner because he was usually on the sidewalk and I just stopped and picked him up."

"Were you later than usual that morning?"

"No, sir, I don't believe we were, because we got to work on time. I say, when I looked at the clock, after I glanced he was there a split second, and I just turned around and looked at the clock to see what time it was, and it was right around seven-twenty-one then, and I went in and brushed my teeth real quick and running through the house put my coat on and we left."

"You both got in the car about the same time?"

"Right."

"All right. When you got in the car did you say anything to him, or did he say anything to you?"

"Let's see, when I got in the car I have a kind of habit of glancing over my shoulder and so at that time I noticed there was a package laying on the back seat. I didn't pay too much attention and I said, 'What's the package, Lee?'

"And he said, 'Curtain rods,' and I said, 'Oh, yes, you told me you was going to bring some today.'

"That is the reason, the main reason he was going over there that Thursday afternoon when he was to bring back some curtain rods, so I didn't think any more about it when he told me that."

"What did the package look like?"

"Well, I will be frank with you. I would just—it is right as you get out of the grocery store, just more or less out of a package—you have seen some of these brown paper sacks you can obtain from any, most of the stores, some varieties—but it was a package just roughly about two feet long."

"It was—what part of the back seat was it in?"

"It was in his side over on his side in the far back."

"Do you remember any conversation on the way in about anything?"

"Yes, sir, I asked him did he have fun playing with them babies, and he chuckled and said he did. And so that morning I said just a few minutes after we started, you know it was a cloudy day and it started misting and rain, and by the time we got out on the freeway I said, you know, how those trucks throw that grime on the windshield, and finally it was getting pretty thick on there with spots of rain, and I turned on the windshield wiper and you know how grime spatters your windshield and I said, 'I wish it would rain or just quit altogether. I wish it would do something to clear off the windshield.' And the drops started getting larger, so eventually it cleaned off the windshield, and by the time I got down to Dallas there I just turned off the windshield.

"Just a few clouds, and rained a little bit to get out of it. But other than that just saying the weather was messy, that is about all."

"Was it foggy?"

"No, sir, not in too particular. I say in other words, just old cloudy, dull-looking day, and like I say fine mist of rain, and after we got a little bit further we got into larger drops."

"Was there anything said about the President coming to Dallas that day?"

"No, sir, it wasn't."

"Did he say anything about that the day before?"

"No, sir."

"Did you ever have any conversation with him with reference to the President's visit to Texas?"

"No, sir."

"When you got to the parking lot who got out of the car first?"

"He did."

"You didn't get out immediately then?"

"No, sir, I was sitting there, say, looked at my watch and somewhere around seven or eight minutes until, and I saw we had a few minutes and I sat there, and as I say you can see the freeway, Stemmons Freeway, from the warehouse, and also the trains coming back and forth and I was sitting there.

"What I was doing glanced up and watching cars for a minute, but I was letting my engine run and getting to charge up my battery, because when you stop and start you have to charge up your battery."

"What did he do about the package in the back seat when he got out of the car?"

"He put the package that he had, you know, that he told me was curtain rods up under his arm, you know, and so he walked down behind the car and he started walking off, and so I followed him in."

No curtain rods were ever found in the Texas School Book Depository or Lee's roominghouse. The Mannlicher-Carcano rifle, serial

334

number C2766, which until that morning had been wrapped in a blanket in the Paines' garage, was found on the sixth floor. Unwittingly Wesley Frazier had delivered the assassin and his murder weapon that "ordinary" morning.

CHAPTER 25

DALLAS—THREE DAYS
IN NOVEMBER

From the moment the shots rang out from the Texas School Book Depository until the murder of Lee Harvey Oswald by Jack Ruby—the events of these three days have been retold in the minutest detail. The report of the Commission follows minute by minute and foot by foot the flight of Lee Oswald from the building, his race to his roominghouse, his encounter with and cold-blooded murder of Officer Tippit and his swift apprehension at the Texas Theatre. Giving icy reality to the impossible succession of events are thousands of feet of film and tape, much of it seen by millions of viewers within moments of occurrence. The tragic story is all too vivid in the memories of Americans. By midnight the Dallas authorities believed they had an open-and-shut case against Lee Harvey Oswald. The mere fact that he was so swiftly caught, so quickly implicated in a crime of such fantastic proportions made it more unbelievable to the public. Could a man individually commit so great a crime without accomplices? Was it possible that a motivation so obscure and pointless could explain the murder of a President so generally beloved? The great swell of human emotions that this tragedy evoked was like a tidal wave of sorrow engulfing everyone. Even without the compounded villainy of Jack Ruby's act, it was too much to expect anyone to believe that one man at one instant of time had wrought so much meaningless misery with three bullets fired from a rifle. And for what purpose? Speculations ran riot, but they were all unconvincing. How could such a thing be?

The President's Commission went about its task of trying to establish the truth with the same forthright purpose that any seven ordinary citizens might have undertaken the assignment. The report, and the twenty-six volumes of exhibits and testimony, back their conclusions. Every American is entitled to judge for himself whether the record substantiates the report. However, one gets the feeling there are still scores of theorists, writers and speculators who view with skepticism the work of the Commission. Let it be said, however, that above all else it is not fair to the work of the Commission or the conscience of the world for these conjectures to be given credence unless the authors of these speculations have labored hours over all the testimony as have the members of the Commission. The record is monumental in its scope. And in fairness to the people whose lives were blighted by these events in which they became innocently involved, their feelings deserve understanding.

Not just Lee Oswald and Jack Ruby were suddenly cast into the limelight but all the others whose inadvertent roles placed them at the burning focus point of the lens. Suddenly there was Marguerite Oswald in the picture and Lee's brother Robert. The kindly Quaker housewife, who had her own problems, became a center of curiosity. Ruth Paine took the brunt of many suspicions and criticisms. An Australian girl who had happened to ride a bus to Mexico City would be trailed halfway around the world, as well as an Englishman who happened to be sight-seeing on that same trip. Schoolteachers who had long since forgotten Lee Harvey Oswald would be asked to tax their memories—truant officials in New York City, Marine Corps associates of Oswald's, immigration officials, State Department authorities, retired FBI men, Secret Service agents. All at once, each is mercilessly asked to render an account of every second of experience he or she once accidentally had with an assassin. To stand in harsh judgment of the roles played by any of these individuals was not the purpose of the Commission. And yet these people's stories had to be meshed into the whole story so that in the final analysis rational human beings could understand how such a thing could come about. In hours the Dallas police knew that Lee Harvey Oswald had purchased the fatal rifle from a mail-order house in Chicago; his alias, "A. J. Hidell," was on the order blank. Before the first frightful day was out, a troop of witnesses had identified him in the show-up as the murderer of Officer Tippit. Eventually ballistics, fingerprints, fiber tests, all came from experts to confirm the suspicion of Oswald's guilt. In fact it appeared, aside from his denials, which were meaningless considering his habitual lack of veracity, that Lee Oswald had made no earnest effort to disguise his moves or plan an escape. It looked as if he had achieved that which he wanted—fame, or infamy, at any price. Had he sought to pay society back? Had he sought to avenge himself on Marina? It seems improbable that these things would ever have been confessed even if he had lived to have the chance. The pattern of Lee Oswald's life was one of defiance of society. This was to have been his greatest hour of defiance.

How, then, did an open-and-shut case become so complex?

There were many reasons. Lee Oswald's short life was, as we have seen, vastly complex. He cloaked his own acts in an air of mystery. He nurtured his own sense of self-importance with deliberate nonconformity. He antagonized almost everyone he came in contact with by challenging them and their ideas. "Bonnie Ray" Williams' testimony of how Lee Oswald would chuckle with contempt when he read some political article in the newspaper and yet smugly say nothing to his associates was a measure of the conceit he liked to revel in. He hugged his own egotism, and even the pride he took in mastering a difficult language like Russian was more for the purpose of proving to others his superiority than for its practical use.

One could easily make too much of the testimony Marina gave of his interest in TV suspense stories and tales of assassinations. Most Americans have at one time or another watched such shows. But most Americans do not exult in using aliases, plotting murders of generals or practicing the bolt action of a rifle on shadowy porches. Quite indicative of the way in which Oswald's mind sometimes operated was the testimony of his fellow employee at the Reily Company in New Orleans who described his little prank of taking aim with his forefinger and solemnly saying, "Pow." For a fourteen-year-old a gesture of this sort would be normal for a game of cowboys and Indians—but for an adult man? No wonder Charles Le Blanc wondered if Oswald was all right in his mind.

The case was also made extremely complex by the nomadic course of his wanderings. The mere fact that he had defected to Russia was in itself enough to raise many, many questions. Then there was the appearance that when he returned to the United States he jumped from one job to another, one city to another. It was the classic conduct for someone who really was involved in plots, or espionage, or other suspect activities. On the surface there seemed little reason for these meanderings, and wherever he went he became involved in veiled activities. He seemed to hide behind post-office box numbers, and his secretive manner added to the appearance that indeed here was a mysterious character. Lee Oswald was mysterious, but not in the way he appeared in the early stages of the investigation. As the investigations of the Commission added depth to the understanding of this man, his acts became more understandable. He did not move to New Orleans for the specific purpose of joining an organized Castro intrigue. He moved to New Orleans to get away from the heat of his Walker murder attempt. And there is no evidence that he went to Mexico to carry on secret negotiations with the Cuban underground, because when he got there he was flatly rejected. His associations with American Communists were zero, except for an occasional letter he wrote hoping to be recognized as a very important person. However, much of this information was not known for months to come. With so many loose ends of suspicious information available to the press and news media, the case was bound to become more and more bewildering.

And imagine the confusion and disbelief of his own immediate family and acquaintances! Each of them testified that he or she had never dreamed this man was capable of such a violent act. In Haiti, George de Mohrenschildt was quoted as saying the whole thing must have been a "frame-up." Oswald could not have done such a thing. In the frenzy of the next few days, few observers were interested in the reactions of the other human beings whose lives were paralyzed by these events. The Commission found, however, that some of the most complicating problems were created by the natural reactions of people who thought they knew the man, Lee Harvey Oswald, but who in reality knew him not at all. It can be seen now that except for Marina Oswald there was no one who really knew the magnitude of this man's ill will and lack of conscience. He was of their flesh and blood, or had moved among them as a taciturn, sometimes unpleasant figure, but they did not know, nor could they dream of, the proportions of his malevolence.

The news that Lee Harvey Oswald was implicated in the murder of Officer Tippit, and shortly thereafter in the assassination of John F. Kennedy, came to them as a stunning blow. Their lives were going along a normal course, and suddenly they were thrust into this searing hell of unreality. Murder, assassination and the countermurder. Nothing was real in the midst of this panic of events except the feeling, "It can't be. It can't be." But it was! And the crushing truth was most obvious to Marina. She knew more of the facts of Lee's twisted life than anyone else—many facts she would not reveal for months to come.

"I was watching television, and Ruth by that time was already with me, and she said someone had shot at the President."

"What did you say?"

"It was hard for me to say anything. We both turned pale. I went to my room and cried."

"Did you think immediately that your husband might have been involved?"

"No."

"Did Mrs. Paine say anything about the possibility of your husband being involved?"

"No, but she only said that 'By the way, they fired from the building in which Lee is working.'

"My heart dropped. I then went to the garage to see whether the rifle was there, and I saw that the blanket was still there, and I said, 'Thank God.' I thought, 'Can there really be such a stupid man in the world that could do something like that?'

"But I was already rather upset at that time—I don't know why. Perhaps my intuition. I didn't know what I was doing."

"Did you look in the blanket to see if the rifle was there?"

"I didn't unroll the blanket. It was in its usual position, and it appeared to have something inside."

"Did you at any time open the blanket to see if the rifle was there?"

"No, only once."

"You have told us about that."

"Yes."

"And what about Mrs. Paine? Did she look in the blanket to see if the rifle was there?"

"She didn't know about the rifle. Perhaps she did know. But she never told me about it. I don't know."

"When did you learn that the rifle was not in the blanket?"

"When the police arrived and asked whether my husband had a rifle, and I said, 'Yes.' "

"Then what happened?"

"They began to search the apartment. When they came to the

garage and took the blanket, I thought, 'Well, now they will find it.'

"They opened the blanket, but there was no rifle there. Then, of course, I already knew that it was Lee. Because, before that, while I thought that the rifle was at home, I did not think that Lee had done that. I thought the police had simply come because he was always under suspicion."

"What do you mean by that—he was always under suspicion?"

"Well, the FBI would visit us."

"Did they indicate what they suspected him of?"

"They didn't tell me anything."

"What did you say to the police when they came?"

"I don't remember now. I was so upset that I don't remember what I said."

"Did you tell them about your husband leaving his wedding ring that morning?"

"No, because I didn't know it."

"Did you tell them that you had looked for the gun you thought was in the blanket?"

"No, it seems to me that I didn't say that. They didn't ask me."

"Did you watch the police open the blanket to see if the rifle was there?"

"Yes."

"Did Mrs. Paine also watch them?"

"It seems to me, as far as I remember."

"Do you recall the exact time of the day that you discovered the wedding ring there at the house?"

"About two o'clock, I think. I don't remember. Then everything got mixed up, all time."

"Did the police spend considerable time there?"

"Yes."

"Do you remember the names of any of the officers?"

"No, I don't."

"How did they treat you?"

"Rather gruff, not very polite. They kept on following me. I wanted to change clothes because I was dressed in a manner fitting to the house. And they would not even let me go into the dressing room to change."

"What did you say about that?"

"Well, what could I tell them? I asked them, but they didn't want to. They were rather rough. They kept on saying hurry up."

"Did they want you to go with them?"

"Yes."

"Did you leave the house with them right soon after they came?"

"About an hour, I think."

"And what were they doing during that hour?"

"They searched the entire house."

"Did they take anything with them?"

"Yes—everything, even some tapes—Ruth's tapes from a tape recorder, her things. I don't know what."

"Did they take many of your belongings?"

"I didn't watch at that time. After all, it is not my business. If they need it, let them take it."

Ruth Paine's account of these moments filled out Marina's harassed recollections.

"I went to the door. They announced themselves as from both the Sheriff's office and the Dallas Police office. I was very surprised."

"Did you say anything?"

"I said nothing. I think I just dropped my jaw. And the man in front said by way of explanation, 'We have Lee Oswald in custody. He is charged with shooting an officer.' This is the first I had any idea that Lee might be in trouble with the police, or in any way involved in the day's events. I asked them to come in. They said they wanted to search the house. I asked if they had a warrant. They said they didn't. They said they could get the Sheriff out here right away with one if I insisted. And I said no, that was all right, they could be my guests.

"They then did search the house. I directed them to the fact that most of the Oswalds' things were in storage in my garage and showed where the garage was and to the room where Marina and the baby had stayed where they would find the other things which belonged to the Oswalds. Marina and I went with two or three of these police officers to the garage."

"How many police officers were there?"

"There were six altogether, and they were busy in various parts of the house. The officer asked me in the garage did Lee Oswald have any weapons or guns. I said no and translated the question to Marina, and she said yes, that she had seen a portion, had looked into, she indicated the blanket roll on the floor."

"Was the blanket roll on the floor at that time?"

"She indicated the blanket roll on the floor very close to where I was standing. As she told me about it I stepped onto the blanket roll."

The Commission furnished the blanket so that Ruth Paine could re-enact her part. Even in the quiet atmosphere of the Commission hearing room this re-enactment was dramatic. I could easily visualize the shocking conclusions those standing in the Paine garage that November afternoon came to as the blanket incident developed.

"This might be helpful. You had shaped that up yesterday and I will just put it on the floor."

"And she indicated to me that she had peered into this roll and saw a portion of what she took to be a gun she knew her husband to have, a rifle. And I then translated this to the officers that she knew that her husband had a gun that he had stored in here."

"Were you standing on the blanket when you advised—"

"When I translated. I then stepped off of it and the officer picked it up in the middle and it bent so."

"It hung limp just as it now hangs limp in your hands?"

"And at this moment I felt this man was in very deep trouble and may have done—"

"Were the strings still on it?"

"The strings were still on it. It looked exactly as it had at previous times I had seen it. It was at this point I say I made the connection with the assassination, thinking that possibly, knowing already that the shot had been made from the School Book Depository, and that this was a rifle that was missing. I wondered if he would not also be charged before the day was out with the assassination."

"Did you say anything?"

"No, I didn't say that. Marina said nothing at this time. She was very white, and of course I judged—"

"Did she blanch?"

"She is not a person to immediately show her feelings necessarily. She was white. I wouldn't say that it was a sudden thing. I can't be certain that it was sudden at that point."

"How close was she standing to it?"

"From here to there. About six feet."

The shock that came over Ruth Paine as recent events fell into place caused Marina to say, "Your Russian has suddenly become no good at all." And well it might have failed in the confusion of that hour. Six policemen were ransacking the house. Here she was, a person whose Quaker pacifism extended to all personal relationships—even to coping with gruff policemen—and she now realized she was involved in a crime of frightful violence. This was why Lee Oswald lived in Dallas under an alias! Could this be why he wrote strange letters to the Russian Embassy? And she recalled now that she had found a light on in the garage after she had turned it off the night before. Lee had indeed gone to the garage at some time while they were asleep and taken an assassination weapon that had lain in her garage for weeks unbeknown to her! Small recollections added up quickly to a mountain of proof. And this was the harvest of her charity to him! To remember English words alone would have been a test of wit in these circumstances—but Russian? Her vocabulary vanished.

"The officers then said they would like me and Marina to go down to the police station, and I said, well, I would seek to try to get a baby sitter. About this time we then left the garage as I recall, because then Michael Paine arrived at the front door. I was in the living room when he came. And I said, 'How did you know to come?' And he said that he had heard Oswald's name mentioned on the radio and had come over directly, for which I may say I was very glad."

"All right, proceed."

"The police officers then asked if Michael would also accompany us to the police station and he said he would. I changed clothes to a suit from slacks and went to the house of my baby sitter. She has no phone. I need to walk to her."

"Where was Marina in the meantime?"

"Marina remained in the house with the children."

"So then I went to the home of the person I normally have for a baby sitter. It was now after school or this baby sitter would not have been there, which brings us to three-thirty perhaps. And I asked the mother if the young girl, teen-age girl, could come and stay at the house. I was accompanied to the house by one of the officers. As we left the house I said, 'Oh, you don't have to go with me.' Oh, he said, he'd be glad to. And then it occurred to me he had

344

been assigned to go with me, and I said, 'Come along.' It was the first I have ever experienced being in the company of people who suspected me of anything, and of course that is their business.

"We did arrange then for the girls to come back, one or two. I forget whether it was two of the daughters or one that came then to my house to stay with the children. As I came back, I noticed the officers carrying a number of things from the house, and I looked into the back of one of the cars—it was across the street from my house—and saw he had three cases of seventy-eight records of mine, and I said, 'You don't need those, and I want to use them on Thanksgiving weekend. I have promised to lead a folk-dance conference on the weekend. I will need those records, which are all folk-dance records, and I doubt that you might get them back at that time.'

"And I said, 'That is a sixteen-millimeter projector. You don't want that. It is mine.'

"And he took me by the arm and he said, 'We'd better get down to the station. We have wasted too much time as it is.' And I said, 'I want a list of what you are taking, please.' Or perhaps that was before. As much answer as I ever got was 'We'd better get to the station.' Then I evidently had made them nervous because when we got back from this car to the house, Marina wanted to change from slacks as I had already done to a dress. They would not permit her to do that. I said, 'She has a right to, she is a woman, to dress as she wishes before going down.' And I directed her to the bathroom to change. The officer opened the bathroom door and said no, she had no time to change. I was still making arrangements with the baby sitters, arranging for our leaving the children there, and one of the officers made a statement to the effect of 'We'd better get this straight in a hurry, Mrs. Paine, or we'll just take the children down and leave them with juvenile while we talk to you.'

"And I said, 'Lynn, you may come too,' in reply to this. I don't like being threatened. And then Christopher was still sleeping, so I left him in the house, and Lynn, my daughter, and Marina took her daughter and her baby with her to the police station, so we were quite a group going into town in the car. Michael was in one car, Marina and I and all the children were in another with three police officers as I recall. One of them spoke some Czech, tried to understand what was being said. The one in the front seat turned to me and said, 'Are you a Communist?' and I said, 'No, I am not, and I don't even feel the need of a Fifth Amendment.' And he was satisfied with that."

Peace and good will—the dedication of a sincere Quaker—had been mocked by a man of violence and misanthropy whom she had helped to shelter. Three small bullets from a rifle and the whole course of the world had been changed! And here was Ruth Paine, a person who could never have imagined herself involved in a crime en route herself to be questioned. In a lifetime of striving to do the right thing she had never dreamed she would see the inside of a jailhouse. She was not fearful for herself. Her conscience was clear.

It sent a chill down her spine to hear Marina say, "Isn't it true that the penalty for shooting someone in Texas is the electric chair?"

CHAPTER 26

HOUR OF BLACK NEWS

As Ruth Paine and Marina were being sped to the Dallas police station, two other members of the Oswald family got the shocking news. Robert, Marguerite, Lee and Marina had not been together for more than a year, and suddenly they were reunited by murder.

Normally a mother has some idea of a son's activities. A brother may not be close to a sister but will keep track of her doings. A family is a network of natural communications, but in the Oswald family it was not. Thus when they were all brought together at the Dallas police station, in many ways they were like strangers. The intervening year separated them from Lee farther than they could have believed. As far as either Robert or Marguerite knew, Lee was living in the Dallas–Fort Worth area pursuing his job. They were both busy with their normal pursuits.

Now with their sudden coming together many strange things happened. Robert and Marguerite entered in the middle of the reel and knew nothing of the events in the reel just before. They were thrust among a cast of characters unknown to them. The action had been headed in a dangerous direction for some time. They knew nothing about it. In trying to catch up with the story they had only the past and their instincts to go by. In the hours of reunion of these unhappy people, a series of misunderstandings arose which fired a fuse of events so complex as to make an involved mystery story seem simple.

The unraveling of these matters became an important charge of the Commission because only after months of study and the careful reconstruction of events was it possible to understand where all the false leads had come from. The Commission had had its first shock when the Attorney General of Texas officially raised the alarm that Lee Oswald might have been working for the FBI. How did this story get its start? In the dark hours of the forced reunion of Lee

Oswald, his family and innocent associates, many of these speculations had their beginning.

Marguerite Oswald told the Commission how she had learned about her son's involvement. She also had some definite ideas about what might be behind his actions.

"Well, I was on a case in a rest home, and I had a three-to-eleven shift. I was dressed, ready to go to work. I was watching—I am a little ahead of my story.

"I watched the television in the morning before I was dressed. And Richard Nixon was in Dallas, and he made a television appearance approximately two hours before President Kennedy was to arrive in Dallas. And as a layman, I remember saying, 'Well, the audacity of him, to make this statement against President Kennedy just an hour or two before his arrival in Dallas.'

"And then I had my lunch, and I dressed, with my nurse's uniform on, to go to work, for the three-to-eleven shift. And I have to leave home at two-thirty. So I had a little time to watch the Presidential procession.

"And while sitting on the sofa, the news came that the President was shot. And there was a witness on television, a man and a little girl on television. However, I could not continue to watch it. I had to report to work.

"So I went in the car, and approximately seven blocks away I turned the radio on in the car. I heard that Lee Harvey Oswald was picked up as a suspect.

"I immediately turned the car around and came back home, got on the telephone, called Acme Brick in Fort Worth and asked where Robert was, because he had been traveling, and I must get in touch with Robert immediately, because his brother was picked up as a suspect in the assassination. So they had Robert call me.

"Robert didn't know that Lee was picked up.

"Now, Robert is in Denton. So I called the *Star Telegram* and asked that—if they could possibly have someone escort me to Dallas, because I realized I could not drive to Dallas. And they did. They sent two men to escort me to Dallas.

"The name of one is Bob Shieffer, and the other name I will have for you gentlemen.

"Now—"

"Who are those? Are those reporters?"

"*Star Telegram* reporters, sent by the *Star Telegram* editor to escort me to Dallas.

"Now, upon arriving in Dallas, I did not ask—I did not want to talk to the police. I asked specifically to talk to FBI agents. My wish was granted. I was sent into a room. I have to backtrack my story.

"The policemen do not know I am here—'I want to talk to FBI agents.' "

"What time of the day is this?"

"This is approximately three-thirty. So I am escorted into an office and the two Brown FBI agents—they are brothers, I understand— and there was another man that I do not know the name."

"By that you mean their names were Brown?"

"Their names were Brown. And I have the correct names also. But we were in this room, and I told them who I was. And I said, 'I want to talk with you gentlemen because I feel like my son is an agent of the Government, and for the security of my country I don't want this to get out.'

"But first I said to them, 'I want to talk to FBI agents from Washington.'

" 'Mrs. Oswald, we are from Washington. We work with Washington.'

"I said, 'I understand you work with Washington. But I want officials from Washington,' and I believed they would be in town because of protecting the President.

"I said, 'I do not want local FBI men. What I have to say I want to say to Washington men.'

"Of course they wanted the news. They said, 'Well, we work through Washington.'

"I said, 'I know you do. But I would like Washington men.'

"So I had no choice."

"Did you tell them why you thought he was an agent?"

"Yes, sir. I am coming to this.

"So I said, 'I have information that'—I told him who I was. I said, 'For the security of my country, I want this kept perfectly quiet until you investigate. I happen to know that the State Department furnished the money for my son to return back to the United States, and I don't know if that would be made public what that would involve, and so please will you investigate this and keep this quiet.'

"Of course that was news to them. They left me sitting in the office. And I also told them that Congressman Jim Wright knew about this.

" 'You can be sure we will question Jim Wright.'

"And I gave them the names of the four men I had talked with while in Washington. Would you like those four names now?"

"Yes."

"One is Mr. Boster, who was special counsel in charge of Soviet affairs. One was Mr. Stanfeld. I should know the names.

"Well, Gentlemen, Mr. Doyle [the attorney appointed to represent Mrs. Oswald] will see that I gave you the names of these men. I had it in a little card and carried it all these years from my Washington trip, and gave it to the FBI men to investigate.

"So they left me."

"When you say you understand that the State Department paid your son's way back from the Soviet Union—"

"Yes, sir."

"Did you ever learn that that was a loan?"

"I have the document to state that they loaned Lee the money to come back."

"But you didn't know that at the time?"

"Yes, sir. But I stated—you see, I was worried about the security of my country. I didn't know if the public would find out—how they would take the news that the State Department loaned him the money, since now he is a Marxist and an accused assassin.

"I was worried about my country. And I didn't want the public to know. I wanted the FBI, not the police, to know."

"Did you know anything else that you told them about why you thought he was an agent?"

"No, I didn't tell them anything. But they questioned me, started to question me.

"One of them said, 'You know a lot about your son. When was the last time you were in touch with him?' That wasn't the Browns. That was the other man. I said, 'I have not seen my son in a year.' He said sarcastically, 'Now, Mrs. Oswald, are we to believe you have not been in touch with your son in a year? You are a mother.'

"I said, 'Believe what you want. But I have not been in touch with my son in a year. My son did not want me involved. He has kept me out of his activities. That is the truth, God's truth, that I have not seen my son in a year.'

"And the gentlemen left, and I did not see them after that. They sent the stenographer that was in the outer office to sit with me, and she started to question me. I said, 'Young lady, I am not going to be questioned. You may just as well make up your mind that I am just going to sit here. What I want, if you will relay—have these two *Star Telegram* men come in here, please. I would like to ask them something.'

"So they came in. And I said, 'Bob, I have rights and I want to see Lee.' And I sat in the office two or three hours.

"Every now and then I would walk up to the outer corridor and say to whoever was there, 'Now, listen, I am getting tired of this. I want to see Lee.' "

"What office was this?"

"The courthouse in Dallas."

"Were you there when he was questioned?"

"No, sir. And I will state now emphatically that I have never been questioned by the FBI or the Secret Service—never, Gentlemen. If they can produce my voice or anything, they can produce it.

"So then I was escorted into the office where Marina and Mrs. Paine was. And, of course, I started crying right away and hugged Marina. And Marina gave me Rachel, whom I had never seen. I did not know I had a second grandchild until this very moment. So I started to cry. Marina started to cry. And Mrs. Paine said, 'Oh, Mrs. Oswald, I am so glad to meet you. Marina has often expressed the desire to contact you, especially when the baby was being born. But Lee didn't want her to.'

"And I said, 'Mrs. Paine, you spoke English. Why didn't you contact me?' She said Marina didn't know how to get in touch with me. She said, 'Well, because of the way they lived, he lived in Dallas, and came home to my home on weekends, I didn't feel like I wanted to interfere.'

"And she acted as—excuse me, Gentlemen, but this is very, very emotional."

"That is all right."

"She acted as interpreter for Marina. We are in the courthouse now, in the jailhouse. So her testimony, Gentlemen [Marina's], the testimony that the Dallas police have is the testimony of Mrs. Paine.

"Could we state now maybe it is not the correct testimony that Marina gave—just one interpreter, and Marina's friend, is the testimony that the Dallas police have. I have no way of knowing, and you have no way of knowing, Gentlemen, whether it is the correct testimony."

Marguerite's concern that Ruth Paine might have interpreted incorrectly was understandable. The whole story of Marina's and Lee's life since they had met the Paines was unknown to Marguerite. Here she was, the mother of the accused, and upon arriving at the police station she found her daughter-in-law under the wing of a total stranger. How had this all come about? Who was Ruth Paine? What connection did she have with these events?

She asked Mrs. Paine sharply why she hadn't been advised of the birth of Rachel. It wasn't normal not to let a grandmother know a new child had been born. And what did these strangers know about Lee's work with the State Department? When the truth was established, Lee would be found innocent. Was someone trying to frame him and force Marina into a confession of something untrue?

If Marina wouldn't rise to the defense of Lee, Marguerite Oswald most certainly would. After all, Marina still couldn't say more than a few words of English—or could she? That question began to trouble Marguerite. She recalled times when Marina did seem to understand more English than she admitted.

Any normal human being thrust into this bewildering plight—a son accused of murder, a daughter-in-law who spoke a foreign language dependent on an interpreter, a grandchild one had never seen —would be at her wit's end to place facts in an orderly relationship.

In the midst of that frenzy in the Dallas police headquarters no one had time to explain all the evidence against Lee Oswald that was being piled up. If the FBI seemed to let her sit outside momentarily, not really knowing what was going on, it was understandable. They were busy with the interviews with the assassin himself. They were dispatching inquiries in all directions, tracing the spurious papers in Lee's possession. Already the atmosphere was darkly clouded by Marguerite's own allegations. A plot? Who was in the plot— Moscow, Washington, Cuba, the FBI, Secret Service, CIA? Lights were burning now all over Washington. Experts were frantically going through records, poring over files, minutely scrutinizing evidence under microscopes. And from the moment Marguerite raised the question of Lee's relationship to the Government, no agency could work with total faith in the other.

Marguerite Oswald was not the only person who suffered from the stunning blow. Robert Oswald learned the news as bluntly as she had. He told the Commission how he received the news and groped for his bearings. Conscious of the magnitude of the events he now found himself ensnarled in, he made mental notes of all that happened and later jotted down the facts in a notebook, which is part of the public record.

"For the history of the past two weeks as seen through my eyes and heard with my ears and felt with my body, I write for future reference for myself and future members of the family."

Friday, November 22, 1963

"I was out to lunch, on this never to be forgot day, with Bill Darwin, Burnett Henry, Bob Oech, and Bud Adams, all of the Acme Brick Company. As we were leaving the Jay's Grill, in Denton, the cashier commented, 'Have you heard (speaking to all of us) that the President has been shot?' This was approximately 1:00 P.M. As we walk to the car generally we all had doubts if it were true or not. Soon as we entered the car, the radio was turned on and it was real enough, but at the time the reports were not stating how serious the President was or Gov. Connally.

"After about ½ hour in the office we went out in the yard at the new plant and returned to the office approximately ½ to ¾ of an hour later.

"I returned to my desk and worked on some papers for about 15 minutes and left my office and walked up to the front desk or rather into Marvin Ellis's office. And Nina Providence (the receptionist is located there also) had a portable radio going. I remember that the radio announcer said Lee's name and Miss Providence said 'Oswald' with shock and realization on her face—then the second time. Lee's name—then it hit me. My statement was, 'That's my kid brother.'"

"Now, would you give us your immediate mental reaction when you heard that?"

"I believe, sir, my reaction to that would be somewhat stunned."

"Stunned in the sense of disbelieving? You just could not absorb it?"

"No, sir, not to that extent. If I may say this: My own personal mental attitude, through my entire life, seems to react to trouble to the extent that I do not perhaps go to pieces, so to speak, that I react apparently calmly in the face of adversity."

"You were disbelieving, but it might have been—at least your thought was that it was possible, though you were disbelieving at the moment?"

"That is right."

"I turned and went to my phone and called Vada and asked her if she had heard. She had not. I explained briefly and told her I would be home shortly.

"I received, before leaving the office, a phone call from Wilt Dubose, credit manager in Fort Worth, stating, 'Bob, brace yourself. Your brother has been arrested,' to which I replied, 'Yes, I know. I just heard.' He advised me that my mother was trying to reach me and gave me a number to call. I called and we agreed to meet in the Baker Hotel in Dallas, and that a *Star Telegram* reporter would take her there.

"I left the office and came home, and on arrival Vada and I agreed, best to call her folks and have them pick up the kids and herself. At first Vada insisted on going with me—I am thankful I would not let her go.

"I called the Fort Worth general office and asked for Harry Reger, but he was on a long-distance call, so I asked for Bill Darwin and advised him I needed to go to Dallas, and he stated, yes, he had heard and something like 'Do what you need to do and don't worry about the office.' Also the FBI had called the office for me.

"I called the FBI, Fort Worth office, and spoke to a Mr. Jennings and informed him that unless he wanted me to do something else, I was going to Dallas, and he asked that I go to the FBI office in Dallas as soon as possible. I advised him I would arrive around five P.M.

"It was approximately five-fifteen as I rang the night bell at the FBI office. Strange, but I do not recall the agent's name who interviewed me for two hours or when was the last time I saw Lee. Or when was the last time I wrote him or heard from him. This was an interview with no pressure applied to me. His first statement was, I had a right not to answer any questions. My reply was I didn't need a lawyer and he could feel free to ask any question. On completion of our talk, I asked him where Lee was kept, and he said Dallas City Jail or police station.

"I walked into the police station around seven-fifteen P.M. and went up on an elevator, but it was the wrong floor.

"I found a captain of police in traffic division eating his dinner and asked where I could find someone in charge of the case. I then introduced myself. He stopped eating and tried to call upstairs, but all the lines were busy, so he said he would take me up. As we stood waiting for the elevator, I reach into my left-hand rear pocket for a hand-kerchief and apparently, or at least I feel almost certain that the captain thought I was reaching for a gun, because he turned as to prepare himself, but then he saw it was a handkerchief. We went up-stairs and he found a Captain Fritz, who was in charge of the case. We shook hands and he asked that I wait in another office. The office I went into was where Mother was and a *Star Telegram* reporter and two or three FBI agents. Two of the agents were named Brown.

"Mother and I talked briefly and after about thirty minutes we were taken across the hall to where Marina and the two children were—this was the first I knew of the new baby. A Mrs. Paine was also present. We talked a little and shortly Mr. Paine, who the police had been talking to, came out of the office and Mrs. Paine introduced us. I did not like the appearance of Mr. Paine, nothing really to put my finger on, but I just had a feeling.

"I still do not know why or how, but Mr. and Mrs. Paine are somehow involved in this affair."

Robert now made a perfectly natural mistake. He knew nothing of the Paines, how they had come to befriend Marina, the repeated generosities they had shown her in the face of Lee's erratic conduct. He knew that the burden would fall on him to make many critical decisions in the next few days. He was at a loss to explain his brother's involvement in such a tragic affair.

He described his reasons for viewing Michael Paine with suspi-cion:

"His handshake was very weak, and what I might term a live-fish handshake. And his appearance, his face and most particularly his eyes to me had what I would term a distant look to them, and that he wasn't really looking at you when he was."

Robert Oswald immediately distrusted Michael Paine, and the de-cision he was to make based on this visceral feeling he had led to many other rumors of plots and counterplots.

CHAPTER 27

ROBERT'S NIGHTMARE

Robert Oswald had commented to the Commission that through his entire life he had been able to meet unforeseen difficulties without going to pieces. Now in the face of a deepening realization that Lee was very much involved in this foul business he had need of all his strengths and reserve. His distrust of the Paines was intangible. To this moment, what he knew about the crime was the little he had heard on the radio and a few fragments of information he had picked up since his arrival at the police station. Here he sat in the police station. There was Marina. There was the new baby he had never seen before. There was his mother, and the Paines. A President was dead, and there he was, involuntarily related to this ghastly truth. It was unreal but inescapable.

Robert struggled to collect his thoughts. His mother was doggedly maintaining Lee's innocence. Marina seemed quiet and resigned. Long ago he had learned in the Marines, slithering on his belly while a flack of machine-gun bullets sped overhead, that to make a rash move meant death. It didn't seem possible that Lee could be involved alone. Only once had it ever occurred to him Lee might be involved as some sort of an agent; that was when he first came back from Russia. But conceivably the Paines? Why would they befriend Marina? Why were they all so close to Marina? Robert knew he had to reserve judgment. His mother was already showing the signs of the strain on her. In this crisis she couldn't be expected to carry the burden. He would have to shoulder this one whether he liked it or not.

It was getting late now and Mrs. Paine had suggested that if they were no longer wanted, she should take Marina and the children back to Irving. The children were exhausted. It was also suggested that Marguerite join them if she didn't mind sleeping on the couch. She insisted she would not leave the Dallas area. She was going to be on hand to look out for Lee. They weren't going to frame him without getting to the bottom of this business.

Robert agreed that was the best thing. He would keep the vigil and meet them tomorrow. They left.

Robert recorded his feelings:

"I stood around for a short while, and finally started a conversation with a Cummings (I believe that was his name). We of course discuss the happenings of the day, and I do not feel we were in any type of 'formal interview.' We were just talking. This officer did state he did arrive at the movie show shortly or during Lee's arrest. He did give me my first hand report, and generally it was as announced on the radio and through the press. That he was captured in the theatre after shooting a policeman later identified as Tippit. Also he was thought to be involved with the President's death. We talked about 35-45 min. and I finally decided I could gain nothing this night—this night of unspeakable horror.

"I walked to my car about 7 blocks away (I was not known to reporters at that time and was not bothered at all) and I just started to drive—to drive down Highway 80 to Fort Worth."

Why was he going to Fort Worth? He didn't know. The sense of motion at least calmed his nerves, and it was doing something. How could that night ever pass? Reaching Fort Worth, he turned around and headed back to Dallas. He stopped once to get gas. He commented, "I do not recall my thoughts other than I was attempting to arrange my thoughts and my fears in my own mind."

During these agonizing hours while Robert was struggling to arrange his thoughts, a situation had developed at the Paines' home that was to affect the relationships of Marina, Ruth and Marguerite and in turn add to the complexity of events. Marguerite's version implies a harsh judgment on Ruth Paine, but it must be understood they were strangers of markedly different temperaments.

"We went to Mrs. Paine's home. I am going to say again, I did not see my son. So—I had my nurse's uniform on for three days."

"What day was this at Mrs. Paine's?"

"That was the night of Friday, November twenty-second. We arrived there approximately six o'clock. Upon entering the home, about five minutes after I was in the home, there was a knock on the door.

"Now, this is a little vague. On the way leaving the courthouse we

357

may have been in the company of the two *Life* representatives. They may have taken us to Mrs. Paine's home. I did not ask who was taking us to Mrs. Paine's home because I was holding my grandbaby and talking to Marina and sitting in the back of the car. And it didn't interest me at the time how I was getting to Mrs. Paine's home.

"Why I am bringing this up was because after I was in her home, about five minutes, there was a knock on the door, and these two *Life* representatives entered the home. The name of the men, one is Allen Grant and the other is Tommy Thompson.

"And I was not introduced."

"Had you ever seen them before?"

"No, I had never seen them before. As I say, they could have been the men driving the car. But I want you to understand at the time I didn't notice that, because I was holding my new grandbaby, and comforting my daughter-in-law, and talking to Mrs. Paine in the back seat of the car.

"So Mrs. Paine sat on the floor. And she said to the photographer —he had a camera in front of him—'Now, I hope you have good color film, because I want good pictures.' "

"What time of the day was this?"

"This was approximately six-thirty. We had just arrived in Mrs. Paine's home—I would say six and seven o'clock, approximately, between that time. We are home five minutes when they knocked on the door.

"Mrs. Paine immediately says, 'Gentlemen, I hope you have colored film so we will have some good pictures.' I didn't know who they were. But then I knew they were newsmen, because of her statement and the camera. So Tommy Thompson started to interview Mrs. Paine. He said, 'Mrs. Paine, tell me, are Marina and Lee separated, since Lee lives in Dallas?'

"She said, 'No, they are a happy family. Lee lives in Dallas because of necessity. He works in Dallas, and this is Irving, and he has no transportation, and he comes every weekend to see his family.'

" 'Well,' he said, 'what type family man is he?'

"She said, 'A normal family man. He plays with his children. Last night he fed June. He watches television and just normal things.'

"She went on.

"So he said, 'Mrs. Paine, can you tell me how Lee got the money

358

to—' I am sorry—'can you tell me how Lee was able to return back to the United States financially?'

"She said, 'Oh, yes, he saved the money to come back to the United States.'

"Now, while this little episode went on, I was fuming, Gentlemen, because I didn't want this type of publicity. I thought it was un-called for, immediately after the assassination, and the consequent arrest of my son.

"But I was in Mrs. Paine's home. Now I had an opportunity to be gracious. I spoke up and I said—I am ahead of myself.

"She answered that he saved the money.

"I spoke up and I said, 'Now, Mrs. Paine, I am sorry. I am in your home. And I appreciate the fact that I am a guest in your home. But I will not have you making statements that are incorrect. Because I happen to know you have made an incorrect statement. To begin with, I do not approve of this publicity. And if we are going to have the life story with *Life* magazine'—by that time I knew what it was —'I would like to get paid. Here is my daughter-in-law with two small children, and I, myself, am penniless, and if we are going to give this information, I believe we should get paid for it.' "

"Did you think Mrs. Paine was trying to get paid for it?"

"Possible. But I do know this. It was prearranged. That is the point that is important. That after a few hours' time, the *Life* repre-sentatives were invited to her home, into her home, because she ex-pected them, you see."

"Were they talking to each other, Marina and Mrs. Paine, while you were there?"

"Yes, they talked in Russian. And that is a difficult part. I didn't know Russian.

"Then, with that, the *Life* representative got up and said, 'Mrs. Oswald, I will call my office and see what they think about an ar-rangement of your life story.'

"So he did call the office. He closed the door and called in private. And nothing was said—in the living room.

"When I say nothing was said, it was between myself and the other representative. Mrs. Paine was talking to my daughter-in-law in Russian. I was talking to my daughter-in-law in English. It was a regular general conversation, so far as I knew.

"He came out from the telephone conversation and said, no, that the company would not allow him to pay for the story. What they would do—they would pay our expenses while in Dallas, and our food and expenses, hotel accommodation.

"So I told him that I would think about it.

"Now, they continued to hang around. And they were taking pictures continuously, all the while this was going on—the photographer, Mr. Allen [Grant] was continuously taking pictures. I was awfully tired and upset. I rolled my stockings down, and the picture is in *Life* magazine. And he stopped that. So I got up and said, 'I am not having this invasion of privacy. I realize that I am in Mrs. Paine's home. But you are taking my picture without my consent, and a picture that I certainly don't want made public.' It is the worst—with me rolling my hose. I wanted to get comfortable.

"He followed Marina around in the bedroom. She was undressing June. He took pictures of everything. And Mrs. Paine was in her glory—I will say this. Mrs. Paine was very happy all these pictures were taken. And I had to go behind Marina to see that the photographers were not taking her, and they were taking me. And it was just a regular—the home was a living room and a hall and a bedroom and kitchen, and we were all going around in circles.

"And the photographer was taking pictures. Until finally I became indignant, and said, 'I have had it. Now find out what accommodations you can make for us, for my daughter-in-law and I so that we can be in Dallas to help Lee, and let me know in the morning.'

"So they left. However, about an hour later there was a telephone call to Mrs. Paine from a *Life* representative. I know by her conversation who she was talking to."

"Who was that?"

"One of the men—either Allen Grant or Tommy Thompson. And after the conversation, I said to her, 'Was that one of the *Life* representatives?' And she said, 'Oh, yes, he just was a little upset about what happened.' So I got no information there."

"This is on the day of the assassination?"

"Yes, sir—the twenty-second, Friday the twenty-second. I am worried because Lee hasn't had an attorney. And I am talking about that, and Mrs. Paine said, 'Oh, don't worry about that. I am a member of the Civil Liberties Union, and Lee will have an attorney, I can assure you.'

"I said to myself, but when? Of course, I didn't want to push her, argue with her. But the point was if she was a member of the Union, why didn't she see Lee had an attorney then? So I wasn't too happy about that.

"Now, Gentlemen, this is some very important facts. My daughter-in-law spoke to Mrs. Paine in Russian, 'Mama,' she says. So she takes me into the bedroom and closes the door. She said, 'Mama, I show you.' She opened the closet, and in the closet was a lot of books and papers. And she came out with a picture—a picture of Lee with a gun.

"It said, 'To my daughter June'—written in English. I said, 'Oh, Marina, police.' I didn't think anything of the picture.

"Now, you must understand that I don't know what is going on on television—I came from the jailhouse and everything, so I don't know all the circumstances, what evidence they had against my son by this time. I had no way of knowing. But I say to my daughter, 'To my daughter, June,' anybody can own a rifle, to go hunting. You yourself probably have a rifle. So I am not connecting this with the assassination—'To my daughter, June.' Because I would immediately say, and I remember—I think my son is an agent all the time—no one is going to be foolish enough if they mean to assassinate the President, or even murder someone to take a picture of themselves with that rifle and leave that there for evidence.

"So I didn't think a thing about it. And it says, 'To my daughter, June.' I said, 'The police,' meaning that if the police got that, they would use that against my son, which would be a natural way to think.

"She says, 'You take, Mama.' I said, 'No.' 'Yes, Mama, you take.' I said, 'No, Marina. Put back in the book.' So she put the picture back in the book. Which book it was, I do not know.

"So the next day, when we are at the courthouse—this is on Saturday—she—we were sitting down, waiting to see Lee. She puts her shoe down, she says, 'Mama, picture.' She had the picture folded up in her shoe.

"Now I did not see that it was the picture, but I know that it was, because she told me it was, and I could see it was folded up. It wasn't open for me to say. I said, 'Marina.' Just like that. So Robert came along and she says, 'Robert.' I said, 'No, no, Marina.' I didn't want her to tell Robert about the picture. Right there, you know. That was about the picture."

"Did you ever tell her to destroy the picture?"

"No. Now, that was in Mrs. Paine's home.

"I want to start to remember—because when we leave Mrs. Paine's home we go into another phase, where the picture comes in again. So I have to tell the—unless you want to ask me specific questions."

"No, you go right ahead."

"Mrs. Paine, in front of me, gave Marina ten dollars. Now, Mrs. Paine, when I said, after the representatives left—I said, 'You know, I do want to get paid for the story, because I am destitute, and here is a girl with—her husband is going to be in jail, we will need money for attorneys, with two babies.'

"She said, 'You don't have to worry about Marina. Marina will always have a home with me, because Marina helps.'

"Now, Mrs. Paine speaks Russian fluently. 'She helps me with my Russian language. She baby-sits for me. And helps me with the housework, and you never have to worry about Marina. She will always have a home with me.'

"Now, Mr. and Mrs. Paine are separated. Mr. Paine does not live here. So it is just the two women. So Mrs. Paine didn't graciously do anything for Marina, as the papers stated—that Lee never did pay Mrs. Paine for room or board. Mrs. Paine owes them money. That is almost the kind of work that I do, or the airline stewardesses do, serve food and everything. Marina was earning her keep and really should have had a salary for it—what I am trying to say, Gentlemen, Mrs. Paine had Marina there to help baby-sit with the children, with her children—if she wanted to go running around and everything. So actually she wasn't doing my son or Marina the favor that she claims she was doing.

"But the point I am trying to stress is that she did tell me Marina would never have to worry, because Marina would have a home with her."

Marina testified more briefly on the events of that evening. Among other matters she claimed she not only showed Marguerite the now famous picture of Lee holding the rifle but also she told Marguerite Lee had taken a shot at General Walker.

This information did not come to the attention of the authorities until ten days later. Perhaps Marguerite did not understand what Marina was trying to tell her. She never mentioned it, nor did Marina until circumstances forced the truth into the open.

About the night of the assassination, Marina was asked, "Now, the evening of November twenty-second, were you at Ruth Paine's house?"

"Yes."

"At that time did the reporters come there and the *Life* reporters and ask you and your mother-in-law and Mrs. Paine about what had happened?"

"Yes."

"We have a report that there was quite a scene between Mrs. Paine and your mother-in-law at that time. Was there such an event?"

"I did not understand English too well, and I did not know what they were quarreling about. I know that the reporters wanted to talk to me, but his mother made a scene and went into hysterics and said I should not talk and that she would not talk."

"Did she say why she would not talk?"

"Perhaps she said it in English. I didn't understand. She talked to the reporters."

"Did she say anything about being paid if she was going to tell any story?"

"She has a mania—only money, money, money."

"Did you understand that she was quarreling with Ruth Paine about something concerning the interview?"

"Yes, it appeared to be a quarrel, but what they quarreled about, I don't know."

"And after the quarrel, did you leave there?"

"I went to my room. But then I showed Lee's mother the photograph, where he is photographed with a rifle, and told her he had shot at Walker and it appeared he might have been shooting at the President. She said that I should hide that photograph and not show it to anyone.

"On the next day I destroyed one photograph which I had. I think I had two small ones. When we were in the hotel I burned it."

"Did you say anything to her about the destruction of the photographs when she suggested that?"

"She saw it, while I was destroying them."

Ruth Paine gave a third and somewhat different version of the tense evening at her home the night of the assassination. No matter which version was correct, obviously Robert would have his hands full deciding the future of Marina's welfare, especially with his intuitive distrust of the Paines.

Ruth Paine recalled, "The police officers brought us back to my home. It was by this time dark, and I think it was about nine o'clock in the evening. I asked Michael to go out and buy hamburgers at a drive-in so we wouldn't have to cook, and we ate these as best we could and began to prepare to retire. We talked. I have a few specific recollections of that period that I will put in here.

"Just close to the time of retiring Marina told me that just the night before Lee had said to her he hoped they could get an apartment together again soon. As she said this I felt she was hurt and confused, wondering how he could have said such a thing which indicated wanting to be together with her when he must have already been planning something that would inevitably cause separation. I asked her did she think that Lee had killed the President, and she said, 'I don't know.'

"And I felt that this was not something to talk about really anyway. But my curiosity overcame my politeness.

"Now, back a little bit to the time in the living room. Mrs. Oswald and Michael and Marina and I were all there, and Mrs. Oswald, I recall, said—I mean, of course, Mrs. Marguerite Oswald—"

"Yes."

"—that if they were prominent people there would be three of the lawyers down in the city jail now trying to defend her son and coming to his aid.

"She felt that since they were just small people that there wouldn't—they wouldn't get the proper attention or care, and I tried to say this was not a small case. That most careful attention would be given it, but she didn't feel that way."

"You made no impression on her?"

"I made no impression on her."

"I take it—"

"She made an impression on me."

"I think we would prefer if you would call her Marguerite. It would avoid confusion."

"All right.

"Somewhere in that evening before we retired and after we had eaten, the doorbell rang and two men from *Life* magazine appeared. I was—"

"Had you had any advance notice?"

"We had had no advance notice."

"Nobody did?"

"Nobody did."

"You in particular, and none of the others in the room?"

"None of the others."

"That was your impression?"

"I would be quite certain that none of the others and myself—"

"At least that was your impression at the moment?"

"—that they had no prior information that these people might come. I will say I was not surprised that anyone of the press found his way to our door at that point. If anything, I was surprised there weren't more. *Life* magazine was the only company or group to appear that evening. I permitted them to come in, and I felt that Mrs. Marguerite Oswald was interested in the possibility of their buying the story, or paying for what information she and Marina might give them."

"Had that occurred to you?"

"Had that occurred to me? No. But then, too, I wasn't thinking about pay for lawyers, but she made that connection verbally in my presence."

"What connection?"

"Between the need for money."

"Yes."

"The availability of *Life* magazine and the need to pay for a lawyer."

"And she was the one who raised that subject?"

"Yes, she raised it."

"For commercialization of the story?"

"I recall now she raised it definitely enough that Mr. Tommy Thompson of *Life* called I believe still that evening to see if he could offer anything, or what he might be empowered to offer."

"That was all instigated by her?"

"Yes, very much so. I noticed that the other man, whose name I forget, had a camera and I was amazed, and I also saw he took a picture and I was amazed—he tried with a dim light in the room."

"When you say he took a picture, you don't mean he took a picture from your living room?"

"He took a picture in my living room. He photographed. I saw him wind his roll."

"Thank you."

"I made the mistake I now think of turning another light on simply as an act of hostess—it was dim in the living room—but I hadn't realized until later that I was making it possible for him to take a picture.

"I didn't know what was best for me to do as hostess. It seemed to me that Mrs. Oswald, Sr., Mrs. Marguerite Oswald, was both interested in encouraging the *Life* magazine representatives and still didn't really want her picture taken, and I had no personal objection to their being there. But I considered the Oswalds my guests, and I didn't want to have the *Life* magazine people there if they didn't want them. But they left fairly promptly, saying that they would come back in the morning."

Back in Dallas at the police station, the case against Lee Oswald was piling up. He had been before the "show-up" a number of times, and Helen Markham, an eyewitness to the Tippit shooting, had identified him positively. In the interrogations by the police and the FBI Oswald denied facts which even Marina had admitted—namely, that he owned a rifle and kept it in the garage. Having been apprehended in the Texas Theatre with the revolver in his possession, he could scarcely deny owning that, but he offered no explanation for the whimsy of carrying a gun into a theater. His denials were persistent, but they did not stand up. For example, he denied he had told Wesley Frazier he was going home Thursday night to pick up "curtain rods." He denied carrying a package into the Texas School Book Depository despite Frazier's contrary testimony about these events. In the face of mounting and reliable evidence, he refused to talk. Lee Oswald would show the authorities what it was to be an iron man of silence.

By 10:30 P.M. Robert had arrived back in Dallas. His fears and apprehensions were not to be alleviated. He checked into the Statler-Hilton Hotel across from the police station. He wrote:

"After checking in I went to my room, and then decide to eat something which I did in the coffee shop. I had a ham sandwich.

"After eating I decide to go back to the Police Station. This was approximately 11:15, maybe 11:30 P.M. Anyway, I asked to see Captain Fritz again, and was taken to his office, however as I stood outside of the office an FBI agent whose name I do not recall asked if he could not speak with me and of course I said yes. We sat in a small office and another FBI agent came in and we covered more or less the same ground covered by the original interview with the exception of one thing: the man who had come to my home in Fort Worth while Lee was there. This was Mr. Peter Gregory (I later become to know him, at least a little bit and find him to be a fine person). At approximately 11:55 one agent left and returned and said 'Robert you might as well know now they are charging your brother with the President's death.' (He had already been charged with Policeman Tippit's death.) I looked at my watch. It was a few minutes after twelve midnight.

"I left the police station a few minutes later and as I walked to the hotel approx. ½ block away my body suddenly began to shake all over—however, I regained control by the time I reach the entrance to the hotel. This young body of mine had then started to react to this unbelievable day and during the next 7 days especially my young body, mind and soul was aged a great deal. I went to bed this Friday night of November 22, 1963 but I never really went to sleep."

Thus began Robert's nightmare, a ghastly dream from which he would never quite awaken.

CHAPTER 28

MARGUERITE TAKES OVER

SATURDAY MORNING, November 23, Marguerite decided to take over. She felt that Mrs. Paine had said some things to the *Life* people that were untrue. *She* was the mother of these children in trouble. It was up to her to make the decisions.

"So the next morning the two representatives of the *Life* magazine, Mr. Allen Grant and Mr. Tommy Thompson, come by at nine o'clock with a woman Russian interpreter, a doctor somebody.

"During the night I had decided I was going to take up their offer, because I would be besieged by reporters and everything. So why not go with the *Life* representatives and let them pay my room and board and my daughter-in-law's. They came by at nine o'clock, without calling, with this Russian interpreter. So Marina was getting dressed and getting the children dressed. He was taking pictures all the time."

"They came by where?"

"Mrs. Paine's home. And there was no hurry, though, to leave the home, because Mrs. Paine was most anxious for the *Life* representatives to talk to her and get these pictures and everything—whether Marina has any part in this, I don't know, because they spoke Russian, and she didn't tell me about it. But I know Mrs. Paine did.

"We left with the two *Life* representatives. They brought us to the Hotel Adolphus in Dallas. I immediately upon entering the hotel picked up the phone and called Captain Will Fritz to see if Marina and I could see Lee at the jailhouse."

"Who is he?"

"He is one of the big men in Dallas on this case."

"The Chief of Detectives, or something like that?"

"Yes. And I called him from the hotel, and the man that answered the phone said he would relay my message to him, that I wanted to see if Marina and I could see Lee. I waited on the phone. He came back and said, 'Yes, Mrs. Oswald, Captain Fritz said you may see Lee at twelve o'clock today.' "

Now things were getting somewhere! If she had a chance to talk to Lee, certainly he would give her some intimation of what this was all about.

That morning Robert got up at the Statler-Hilton Hotel across from the Dallas police department and went to the barbershop for a shave. He sat as calmly as he could while two barbers discussed Lee's case.

"No matter what this Oswald did, he deserves a fair and square trial like anyone else," the barber shaving Robert opined. Robert tipped the barber fifty cents and left for the police station.

Across the street he did not learn a great deal new except that the prosecutor, Mr. Wade, explained to him that Lee's trial would not be in a Federal court. It sounded ironic to hear Wade say, "You see, killing a President is not against the law—the Federal law, that is."

Marguerite called from the Adolphus. Robert agreed to meet them and go together at noon to see Lee.

When Marina left Ruth Paine's that morning, Ruth had no idea that this was the end of an association with Marina that had meant a great deal to her. Nine months had gone by since they had met at the party at Glover's.

On several occasions in her testimony before the Commission Ruth Paine responded to questions about the abrupt break-off in relations with Marina. In each case I could feel that Mrs. Paine was perplexed, hesitant and initially at a loss for the right words to explain what caused the termination. I sensed in the way she spoke and acted on the witness stand a deep regret, not bitterness, despite her generous hospitality to the Lee Oswald family. She and Marina had shared their griefs, commiserated with each other and been friends in a way Ruth thought would be everlasting. She had lived Marina's problems as if they had been her own. She had doubted Lee from time to time, but she had never questioned Marina. Even now when some dreadful things had come to light and it appeared Marina knew much more about Lee's doings than she had ever admitted, Ruth could not bring herself to criticize Marina. At this moment only one fact had come out that might have made her wonder. Should Marina have told her that Lee kept that rifle in the garage? She had felt silly telling the police Lee didn't have a rifle, only to be corrected. It was like innocently being made a liar of, and Ruth Paine didn't like lies. But that was a minor thing. Many men had hunting rifles. Nothing factual had been revealed as yet about the Walker incident. That secret was locked in Lee's and Marina's memories. Ruth had not yet realized that Lee actually had gone to Mexico, although she did give the draft and her copy of Lee's strange letter to the Russian Embassy to the authorities.

Ruth Paine remembered the last time she saw Marina:

"They left quite soon. I remember wishing Marina had taken more time to have more breakfast since it was going to be a trying day, and that is the last I saw her until March ninth, in the evening, very recently.

"March ninth, 1964?"

"Yes."

"Just a week or so ago?"

"That is right. She left, of course, expecting to come back. She took only the immediate needs of the baby's diapers and bottle, and I fully expected her to come back later that same day.

"I don't really recall. I think there must have been some newsmen out then that morning, later that morning."

"To see you, at your home?"

"At my home. I would be certain of that. The Houston *Post*— well, yes. And Michael was there also, at least in the morning, as I recall, and talked with these people.

"I believe the local paper, Irving *News*, was there. Then Michael, as I recall, went to do something related to his work, or had to do some shopping."

"He left your home?"

"Anyway, in the afternoon I was the only one there, and I felt I had better get some grocery shopping done so as to be prepared for a long stay home just answering the doorbell and telling what I could to the people who wanted to know. I was just preparing to go to the grocery store when several officers arrived again from the Dallas police office and asked if they could search.

"This time I was in the yard, the front yard on the grass, and they asked if they could search, and held up their warrant, and I said yes, they could search.

"They said they were looking for something specific and I said, 'I want to go to the grocery store. I'll just go and you go ahead and do your searching.'

"I then went to the grocery store and when I came back they had finished and left, locking my door, which necessitated my getting out my key. I don't normally lock my door when I go shopping."

"Did you take your children shopping?"

"Always. Then about three-thirty or four I got a telephone call."

"The phone rang?"

"The phone rang. I answered."

"Did you recognize the voice?"

"I recognized the voice, but I don't recall what he said."

"What did the voice say?"

"The voice said, 'This is Lee.' "

"Give your best recollection of everything you said, and if you can, please, everything he said, and exactly what you said."

"I said, 'Well, hello.' And he said he wanted to ask me to call Mr. John Abt in New York for him after six P.M. He gave me a telephone number of an office in New York and a residence in New York."

"Two telephone numbers he gave you?"

"Yes."

"One office and one residence of Mr. John Abt. Did he say who Mr. John Abt was?"

"He said he was an attorney he wanted to have."

"Represent him?"

"To represent him. He thanked me for my concern."

"Did he tell you or ask you what you were to do or say to Mr. Abt if you reached him?"

"I carried the clear impression I was to ask him if he would serve as attorney for Lee Oswald."

"All right. Have you given the substance of the conversation in as much detail of the entire conversation as you now can recall?"

"There is a little more that is—"

"Why don't you just go ahead and tell it as you remember it, everything that he said and you said?"

"I can't give the specific words to this part, but I carry a clear impression, too, that he sounded to me almost as if nothing out of the ordinary had happened.

"I would make this telephone call for him, would help him, as I had in other ways previously. He was—he expressed gratitude to me. I felt but did not express considerable irritation at his seeming to be so apart from the situation, so presuming of his own innocence, if you will, but I did say I would make the call for him.

"Then he called back almost immediately. I gather that he had made the call to me on the permission to make a different call, and then he got specific permission from the police to make a call to me and the call was identical."

"This is speculation?"

"This is speculation, but the content of the second call was almost identical."

"The phone rang?"

"He asked me to contact John Abt."

"He identified himself and he asked you to make the call?"

"Yes."

"What did he say?"

"He wanted me to call this lawyer."

"Did you express any surprise for him to call back almost immediately giving you the same message that he had given previously?"

"I think somebody must have said that the officers had said he could call, make this call."

"Did you say anything about the fact that he had already just called you about the same subject matter?"

"He may have added."

"Did you, please?"

"No. I was quite stunned that he called at all, or that he thought he could ask anything of me, appalled, really."

"Did he say he was innocent, or did he just have this conversation with respect to the retention of a counsel?"

"That is all."

"At no time during either of those conversations did he deny that he was in any way involved in this situation?"

"He made no reference to why he was at the police station or why he needed a lawyer."

"He just assumed that you knew he was at the police station, did he?"

"That is right."

"While you were shopping, and after the officers had come with a warrant, they went in the house, no one was in the house?"

"For a portion of the time they were looking, no one was in the house."

"Do you know what they took on this occasion, or did they tell you what they were coming for?"

"No, I do not. Before I left they were leafing through books to see if anything fell out, but that is all I saw."

"All right."

"In this interim then I suppose I talked to some more news people, but I want to get to the next important point, which was that Lee called again."

"A third time?"

"I really call the first two one, but it was twice dialed."

"Fix the time, please."

"It was around nine-thirty in the evening."

"Who was home? Was your husband there on that occasion?"

"I don't recall."

"Was anyone else other than your children and yourself in your home at the time of the receipt of the call in the evening?"

"It could only have been Michael. I would remember someone else."

"All right. The phone rang, you answered it."

"Yes."

"Did you recognize the voice?"

"I recognized the voice."

"Whose was it?"

"It was Lee Oswald's."

"What did he say and what did you say?"

"He said, 'Marina, please,' in Russian.

"Did you speak to you in English in the conversations in the afternoon or in Russian?"

"He spoke in English the entire conversation."

"The two in the afternoon?"

"Yes."

"Now, however, he resorted to Russian, did he?"

"Yes. He planned to speak to Marina, and this opening phrase was one he normally used calling as he had many previous times to speak to her."

"He was under the assumption you gathered that Marina was in

373

your home?"

"He certainly was."

"All right."

"And I would be fairly certain that I answered him in English. I said she was not there, that I had a notion about where she might be, but I wasn't at all certain. That I would try to find out. He said he wanted me to; he said he thought she should be at my house. He felt irritated at not having been able to reach her. And he wanted me to—"

"Did he sound irritated?"

"Yes, he sounded just a slight edge to his voice. And he wanted me to deliver a message to her that he thought she should be at my house."

"And he so instructed you?"

"Yes."

"That is what he said?"

"Yes. That was, so far as I remember, the entire conversation."

While these events were taking place in Irving at Ruth Paine's, Marguerite was in full charge at the Adolphus. Robert was on his way downtown to join his mother and Marina.

Marguerite recalled, "An FBI agent, Mr. Hart Odum, entered the room with another agent and wanted Marina to accompany him to be questioned."

"Were these FBI agents?"

"Yes, sir—Mr. Hart Odum is an FBI agent. And I said, 'No, we are going to see Lee.' We were all eating breakfast when he came in. I said, 'No, we have been promised to see Lee. She is not going with you.'

"So he said, 'Well, will you tell Mrs. Oswald, please,' to the interpreter, 'I would like to question her, and I would like her to come with me to be questioned.'

"I said, 'It is no good. You don't need to tell the interpreter that, because my daughter-in-law is not going with you. We have been promised to see Lee. And besides, Marina has testified, made her statement at the courthouse yesterday, and any further statements that Marina will make will be through counsel.'

"Mr. Odum said to the interpreter, 'Mrs. Oswald—' to the interpreter—'will you tell Mrs. Oswald to decide what she would like to do and not listen to her mother-in-law.'

"I said, 'It is no good to tell my daughter-in-law, because my daughter-in-law is not leaving here with you, Mr. Odum, without counsel.'

"And I had been telling Marina, 'No, no.'

"She said, 'I do, Mama,' she kept saying.

"Just then my son Robert entered the room, and Mr. Odum said, 'Robert, we would like to take Marina and question her.'

"He said, 'No, I am sorry, we are going to try to get lawyers for both she and Lee.'

"So he left.

"We went to the courthouse and we sat and sat, and while at the courthouse my son Robert was being interviewed by—I don't know whether it was Secret Service or FBI agents—in a glass enclosure. We were sitting—an office, a glass-enclosed office. We were sitting on the bench right there."

"Where was this?"

"In the Dallas courthouse, on Saturday. So we waited quite a while. One of the men came by and said, 'I am sorry that we are going to be delayed in letting you see Lee, but we have picked up another suspect.'

"I said to Marina, 'Oh, Marina, good, another man they think maybe shoot Kennedy.' "

"Did you ask anything about who this suspect was?"

"No, sir, I did not. He just gave the information why we would be delayed. We sat out there quite a while. The police were very nice. They helped us about the baby. We went into another room for privacy, for Marina to nurse Rachel. It was two or three hours before we got to see Lee. We went upstairs and were allowed to see Lee. This was in the jail—the same place I had been from the very beginning, and we were taken upstairs. And by the way, they only issued a pass for Marina and myself and not for Robert. And Robert was very put out, because he thought he was also going to see his brother. Whether Robert saw his brother or not, I do not know."

"About what time of the day was this?"

"Just a minute now. We arrived there at twelve o'clock. This would be about four or four-thirty in the afternoon, before we got to see Lee."

"Was anyone else present when he saw you?"

"No. Marina and I were escorted back of the door where they had an enclosure and telephones. So Marina got on the telephone and talked to Lee in Russian. That is my handicap. I don't know what was said. And Lee seemed very severely composed and assured. He was well beaten up. He had black eyes, and his face was all bruised and everything. But he was very calm. He smiled with his wife and talked with her, and then I got on the phone, and I said, 'Honey, you are so bruised up, your face. What are they doing?'

"He said, 'Mother, don't worry. I got that in a scuffle.'

"Now, my son would not tell me they had abused him. That was a boy's way to his mother—if he was abused, and it was shown in the paper his black eyes—he wouldn't tell me how he got that. He said that was done in the scuffle. So I talked and said, 'Is there anything I can do to help you?'

"He said, 'No, Mother, everything is fine. I know my rights, and I will have an attorney. I have already requested to get in touch with Attorney Abt, I think is the name. Don't worry about a thing.'"

"Did you say anything to him about another suspect?"

"No, sir, I did not. That was my entire conversation to him.

"Gentlemen, you must realize this. I had heard over the television my son say, 'I did not do it. I did not do it.'

"And a million of the other people had heard him. I say this. As a mother—I heard my son say this. But also as a citizen, if I had heard another man say, I didn't do it, I will have to believe that man, because he hasn't been—hasn't had the opportunity to present his side of the case. So here is my son. When I saw him, people had said, 'Did you ask him if he did it?'

"No, sir. I think by now you know my temperament, Gentlemen. I would not insult my son and ask him if he shot at President Kennedy. Why? Because I myself heard him say, 'I didn't do it, I didn't do it.'

"So that was enough for me. I would not ask that question."

"Who told you that there was—they had found another suspect?"

"One of the officers. That, sir, I don't know. He just walked in real fast while we were sitting down and said they had picked up another suspect, and it was in the paper that they had picked up another suspect at that particular time, which would have been approximately one o'clock that day."

"But you don't remember the officer's name?"

"No, sir, that is all he said and he left. He was just relaying why we would be delayed. But it was also published. I do not have the paper or the information. But I do know from the reporters, when I told my story, that part to them—they said that substantiates the newspaper story that they did pick up a suspect at that time."

"About how long did you and Marina spend there with your son?"

"I would say I spent about three or four minutes on the telephone, and then Marina came back to the telephone and talked with Lee. So we left. So Marina started crying. Marina says, 'Mama, I tell Lee I love Lee, and Lee says he love me very much. And Lee tell me to make sure I buy shoes for June.'

"Now, here is a man that is accused of the murder of a President. This is the next day, or let's say about twenty-four hours that he has been questioned. His composure is good. And he is thinking about his young daughter needing shoes.

"Now, June was wearing shoes belonging to Mrs. Paine's little girl. Marina told me—they were little red tennis shoes, and the top was worn. They were clean, and the canvas was showing by the toe part, like children wear out their toes.

"I ask you this, Gentlemen. If Marina had a hundred and some odd dollars in the house, why is it necessary that my son has to tell her at the jailhouse, remind her to buy shoes for his baby, for their child? Just a few dollars out of that hundred and some odd dollars would have bought shoes for this particular child.

"Another way to look at this, as I stated previously—that the boy is concerned about shoes for his baby, and he is in this awful predicament. So he must feel innocent, or sure that everything is going to be all right, as he told me."

"Now, in this telephone conversation, when you talked to your son, can you explain a little bit to the Commission how that is? Was your son on the other side of a wall or something?"

"Yes, sir. My son was on the other side of the wall, and then back of the wall was a door with a peephole, where an officer was.

"Now, we are going to come from the door, with the peephole and the officer, to my son. Then a glass partition, and then glass partitions like telephone booths. But not really enclosed—just a little separation."

"So you could not reach in there and take your son's hand?"

"No, sir, we talked by telephone."

"And he had a telephone on his side, and—"

"And he had a telephone."

"And you talked back and forth?"

"Back and forth, that is right. That is the way we talked. And the boy was badly beat up. I have proof in the papers—his face, black eyes, all scratched up, his neck was scratched. He was badly beat up. But he assured me they were not mistreating him, that he got some of the bruises in the scuffle. As I say, the boy, if he was being mistreated, would not tell his mother that."

"And whatever Marina said to him was in Russian, and you didn't understand it?"

"No, sir, I did not understand. But I would say this: it seemed to be just an ordinary pleasant conversation. He was smiling. And she told me he said he loved her very much, she said she loved him, and told about buying the shoes for the baby. That is all she said. She did not tell me any other part of the conversation. And they talked quite a while. She talked with him twice. She talked with him the first time. I got on the phone. Then she talked to him again."

"Did it sound like there was any dispute or argument?"

"No. It was a pleasant conversation. But she did not volunteer to tell me what was said, and I did not ask her what was said."

"What did you do after that?"

"So then after that we went back to the Adolphus Hotel. And upon arriving at the hotel—I am a little ahead of my story.

"The police and the detectives at the Dallas jail were most courteous to Marina and I. There were hundreds of reporters out in the corridor. And we were getting ready to leave, so they said that they would take us down the back way—incidentally, the same place where my son was shot. And they had arranged for two to go down and to get a car and to bring into this basement, and take us down the back elevator, and try to avoid the reporters. And there were approximately six or seven in the elevator. When we got down there, there were just a few reporters, and they went way out of their way to elude any reporters. We were at the Adolphus Hotel as I explained to you. And instead of from the jail straight to the Adolphus Hotel, they drove around twenty or twenty-five minutes' time

378

in circles in order to lose anybody who might be following Marina and I.

"So, as we got to the floor of the Adolphus Hotel, we knocked on the door where we were, and no one answered. We were with two men. Immediately around the corner comes Mr. Tommy Thompson, the *Life* representative."

"What two men were you with?"

"Two men from the Dallas courthouse."

"From the police?"

"Yes, from the police. So Mr. Tommy Thompson came and they asked for his credentials. I had never even—as thorough as I am trying to be—I am trying to tell you there are some things I don't know because of the confusion—I didn't ask for the credentials. I could have been with anybody. I just assumed they were *Life* representatives. I had not asked. But these Dallas detectives or police, in plainclothes, asked Mr. Tommy Thompson for his credentials, and then left us in his care again.

"Immediately Mr. Tommy Thompson said, 'Mrs. Oswald, what do you plan to do now?'

"The interpreter was gone, and so was the other representative, Mr. Allen Grant. I said, 'Well, the arrangement was that we were going to stay here in the hotel for a few days, and you were going to pay expenses.' He said, 'But you have not given us any facts.'

"They were not interested—and to me it seems very strange that they were not interested in my conversation at the jail with my son. They did not even ask if we saw Lee. Yet they knew we left the Adolphus Hotel in order to go see Lee. But they did not even ask if we saw Lee. And I have often wondered about that.

"So when I told him that we expected to stay there, he said, 'Well, Mrs. Oswald, the reporters will be coming in flocks; they know where you are. Just a minute.'

"He got on the telephone. Mr. Allen Grant—they had a *Life*—the *Life* representatives had a room on the ninth floor where they had a lot of men working on this case, and we were on the eleventh, I believe. So Mr. Allen Grant came down from the ninth floor with another man—I do not know his name—because the baby's diapers had to be changed and things of that sort. Tommy Thompson said, 'Mrs. Oswald, what we are going to do is get you on the outskirts of town, so the reporters won't know where you are, and here is some money for your expenses in case you need anything.'

"Well, I took the bill, and I put it in my uniform pocket without looking at it. That may sound strange to you, Gentlemen, but this is confusion. I knew it was money, and I just put it in my uniform pocket.

"So Mr. Allen Grant escorted my daughter-in-law and I out of the hotel, the Adolphus Hotel, and took us to the Executive Inn, which is on the outskirts of Dallas. We sat in the car. He went in and came out then and said, 'Mrs. Oswald, I have arranged for you all to stay here for two or three days. I have to be back in San Francisco. Anything you want you have your cash that Mr. Tommy Thompson gave you. And he will be in touch with you.'

"Well, I didn't think too much of it. He escorted us with a porter up to our room.

"We had two beautiful suites—two, not one—complete rooms and baths, adjoining, at the Executive Inn. And that was the last time I had seen either representative. I was stranded with a Russian girl and two babies!"

Robert did not return to the Adolphus or take part in Marina and Marguerite's move to the Executive Inn. He had not been issued a pass to see Lee when the others had, and so he waited his turn at the police station. Meantime he was interviewed in a friendly manner by Mike Howard and a Mr. Kelly of the Secret Service.

"Mike Howard, Mr. Kelly and myself talked about whether or not Lee, upon seeing me, would say anything to me because he did not at any time admit to any part of the whole unbelievable mess. I stated I would do my best. Do not misunderstand here. My whole intention then, as now, was to find out the truth and nothing else.

"Approximately 3:15 P.M. I went up to see Lee. We came face to face through the glass. He motioned for me to pick up the telephone which we were to talk through. His first statement to me was 'How are you?' I replied, 'O.K.' and I asked him if he was O.K., and that they were 'treating me well.' I do not recall everything we say. I did try to point out to him that the evidence was overwhelming that he did kill the police officer Tippit and possibly the President. To this he replied, 'Do not form any opinion on the so-called evidence.'

"All the time we were talking I searched his eyes for any sign of guilt or whatever you call it. There was nothing there—no guilt, no shame, no nothing.

"Lee, finally aware of my looking into his eyes, stated, 'You will not find anything there.' "

Robert did not comment on Lee's expression when he said this, but it must have been one of those stony looks so practiced with Lee Oswald. There could have been a curl of wry contempt in the corners of his mouth.

"I tried to talk about his family and Marina and the babies. He said, 'How about the little one? I want a boy but you know how that goes.' He asked that I not come every day to see him, but he did want me to come though and visit with him. He talked about the Paines as his friends and that they would take care of Marina and children. I stated who he considered to be his friends were not necessarily mine. I did this to try to get through to him. To me his answer was mechanical, and I was not talking to the Lee I knew.

"A police officer finally tapped Lee on the shoulder and Lee said that was all, and his last words were 'See you.'

"These were the last words I would ever hear from him."

CHAPTER 29

STRANGE INTERLUDE

Less than twenty-four hours later Lee Oswald was dead.

As one of the agents remarked to Robert, "Violence breeds violence."

Jack Ruby had taken matters into his own hands, robbing American justice of its mantle of dignity.

In the midst of mourning a President, few mourned the demise of his killer. Yet the way in which it occurred was shocking. Something that couldn't happen in America had happened.

Beside the awful feeling of doom those hours evoked, the seeming mystery of the succession of events was intensified. Bewildering enough had been the questions raised by Lee Oswald's acts. Now added to the atmosphere of intrigue were all the baffling circumstances clouding Ruby's motives. To discount the possibility of a plot now was intolerable. When the Dallas authorities announced that the "case is closed," those ill-chosen words stung. Closed! The case had just begun.

If the mystery of all the skeins spun into this dark web baffled the average bystander, they more deeply troubled those directly connected with Lee Oswald. Eventually each person would come to mistrust the other; every person would be wounded by the other's mutual suspicion. Already Robert had become deeply distrustful of the Paines and had told Lee his friends were not necessarily Robert's. Although Marina testified she immediately thought Lee had shot the President, his cool composure at the station could not help but make her wonder about the possibility of a plot she knew nothing of. Those who had known Oswald for the past seventeen months tried to fit parts of conversations and experiences with him into a meaningful pattern. Reporters rushing about in their frenzied efforts to piece a story together latched onto wisps of truth and tried to weave them into whole cloth. And Marguerite, the mother of the man who had precipitated this mournful cataclysm, stood unrelenting in the belief that her son was a good boy. It could not be otherwise, and she felt she had every reason to suspect others. The idea of intrigue in the relationships of her son to the Government was an obsession fixed through the years. It became more fixed now. Even the day before Lee was murdered by Ruby, small incidents seemed to give "proof" to her that dire plots were going on around her. Under the strain of the next few days she would see sinister meanings everywhere. Her imagination ran riot.

In the simple act of Ruth Paine following up Lee's telephone requests Marguerite sensed deceptive purposes. Also she thought the FBI was acting most suspiciously.

Ruth Paine's account, however, of how she sought to reach Marina was disingenuous and straightforward:

"I then tried the only thing I knew to do to try to reach Marina. I had heard one of the FBI agents try to find her when he was at my home; had dialed the hotel where the *Life* people were staying and asked to be put in contact with Marina, and was told, I judge, because he repeated it and wrote it down, Executive Inn. Here I am turning detective in this small way."

"You also mentioned now for the first time there were FBI agents in your home?"

"That day."

"During the course of the day?"

"Yes. I then dialed—"

"You shook your head—did you shake your head in the affirmative?"

"Yes, there were FBI agents in my home during the day. One I recalled made this telephone call. I was waiting to hear from Marina to see if she wanted to talk with me. I had no desire to press her or to attempt to reach her unless she wanted to reach me, but then with this message I went ahead and dialed the Executive Inn and asked for Tommy Thompson, and Marguerite Oswald answered, and I said I would like to talk to Marina, and she said, 'Well, Marina is in the bathroom.' "

Ruth Paine had no reason to believe she was under suspicion by either Marina or Marguerite or that she was being avoided. It would have been incredible to her after all she had done for Marina.

I observed her carefully as she testified. Particularly in the mannerisms and tone of voice as she spoke to the members of the Commission and its staff it seemed to me that a person with her knowledge of the circumstances would have been struck dumb by any accusations.

Ruth Paine continued, "I said to Marguerite that Lee had called me, that he wanted me to deliver a message to Marina, that he wished for her to be at my home, and Marguerite Oswald said, 'Well, he is in prison; he don't know the things we are up against, the things we have to face. What he wants doesn't really matter,' which surprised me.

"And I again asked to speak to Marina and waited until I did speak to her, and delivered the same message in Russian to her, but there was no further—"

"What response did Marina make to the message that you conveyed to her?"

"She said she was very tired and wanted to get to bed, as I recall, and thought it was certainly best to stay there that night."

In the next days, weeks and months, Marina's glacial cutoff of Ruth Paine became incomprehensible to her. In fact, Ruth's anxieties over Marina's well-being would create another plot theory which, when added to all the rest, became a spider's nest of apparent machinations.

Marguerite continued with her side of the story of events Saturday night at the Executive Inn. Part of the dramatics of the situation became intensified in retrospect, but she was alone with Marina in a world that was certain to feel hostile toward her as the mother of an alleged assassin. Furthermore, her ability to communicate with Marina was monosyllabic.

"I sensed we were alone. And there I was with a Russian girl. And I didn't want anybody to know who we were, because I knew my son had been picked up.

"So this is where the picture comes in.

"While there, Marina—there is an ashtray on the dressing table. And Marina comes with bits of paper and puts them in the ashtray and strikes a match to it. And this is the picture of the gun that Marina tore up into bits of paper and struck a match to it.

"Now, that didn't burn completely, because it was heavy—not cardboard—what is the name for it?—a photographic picture. So the match didn't take it completely."

"Had you said anything to her about burning it before that?"

"No, sir. The last time I had seen the picture was in Marina's shoe when she was trying to tell me that the picture was in her shoe. I state here now that Marina meant for me to have that picture, from the very beginning, in Mrs. Paine's home. She said—I testified before —'Mama, you keep picture.'

"And then she showed it to me in the courthouse. And when I refused it, then she decided to get rid of the picture. She tore up the picture and struck a match to it. Then I took it and flushed it down the toilet."

Marina's and Marguerite's efforts to protect Lee by destroying this picture proved fruitless. The police discovered in the Paine garage two copies of a similar photograph, each showing Oswald with a rifle and a pistol. When he was confronted with these at the police station he sneered and said the police had superimposed the rifle and the revolver on pictures of him they had taken the day before. But in the garage the police also found the original negatives of one of these pictures. Expert testimony proved that it had been taken by Oswald's Imperial Reflex camera. Marina later admitted that she had snapped the photographs herself.

The paradox of Marina Oswald's behavior in the next few months, however, comes out in this incident. She had felt certain of Lee's guilt the moment the rifle was not in the blanket. But frequently she tried to screen this man she knew had a will to kill. Why? Self-preservation? Fear of recrimination against her? Her tragic role was one for which it would be hard to find an equal in fact or fiction. Who in history has ever had to play a role so complex, so torn from every direction?

"Now, Mr. Hart Odum, the same FBI agent that insisted upon my daughter-in-law going with him from the Adolphus Hotel, knocked on the door at the Executive Inn. I had had my robe and slippers on, and I pushed the curtain aside when he knocked. He said, 'This is Mr. Odum.'

"So I opened the door. This is very important. I would like to not talk about it. I would like to show you what I did. This is so important."

Marguerite now acted out an incident she considered to be highly significant. It would have been had her suspicions been well founded in fact. The Commission thoroughly investigated the matter and found that the picture in question was not a picture of Jack Ruby. It had nothing to do with Ruby. It was a person the FBI thought might possibly have something to do with the assassination but later proved to be entirely unrelated. Marguerite fixed on this incident to bolster her claims that Lee was somehow an agent of the Government. This persistent belief gained increased credibility to her as she fed her imagination on half-understood events.

"I opened the door just a little, because I had the robe off and I didn't want anybody to come in. The door is just ajar—I am going to take my shoes off, Gentlemen, because I have this worked out. This is my height. He said, 'Mrs. Oswald, we would like to see Marina.'

"I said, 'Mr. Odum, I stated yesterday you are not going to see Marina. We are awful tired.'

" 'Well, we just want to ask her one question.'

" 'Mr. Odum, I am not calling my daughter. As a matter of fact, she is taking a bath.'

"She wasn't.

"He said, 'Mrs. Oswald, I would like to ask you a question.'

"I said, 'Yes, sir.' The door is ajar. This is my height. I wear bifocals, which enlarges things. And in his hand—his hand is bigger than mine—in the cup of his hand, like this, is a picture. And the two corners are torn off the picture. This is a very glossy black-and-white picture of a man's face and shoulder.

"Now, Mr. Odum wasn't too tall. I need somebody else. Mr. Odum's hand with the picture—what I am trying to say—he is facing this way—showing me. So my eyes are looking straight at the picture. And I have nothing else to see but this hand and the picture, because the door is ajar. And this is nothing on the picture but a face and shoulders. There is no background or anything. So I can identify this picture amongst millions of pictures. I am so sure of it. It was a glossy black-and-white picture. So I said, 'No, sir, believe me. I have never seen this picture in my life.'

"With that, he went off. There was another man with him.

"About an hour later the telephone rang, and it was Mrs. Paine. She said, 'Mrs. Oswald, Lee called and he was very upset because Marina was not with me, and he asked me to get a lawyer for him, a Mr. Abt. I would like to talk to Marina.'

"So I put Marina on the telephone, and Marina said about two or three words. So when she got off the telephone, I said . . . Now,

Marina talks in Russian, Gentlemen. I said, 'Marina, Mrs. Paine told me that Lee called and you were not home at Mrs. Paine, and Lee tells Mrs. Paine to get a lawyer.'

"Marina didn't answer.

"And I then sensed—well, now, why isn't she answering me? This is very peculiar. And there was no more said about that conversation."

It seemed now Marguerite began to suspect that Marina, too, was in some kind of covert maneuver with the FBI.

"Did you ask her about this lawyer?"

"Ask Marina?"

"Yes."

"No, sir. There was no more said about this conversation."

"You didn't say anything about Mr. Abt to her then?"

"No, sir. But the point I am going to make is that the picture was tried to be shown to Marina before the telephone conversation.

"Now, if there are any questions why I say that, I would be happy to answer."

"Yes—why do you say that?"

"Because they wanted Marina—"

"Could we get what picture this is? Is that the picture held in the hand?"

"Yes, sir—the picture that is held in the hand, that the FBI agent, Mr. Hart Odum, showed me."

"I understand you didn't recognize who the picture was at all."

"No. I told Mr. Hart Odum I had never seen the man before. 'Believe me, sir,' and he left.

"So the picture was shown—was tried—had tried to be shown to my daughter-in-law, but they were not successful.

"So then they received—Marina receives a telephone call. Now, I am under the impression, since I know it was Mr. Jack Ruby's picture I saw—at the time I didn't."

"How do you know that?"

"Because I have seen his picture in the paper. Now I know it is Mr. Jack Ruby.

"I am under the impression that Marina was threatened—"

It was never entirely clear just how Marguerite visualized the details of this suspected intrigue. Did she think Ruth Paine threatened Marina in some way when she called and spoke in Russian? Did she think Marina was warned not to identify the picture which Marguerite claimed was Jack Ruby? The implication is that if the FBI had a picture of Jack Ruby, they knew in advance he was going to kill Lee. Marguerite never made her suspicions in this and other matters quite lucid. She believed in Lee's innocence. Somehow if she could start a corner to unravel, the whole fabric of things would open up.

Marguerite's intense emotional display as she related the picture-showing incident was testimony not to be forgotten. This whole sequence covered a very limited number of minutes, possibly even seconds, but it made a deep impression on Lee's mother and her every action and word before the Commission graphically demonstrated the depth of her feeling.

"And the next day my son was shot.

"Now, it's now that I have done investigation of this case that I believe that the picture was meant for Marina to see."

"Why do you think that?"

"Because now it has been proven that Jack Ruby killed my son. And I think there is a connection there. Because Marina did not tell me about her conversation. And you men hold the answer whether Lee used the telephone from the jailhouse. I don't know that.

"So that night I was very upset and very worried. I realized that we were there alone. And we were not going to go in town, into Dallas. I wasn't going to take this Russian girl and the two babies. And the babies were all chapped. We had no diapers. We were not prepared for this. And it was hectic, Gentlemen.

"So all night long I am wondering how can I get in touch with Robert, what can I do. And I was a little suspicious of Mrs. Paine. I was suspicious of Mrs. Paine from the time I entered her home."

"Had you found out how much money the *Life* man gave you?"

"No, not even yet."

"All right."

"So I signed for the food. I called the operator and I asked the operator what name the room was registered under. She said, 'Well, this is an unusual request. Don't you know what room—what name?'

"I said, 'Frankly, I don't. We are three couples. I don't know which name they used.'

"So she told me that the room was registered under Mrs. Allen Grant, which is the name of the *Life* representative. So I charged and signed. And they would have that for proof—Mrs. Allen Grant, on the food."

"Why did you say three couples?"

"I just said that to the operator, because I had to give her a reason why I didn't know which name the room was registered under. So I just wanted to elaborate a little bit—let her know. I didn't want to give my name. Because I was by this time a little concerned about the situation.

"During the night I thought, 'We are in a position here. I am in a position with a Russian girl and two babies, and I just don't know what to do.'

"I had no contact with Robert. Robert was trying to get an attorney. And I didn't know if Robert knew where we were. And I did not want to call Mrs. Paine. I wanted to stay clear of Mrs. Paine."

CHAPTER 30

AN EYE ON DEATH

LOOKING BACK from the calm distance of the intervening time, Marguerite's imagination may seem fantastic and overwrought. But the pressures upon this woman alone with two babies and a Russian daughter-in-law were real. How alone she was in the world is difficult for many to imagine. As she told the Commission: "I have no friends in Fort Worth. I never—I live a very lonely life. I am not lonely. But I live to myself. I am kept very busy. I had my work, twenty-four-hour duty. So really I have no friends. And because of Lee's defection, I didn't make any new friends."

Marguerite's life had been a hard one, and she had toughened to the challenge of it. To me it appeared at times from her words on the printed page and her actions that she had been able to steel herself against her trials and tribulations, but her personal appearance before the Commission gave away some inward softness. During her days of testifying I listened and saw at close hand this woman, and she does have on occasion another side which is sympathetic. That night at the Executive Inn, as she worried her way through troubled sleep, her memories of her hardships could never be quite blotted out.

Yes, she had been married three times, but if the truth were told, there was nothing so unusual about that in this day and age. Her first marriage to Mr. Pic had not failed because of Marguerite alone. It had been a mistake, yes, but not of her own making. She was young at the time, and it may have been a typical romance of youngsters who are infatuated with each other. Who can tell you anything when you are that young? Well, they were both young, and perhaps she was a little immature, but she felt Pic simply hadn't wanted any responsibility at all—least of all children. When he found that Marguerite was going to have a baby, she said he had just walked out—that was all—and she thought that had it not been for his family

390

assuming some responsibility, she wouldn't have had any help. So that was past history, a long, long time ago, and she thanked heaven at least that from that marriage she had had one very fine son, John Pic, and there was nothing in this to be ashamed of.

No, in Marguerite's opinion her youth and her life as a young lady had been very normal and very happy. She resented all these so-called psychological experts delving into her past and trying to make her out as a freak. Speaking of her own youth, Marguerite had this to say and she said it to the Commission at the hearing with a conviction: "I had a very happy childhood. I sang. I sang from kindergarten at grammar school, and all through grammar school I was the lead singer. I was one of the most popular young ladies in the school." She continued with her reminiscences: "At grammar-school graduation I had the honor of wearing a pink dress instead of a white dress and sang the song, 'Little Pink Roses.' So I had a very happy childhood and a very full childhood. I played the piano. We had house parties in those days, and it was everything Marguerite—and I also played a ukulele, so I have a very full, happy childhood."

How the years had inexorably passed by the image of a happy child singing "Little Pink Roses"! She had somehow or other had many misfortunes, one after another, it seemed. It is only too easy to look at someone else's life from a safe vista of comfort and success and pass judgment. Often it is the brightness of memories of a happy time that saves each and every one of us from getting lost in the plunging events of our adult lives. Everything seems so orderly in the time of our youth. What happens in the outside world happens to "other people," not to us. Hardship, wars, assassinations—these are things that in time belong to history, not to us as individuals. But when they impinge on our lives, unexpectedly, they come as hard to one as to another. In the overwhelming emotion of our own grief over the death of a President, it would be wrong to overlook the shock Marguerite felt at the involvement of Lee in these happenings. None of us could feel the sorrow and confusion she must have felt alone that night at the Executive Inn.

Her son was accused of being a murderer, and they were even trying indirectly to blame it on her because she had neglected, they said, to provide Lee with a decent childhood environment. Well, they ought to know about that; they ought to know the truth, and if all this was so bad, why was John Pic a respected member of the

United States Air Force and Robert an upstanding young man who was making his way just fine in life? Just fine. Marguerite had had troubles, plenty of them, but she had battled for her children; she'd like to know what one of those fine society ladies would do with her children if she had to face the hard times she had known! And it could have been all so different!

Her second marriage to Robert Edward Lee Oswald had been a very good marriage. She was more grown up when she married the second time, and life had once more looked as if there would be long years of happiness and good times. Mr. Oswald liked children, and she could fulfill her role at last by having a home, a family, security and all those things she had hoped for when she was a young lady. Her heart could sing again, and when she was particularly happy about her marriage to Robert Oswald, she could look back on that grammar-school graduation and feel the same kind of happiness she had felt when she sang "Little Pink Roses." Maybe life wasn't so cruel after all. There had been times after her divorce from Pic when she nearly lost all of that gaiety. There had been times when she was plunged in discouragement and felt so depressed she wondered if she would ever get that bright, cheerful outlook of youth back again. It had been a pretty rough kick—to start out so optimistically with a feeling of love and adventure and enthusiasm and to have it end so miserably. But now she had a good marriage, and it was going to remain a good marriage. Life was not so bitter after all.

When she had told Robert E. Lee Oswald that she was going to have a baby, he had been pleased. He had been the proudest father this side of Ponca City. He had made her feel like a woman, and he had loved Robert, and he wasn't for a minute hesitant about having another son. He wasn't well-to-do by any means, but he had a good job, and he was providing for them and was on the way up. After all, working for the Metropolitan Life Insurance Company was no menial employment. People respected a man who worked for the Metropolitan; she was never ashamed when her neighbors asked her what Oswald did to say, "He's a Metropolitan man." And she liked New Orleans, where she lived. The Murrets, her relatives, had come from an old French family, and she had some position and self-respect and company among her kin.

So once again her life looked as though it had order and stability.

And then Robert E. Lee Oswald died of a heart attack. His heart had stopped, and now he was a body without a life, and it seemed to her that with his death even the young unborn child stirring within her would die. How could anything quite so terrible happen to her? Hadn't she suffered enough?

Sorrow? It was impossible to feel sorrow. It was just a numb, dumb sensation of shock.

These, then, were some of the experiences that had toughened Marguerite to life. After Robert E. Lee Oswald's death she braced herself for loneliness and hardship. Lee was born without a father.

If her manner of walking changed a little, it wouldn't have been surprising. She walked more purposefully. If her manner of speaking became a little more positive, why not? She was no longer a school girl, and she now faced a life alone which she would have to deal with realistically. Three boys—one an infant in a crib, the second just getting started in school and the third, John Pic, eating her out of house and home. She had a little money from insurance, but not enough to sit around indefinitely doing nothing. Furthermore, she had learned a harsh lesson. Life does not necessarily bring to people joyous things. One goes out and meets the realities of the world head on. Marguerite, as soon as she could arrange for the care of the children, went out to meet new realities.

She worked hard, and she provided for her children in the best way she knew how.

Then there was a third marriage near the end of the war that had turned to chalk. She thought he was disloyal to her, and they were divorced. After that she had been on her own all these years.

Marguerite's loneliness was real, but she never lacked courage. Tomorrow she would have to face the problems of a place to stay more permanently, because Lee's trial would probably go on for months. Tomorrow she would have to start thinking how she would raise the money for his attorneys. No time for softness or self-sympathy. It was frightening but she had faced terrors of the night before. She could face them again.

The next morning was Sunday, and Marguerite was up bright and early. At 6:30 A.M. she was on the phone seeking help. She called Mr. Peter Gregory, the same gentleman Lee had first contacted on his return to Fort Worth from Russia. It was through Peter Gregory that Lee had become acquainted with George Bouhe and the other Russians. She explained how she had happened to call Mr. Gregory:

"Now, I have to go back a little bit. But believe me, Gentlemen, the story will get together for you to understand.

"About one month prior to this there was an ad in a Fort Worth paper that the public library was going to have language lessons, and one was Russian classes.

"Well, then, as I told you—I was employed for the three-to-eleven shift. And I was getting a day off. And this would have been a steady job because this woman was not that sick, just an invalid.

"So I decided on my day off I wanted to do something. So I decided I would call up about it, and on my day off—make Tuesday my day off—and take up Russian in case, because I had always hoped in my heart that Marina and Lee would contact me some day. After all, I am a mother first.

"So I went to the library. And Mr. Peter Gregory was the instructor. I went to the second class. My car broke down just one block from the library, and I had to have it towed, and I went to the class. And Mr. Peter Gregory was there, and several of the women were waiting for his classes to start. I said I don't imagine I will learn anything, because my car has broken down and I am pretty upset. And Mr. Gregory said, 'Where do you live, Mrs. Oswald? Maybe I could help you and take you home.' And the other couple said, 'We would be happy.'

"And I said I live in Arlington Heights. And he happens to live about ten blocks away.

"Now, I have to go back.

"The point I am going to make is this: Mr. Peter Gregory is the engineer who knew my son Robert who was friends with Lee and Marina. Yet when I registered for a class and the librarian had come back down before the class and read off the names of the people that were going to take the lesson, isn't it peculiar that Mr. Gregory did not remember me as the mother of Lee, didn't acknowledge me as the mother of Lee? I find that very peculiar.

"Even the second lesson, there was no acknowledgment.

"So I went home with Mr. Peter Gregory. And there was still no acknowledgment.

"So we were talking about the Russian language, that it is very hard to learn. And I said, 'I am sure I will never master it.' And I thought I think I will tell him why I want to take lessons is because of my Russian daughter-in-law, and my son speaks Russian. But I didn't do it.

"But I am going to point out again that Mr. Gregory did not acknowledge me.

"I am going to give and take. Maybe he didn't connect me. But it would seem very odd—Mrs. Marguerite Oswald was the name—that he didn't connect as Marina's mother-in-law and Lee's mother, when he was such a friend with them."

Was Marguerite implying that Peter Gregory was in some kind of plot too?

"Now, believe me, Gentlemen—and I will swear again, if you want me to—nothing was said about Mr. Gregory and Marina being friends. But I do have a guardian angel. And, as I go along, some of the things I know have been from this guardian angel.

"So I am wracking my mind who can I call for help. And I think of Mr. Peter Gregory. So I call Mr. Peter Gregory at six-thirty in the morning, Sunday, the twenty-fourth—Sunday morning, the twenty-fourth.

"And I didn't want the hotel operator to know who I was. So I gave a fictitious name. And he said, 'I am sorry'—I said, 'I can't tell you who I am, Mr. Gregory.'

"I am ahead of my story.

"When I said, 'Marina, we need help, honey. I am going to call a Mr. Gregory.' And I told her about me taking Russian lessons.

" 'Oh, Mama, I know Mr. Gregory, Lee know Mr. Gregory, the man at the library that gives Russian lessons.'

"So I find that very much of a coincidence.

"So I called Mr. Gregory. I said, 'Mr. Gregory, I won't say who I am, but you know my son and you know my daughter-in-law, and I am in trouble, sir. I am over here.'

"He said, 'I am sorry, but I won't talk to anybody I don't know.'

"And I said again, 'Well, you know my son real well.'

"He said, 'Oh, you are Mrs. Oswald.'

"I said, 'Yes, sir, this is Mrs. Oswald. We are at the Executive Inn in Dallas, stranded. And do you know of anyone who would give my daughter-in-law and I a home and put us up for the time that this is going on, so we can be near Lee at the courthouse? I need help, Mr. Gregory.'

"He said, 'Mrs. Oswald, what is your room number? I will help you. Hold still. Help will be coming.'

"And so that was the end of my conversation with Mr. Gregory."

I could visualize him saying this or something comparable. When Peter Gregory later testified before the Commission his whole demeanor as a witness was that of a fine citizen willing to help a person in need.

Marguerite went on: "At eleven-thirty Sunday, November twenty-third, my son Robert and Mr. Gregory came to the Executive Inn, all excited. We had diapers strung all over the place. My uniform was washed. I had no clothes with me.

" 'Hurry up, we have got to get you out of here.'

"I am not one to be told what to do, and you gentlemen know that by this time. I said, 'What's your hurry? We have the diapers and all. I want to tell you what happened.'

" 'Mother, Mother, stop talking. We have to get you out of here.'

"Mr. Gregory said, 'Mrs. Oswald, will you listen and get things together. We have to get you out of here.'

"I said, 'That is all we have been doing since yesterday, running from one place to the other. Give us just a minute. We are coming, but we have to pack things.'

" 'Hurry up.'

"I said, 'I want you to know how we got here. I was shown a picture of a man last night. And Mrs. Paine called and said that Lee called.'

"I told him exactly.

"So Mr. Gregory and Robert knew about the things I told you. I told him that while I am gathering up the things.

" 'Mrs. Oswald, we will talk later. We have to get you out of here.'

"I have found out since that my son was shot. But they did not tell us."

"Did you have a television in this room?"

"Yes, sir.

"Now, here is another godsend. We watched the television, Marina and I. She watched more than I did. We were very busy, Mr.

Rankin. The babies had diarrhea and everything. I was very busy with the babies and the Russian girl. We were just getting snatches of it. But Marina wanted to know. 'Mama, I want see Lee.' She was hoping Lee would come on the picture, like he did. So this morning, Sunday morning, I said, 'Oh, honey, let's turn the television off. The same thing over and over.'

"And I turned the television off. So Marina and I did not see what happened to my son. We had the television off. So we did not know.

"But frantically Robert and Mr. Gregory kept insisting that we pack and run. So when we get downstairs, here was Secret Service men all over."

"Now, before you leave that, what did Robert say about the story about the picture, when you told him that? Did he say anything?"

"No. He and Mr. Gregory both didn't want to listen to me. I told them, but they didn't want to hear my story. They wanted to get us out of here."

"They didn't say anything about it?"

"No, sir, not that I can recall. And I don't believe they did. They didn't want to hear what I had to say. They kept fussing at me and saying, 'Mother, stop talking. Hurry up. We have got to get you out of here.'

"I kept saying, 'All we have been doing is run from one place to the other. The diapers are wet.'

"I was kind of having my way about this.

"So when we get downstairs, there is Secret Service all around.

"I am ahead of my story.

"Robert went downstairs to pay the bill, and that is when I gave Robert the money, and it was a fifty-dollar bill that the *Life* representative had given to me.

"Then Robert got in a car with Secret Service, and then Marina and I and Mr. Gregory were in another car, with two Secret Service agents in the front."

"Did you go some place?"

"Here comes me again. They wanted to take us—as soon as we got in the car Mr. Gregory says, 'We are taking you to Robert's mother-in-law's house.'

"Now, they live out of Boyd, Texas, in the country. Boyd, Texas, is a little bit of country town. But they live in a little farmhouse.

They are dairy people, Robert's in-laws. And they wanted to take us there, which would have been approximately forty-five miles from Dallas.

"And I said, 'No, you are not taking me out in the sticks, in the country. I want to be in Dallas where I can help Lee.'

" 'Well, for security reasons, this is the best place. Nobody would ever find it.'

"And I said, 'Security reasons? You can give security for me in a hotel room in town. I am not going out in this little country town. I want to be in Dallas where I can help Lee.'

"And so I am not being well liked, because all the arrangements was made, that we were going to go to this little farmhouse. But I would not go.

"I could not survive if I was forty or fifty miles away and my son was picked up as a murderer. I had to be right there in Dallas."

"Now, this was after—"

"When they left the Executive Inn, when we got in the car."

"And this was after your son was killed?"

"Well, yes, but we didn't know this. They kept it from us—I guess being women. Marina and I did not even know that he was shot."

"The Secret Service people didn't tell you either?"

"No, sir. Nothing was said. They wanted us for security reasons . . . This has to go in sequence, sir. Lee was shot, or else we wouldn't have had all these Secret Service men around. But I know then after that Lee was shot. Not now—I do not know this.

"Are there any questions? I am willing to answer anything you want to ask.

"If you will bear with me, I can go into—"

"Now, after you told them that you wanted to stay in a hotel, you could be protected there, what happened?"

"Then, of course, nothing was said that they were going to give me my way. But we needed clothes—Marina and the baby needed clothes. So then they decided that they should go to Irving, through my suggestion and so on, and pick up clothes for Marina and the baby, because we were short on diapers. So they are going to Irving.

"We got to Irving. There is police cars all around. So that is why I feel sure my son was shot."

"How far away is that from this Executive Inn?"

"I would think—now, this is just hearsay. But I would think it is about twelve to fifteen or eighteen miles.

"When we reached there, they brought us to the chief of police's home. And there were cars all around.

"As soon as the car stopped, the Secret Service agent said, 'Lee has been shot.'

"And I said, 'How badly?'

"He said, 'In the shoulder.'

"So Marina went into the chief of police's at Irving home to call Mrs. Paine to get the diapers and things ready. They decided and told us, with me in the car and Marina, that it would not be a good thing for us to go to Mrs. Paine's home and get these things, that Marina should go in the chief of police's home and call and tell Mrs. Paine what she wanted.

"And one or two of the agents would go and get the things for Marina.

"So I am sitting in the car with the agent. Marina is in the home now—remember.

"So something comes over the mike, and the Secret Service agent says, 'Do not repeat. Do not repeat.'

"I said, 'My son is gone, isn't he?'

"And he didn't answer.

"I said, 'Answer me. I want to know. If my son is gone, I want to meditate.'

"He said, 'Yes, Mrs. Oswald, your son has just expired.' "

"Now, about what time on that Sunday did you learn of your son's death?"

"Well, now, here is your time element. I said Robert and Mr. Gregory and the Secret Service were there approximately from eleven-thirty. And I knew nothing about the shooting. And then we had to go to Irving and everything. Then they told us Lee was shot. So now we are bringing up to the time—it all fits in—which was one o'clock or one-thirty.

"As a matter of fact, then when I got the news, I went into the home, and I said, 'Marina, our boy is gone.'

"We both cried. And they were all watching the sequence on television."

The big electronic eye of the world was on death.

CHAPTER 31

PLOTS AT THE SIX FLAGS

WRACKED BY GRIEF and mercilessly pummeled by this torrent of mishaps, Marina, Marguerite and Robert Oswald fought to keep their equilibrium. Marina and Marguerite had been raced from one hotel to another. Here they had been caught by this latest blow in mid-flight. They were in a stranger's home. Marina literally had no home—no home, no country, no refuge. With one child less than two years old and another barely one month clinging to her hands, she had been rushed from place to place—running, running, running, in cars, out of cars, up stairs, down strange hallways. The frenzy had not let up in forty-eight hours. And even when she was with Marguerite and Robert she was among strangers, because she didn't really know them. How long had she known Robert? Altogether a matter of a few weeks in Fort Worth. The same was true of Marguerite. All the other people were just faces to her: police, Secret Service, newsmen. She didn't even know who they were.

And there was another frightful strain. All she heard was English: talk, talk, talk. It is maddening to hear so much jibbering when you understand only a fraction of what's being said. Here was Marguerite trying to tell her something. She made faces or tried to act out her meaning. The police were trying to get information from her, but without an interpreter she was virtually tongue-tied. They were all coming at her. Questions—hundreds of them. It was exhausting to try to think what they were trying to say to her. And in turn she didn't know what they were saying among one another. What would happen to her now? Would she be accused of something and be put in jail? She was a Russian in a country where Russians were little loved. Would they deport her to the USSR? Surely they would punish her somehow. Her thoughts were trapped in her own consciousness, and there was no way to break through. Even when an interpreter was translating, how did she know he was not telling the others something different? It was painful, head-splitting.

Fortunately the Secret Service now realized the new importance attached to the protection of Marina. As soon as Marguerite had called Peter Gregory in the morning, he in turn had called the Secret Service, and, after making arrangements to meet Robert, they had gone to the Executive Inn. These hapless women, who had been more or less on their own since Friday afternoon, now had the vigilant agents at their side day and night. Marguerite no longer needed to worry about paying bills. The Government took over that burden. They also guarded Marina scrupulously. She was now the only living link to the true facts of her husband's recent past. If anything happened to Marina, the world might never know any of those secrets she had shared with Lee. Marina complimented the Secret Service on their courtesy and watchfulness. Not until after she had made her first appearance before the Commission in Washington was the vigil relaxed at Marina's request.

The unexpected murder of her son by a heretofore unknown night-club operator inflamed Marguerite's already overwrought temper. She believed so ardently that Lee was innocent, and if he could live to explain himself, he would be "the unsung hero of this episode." He had denied his guilt—that was good enough for Marguerite. But now it was obvious to her that someone didn't want him to talk. She began to swing widely between the alternatives she considered possible. She saw the possibility of plots in the unexplained actions of everyone and anyone. The Secret Service, after a trip to the hospital to view the body, made arrangements with Mr. Jim Martin, manager of the Six Flags Motel in Arlington, Texas, to provide adequate rooms for them and the Oswalds until a plan of action could be formulated.

Peter Gregory accompanied them as interpreter. His observations of Marguerite's behavior help to explain some of the chaotic events that followed. His comments were elicited in reply to the question: "There has been a newspaper report, and Mrs. Marguerite Oswald has said that on Saturday night an FBI agent came to the Executive Inn and showed her a picture of a man who she claims to be Jack Ruby. Have you seen newspaper reports to that effect?"

"Yes, I have seen reports to that effect."

"Now, Mrs. Oswald says also that while at the Inn of the Six Flags she observed a newspaper that had Jack Ruby's picture in it, and exclaimed in the presence of other people that that was the same picture as the FBI had showed her—that is what she says. Did you ever hear her do anything like that?"

"No, sir, not to my recollection."

"She never did anything like that in your presence?"

"No, sir."

"After you met Mrs. Oswald, Marguerite Oswald, and had a chance to observe her, did that further your judgment of Lee Harvey Oswald in any way?"

"Yes, sir. I felt that a lot of his, many of his peculiarities possibly were brought on by the influence of his mother.

"To me, she impressed me as being not necessarily rational. She is quite clever, but she certainly is most peculiar. She demands public attention, she wants to be the center of attention. As, for example, standing there in the middle of the room at the motel of that Six Flags, standing in the middle of the room saying, 'I want to make a statement,' and she made those statements throughout the frequent intervals and always she would precede the statement by saying, 'I want to make a statement. I feel that my son can't be buried anywhere but at the Arlington National Cemetery.' "

"And you detected similarities between Mrs. Oswald and Lee?"

"Yes, I felt they both craved public recognition, or to be craving attention or publicity, or whatever you wish to call it."

Marina Oswald added to Peter Gregory's estimate of Marguerite's conduct at the Six Flags during the tense days to follow:

"Will you describe to us your relationship with your mother-in-law now?"

"After all of this happened I met with her at the police station. I was, of course, very sorry for her as Lee's mother. I was always sorry for her because Lee did not want to live with her.

"I understood her motherly concern. But in view of the fact of everything that happened later, her appearances in the radio, in the press, I do not think that she is a very sound-thinking woman, and I think that part of the guilt is hers. I do not accuse her, but I think that part of the guilt in connection with what happened with Lee lies with her because he did not perhaps receive the education he should have during his childhood, and he did not have any correct leadership on her part, guidance. If she were in contact with my children now, I do not want her to cripple them.

"After Lee was in jail I lived with her for some time at that inn."

"The Six Flags?"

"The Six Flags. And inasmuch as I lived with her and met with her every day I could see—I was able to see the change. At least if her relationship with me was good, it was not sincere. I think that she does not like me. I don't think that she simply is able to like me.

"There were some violent scenes, she didn't want to listen to any-one, there were hysterics. Everyone was guilty of everything and no one understood her.

"Perhaps my opinion is wrong, but at least I do not want to live with her and to listen to scandals every day."

A number of other witnesses shared Peter Gregory's and Marina's feeling that at least under the pressure of events at the Six Flags Marguerite was strained to a breaking point. Her charges of plots and counterplots might be disregarded except for the fact that as these incidents found their way to the press, the atmosphere of in-trigue was heightened for the public. Marguerite alone was the source of many rumors that later came back to the Commission in the form of such allegations as those of Attorney General Carr of Texas. It was true that Lee had the telephone number, address and even license number of FBI agent Hosty in his address book. It was true that a high official among Dallas authorities confirmed this to at least one reporter. From these facts, plus the aura of intrigue as-signed to all events by Marguerite, the fantastic improbability of all circumstances surrounding Lee's act and Jack Ruby's blundering deed came the suspicions of the public. Reporters acted in good faith in most cases, but in a free society it is the duty of the press to raise legitimate questions.

Very rapidly the FBI established the basic truths, but when they were later thrown under a cloud of suspicion themselves, their re-ports were doubted. The very fact that the President's Commission had to operate under the ban of "Top Secret" gave the purveyors of lies and rumors months in which to nurture their garden of weeds. Especially true of the groundless speculations in Europe, Margue-rite's insistence that Lee must have been "framed" fed the appetites of mystery lovers. Only by understanding in detail how the "Plots at the Six Flags" came about can the public fully understand the difficulties the Commission had to contend with. Marguerite was convinced she knew more about Lee's activities and background than anyone else, despite the fact she knew nothing of Lee's life in Moscow and Minsk which he confided to his diary. She belittled Marina's profound knowledge of the erratic behavior of her husband, and found it bewildering and suspicious that her daughter-in-law was convinced from the moment the rifle was missing in the Paines' garage that Lee had done this deed. She wanted to talk and be heard in defense of the image of her son. In an indirect sense she was defending herself to the extent people blamed her for Lee's faults. The tragedy of Marguerite Oswald fighting for the dignity of her own life is one of the most heart-rending dramas of fiction or real life a reader is apt to encounter. Marguerite is seldom a sympathetic character because her past experiences had taught her so well that no one would look out for Marguerite but Marguerite. Her personality is the paradox of the human being who wants to be loved but whose need for affection destroys the very opportunity she so much craves. There can be no substitute for the self-portrait revealed by Marguerite herself as she told the Commission about the events of the next few days at the Six Flags.

She wanted to be heard. It seemed to her no one would listen—neither Robert, nor Marina, nor the Government agents.

"I was never questioned by the Secret Service or the FBI at Six Flags. My son, in my presence, was questioned and taped, and Marina was continuously questioned and taped. But I have never been questioned.

"I had all the papers from the State Department, and all of my research from Lee's, I say, so-called defection. And I wanted them to have them. All the papers were at home.

"I told them I thought I could save a lot of manpower, while they were getting the original papers, because I know that each department in the State Department had a reference on Lee, and I had the whole thing condensed, and by them having my papers they could get the picture. They were not interested in any papers I had. They were not interested."

"Were you not questioned on November 22, 1963?"

"No, sir. Here is what you may have on tape. I insisted so much that they talked to me, because I had all this—that Mr. Mike Howard finally agreed—not twenty-second, though."

"This is Mr. Harlan Brown and Mr. Charles T. Brown?"

"That is the two FBI agents, Mr. Brown, questioned me in the office. But all they wanted to know is how did I know my son was an agent, and how did I know that he had the money from the State Department. And I told them Congressman Wright knew and that they would investigate Congressman Wright. That was a very short questioning. I mean I explained that before. I told them I wanted to talk to the FBI, and I did. And it was the two Mr. Browns, and there were two other men."

"Then Mr. Howard was what date?"

"Mike Howard? Mike Howard was toward the end, because I was so persistent in them talking to me that finally he decided he would put me on tape. But I do not consider this questioning. It was the date of the funeral—I remember now."

"November twenty-fifth?"

"Was that the day of the funeral? If this was the day of the funeral—I can tell you why. He decided he would put me on tape. So I started to tell him about my having the papers and Lee's defection. And then Robert came out of the room and was crying bitterly. I saw Robert crying.

"Wait, I am ahead of my story."

At times I and other members of the Commission had difficulty following the sequence of Marguerite's testimony. This moving ahead to one incident and then jumping back to another made it hard to follow. However, I am including a certain amount of this purposely in the narrative to give an indication of Marguerite's state of mind. She was nervous and distraught—terribly anxious to get her involved theories across, and they were complicated, to say the least.

"You have to understand this. As a family we separated—not maybe for any particular reason; it is just the way we live. I am not a mother that has a home that the children can come to and feed them and so on. I am a working mother. I do twenty-four-hour duty. So I am not that type mother, where I am a housewife with money, that the children have a home to come to.

"So I said to Mike Howard, 'I would like Robert to hear this. Maybe he will learn something.' Because Robert never did want to know about my trip to Washington. He doesn't know. Robert never was interested in anything. Lee did not want to know about my trip to Washington. So I thought, well, now, this is an opportunity, since the tragedy has happened, for Mr. Robert Oswald to know some of these things that his mother has known all of these years.

"So I started.

"Then Robert had a phone call and he came out of the room, and he was crying bitterly. So I ended the tape—I would say I talked approximately ten minutes. I ended the tape saying, 'I'm sorry, but my thoughts have left me, because my son is crying.'

"I thought for a moment that Robert was crying because of what I was saying, and he was sorry that he had not listened to me before, because I tried to tell him about the defection and my trip to Washington. But Robert was crying because he received a telephone call that we could not get a minister at my son's grave.

"They had three ministers that refused to come to the ceremony at my son's grave—for church. And that is why Robert was crying bitterly. So that ended the testimony."

"Now, that questioning was a question and answer. You were questioned by the FBI agent, Mr. Howard—"

"No, sir. I was just talking."

"The Secret Service man?"

"Mr. Mike Howard. I was talking on tape."

"Didn't he ask you questions?"

"I don't recall him asking any questions. It could be. But I frankly do not recall him asking any questions. But it was a very short session. And that is the way I ended the tape. I said, 'My thoughts have left me because I see my son crying bitterly.'

"That is the way I ended the tape. And it was a very short tape. I do not remember him questioning me. I think I started to tell my story. And that is the only time.

"It was from my persistence that I got on tape just that little while. They did not want to hear anything from me."

"You don't think, then, that at that time there were questions and answers for about twenty-eight pages taken from you?"

"From me—no, sir. Definitely not. If they have that, what they have is my talking, like I said, when I saw on television. They said— they were showing Lee's gun. And I was not watching television—I am getting snatches of it, and I said, 'Now, how can they say, even though it is Lee's gun, that Lee shot the President? Even being his gun doesn't mean that he shot the President. Someone could have framed him.'

"If they have twenty-eight pages of that, they have me doing that kind of talking, and had the room bugged, or whatever you want to say. But no, sir, I did not sit and testify. I swear before God ten times I never have. And that is the point that has bothered me.

"Even before Lee's defection no one came along to the house. I called Mr. John Fain in the FBI myself to make friends with him. If they have twenty pages of testimony—that is when they got it, my talking. They got it with a tape recorder going. But I did not, no, sir."

"Well, then, what happened after that?"

"Now—we got off of that. About Robert crying?"

"You said that that ended the interview with Mr. Howard."

"Yes, that ended the interview with Mr. Howard, because Robert was crying. I was not consulted. I want you to know this, too. I was not consulted about the graveyard services or any part of my son's funeral.

"What I know—when my son was going to be buried—it was approximately one hour before the time for my son to be buried. My son Robert knew."

"Do you know whether Marina was consulted?"

"I do not know. And I am assuming that she was. But I do not know whether she was consulted or not. But I was not consulted. And since then—we will go on to the story. They have put a marker on the grave. I have not been consulted. I have found out my son is encased in cement, and I did not know anything about it until I investigated and asked the man at the cemetery.

"They did not consult me about anything, never have. I want that made clear—because that is the part I cannot understand."

"You don't know whether the laws of Texas give the widow the right to say what shall be done?"

"Well, naturally, she is his wife, and I am just the mother. But from a moral standpoint, what are they doing to me? Law and right —but from a moral standpoint, I should go out to the graveyard and see a marker? I should find out from strangers that my son is now in a concrete vault?"

"Well, then, did you go to the funeral?"

"Well, let me get—we will get to the story of the ministers."

"All right."

"Now, I was not consulted. Had Robert asked me—they are Lutheran, we were raised Lutherans. I have no church affiliation. I have learned since my trouble that my heart is my church. I am not talking against the church. But I go to church all day long, I meditate. And my work requires that I don't go to church. I am working on Sunday most of the time, taking care of the sick, and the people that go to church, that I work for, the families, have never once said, 'Well, I will stay home and take care of my mother and let you go to church, Mrs. Oswald, today.'

"You see, I am expected to work on Sunday.

"So that is why—I have my own church. And sometimes I think it is better than a wooden structure. Because these same people that expect me to work on Sunday, while they go to church, and go to church on Wednesday night—I don't consider them as good a Christian as I am—I am sorry.

"Well, I would not have let Robert be so upset trying to get a Lutheran minister. If he could not get a Lutheran minister, I would have called upon another minister, because there would have been many, many ministers of many denominations that would have been happy to come and help the sorrowing family.

"Well, a Reverend French from Dallas came out to Six Flags and we sat on the sofa.

"Reverend French was in the center, I and Robert on the side. And Robert was crying bitterly and talking to Reverend French and trying to get him to let Lee's body go to church. And he was quoting why he could not.

"So then I intervened and said, 'Well, if Lee is a lost sheep, and that is why you don't want him to go to church, he is the one that should go into church. The good people do not need to go to church. Let's say he is called a murderer. It is the murderers and all we should be concerned about.'

"And that agent—I am going ahead of my story a little bit—that man right here—"

"You are pointing to—"

"This agent right here. You may pass the picture around."

"The figure on the left hand of the picture you have just produced?"

"Yes, sir. I do not know his name. The man had the decency to stay at the far end of the room, near the entrance door, while the minister and myself and Robert were sitting on the sofa. And when I said to the minister about the lost sheep, this agent, who I will have a much longer story to talk about, left the group and came and sat on the other sofa—there were two sofas and a cocktail table—and he said, 'Mrs. Oswald, be quiet. You are making matters worse.'

"Now, the nerve of him—to leave the group and to come there and scold me.

"This Mr. French, Reverend French, agreed that we would have chapel services, that he could not take the body into the church. And we compromised for chapel services.

"However, when we arrived at the graveyard, we went to the chapel. There is the body being brought into the chapel. There is another picture. Here is another picture of the chapel."

"Before we go on—"

"And the chapel was empty. My son's body had been brought into the chapel, but Reverend French did not show up. And because there was a time for the funeral, the *Star Telegram* reporters and the police, as you see in the picture, escorted my son's body from the chapel and put it at the grave site. And when we went to the cemetery, we went directly to the chapel, because we were promised to have chapel services. And the chapel was empty. My son's body was not in it. Robert cried bitterly.

"Now, I don't remember if I stated while at Six Flags that this particular agent identified as being to the left of the picture, while the television was on continuously—I have stated before I never did sit down and watch it, because we were quite busy. And this was published in the *Star Telegram* by Mr. Blair Justice, and also on the radio.

"He was very, very rude to me. Anything that I said, he snapped. And I took it for quite a while. At this particular time that they showed the gun on television, I said, 'How can they say Lee shot the President? Even though they would prove it is his gun doesn't mean he used it—nobody saw him use it.'

"He snapped back and he said, 'Mrs. Oswald, we know that he shot the President.'

"I then walked over to Mr. Mike Howard and I said, 'What's wrong with that agent? That agent is about to crack. All he has done is taunt me ever since I have been here.'

"He said, 'Mrs. Oswald, he was personal bodyguard to Mrs. Kennedy for thirty months, and maybe he has a little opinion against you.'

"I said, 'Let him keep his personal opinions to himself. He is on a job.'

"Now, there was another instance with this same agent. He followed Marina around continuously. I am going to make this plain. He followed Marina around continuously. The pictures will always show him by Marina.

"We were in the bedroom, and he was in the bedroom. And we were getting ready for the funeral.

"Marina was very unhappy with the dress—they bought her two dresses. 'Mama, too long.' 'Mama, no fit.' And it looked lovely on her. You can see I know how to dress properly. I was in the business world as merchandise manager. And the dress looked lovely on Marina. But she was not happy with it.

"I said, 'Oh, honey, put your coat on, we are going to Lee's funeral. It will be all right.'

"And we had one hour in order to get ready for the funeral.

"I said, 'We will never make it. Marina is so slow.'

"She said, 'I no slow. I have things to do.'

"I am trying to impress upon you that Marina understands English and has always talked broken English.

"Now, this agent was in the room and Robert was on the telephone. That is why he was allowed in the bedroom.

"While Marina was complaining about her dress, my little grandbaby, two years old—and she is a very precious little baby, they are good children—was standing by her mother. And Marina was very nervous by this time. She was not happy with the dress. And Marina was combing her hair. She took the comb and she hit June on the head. I said, 'Marina, don't do that.' And this agent—I wish I knew his name—snapped at me and said, 'Mrs. Oswald, you let her alone.' I said, 'Don't tell me what to say to my daughter-in-law when she was hitting my grandbaby on the head with a comb, in front of Robert Oswald.

"Now, why did this man do these things?"

"Are you saying that the agent did anything improper as far as Marina was concerned?"

"Now, what do you mean when you say improper?"

410

"Was there any improper relationship between them, as far as you know?"

"No. I am saying—and I am going to say it as strongly as I can—that I—and I have stated this from the beginning—that I think our trouble in this is in our own Government. And I suspect these two agents of conspiracy with my daughter-in-law in this plot."

"With who?"

"With Marina and Mrs. Paine—the two women. Lee was set up. And it is quite possible these two Secret Service men are involved."

"Which ones are you referring to?"

"Mr. Mike Howard and the man that I did not—did not know the name, the man in the picture to the left. I have reason to think so because I was at Six Flags and these are just some instances that happened. I have much more stories to tell you of my conclusions. I am not a detective, and I don't say it is the answer to it. But I must tell you what I think, because I am the only one that has this information.

"Now, here is another instance—"

"What kind of a conspiracy are you describing that these men are engaged in?"

"The assassination of President Kennedy."

"You think that two Secret Service agents and Marina and Mrs. Paine were involved in that, in the conspiracy?"

"Yes, I do. Besides another high official. I will tell you the high official I have in mind when we go through that part of the story, if you please."

"Well, now, could you tell us what you base that on—because that is a very serious charge."

"It is a very serious charge, and I realize that. I base that on what I told you, the attitude of this man, and Mike Howard's attitude also.

"Now, I have to continue."

"Have you described that?"

"Yes. I have to continue.

"While at Six Flags, Marina was given the red-carpet treatment. Marina was Marina. And it was not that Marina is pretty and a young girl. Marina was under—what is the word?—I won't say influence—these two men were to see that Marina was Marina. I don't know how to say it. Are you getting the point? Let me see if I can say it better."

"You mean they were taking care of her, or were they were doing more than that?"

"More than taking care of Marina."

"Well, now, describe what more."

"All right, I will describe it for you.

"I am not quite satisfied with the way I said that. Let me get my thoughts together.

"I noticed that—and of course as I have testified, the way the man treated me—and I was told he was a bodyguard for Mrs. Kennedy. We were at Six Flags on November twenty-fourth, at Lee's death, and on November twenty-sixth Marina and I—before November twenty-sixth—Marina and I were very, very friendly, very loving, everything was 'Mama,' 'Mama has a big heart.' And we planned to live together.

"I had an insurance policy that had expired on Lee. I was not able to keep up the premium. And I had eight hundred and sixty-three dollars. But however I had not looked at the policy for some years, and I was not quite sure that it was in force. But otherwise I had no money and no job. I had given up my job to come to the rescue. So I was very anxious to get home and get my papers and let them see the copies of everything I had, and to find out if I had my insurance policy, if it was in force, and also get some clothes.

"From the twenty-fourth until the twenty-sixth I lived in my uniform, Gentlemen. I did not have any clothes at the Six Flags. Yet Robert Oswald was taken to his home a couple of times to get clothes. And when I wanted to go home and get clothes, they put me off. One time I broke down crying. I said, 'I don't understand it. You won't do anything for me, yet you drove Robert all the way to Denton to get clothes.'

"So the night of the twenty-sixth they took me home, and I got my papers. I found that my insurance policy was in force. So I said to Marina, 'Marina, we all right. Mama has insurance policy, eight hundred dollars. You stay home with baby and Mama work, or Mama stay home with baby and you work, and at least we have a start.'

" 'Okay, Mama. I not want big house, Mama. I want small place.'

"And this is the girl that has never had anything, and she only wanted small things. Fine.

412

"On the date of the twenty-seventh, approximately ten o'clock—this was in the morning—I want to say something to Marina, and Marina shrugged me off and walked away.

"That morning I had acted as interpreter for an FBI agent, and Mr. Mike Howard said, 'Would you like us to get a Russian interpreter?' And he said, 'No, Mrs. Oswald is doing fine.' And he took the testimony from me as an interpreter. So, you see, my daughter-in-law did understand English and answered me in her Russian broken English, because the FBI man was satisfied.

"So when Marina shrugged me off, I thought right away that she thought—because I had to use the name Lee so many times—that I was hurting her husband, and maybe that is why she felt this way. So I thought maybe I am just imagining things. So I waited quite a while, I would say half an hour. I went to Marina again. And she walked away and shrugged me off.

"So I walked into the living room, where my son, Robert Oswald, and the Secret Service were, and I said to Robert, 'Robert, something is wrong with Marina. She won't have anything to do with me.'

"He said, 'I know why. Marina has been offered a home by a very wealthy woman'—all of this was done without my knowledge—'by a very wealthy woman who will give her children education, and she didn't know how to tell you.'

"I said, 'Well, Robert, why didn't you tell me?'

"Of course when I said it, I was emotionally upset. I said, 'Robert, why didn't you tell me?'

"He said, 'Because just the way you are acting now.'

"I said, 'What do you mean the way I am acting now? I am acting in a normal fashion. You are telling me that you are taking my daughter-in-law and grandchildren away from me, and I have lost my son, and my grandchildren and daughter are going to live with strangers. This is a normal reaction.'

" 'Well, that is why we didn't tell you. We know you would take it that way.'

"And that is the last time I have talked to my daughter-in-law, Marina. And that is the rift between Marina and I. There is no rift, sir? We were going to live together. But this home was offered Marina—and I will present this in evidence.

"Now, Mr. Gregory is involved—Mr. Gregory did all the Russian talking. They all knew better but me. And I have more to the story.

"Yes, here it is.

"And there are other offers Marina had—other offers.

"So I was not able to be around Marina. The Secret Service saw to it. And they gloated.

"Gentlemen, I am not imagining these things. These two men gloated of the fact that now Marina is going to be fixed—you know, she is fixed financially and otherwise."

"Is this Mrs. Pultz?"

"I didn't even read this, sir, believe me. This was handed to me by a reporter before I left, saying, 'Mrs. Oswald, maybe these things'— because he knows the story. This has all been published publicly in newspapers, what I am saying. The *Star Telegram* could give you all I am saying here. It has already been made public in the paper, all of this. And he handed that to me. I never did see that article until the other day."

"This article refers to Mrs. Oswald being offered a home, and apparently a newspaper account—a newspaper account of the offer, according to this newspaper account—the offer was by a Mrs. Pultz. That is the one that you refer to when you handed this paper to us."

"Yes, sir, that is offering her a home.

"Now, I have not read that. I know she was offered a home by a woman and I will tell you further what I do know about this.

"Now, there were other people that offered her homes."

"But you seemed to think there was something improper or bad about your son Robert wanting to get your daughter Marina taken care of in this manner. I don't understand that. Can you explain it?"

"Yes. Well—no—as I have explained before, Robert and I are not close, we are not close as a family. But Robert is a very easygoing person. He is not opinionated, particularly like I am. My older son and Lee are of my disposition. But because you are a Secret Service man or somebody, if you tell him something, he will go along and 'yes' you. So he was part of this arrangement. They probably had to have his consent. But he knew of the arrangement. They all knew it but me. I was not consulted about this at all."

"Do you think Robert was trying to do something bad by it, or just trying to look out for—"

"He thought it was a good idea, that Marina should go and live in this home. But I took a different attitude. I am not interested in material things, Gentlemen. I then went into my speech, that I thought, as a family, Marina and I should stick together and face our future together. I could see no reason—and I made this at the Six Flags, and have made it public in the newspapers—I could see no reason, no advantage of Marina living with strangers. I said that before. I thought it would be better, original idea, Marina and I had made, to live in my apartment and do the best we can. And I even said—we have eight hundred and sixty-three dollars to start with, and then if we don't make it, 'What about you helping us?'

" 'But give us a chance as a family. Don't put the girl in a strange home, a Russian girl, a foreign girl, taking away from her Mama.'

"Marina has no mother and father—she has a step-father. But I was her Mama up until this time. And I could not see Marina in a strange home.

"Well, I am going to prove this story to you. It is a fantastic story. But as I go along—I have witnesses—and that is why I asked you, sir, I would like these people called to back up these fantastic stories I am telling you. It can be proven, sir.

"So I had no further contact with my daughter-in-law—once they came out and said what they had planned. I had no inkling of it. That was the—they wanted to keep her and the children away from me.

"That night, the night of November twenty-seventh—now, we were in a bedroom with twin beds that we shared. They opened the studio couch in the living room, and rolled June's bed, the baby bed, in the living room, sir."

"What do you mean by 'they'?"

"The Secret Service had the maid come in with sheets and everything and they got—opened the sofa into a bed. The Secret Service rolled the baby bed from the bedroom into the living room. And I knew that I was not wanted or involved. And I have a very dignified way about me. I didn't say a word. What I did, I sat up in a chair all night long in the living room, rather than to be so indignant as to sleep in the bedroom where they had taken my daughter-in-law from me. I sat up in a chair in the living room rather than be pushed aside like I was being pushed aside."

"Well, now, what Secret Service men were these—Mr. Howard?"

"Mr. Howard was involved, and this other man."

"The same man?"

"This same man. And my son is in this, too. Robert was part of this conspiracy that they were going to let her go to a home, and they didn't tell me—and Mr. Peter Gregory."

"And did they move your daughter-in-law out into the living room?"

"Yes, sir, she slept on the sofa. And they moved June's baby bed from the bedroom into the living room, by my daughter-in-law. And I sat in a chair. I can do that. I am a nurse, and I can do without sleep. And I had all the papers. I told you that the night before they took me home to get my papers. And that is why I knew I had the insurance money. So I started to work on the papers. And I sat up all night long."

"What did Marina say about that arrangement?"

"There was nothing said between Marina and I. The last time I had seen Marina was when she shrugged me off, and then this came out why she shrugged me off. I have had no contact with Marina since."

"Now, why do you think there is a conspiracy about this? Can you explain that to us?"

"About this particular instance?"

"Yes."

"Well, I don't say that is a particular instance. But it is certainly a very unusual way to do a thing, a very unusual way—not to consult me. Marina and I were friends. She was going to come and live with me. I was going to share my money with her. And then they went ahead and planned all this without my knowledge.

"Maybe you know the answer to it, I don't know. But there was no hard feelings—even now I love Marina and I would take and help her any way I can.

"So I don't understand these things. But I am telling you the way things happen, the way I was excluded. And your Secret Service agents had part of this."

"Well, this plan to have your daughter-in-law go and live with another lady—this Mrs. Pultz—you said you did not think it could be innocent or in good faith?"

"Yes—because then this same Secret Service man, that I don't know the name—now, I may be wrong about this—just a moment. No, this is not the same man.

"One of the other Secret Service men had gone to talk to Robert's boss, because Robert was worried about his job. So this happened in the afternoon. I had no contact with Marina. And he came in and in front of me he patted Robert on the shoulder and said, 'Now, Robert, I have talked to your boss and you are all right. I assured him you are not involved in any way.'

"So, Gentlemen, Marina is taken care of; Robert is taken care of— I am not feeling sorry for myself, believe me, because I can take care of myself. But here is a mother who has come to the rescue, lost her job, offered her good love and insurance money, and nobody has wondered what is going to become of me."

As I recall, Marguerite, sitting in the witness chair, almost broke down with a real display of emotions as she said these words.

"Well, did you think it was improper that the Secret Service man would go to Robert's boss and tell him he was not involved, that there was nothing improper?"

"No, sir, I do not. I think it was a fine gesture. And that is the point I am trying to make out. Why are these fine gestures to see that Marina is going to have a home and be taken care of, and Robert's job is secure—but I am nothing. I was not included in the plans. And what is going to become of me? I have no income. I have no job. I lost my job. And nobody thought about me.

"I don't mean to imply I'm sorry for myself. I am trying to bring out a point that through all of this that I have not been considered, even as much as to testify. I want to know why. I don't understand why.

"It is very strange.

"I packed during the night, sat up in the chair, as I said.

"So the next morning I am on my way home. I have no purpose to be there. I was helping my daughter-in-law and helping the children. But now I am out of everything, so I insist on going home.

"Before going home I asked to tell Marina goodbye, and my grandchildren, and what they have done this morning—they have taken her out of these quarters and brought her next door, to the other quarters of the Inn—it is just one door and a little courtyard to the other door."

"What day is this?"

"This is the twenty-eighth. So the agent that was taking me home —I'm sorry, but I'm very bad at names, and there were so many agents, it is awfully hard for me to remember it all. I told him that I wanted to tell Marina that I was going. He knocked on the door. The Russian interpreter from the State Department, Mr. Gopadze, came to the door, and the agent said, 'Mrs. Oswald is going home and wants to tell Marina and the children goodbye.' "

"He said, 'Well, we are interviewing her, and she is on tape. She will get in touch with you.'

"So I never saw Marina after that time."

CHAPTER 32

MARINA INCOMMUNICADO

MARINA DID NOT go to live with the Mrs. Pultz who had been mentioned in the newspapers. Perhaps Marguerite misunderstood the exact explanation Robert had given of Marina's plans. Instead after a few days she went to live with the manager of the Six Flags Motel and his family, Mr. and Mrs. Jim Martin. How this came about, Jim Martin explained to the Commission:

"Well, I was called by the Tarrant County Sheriff on Sunday, November twenty-fourth."

"Who was that?"

"Lew Evans."

"Yes."

"About eleven o'clock in the morning, and they wanted a room where they could question the Oswald family. I told them they could have it, and about four o'clock, I guess, four or four-thirty—I don't know the exact time they came in with the whole family—and we gave them several rooms to accommodate the family."

"Were you introduced to Marina Oswald at that time?"

"Well, I don't believe I was ever really introduced to her."

"How did you come to know her, then?"

"Well, just through association."

"I see. Did you know the County Sheriff before that?"

"Vaguely, not to any great extent."

"Do you know of any particular reason why he chose your establishment?"

"Because of the central location between Dallas and Fort Worth and the isolation of it."

"At that time who came to stay with you at the Six Flags Inn, Marina and some of her family?"

"Well, Marina and the two children and Robert and Marguerite Oswald."

"Did they have several suites there?"

"They had one room. Well, one suite, Room four-twenty-three and four-twenty-four, and then we gave them two other rooms for the Secret Service."

"Did anyone make arrangements with you besides the County Sheriff about how this would be handled?"

"Yes, Secret Service."

"Who for the Secret Service?"

"Let's see. Charles Kunkel, and Howard—I can't remember his first name."

"Secret Service man?"

"Yes."

"Where was this arrangement made?"

"Well, down in the room in the suite."

"There at the Six Flags Inn?"

"Yes."

"And the three of you were there together, were you?"

"Yes, there were also Arlington police officers and several other Secret Service men."

"Who participated in the conversation?"

"Well, I don't know who else was in the conversation. It was primarily between Kunkel and Howard and myself."

"What was said in regard to this arrangement at that time?"

"Well, they said that they would need these rooms to accommodate the family, and they had no idea how long they would need it."

"Was anything said about the price and who would make payment?"

"Yes, they said that the Government would take care of the room rate on it."

"Did you have to submit this matter to any of your superiors, or did you make the decision at that time?"

"No, I made the decision."

"Had you had any prior deals with the Secret Service people before that?"

"No."

"How long did Marguerite Oswald stay there?"

"I believe she left on Friday."

"What day?"

"Or maybe Thursday. Would be the twenty-eighth or twenty-ninth. I am not certain as to the exact date."

"Do you recall any incidents where Marguerite Oswald sought to leave prior to the Thursday or Friday that she left?"

"No, I don't recall anything like that."

"Have you ever assisted the local police officers in any other way at your Six Flags Inn before that?"

"Yes."

"In a general way what was the nature of that assistance?"

"Well, of course, I can't recall any specific instances. I know we cooperate with the law-enforcement officers in anything they have to ask us, and we cooperate with them, giving them the information. I don't know of any particular incidents other than—"

"Would you describe briefly just where these rooms were in your inn, and where the Secret Service were compared with Marina Oswald's rooms?"

"Well, Marina Oswald was in Room four-twenty-three and four-twenty-four, which were connecting rooms, and the rooms faced away from the entrance to the motel. And then the Secret Service had four-twenty-two and four-twenty-one also. They were rooms next door to it, but not connecting."

"After Marina first came there, did the Secret Service have someone on duty while she was at the Six Flags?"

"Yes."

"All the time?"

"Yes."

"Do you recall who that was?"

"Let's see—well, I remember his first name now, Mike Howard, and Charles Kunkel. Lee Gopadze was there part of the time. They seemed to change quite frequently."

"Did they have someone there twenty-four hours of the day?"

"Yes, sir."

"During this early period did you ever talk to Marina?"

"No, except to say hello."

"Do you know whether she talked English much at that time?"

"From all appearances, she didn't."

"Did anyone visit you while she was there at the Six Flags during this early period that you recall?"

"Not to my knowledge other than the FBI."

"Did you invite Marina and her family to come to your home for Thanksgiving?"

"Yes."

"Will you tell us how that happened?"

"Well, it just happened, I don't know. I think I asked Robert if he would like to come out for dinner, Thanksgiving dinner. They weren't going to have a very happy Thanksgiving, and living in those rooms was pretty cramped."

"When was this that you asked Robert?"

"I believe on Wednesday."

"Did you include Robert and his wife as well as Marina and her family in the invitation?"

"Well, Robert's wife wasn't there, but I included Robert. He came out to the house also."

"Did Marina then come to your house for Thanksgiving?"

"Yes."

"Who all came at that time?"

"Let's see, there were Marina and June Lee, and Robert, Charlie Kunkel, and one Arlington police officer. I don't recall his name."

"What time of the day did they come?"

"I believe it was three or four o'clock in the afternoon."

"Did you invite Marguerite Oswald to Thanksgiving dinner at that time, too?"

"No."

"Did you say anything to her about it?"

"No. As I recall I just asked, I believe I just asked Robert if they would like to come, they were welcome if they would like to come."

"You mean by that that you included Marguerite Oswald in your invitation?"

"I don't think I named her. I don't know if she had left by then."

"You didn't deliberately exclude her from the invitation?"

"No."

"Then did you at some time discuss with Marina the possibility of her staying at your home rather than at the Six Flags Inn?"

"No, I discussed it with Secret Service first."

"When was that?"

"Thursday or Friday."

"Before this Thanksgiving dinner or afterwards?"

"I don't recall. I know the Secret Service made a statement that they were quite concerned as to where Marina would go after she left the inn. They had no place to put her and they had no idea where she was going to go."

"Do you recall when they made that statement?"

"No, it was Wednesday or Thursday."

"At that time did you say anything about that?"

"I told them that if they couldn't find any place for her that I would be glad to take them into my home."

"Was anything said about what compensation you would receive for that?"

"No. There was no compensation considered."

"You didn't suggest any and they didn't, is that right?"

"That is correct."

"Did you discuss that idea with Marina at all?"

"No. They, the Secret Service, told Robert about it, and—"

"How do you know that?"

"Because he told me they had. And then Robert thanked me and said that it would work out all right."

"Before you made that suggestion had you had any discussions about selling any rights to Marina's stories or anything of that character?"

"No."

"With any media?"

"No."

"How did you happen to make this offer?"

"I felt sorry for her."

"Did you limit the offer to Marina and her children?"

"Yes."

"Was there any talk at that time about Robert living at your home, too?"

"No."

"Anything about Marguerite living there?"

"No."

"Did you discuss this proposal with your wife before you made it?"

"No."

Through these circumstances Marina and the children went to live with the Martins. Jim Martin later became her business manager, with a contract to share in monies earned in her behalf. He was with her when she made her first appearance in Washington. He testified at a later date—after Marina gave him his walking papers which led to a lawsuit with him. At this time she accepted the suggestion she go to live among strangers.

To me Jim Martin looked like a successful young businessman, above average in height, rather handsome and pleasant in manner. I could see how his hospitality and friendship would be welcome.

Marina had spent considerable time among strangers since she had arrived in America. She had lived with Elena Hall, Anna Meller, Mrs. Declan Ford, Anna Ray and Ruth Paine during various periods of separation from Lee. Now again she preferred to live with strangers rather than Marguerite or Ruth Paine. They both found this remarkable—difficult to understand. Obviously after the series of killings that had happened, the Secret Service was anxious to keep Marina out of the line of fire and away from the harassment of newsmen. Ruth Paine could hardly help being bewildered, however. Marina had left that morning simply to make a visit to Lee at the police station. Since that time she had talked with Marina only at the Executive Inn and again a few hours after Lee's murder when she was asked to get together some clothes for Marina and the children. How could she know that Robert had planted a seed of suspicion in Marina's mind that, together with all the other bewildering circumstances, caused Marina to wonder? Marina's predicament was a very difficult one. She needed time to get her bearings.

There can be no question that Ruth Paine had a genuine affection for Marina. Marina had seemed to return these warm feelings. Ruth Paine still had that letter Marina had written her from New Orleans which said in part, "Sweet Ruth, I am so thankful to you for your good and sympathetic heart. And wherever I am I will always say that plain Americans are good, peaceful and intelligent. You see what emotions your invitation and attitude towards me have evoked. It is your fault! Ha-ha!" This had been a kind letter, an affectionate letter; at face value, one would expect such a person always to be warm and appreciative. As the days numbered upward from that terrible Friday afternoon when they had been together at the police station, Ruth became more and more baffled why she did not have any direct word from Marina. At first she didn't even know where Marina was staying. After the conversation—which had been brief and edged with frost—at the Executive Inn, Marina had simply dropped out of her world. What was the meaning of this? Rumors were going around Dallas that for dubious reasons Marina might be held incommunicado by the Secret Service. Why would they hold her incommunicado?

So straightforward and unsuspecting was Ruth Paine by nature that it was unlikely she visualized herself as being under suspicion by anyone. She had told the police all she knew; she had cooperated in every way with the FBI and other law officials. Her life was an open book to them or anyone else who had a legitimate reason to ask, and she had nothing to hide. Actually she knew very few of Lee's dark secrets, his only suspicious acts being his letter to the Russian Embassy about a trip to Mexico and his living on Beckley Avenue under an alias. One other matter had come to her attention which she promptly recalled for the police. Lee had mildly annoyed her one day by using Michael's power drill in the garage to bore a hole in a foreign coin he put on a chain for Marina. When this coin turned out to be Mexican it seemed to confirm that he really had been in Mexico sometime after leaving New Orleans. Did Marina know he had been there and failed to tell her the truth?

But the matter of Marina's being held incommunicado became a growing anxiety as the weeks went by. Both Michael and Ruth were very earnestly interested in civil rights and the matter of personal freedom. Michael, in fact, was a member of the American Civil Liberties Union and had taken Lee to a meeting a month before the assassination.

It was about Christmas time that Marina did write Ruth Paine a brief letter. Ruth now knew Marina was with the Martins. Ruth responded immediately.

December 27, 1963

"MARINA, DEAR,

"Truly, I don't know what to say. I don't know whether it is better to be quiet or to speak. Things are already difficult for you, and I don't want to trouble you. I want to explain that I felt lonely when I read through your letter to me. I was very happy to see the letter, but when I had read it I knew nothing further about you. You wrote me as if I were an old grandmother and not a friend. You closed your face to me. Is it true, have I offended you? If so, excuse, forgive me, please. I did not want to offend and do not wish to. But I am coarse and stupid, especially in Russian. But perhaps you don't want my friendship—it is of course your business, and

I can do nothing. But I want you to understand me and know what I think, and not drop me without knowledge of my thoughts.

"Another matter bothers me. I have been sending you letters from fine people who wrote me saying that I am good in that I gave you a place to live and was a friend to you. In the letters there was also money for you. I wanted for you to see who the money was from, and see how kind people are. *But don't think* that I consider that I have done anything for you especially, nor that it is necessary for you to be grateful. Certainly not. Such thoughts interfere with friendship and also are not true. How many times have I said when you were here, that I was giving nothing more than I received. You never understood how useful it was to me to speak Russian every day. Also, I was alone at home, and it was very pleasant to speak and chat with you in the evening and especially pleasant to have companionship. You know that I received no more money from Michael while you lived here, but we had no difficulties with money.

"I want simply to know, Marina, how you are, what you think, feel. But of course it is your business with whom you talk and about what. Is it not so?

Sincerely,
RUTH

"Enclosed: Recipes (in English) for: Meat Loaf
Macaroni and Cheese
Noodles and Tuna Fish

Ruth explained the circumstances of the letter's delivery. "This letter was taken to 11611 Farrar and handed in at the door to Mrs. Martin, about one P.M., December twenty-seventh, along with letters containing contributions to Marina. That day I also took Marina's hair dryer, a package of condiments and other sundries belonging to her found since Mr. Martin, Mr. Thorne and Mr. Robert Oswald came to my house to get the bulk of Marina's things. I also took a package which had come addressed to me and which I had opened but which contained things for Marina.

"Mrs. Martin consulted with Mr. Jamison within the house and told me through the door that they could not accept the package, that it should go via the post-office annex. I had not had an opportunity to explain that the package was open and the contents known to me. It didn't occur to me until later that they may have thought the contents could be harmful, and in any case I didn't want to press, and simply took the package back home with me that day. I sent it later, as I had been sending other things to Marina via the Irving police."

Certainly from Ruth Paine's viewpoint, Marina's refusal to communicate, see her or reply to her letters implied she was being deliberately held incommunicado. If there was something to all these rumors that Lee might have been associated with the FBI, who was trying to cover up what? Although the President's Commission had been announced on November 29, 1963, it had held no hearings. The skeptics immediately raised the hue and cry, "Whitewash!" The fact that such an insinuation was regarded as a personal insult by every member of the Commission who would spend thankless and unpaid hours grinding over the facts of these crimes meant little to those who wanted for their own notoriety and publicity to raise the question. The mere fact that thoughtless opportunists raised this question made every member of the Commission more determined, no matter whose head had to fall, that the whole truth would be published on the record when its deliberations were completed. Ruth Paine was not one who doubted the integrity of the Commission. She cooperated fully. However, the charge of Marina's being held incommunicado muddied the waters even more deeply. How could so many plots be piled upon plots? Each Commissioner spent dozens of wakeful nights fighting to keep abreast of the charges and countercharges. Seldom have public servants worked harder or felt their responsibilities more keenly.

In good faith Ruth Paine puzzled over Marina's silence. She wrote again the next day—followed by a long series of communications Marina did not answer.

December 28, 1963

"DEAR MARINA,

"They say that it is your choice to speak with someone or not to speak. That is, if you want to see me they *then* would give me permission to meet with you. But I do not believe this, while I have not heard it from your lips. For that reason I bother you and want a refusal from you and not only from Secret Service. I also want to know if you received the letter which I carried to Mr. Martin's home on Saturday the 21st of December at about 12:00 noon.

"Your [Christmas] card to me was at the post office at 1:00 o'clock P.M. on the 21st. You wrote it after you received my letter or before? Surely before, is that not so? Did you receive from me the letter which I wrote on the 27th and brought to Martin's home on that date?

"Forgive me, Marina. As I said to Michael last evening, in general I do not try to hold friendship when it is clear to me that a person doesn't want my friendship. But in general it is possible to find out directly from a person, from his face, his words,—if he wants to talk or not. But in this situation I don't know.

Sincerely,
RUTH

"In a letter to me was $10.00 cash from: Doris P. Mowry

Box 441
Slatersville, R. I.

"Very likely it is better to send a check than cash. Here is a check for $10.00. Consider it from Doris Mowry. (This letter stamped and sealed, but given to the hand of John Thorne the morning of Dec. 28th when he met and talked with me in his office.)"

How troubled Ruth Paine became over Marina's incomprehensible silence was described by her husband, Michael:

"Ruth was troubled about that, and so she wrote a series of quite a number of letters, each one referring to previous letters, trying to discover whether they were being withheld, thinking Marina was a responsible person or normally civil person, she would normally respond to or at least acknowledge receipt of them.

"So Ruth didn't know whether she was receiving them or not, and had another—some encounters with Martin and Thorne [the attorney Marina had hired] which didn't put her at ease. She still didn't know whether Marina was receiving them. She saw only some of the checks had been signed by Thorne rather than Marina. Thorne had said that Marina didn't say he had power of attorney, and Marina was trying to do everything that she could which, at least, she could sign her checks, checks or gifts.

"So there were these indications. Ruth was very much in the dark, not knowing why she had received no communication from Marina, and having conflicting reports from Martin. Martin said she had a phone right beside her if she wanted to call."

"How did she receive these checks?"

"I guess Ruth—some of the checks came to Ruth as gifts to her, and Ruth would write her own check so she got her own stub back."

"I see."

428

"Therefore, Ruth had this question of whether she had offended Marina or whether Marina had done something that offended Ruth, or whether Marina didn't like Ruth and had never let on. This would be a great blow to her ego. It had Ruth in great periods of depression and anxiety."

"Did either you or your wife, to your knowledge, know Robert Oswald?"

"We only met him for the first time on the night of the assassination. We both liked him at that time."

Meantime, Marguerite, rejected and provoked, embarked strenuously on her personal crusade to prove Lee's innocence. She had found out that Lee's phone book contained FBI agent Hosty's phone number, license plate and address. This reconfirmed her in her suspicions, knowing nothing about the true origin of those entries. The press leaked these facts; Lonnie Hudkins wrote his article, echoed by others. Allegations went back and forth that agent Hosty had said the FBI had known Oswald was dangerous, a statement he has flatly denied under oath. The upshot was a painful pitch of tension involving everyone.

Ruth Paine asked the American Civil Liberties Union to make official inquiries as to Marina's true status. Was she being held incommunicado?

Because she wanted the letter technically correct when translated into Russian, she asked Mrs. Declan Ford, a native-speaking Russian, to assist her in preparing the letter they would present to authorities demanding clarification of Marina's isolation. Mrs. Ford struck me as an attractive woman, both nicely dressed and well groomed. I think other members of the Commission would agree that she gave an impression of competence. Mrs. Ford testified:

"I did not want to go with them, but I didn't mind translating, so I did translate and they wanted to know if Marina was held incommunicado, and she answered. Mrs. Paine brought me that letter to translate from English to Russian, and the man in charge—I don't know his name. I have forgotten his name; you mentioned it yesterday. If you say it I will remember it."

"Let's come to that in a moment. Let's develop the story first.

"How did the question of the American Civil Liberties question first come up? Did Mrs. Paine bring it up?"

"Yes, that is right, because she tried to write letters to Marina and she wouldn't answer and she thought she was held in sort of a protective custody and couldn't see anybody—that is what she felt—and she was rather imprisoned is what she thought."

"So Mrs. Paine came to you with a letter that was written in English, is that correct?"

"That is right."

"And she asked you to translate into Russian?"

"That is right."

"Was that a letter from Mrs. Paine to Marina, or a letter from the Civil Liberties Union?"

"No, from Civil Liberties Union."

As a result of the mounting pressures thus raised by newspaper speculations, Marguerite's bombardment in the press, Ruth Paine's anxieties and the carefully prepared letter from the American Civil Liberties Union, Marina and her advisers, Jim Martin and Attorney Thorne, agreed on the advisability of a TV program in which Marina would appear with her children and answer reasonable questions about her well-being and status. The program relieved the doubts of many, but Ruth Paine still was concerned and wounded by Marina's rejection of her.

On Monday, February 3, 1964, she wrote again:

"Dear Marina,

"On Wednesday I spoke with Mr. Sorrels, the head of Secret Service in Dallas. He is very nice, and we talked for a long time. He advised me to write you a letter at the Secret Service post office box. I decided not to send a registered letter.

"I simply want to know: Have you received letters from me written on the 21st, 27th, 28th of December and the 3rd, 10th and 23rd of January? Is it true that you can phone me when you wish as Mr. Thorne told me?

"I saw your interview on television. You have learned a lot of English. From this (TV) appearance all will know (as I already knew) that you are very nice, love your children and are grateful to people. It was evident, of course, that it is still difficult for you to speak in English, but all the same you explained your thoughts very clearly and answered the questions very well.

"I am very glad that today will be your interview with President Johnson's commission. I pray that all goes well and that you do not become too tired. After this I think it will be easier to plan to see each other.

"Phone, please, Marina, when you return to Dallas. I don't understand at all why you have neither written nor phoned.

"In another envelope I am sending a (little) book which is necessary to know nearly by heart in order to receive permission to learn to drive a car. I want sometime to do a translation into Russian with you if it would be useful to you. I regret that I have little practice in Russian now; such work (translation) would be useful for me.

Sincerely,
RUTH PAINE

"(I don't know at all how to correctly use the subjunctive in Russian.)"

At last Marina was in Washington. She was testifying before the Commission. One of the important questions the Commissioners wanted to dispel from their own minds was this whole charge of her being mistreated by the Secret Service or being held incommunicado.

Marina was not ceremonious in setting the record straight. She stated flatly that the Secret Service guarding her at Martin's home had treated her very well, that she was indeed free to come and go as she saw fit, to make any phone calls she wished or write letters to anyone. Specifically in regard to Marguerite and her theories of plots involving Lee, she said, "I think that is just simply idle talk, that she didn't have anything.

"Perhaps she does have something.

"But I think that it is only she who considers that she has something that might reveal, uncover this."

"Has there been any time that you wanted to see your mother-in-law that you have been prevented from doing so?"

"Never.

"I don't want to see her, I didn't want to."

"Mrs. Oswald, I am going to ask you about differences between you and your mother-in-law, not for the purpose of embarrassing you in any way, but since we are going to ask her to testify it might be helpful to the Commission to know that background.

"I hope you will bear with us.

"Have you had some differences with your mother-in-law?"

"I am sorry that you will devote your time to questioning her, because you will only be tired and very sick after talking to her. I am very much ashamed to have this kind of relationship to my mother-in-law. I would like to be closer to her and to be on better terms with her. But when you get to know her, you will understand why. I don't think that she can help you."

"You said that you didn't want to see Ruth Paine because you thought she wanted to see you for her own interests. Will you tell us what you meant by that?"

"I think that she wants to see me in her own selfish interests. She liked to be well known, popular, and I think that anything that I should write her, for example, would wind up in the press.

"The reason that I think so is that the first time that we were in jail to see Lee, she was with me and with her children, and she was trying to get in front of the cameras, and to push her children and instructed her children to look this way and look that way. And the first photographs that appeared were of me with her children."

As far as the Commission was concerned, the question of Marina's being held incommunicado went up in smoke with these words from the witness involved. The harshness of judgments people are apt to pass upon one another in a crisis, however, was discomforting to some who heard those words.

CHAPTER 33

DEAD MAN'S COUNSEL

MARINA WAS WRONG when she said she didn't think Marguerite's testimony would be of any help to the Commission. That members would be very tired after listening to three days of her meandering speculations, however, could not be argued. But it was the job of the Commission to sit patiently and listen to everything she had to say. If nothing else, the Commission now had a lucid understanding of the volatile relationships between various members of the Oswald family. One of the deepest mysteries at the outset of the hearings was *why* would Lee Oswald want to kill a President? The initial appearance that no reasonable motive could be found gradually changed. Too often in trying to find an easy explanation for the complex motivations of a fellow human being we look for an obvious answer. Our minds are conditioned to neat psychological phrases. As the Commission has stated in its report, no single motive can explain Lee's urge to kill. But when the whole of his life is spread out, each part of the picture gives intelligibility to the whole. Lee's motivation was the compound of his entire life; no one person, no one thing, no one event explained his deed. He was "all the sums he had not counted." Marguerite's testimony was very helpful in rounding out the picture. She was a significant part of Lee's life, but those who have jumped to the conclusion that it was "all her fault" haven't had the benefit of the record. As the chemistry of our bodies is made up of minute and subtle things, so is the chemistry of our emotions. Lee's deadly instincts were of a complex formula.

Marguerite's testimony was helpful in other ways. Not the least important was helping the Commission understand clearly where so many seeds of rumors and dark plots had come from. It was not Marguerite's imagination alone that stimulated dozens of speculations. It was the interaction of events and the jostling of personalities. For example, Robert's anxiety about the Paines never translated itself into a "plot" theory. He was very cautious in his statements.

But Robert's sentiments in regard to the Paines obviously helped to bring about the separation of Ruth and Marina, which in turn led to the belief that Marina might be held incommunicado. And if Marina was being held incommunicado, didn't this give more grounds to Marguerite's theory that Lee was an agent? Like breaking the first setup on a pool table, theories rolled in every direction—striking each other, ricocheting from the cushions, one thing moving another. Marguerite was not done with her battle to defend Lee's memory. She would find those who were anxious to take up her cause, and in particular she found Mark Lane.

Among the hundreds who swarmed into Dallas after the killings— newsmen, FBI agents, curiosity seekers and amateur sleuths and others—was a New York attorney by the name of Mark Lane. He had felt moved by the mystery of events and Marguerite's stories in the press. Often interesting himself in controversial public issues, he got in touch with Marguerite and listened to her story. She designated him to go before the Commission and represent the killer *in absentia.*

Whatever Mark Lane's motives, he succeeded in injecting a new element of confusion in the public mind. On January 14, 1964, he addressed himself to the Chief Justice as follows:

"DEAR JUSTICE WARREN:

"This letter, following the telegram sent to your office yesterday, serves as the formal notice of appearance in regard to the investigation and hearings being conducted by the Commission. I have been retained by Mrs. Marguerite C. Oswald of Fort Worth, Texas, the mother of the accused assassin, to represent the interests of the deceased Lee Harvey Oswald before your Commission. I enclose herewith an affidavit, signed by Mrs. Marguerite C. Oswald, and duly notarized on the 11th day of January, 1964, within the State of Texas, City of Fort Worth and County of Tarrant. The affidavit states that the deponent is the mother of Lee Harvey Oswald and that on the 11th day of January, 1964, she retained me, on his behalf, for the purposes above stated.

"I enclose also an affidavit signed by Mrs. Marguerite C. Oswald on the 11th day of January, 1964, stating that Marina Oswald told her that the alleged murder weapon displayed to her by the Dallas Police on the 22nd day of November, 1963, was, in fact, not the rifle owned by the deceased Lee Harvey Oswald.

434

"In view of the above I request permission at this time to visit with Mrs. Marina Oswald to determine the nature of her confinement and to discover if unfair and inappropriate methods have been utilized to tamper with or influence her testimony. The very secret nature of her confinement must, of course, raise serious doubts.

"I also request permission to examine the reports thus far submitted to you which make reference to my deceased client and for the right to present witnesses at the hearings that you contemplate holding. Along those lines I request that you inform me of the proposed dates for the hearings.

"I would appreciate it if communication from your office were directed to me at 164 West 79th Street, New York, New York.

Respectfully,
MARK LANE"

On the surface Mark Lane's request might seem altogether reasonable. However, there were two important considerations. In the first place, if anyone had a right to designate an attorney to represent Lee Oswald, it would not have been Marguerite but Lee's widow, Marina. There was no indication that Marina was interested in having Mark Lane represent Lee. Secondly, this was not a trial in any sense of the word; it was a hearing aimed at getting all the facts, not determining the legal guilt of any person, living or dead.

Mr. J. Lee Rankin, General Counsel for the Commission, replied to the Lane request:

"Mr. Mark Lane
164 West 79th Street,
New York, New York.

DEAR MR. LANE:

"On behalf of the Commission I wish to acknowledge receipt of your recent telegram informing the Commission that you have been retained by Mrs. Marguerite C. Oswald to represent her deceased son.

"As you know, the Commission is interested in developing all the pertinent facts relating to the assassination of President John F. Kennedy and the subsequent killing of Lee Harvey Oswald by Jack L. Ruby. Any documentary material which Mrs. Marguerite C. Oswald or others wish to submit to the Commission will receive careful consideration.

"The Commission does not believe that it would be useful or desirable to permit an attorney representing Lee Harvey Oswald to have access to the investigative materials within the possession of the Commission or to participate in any hearings to be conducted by the Commission. I can assure you that every effort will be made to ascertain the facts regarding Lee Harvey Oswald's implication in the assassination of President Kennedy as accurately and fairly as possible.

Sincerely,
J. LEE RANKIN
General Counsel"

In an effort to carry out the purposes of the Commission with all due regard for the rights of everyone concerned, Walter E. Craig, president of the American Bar Association, was asked to participate in the hearings "fully and without limitations." He agreed to serve in this capacity, in effect representing the ethical conscience of the American bar. Mr. Craig's letter of acceptance reads:

American Bar Association
March 23, 1964

The President's Commission

GENTLEMEN:

Pursuant to the request in the statement of the Commission issued February 25, 1964, I have undertaken participation in the hearings of the Commission and have designated Messrs. Lewis F. Powell, Jr., of Richmond, Virginia, Charles S. Rhyne of Washington, D. C., Whitney North Seymour of New York, New York, Charles B. Murray of Washington, D. C., and Edward L. Wright of Little Rock, Arkansas, to assist me.

So that all may fully understand my position and that of my associates, it is pertinent to point out that the proceedings of the Commission are not comparable to a court trial. These proceedings are not adversary in character; rather, they are an independent and impartial inquiry into the assassination of President Kennedy. Of necessity the normal rules of procedure and evidence in a court trial are not applicable.

As stated by the Commission on February 25, 1964, I am, with my associates, adviser to the Commission. We are not counsel for Lee Harvey Oswald. Our function is to make certain that all facts pertaining to the involvement of Lee Harvey Oswald with the assassination of President Kennedy are fully investigated and fairly presented. The assignment undertaken is not to carry out the traditional function of defense counsel in a murder trial, for the very nature of the inquiry by the Commission would make such a role impossible and inappropriate.

436

The participation in the proceedings by me, with my associates, in no way supersedes or replaces the responsibility of the Commission and its staff with respect to the inquiry and resulting report.

Respectfully,
WALTER E. CRAIG

On occasions when he was unable to attend personally, other high members of the bar designated by him were present. As it turned out, every witness who appeared before the Commission, with three minor exceptions, appeared voluntarily and gave testimony without subpoena. When Marguerite Oswald chose not to give certain original papers to the Commission her wishes were respected. When to protect her commercial interests she wanted to retain certain photographs, she was free to do as she wanted.

It is an important fact that the very way in which the Commission conducted its work is proof of the integrity of its conclusions. Each witness was permitted to say anything he thought might shed light on the investigation, even if it took half the night. No American was denied the right to testify if he made a reasonable showing that he or she had something to contribute. Apparently Mark Lane, by the questions he raised here and abroad, seemed to be trying to give the appearance that the Commission was sweeping something under the rug.

Marguerite Oswald did not retain Mark Lane to represent her before the Commission. At her request the Commission called on the services of a distinguished member of the bar. Nevertheless, Mark Lane showed up in Washington in an effort to participate in Marguerite's hearing. The record indicates the disposition of the matter. Marguerite made her own choice. Mr. Doyle was the attorney appointed by the Commission to represent Marguerite.

Chairman Warren: "The Commission will come to order. Are we ready to proceed?"

Mr. Doyle: "If it please Your Honor—"

Chairman Warren: "Mr. Doyle."

Mr. Doyle: "Mr. Mark Lane is present as counsel, as I understand, for Mrs. Oswald. Although I have not talked to Mrs. Oswald about the matter, as I understand it Mr. Lane has represented her from time to time, in one capacity or another in the past.

"I do not know the particulars. Mrs. Oswald or Mr. Lane could better advise the Commission about the point.

"Of course my designation was at the request of Mrs. Oswald to act in her behalf, since there was no counsel of her choice present at the time."

Chairman Warren: "True."

Mr. Doyle: "In view of the appearance—I wonder if it might be straightened out—if Mr. Lane wishes to enter his appearance in the matter.

"Of course I would immediately respectfully move for leave to withdraw."

Chairman Warren: "Mrs. Oswald, what is your wish?"

Mrs. Oswald: "Well, Mr. Lane is just here for a few hours, Chief Justice Warren. He flew in just for a few hours. He is catching a four-o'clock plane out. And I thought—he had asked permission to sit in just for these few hours."

Chairman Warren: "Either he represents you or he does not."

Mrs. Oswald: "No, sir, he does not represent me."

Chairman Warren: "Then we will excuse Mr. Lane."

Mr. Lane: "Mr. Chief Justice—"

Chairman Warren: "Mr. Lane, now really, either you are here as the attorney for Mrs. Oswald or you are not entitled to be in this room—one of the two."

Mr. Lane: "May I ask, Mr. Chief Justice, if it is permissible for me to function at Mrs. Oswald's request as her counsel together with Mr. Doyle, just for an hour or two, and then be excused?"

Chairman Warren: "Mr. Doyle has said that if you are her attorney he is not. And Mr. Doyle is doing this as a public service. We must respect his views in the matter."

Mr. Lane: "I see. I did explain to Mr. Doyle before I came into the room exactly what the situation was. It was not until now that I understood his response.

"Under those circumstances, I wonder if I might confer with Mrs. Oswald for just a minute or two."

Chairman Warren: "If Mrs. Oswald wants to, she may."

Mrs. Oswald: "Yes, thank you."

Chairman Warren: "All right. You may take another room, if you wish."

After a brief recess Mark Lane did not return to represent Mrs. Oswald. Mr. Doyle continued in his properly designated role.

Throughout the nation and in foreign countries Mark Lane traveled, raising his clouds of doubt. On important occasions he would share the platform with Mrs. Marguerite Oswald, who was intent on taking her "case" to the people. What their arrangements were never became quite clear. Mark Lane's testimony in his second appearance before the Commission implied that he was not personally profiting from monies raised by his appearances in Lee Oswald's behalf.

Mr. Lane: "Mr. Chief Justice, I believe I am the only citizen in this country who has devoted six months to securing information at his own expense. You talk about what it cost to go to Europe. I have gone to Europe twice, and I have paid for those trips myself. I have traveled all over this country. I have gone to Dallas five times. I have paid for those trips myself, and I am not in a position financially to do that, but I have done that to give you this information."

Chairman Warren: "Were you getting evidence over in Europe?"

"No; I was discussing this case, because of the suppression in this country of the facts. I felt it important that somehow the American people be informed about what is taking place, and I found that practically the only way to inform the American people is to speak in Europe."

"Have you charged admission for any of your speaking?"

"Have I charged admission?"

"Yes."

"No; I have not charged admission."

"Do you collect any money in this country at the speeches that you made?"

"Did I, personally, collect any money?"

"Did you have money collected?"

"I collected no money."

"Did you have any money collected?"

"I did not."

"Was there money collected at that meeting—at those meetings that you had?"

"I spoke at probably forty different college campuses throughout the United States."

"Was money collected at those places?"

"To my knowledge, at none of those meetings was money collected. At one or two or perhaps three other meetings, funds have been collected for the purpose of paying the salary of the secretary of this citizens committee of inquiry, and to pay the rent."

"Who got the money?"

"The citizens committee of inquiry."

"Who is the head of that?"

"I am the chairman of that."

Mark Lane was well known in the New York area for his many activities, and he became known as a man who raised many questions about the thoroughness of the investigations into the assassination. The implication was that his interrogatories had not been fully pursued. The twenty-six volumes of testimony and exhibits will speak for themselves.

It is now said that one of the areas where the Commission's report is most commonly doubted is in Europe. Mark Lane made his contributions to the aura of suspicion that pervaded Europe. Not content to tell the American people all about the obvious inconsistencies of the tales out of Dallas after the assassination, he stumped Europe peddling his questions. It is most perplexing why he would go junketing around Europe adding to the rumors that something very foul and dastardly was going on in Washington.

Even Mark Lane, who harassed the work of the Commission by innuendo and inference, was given his days, not once but twice and in public hearings at his request, to talk before the Commission. His long list of questions was combined with all the others for the Commission to answer. For several hours he sat at the long table, hunched and reading from his notes, and droned out his case. Surprisingly enough, although he was supposedly retained by Marguerite Oswald, he did not seem to put a lot of credence in her arguments. In his appearances before the Commission he never once alleged that Lee Oswald had ever been in the pay of the FBI. He didn't seem to know anything about the fears of plots which developed at the Six Flags Motel. He didn't say that Lee had gone to Russia in 1959 on a secret government mission. He never once implied that Marina was involved with Robert in some inexplicable scheme. The questions he raised were quite obvious. They were little more than a summary of the most popular questions raised in the press, and for the most part were questions the Commission had been working on for weeks. The

Chairman and other members of the Commission treated Mark Lane with more courtesy than he sometimes showed.

In the first place, the Commissioners soon became convinced that Lee Oswald's employment in the Texas School Book Depository was a sheer coincidence and not part of a plot or prearrangement.

The second major point: the gun recovered on the sixth floor was Lee Oswald's beyond a shadow of a doubt. Marina may have doubted her own identification of the gun, but her own testimony bore out that she knew little about rifles. Perhaps she had let a wish be father to the thought after hearing so many speculations. It would appear that Marina adopted a wait-and-see attitude after her first burst of conviction that Lee was guilty.

Beyond these two basic questions, Mark Lane raised the classic question of the direction from which the bullets had come. This question is so thoroughly covered in the report that it scarcely requires elaboration. However, the actual words of the three key witnesses who were peering out of the fifth-floor windows almost directly below the window from which Oswald fired are so spontaneous and convincing that even the most dubious critic would have been satisfied if he had heard these men recount their experiences. James "Junior" Jarman was a fellow employee of Lee Oswald's at the Texas School Book Depository, and as he testified I made a note on my working papers on the Commission's table—"good memory." Jarman, a veteran of eight years in the Army, was soft-spoken as he described his experiences on the day of the shooting:

"Now, on November twenty-second, what time did you get to work?"

"About five minutes after eight."

"Was Oswald there when you got there?"

"Yes, sir."

"Where did you see him the first time?"

"Well, he was on the first floor filling orders."

"Did you bring your lunch that day?"

"No, sir, I didn't."

"What did you do about lunch that day?"

"I got a sandwich off the carrying truck."

"Did you talk to Oswald that morning?"

"I did."

"When?"

"I had him to correct an order. I don't know exactly what time it was."

"Did you talk to him again that morning?"

"Yes, sir. I talked to him again later on that morning."

"About what time?"

"It was between nine-thirty and ten o'clock, I believe."

"Where were you when you talked to him?"

"In between two rows of bins."

"On what floor?"

"On the first floor."

"And what was said by him and by you?"

"Well, he was standing up in the window and I went to the window also, and he asked me what were the people gathering around on the corner for, and I told him that the President was supposed to pass that morning, and he asked me did I know which way he was coming, and I told him yes, he'd probably come down Main and turn on Houston and then back again on Elm.

"Then he said, 'Oh, I see,' and that was all."

"Did you talk to him again?"

"No, sir."

"What time did you quit for lunch?"

"It was right about five minutes to twelve."

"What did you do when you quit for lunch?"

"Went in the rest room and washed up."

"Then what did you do?"

"Went and got my sandwich and went up in the lounge and got me a soda pop."

"Then where did you go after you got your soda pop?"

"Came back and went down to the window."

"What window?"

"Where Oswald and I was talking."

"Where?"

"Between those two rows of bins."

"Where Oswald and you had been talking?"

"Yes."

"What did you do there?"

"I was eating part of my sandwich there, and then I came back out and as I was walking across the floor I ate the rest of it going toward the domino room."

"You say you wandered around. You mean on the first floor?"

"On the first floor."

"Did you see Lee Oswald?"

"No, I didn't."

"After his arrest, he stated to a police officer that he had had lunch with you. Did you have lunch with him?"

"No, sir, I didn't."

"When you finished your sandwich and your bottle of pop, what did you do?"

"I went out in front of the building."

"With who?"

"Harold Norman and myself and Daniel Arce."

Many European plot theorists tried to make a big thing out of a photograph at the time of the assassination showing the spectators in front of the Depository. They tried to claim that Lee Oswald couldn't have been at the sixth-floor window because he was in that picture. The difficulty with this theory is that the person they point out is not Lee Oswald but Billy Lovelady. Lovelady has confirmed this himself, and Junior Jarman testified where Lovelady was standing at this time.

"What about Billy Lovelady?"

"I didn't go out with them. They came out later."

"Did you see Billy Lovelady out there?"

"Yes, sir."

"Where was he?"

"Standing on the stairway as you go out the front door."

Norman also established the whereabouts of other key witnesses.

"What about Mr. Truly?"

"He wasn't standing close to me."

"Did you see him?"

"Yes, sir."

"Who was he with?"

"He was with the vice-president of the company."

"What is his name?"

"O. V. Campbell."

"Where were they standing?"

"They were standing at the corner of the building in front of the mailboxes."

"You left there, didn't you, and went some place?"

"Yes, sir."

"With whom?"

"Harold Norman and myself."

"Where did you go?"

"We went around to the back of the building up to the fifth floor."

"Why did you go to the fifth floor?"

"We just decided to go to the fifth floor."

"When you got there was there anybody on the fifth floor?"

"No, sir."

"What did you do when you got to the fifth floor?"

"We got out of the elevator and pulled the gate down. That was in case somebody wanted to use it. Then we went to the front of the building, which is on the south side, and raised the windows."

"Which windows did you raise?"

"Well, Harold raised the first window to the east side of the building, and I went to the second rear windows and raised, counting the windows, it would be the fourth one."

"It would be the fourth window?"

"Yes."

"Did somebody join you then?"

"Yes, sir, a few minutes later."

"Who joined you?"

"Bonnie Ray Williams."

Harold Norman, the second of the young men on the fifth floor during the shooting, recounted how he in turn happened to be there, and his recollection substantiates that of Jarman.

Norman's appearance before the Commission indicated to me, as I listened to his words, clearly that he was a young man who wanted to be most helpful. On occasion this short but sturdy witness was handicapped by his awe of the Commission, but his recollections were vital.

"Where was James Jarman when you got together with him?"

"He was somewhere in the vicinity on the telephone, I believe. I am not for sure."

"Out near the bins?"

"Yes."

"What do you call James Jarman?"

"Junior."

"And you and Junior did what?"

"We went outside."

"You went out the front door, did you?"

"Yes."

"That is the Elm Street?"

"Yes, sir."

"Where did you stand?"

"We stood on the Elm Street sidewalk."

"What time was it that you went out there?"

"Oh, I would say—I don't know exactly—around twelve or twelve-ten—something like that."

"Who was standing with you when you were standing on the sidewalk, on the Elm Street sidewalk?"

"I remember it was Danny Arce."

"And who else?"

"I remember seeing Mr. Truly and Mr. Campbell. They were standing somewhere behind us, not exactly behind us, but they were back of us."

"Anybody else?"

"Well, I believe Billy Lovelady, I think. He was sitting on the steps there."

"Did you stay there?"

"Well, we stayed there I believe until we got the news that the motorcade was coming down—let's see, is that Commerce?—no, Main, because Commerce—we went back in the building, James Jarman and I."

The two employees then went to the front windows overlooking the parade route. Meantime, Bonnie Ray Williams, having finished his lonesome lunch on the sixth floor above, joined his friends on the fifth. The window sills there go near to the floor, so the young men flung the windows open and either squatted or rested on their knees, leaning on the sills. They craned their necks to get a good view of the motorcade coming toward them. They watched the President greeting the crowds. The motorcade slowly turned the corner below them and headed for the Triple Underpass. Junior Jarman recalled what happened next:

"After the motorcade turned, going west on Elm, then there was a loud shot, or backfire, as I thought it was then—I thought it was a backfire.

"And then the second shot was fired, and that is when the people started falling on the ground and the motorcade car jumped forward, and then the third shot was fired right behind the second one."

"Were you still on your knees looking up?"

"Well, after the third shot was fired, I think I got up and I run over to Harold Norman and Bonnie Ray Williams and told them, I said, I told them that it wasn't a backfire or anything, that somebody was shooting at the President."

"And then did they say anything?"

"Hank said, Harold Norman rather, said that he thought the shots had come from above us, and I noticed that Bonnie Ray had a few debris in his head. It was sort of white stuff, or something, and I told him not to brush it out, but he did anyway."

"He had some white what, like plaster?"

"Like some come off a brick or plaster or something."

"Did Norman say anything else that you remember?"

"He said that he was sure that the shot came from inside the building because he had been used to guns and all that, and he said it didn't sound like it was too far off anyway. And so we ran down to the west side of the building."

"Did Norman say anything about hearing cartridges or ejection or anything like that, do you remember?"

"That was after we got down to the west side of the building."

Because the motorcade had picked up speed and the President's car was racing to Parkland Hospital, they ran to that end of the building to see what had happened. Again they flung open the windows on the west side of the building.

"And what did you do after you opened the window?"

"I leaned out and the officers and various people was running across the tracks, toward the tracks over there where they had the passenger trains, and all, boxcars and things."

"Where were you when you heard Harold Norman say something that he had heard cartridges?"

"All that took place right here in this corner after we had went to this window."

"What did you hear him say?"

446

"He said it was something sounded like cartridges hitting the floor, and he could hear the action of the rifle, I mean the bolt, as it were pulled back, or something like that."

"Had you heard anything like that?"

"No, sir, I hadn't."

"Had you heard any person running upstairs?"

"No, sir.

"Well, after Norman had made his statement that he had heard the cartridges hit the floor and this bolt action, I told him we'd better get the hell from up here."

"Did anybody suggest you go up to the sixth floor?"

"No, sir."

"And where did you go then?"

"We ran to the elevator first, but the elevator had gone down."

"Where did you go?"

"Then we ran to the stairway and ran downstairs."

Harold Norman told his version of the events, which substantially confirmed Jarman's version.

"I can't remember what the exact time was, but I know I heard a shot, and then after I heard the shot, well, it seems as though the President, you know, slumped or something, and then another shot and I believe Jarman or someone told me, he said, 'I believe someone is shooting at the President,' and I think I made a statement, 'It's someone shooting at the President,' and I believe it came from up above us.

"Well, I couldn't see at all during the time, but I know I heard a third shot fired, and I could also hear something sounded like the shell hulls hitting the floor and the ejecting of the rifle, it sounded as though it was to me."

"How many shots did you hear?"

"Three."

"Do you remember whether or not you said anything to the boys then as to whether or not you heard anything from above you?"

"Only I think I remember saying that I thought I could hear the shell hulls and the ejection of the rifle. I didn't tell I think I hear anybody moving, you know."

"But you thought, do you remember you told the boys then that you thought you heard the ejection of the rifle?"

"Yes, sir."

447

"And shells on the floor?"

"Yes, sir."

"Falling?"

"Yes."

"Did anybody say anything as to where they thought the shots came from?"

"Well, I don't recall of either one of them saying they thought where it came from."

"But you did?"

"Yes."

"And you said you thought it came from where?"

"Above where we were, above us."

"Did you see any dust or dirt falling?"

"I didn't see any falling, but I saw some in Bonnie Ray Williams' hair."

"Did anybody say anything about it?"

"I believe Jarman told him that it was in his hair first. Then I, you know, told him it was and I believe Jarman told him not to brush it out of his hair, but I think he did anyway."

Bonnie Ray Williams, who had eaten his chicken on the sixth floor and had been the last to join the group, told his version. I distinctly recall from his appearance that he had a small mustache and was very neatly dressed in a gray suit and black tie. His replies to questions were rapidly given and surprisingly frank when prodded a bit.

"After the President's car had passed my window, the last thing I remember seeing him do was, you know—it seemed to me he had a habit of pushing his hair back. The last thing I saw him do was he pushed his hand up like this. I assumed he was brushing his hair back. And then the thing that happened then was a loud shot. First I thought they were saluting the President, somebody—even maybe a motorcycle backfire. The first shot—there was two shots rather close together. The second and the third shot was closer together than the first shot and the second shot, as I remember."

"Now, was your head out the window?"

"I could not say for sure. I do not remember."

"Did you notice—where did you think the shots came from?"

"Well, the first shot—I really did not pay any attention to it, because I did not know what was happening. The second shot, it sounded like it was right in the building, the second and third shot.

And it sounded—it even shook the building, the side we were on. Cement fell on my head."

"You say cement fell on your head?"

"Cement, gravel, dirt or something, from the old building, because it shook the windows and everything. Harold was sitting next to me, and he said it came right from over our head. If you want to know my exact words, I could tell you."

"Tell us."

"My exact words were 'No bull shit.' And we jumped up."

"Norman said what?"

"He said it came directly over our heads. 'I can even hear the shell being ejected from the gun hitting the floor.' But I did not hear the shell being ejected from the gun, probably because I wasn't paying attention."

"Norman said he could hear it?"

"He said he could hear it. He was directly under the window that Oswald shot from."

"When the cement fell on your head, did either one of the boys notice it and say anything about it?"

"Yes, sir. I believe Harold was the first one."

"That is Hank Norman?"

"I believe he was the first one. He said, 'Man, I know it came from there. It even shook the building.' He said, 'You got something on your head.' And then James Jarman said, 'Yes, man, don't you brush it out.' By that time I just forgot about it. But after I got downstairs I think I brushed it out anyway."

"Well, did Norman say anything about hearing the bolt of the rifle?"

"I don't remember him saying anything about it."

"But you heard him say he could hear the cartridges?"

"I heard Harold Norman—pardon me, I thought you were saying James Jarman."

"Did Norman say anything about the bolt?"

"Yes. He said he could hear the rifle, and it sounded like it was right above. He said he could hear the rifle being ejected, the shells hitting the floor."

"How did you know the President was shot at this time?"

"We heard the shots, and we assumed somebody had shot him. And we decided to run down that way."

"Why didn't you go up to the sixth floor?"

"I really don't know. We just never did think about it. And after we had made this last stop, James Jarman said, 'Maybe we better get the hell out of here.' And so we just ran down to the fourth floor and came on down. We never did think about it, going up to the sixth floor. Maybe it was just because we were frightened."

The men hastened to get out of the building, but en route Junior Jarman recalled one other important piece of testimony. He remembered meeting another witness who confirmed that the shots came from the sixth floor. It was Howard Brennan who had seen all that had happened from outdoors. Jarman reinforced Brennan's account of what he did immediately after the shooting. Although he did not at that time know Brennan, he identified him by the "silverlike helmet" he wore.

"He ran up to the police officer and was telling him about the man sticking a gun out the window. And I heard him telling the officer that.

"And I told him that I thought the shots came from inside, too."

The testimony of Jarman, Norman, Bonnie Ray Williams and Howard Brennan coincided in every major detail. No credible witness the Commission could find believed that the shots came from the Triple Underpass or from any place other than the Texas School Book Depository.

CHAPTER 34

THE MANY FACES
OF MARINA OSWALD

VOLUNTARY WITNESSES like Harold Norman, Junior Jarman and Bonnie Ray Williams burned their testimony into the record in a way that will be virtually impossible for speculators of the future to obliterate. Each spoke with candor, artlessness and bluntness that no man can assign to calculation. They called the events as they saw them and, without knowing, they proved facts which had been widely distorted in the foreign press. They confirmed the spontaneous reactions of witness Brennan as he rushed forward to tell the police he had seen the gunman in the sixth-floor window. They corroborated the fact that Billy Lovelady was standing in front of the Depository in the exact spot others tried to maintain Lee Oswald occupied. They attested to the fact that the building manager, Roy Truly, was watching the motorcade as he said he was. How difficult then for the exponents of intrigue to say this was all planned and precalculated by a clandestine group who arranged matters for their dastardly purposes! Twenty-six volumes of testimony, depositions and exhibits like this would undercut the speculations of the Mark Lanes, Sauvages, Feldmans, Buchanans, et al. The most insidious schemer in the world could hardly rig the statements of 552 witnesses. Let those who scoff at the report bury themselves for ten months in the monumental record. After that, if they persist in their skepticism, that's their privilege. May they add to the truth so long as it is the truth and not mere speculation.

In general, witnesses were found to be honest. Some erred simply because memory is fallible; others definitely mistook identities. A number of witnesses who had been reported in the press as knowing this or that key fact turned out to have been misquoted. For example, the well-advertised "mind reader" who was alleged to have seen Oswald in the Carousel Club while performing his act explained that he had indeed seen a man who resembled the pictures of

Oswald. He explained that he did not, nor could he, make a positive identification. He had commented that the person looked like Oswald, but beyond that he made no claims. When asked, "Are you a memory expert?" he explained frankly that his act was just a "gimmick." He was frank to say his memory was no better than the average person's, and the Commission restrained itself from prying into his professional secrets of just exactly how his "gimmick" operated. No evidence could be found that Oswald ever knew Ruby or that he was ever in the Carousel Club.

Of all the witnesses, Marina Oswald was perhaps the most difficult to deal with. Much of this can be assigned to the obstacle of translation. No two languages are identical, and particularly when the fine nuance of an idea hinges on words that do not exist in English. In reading her testimony it must be remembered that with the exception of the third hearing, all questions were asked in English, translated into Russian and vice versa with her replies. Competent translators were employed. However, errors can and do occur. This made the taking of her testimony slow and difficult. But the language barrier was not the only problem with Marina. At her third hearing she explained that some of her previous inaccuracies were made when she was in a state of shock. The word "shock" would seem inadequate to express the dilemma of her position and the frightful pressures she was under.

Ruth Paine, who knew Marina as intimately as anyone, was asked, "What is your opinion as to whether Marina Oswald would tell the truth and the whole truth under oath in response to questions put to her?"

"I would expect that she would make a dedicated attempt to tell the truth. Just looking at the amount of time I have testified, as opposed to the amount of time she testified, relative to the amount of things she knows and the amount of material that I have that is any use to the Commission, she could not have yet told the whole truth, just in terms of time."

"Well, that may be affected—of course, you must understand—by the questions put to her and the subjects that were opened on her examination."

"Right."

"But subject to that, it is your feeling that she—there is a—"

"Subject to that, I really cannot answer. I don't know what her attitude is towards her situation, which is a rather remarkable one in this case. I would guess that it is helpful to her telling the whole truth that Lee is now dead.

"I might say I am affected in that judgment by having been present when she could not positively identify her husband's—what was thought to be his rifle at the police station, whereas I read—and perhaps it is not so—but I read that she positively identified it here at the Commission."

"But you were present when she, in your presence, was unable to identify with reasonable certainty that the weapon exhibited to her was her husband's rifle?"

"That is right."

"And you attribute that largely to the fact that his now being deceased has in her mind released her, so that she may without fear of implicating him, were he alive, to speak fully her opinions on subjects such as that?"

"That would be my opinion."

"I see."

Ruth Paine's steadfast loyalty to Marina loomed in stark contrast to some of the things Marina said to the Commission about her former mentor.

After the report of the Commission was released, Senator Richard B. Russell commented on Marina's appearance. In an article it was reported that "he was particularly struck by the baffling behavior of Marina Oswald. Her attitude changed markedly between her two appearances. She talked freely at her first appearance, seemed coached and elusive the second time." This is indeed a conservative statement of the many-sided picture one gets of Marina when the whole record is taken into consideration.

What went on in Marina's mind during those weeks of tension after the assassination? Did Ruth Paine's speculation explain one aspect of her seeming inconsistency? There was one Marina Oswald while Lee was alive—the Marina who seemed to want to escape Lee's tyranny and yet could exclaim with undisguised enthusiasm "Papa loves us!" when the phone rang from New Orleans. And then there was another Marina when Lee had died who positively identified his rifle. There was a Marina Oswald who de Mohrenschildt said was remarkably lazy, and contrasting with this was Ruth Paine's observation, "I respected what I saw in her, her pride, her wish to be independent, her habit of hard work." Marina's apparent complexity does not connote glamour, but as the witnesses saw her, she changed like the glass patterns in a kaleidoscope. And the Commission more than once had to cope with this changeability.

The first day of her testimony she was asked, referring to FBI and Secret Service interviews she had previously had, "As far as you can recall now, do you know of anything that is not true in those interviews that you would like to correct or add to?"

"Yes, I would like to correct some things because not everything was true."

"Will you tell us—"

"It is not just that it wasn't true, but not quite exact."

How complex truth can be when one's emotions are under stress!

Ruth Paine testified in late March, and she still did not know for sure whether Lee had really been in Mexico.

As far as the Commission was concerned, Marina said she did not tell the FBI and other investigators everything because she wanted to save something to tell the Commission. Marina often used the expression "That's somewhat boring" or its equivalent. If her purpose in holding back information was to keep the Commissioners from getting bored, there was little danger of that.

Prior to coming before the Commission Marina had denied to investigating authorities in Dallas that she knew anything about his having been in Mexico. Unfortunately for her the coin Lee had drilled for a neckpiece was left at Ruth Paine's house and it was soon found. She could then do little else but divulge the deception she had worked on Ruth Paine.

Jim Martin, with whom Marina Oswald took refuge, having decided not to go back to Ruth Paine's, made these observations to the Commission. He was asked, "Did you ever have any reason to believe that she was anything other than what she appeared to be—namely, an ordinary housewife who had come to this country as the wife of an American whom she married?"

"Looking back on the whole picture, she doesn't seem quite right. I mean she doesn't fit."

"What do you mean by that?"

"As a mother and a housewife. She is too cold for one thing."

"Cold in what way?"

"Emotionally. This thing. I don't know whether it is the Russian woman or what, but this thing would have terrifically upset an American woman, and she was not very upset at all."

"Not upset about the assassination?"

"About her husband."

"About her husband's subsequent death?"

"Well, now—She was to a degree. But it didn't ring true."

"So what do you mean by that? Do you mean that because of her coolness under very terrific, very difficult conditions and a very difficult situation, that maybe she was not just what she appeared to be, and if not, what do you think she was?"

"I have no idea. It is the way she treated, the way she treated contributions, for instance. Someone would send a dollar, I don't know, maybe it was her last dollar, and she would look at it and throw it aside and say, 'Oh, it is just a dollar.' And John Thorne and I kind of built up an image for her or of her for the American public and she is not exactly as we picture her in the news articles."

"Would you spell that out in more detail?"

"Well, for one thing, I recall instances that she was reported to have read the Bible every day. She didn't crack a Bible. She got up between ten and eleven o'clock every morning. The only household chore she did was wash the evening dinner dishes, and occasionally she would vacuum."

"This may be attributed to lack of energy or laziness."

"Well, yes, that is true, but she is not a humble person at all."

"Did you ever see her cry or show any comparable emotions?"

"No. The closest I ever saw her to really showing any emotion at all was when—it was about a week after she had been there—she saw a picture, of Jackie Kennedy's picture—a picture of Jackie Kennedy. I don't know whether it was *Life* magazine or what."

"You have said she is too cold, you have said you thought that all this was preplanned. Is there anything specific in anything that she told you or in any of her actions which would lead you to believe that she has withheld certain information from you concerning, or this Commission, concerning her knowledge about the assassination?"

"No, except she made a remark to me one time that she didn't volunteer anything. She only answered questions."

"This was after the return from the Commission hearing?"

"No, this was some time ago. That was before—"

"Before the Commission hearing where she appeared?"

"Yes. I don't remember what brought it up even. She didn't like the FBI. She said that. And she didn't like to answer questions."

"Did she tell you why?"

"No. She just didn't like them. Boguslav in particular."

"But her remark was made before her hearing before this Commission?"

"Yes."

"And did not relate then to that hearing?"

"No."

"Did she indicate to you she had revealed everything that there was to reveal before this Commission?"

"Yes. There again I didn't question her about anything that she said in the Commission. I didn't feel it was any of my business, for one thing, and all I asked her is how it went, and she would say fine, and that would be the end of it. That is the limit of my questioning her as far as testimony within the Commission was concerned."

"Mr. Martin, you said earlier in your testimony that you were building a public image of Marina Oswald?"

"Yes."

"Would you tell the Commission what you mean by that?"

"Well, in this type of thing—we were trying to create in the public mind an image of a bereaved widow and a simple lost girl. And I think we did actually. This was for her, as I say, for her benefit. She has received some sixty-eight thousand dollars in contributions, and the image is not all true."

"Would you tell us in respect to which in your opinion the image is not true?"

"Well, as I mentioned before about the Bible. This is a very small incident. She has received numerous Bibles in the mail, and to my knowledge has never read the first page of one, and most of them are in Russian.

"This is a small thing really, but it is part of her image, that she is a religious person.

"She wants to be thought of as we have built her now, but she doesn't conform to that image."

"In what way, how?"

"Well, she is lazy, for one thing."

"Lazy in what respect?"

"Well, as far as even taking care of the children. The children bother her—I mean to her they are a constant upset. When she left our home to go up to Denton, my wife offered to keep the baby there at the house if she liked, and Marina took her up on it and then Robert told her she had better take the baby with her. She hadn't seen the baby for over a week. And the first day she was back she was willing to leave the baby again."

"Is there anything else?"

"Her lack of, well, humbleness as far as all these contributions are concerned. She takes it as a matter of—she takes it for granted. She is quite unhappy when the contributions slack off."

"Has she discussed the amount of contributions with you?"

"I have kept her informed all along on it."

"Has she indicated that there is some relationship between the story that she reveals to the public and the contributions which she will receive?"

"Yes."

"Would you be more specific about that?"

"Well, she has read newspaper articles, for instance, that I haven't written but I have directed."

"Directed?"

"By giving them information."

"What is the nature—"

"To build it up."

"What is the nature of these articles?"

"Well, I recall one—I wonder if I have it; I guess I don't have it—that was written by Bill Burrus of the *Times Herald* in Dallas. It was a very good article, and not quite true, we will say. It is shaded in truth."

"Do you have the article with you?"

"Here is one Bill Burrus did that is when she went to midnight Mass."

"Will you tell us in what respects this article is not true?"

"Well, I wouldn't say it is strictly not true. But it embellishes the truth."

"Could you be specific in terms of references to the particular article?"

"Well, for instance, let's see, is this where she went to church?"

"Did she go to church?"

"Yes. It is my partner's church.

"Well, for instance, 'She wandered around the secret quarters for long periods of time, sometimes she listened to Christmas carols over radio or television,' which I believe is not true. I don't believe I told that; that was just added in there.

" 'Marina continued her studies of the English language and watched television, including her favorite Steve Allen show.' She doesn't even like Steve Allen. And, of course, she is never studying English."

"Was this information that you gave to Mr. Burrus?"

"No. That is the trouble with newspapers. I have told Bill Burrus that she watches Steve Allen. She does, but just for lack of anything else to do.

"Now I didn't say anything about the Christmas carols nor about studying the English language."

"You say she has not been studying the English language?"

"No, she is learning it quite rapidly because she had to in her own defense in order to converse with people. When she was living with us, there was no one there that spoke Russian, so she had to learn English in order to converse.

"Here is a sentence in here. 'She pores over the letters reaching her, more than a thousand so far, and is choked with emotion by the compassion and support they express.' The only thing she did actually was to open the letters and did not open all of them. The only letters she read or attempted to read were ones written in Russian."

"What was her reaction to those letters?"

"Acceptance of it, but no real thankfulness. The further it went, the longer it went, it seemed the less she cared."

"But you can't recall anything specific that she said which would indicate this lack of compassion?"

"No, other than 'the American people are crazy for sending me that money.' "

"Is that a quotation from Mrs. Oswald? She said the American people are crazy for sending this money?"

"Yes."

It must be borne in mind that this testimony was given by Jim Martin after he and Marina had had their falling out. However, it does show that each of us probably has as many images as there are eyes of beholders to view.

Between the pages of a book in Ruth Paine's house a letter had been hidden for many months. It began with those now famous words, "This is the key to the mailbox which is located in the main post office . . ." It was Lee's farewell note to Marina the night he went out to shoot General Walker. She had saved it to use in case Lee did some crazy thing again.

It was now December 2, 1963. Marina had told the FBI many things. Her husband had been dead more than a week—no danger of retaliation from him. She must have been terribly frightened, afraid to tell the truth for fear she personally would be implicated in some fashion.

Ruth Paine thought Marina needed some more supplies at the Martins'. She bundled up some things, among them the *Book of Useful Advice* she thought Marina might need. She delivered her token of good will. On inspection of these things by the Secret Service the letter was discovered.

For the first time Marina confessed the whole episode of a murder that had failed. Lee Oswald was the would-be killer of Major General Edwin A. Walker.

CHAPTER 35

MURDER—THE CONSTANT THREAT

Wᴵᵀᴴ ᴛʜᴇ ꜰᴵʀꜱᴛʜᴀɴᴅ disclosure of all the details of the Walker affair recounted by Marina before the Commission, the mountains of testimony of other witnesses, the exhaustive studies of the FBI, Secret Service, CIA, State Department, local police, Treasury Department, Postal Department, Immigration Service, foreign intelligence reports, Western Union, Marine Corps, it seemed that little could be added to a record that would weigh the shelves of the National Archives.

History is replete with murders of great leaders. But as members of the Commission read depositions of witnesses until hours long past midnight the mystery of destiny acquired a new meaning. Each member of the Commission had served in public life; each man, now pondering the meaning of this welter of fact, understood that "There but for the grace of God go I." But the meaning was deeper than the response of any individual member of the Commission. The meaning was really universal. Who could really say that he was not an integral part of these events? Of all the complex personalities in this drama, who could say there is not a little portion of this or that in every one of us? Don't we all have the generous impulses from time to time of Ruth Paine, even though we know nothing about the gestures? Does not everyone have the frustrations in a little way of Marguerite? Are we not sometimes bewildered and forced to a philosophy of survival as that which seemed to motivate Marina? Are we not all sometimes embittered and provoked to wonder with men like Jim Martin whether we put our trust in a fiction? Such an array of colorful people—well-meaning Ruth Paine; guileless Robert; kind, sympathetic George Bouhe; boisterous, energetic and self-confident de Mohrenschildt; responsive Anna Meller. These are real people of our generation, people whose good points and bad we all share. Like an earth-bound last judgment, each member of the

Commission could feel that literally hundreds of witnesses had bared themselves in a procession of testimony that was like the summation of human nature. It was a deeply felt experience. It was above and beyond the humdrum play of politics. No member of that Commission took a political stance. Though he came to that session fresh from the fray of partisan debate on the floor of the House or Senate, this responsibility was in another sphere.

But as extensively as the witnesses documented the record of the facts surrounding the death of John F. Kennedy, it seemed that at every turn of the way lay another surprise. When Marina completed her third day of testimony I honestly believed she had told all she knew. Matters she had previously held back either from Ruth Paine or the FBI were now clarified. In addition to the work of the Commission regular investigating agencies had continued their intensive inquiries. It just seemed there couldn't be another surprise, but there was. This particular incident, the Commission decided, had "no probative value in the Commission's decision concerning the identity of the assassin of President Kennedy." In my own opinion, however, it was like the final twist of an already unbelievable story of fate. Perhaps it did not prove anything in a factual sense, but it seemed to round out the portrait of an assassin. My personal feeling is that although the facts will always remain somewhat confused, the occurrence of the incident is not likely to be questioned.

On the final day of Marina Oswald's first appearance before the Commission she was asked, "Do you remember any information or documents under your control or in your possession which would relate to or shed any light on the matters we have been examining which you have not presented here?"

"I have nothing else. Everything has been taken from me."

Marina had spent three long days answering questions, and although she had admitted at the outset that not everything she had said previously was true, she now appeared to have made a clean record.

One of the members probed this cautiously. "I would just like to suggest that if Mrs. Oswald does wish to revise any of her testimony that this be called to the attention of the Commission through her attorney, Mr. Thorne."

The Chairman followed up this observation: "Yes, of course, that is the proper procedure. Now, Mr. Thorne, you have been very cooperative with the Commission. We appreciate that cooperation. We hope that if anything new should come to your attention that would be helpful to the Commission, you would feel free to communicate with us."

"Certainly, Mr. Chairman."

Marina's ordeal was apparently over.

Her attorney closed with these comments:

"During the noon recess, Mrs. Oswald made four requests of me to make before this Commission. You have anticipated several of them, but I think there are one or two that need to be covered.

"To begin with, she wanted me to express to you, Mr. Chairman, and members of your Commission, her extreme gratitude to you for the consideration and kindness that has been shown to her in these proceedings. She feels you have certainly gone out of your way to make her comfortable, and she has been comfortable in spite of the sad and tragic events we have been discussing.

"Point number two. She did want to make it quite clear to the Commission that in the event her testimony was needed for rebuttal or whatever on down the line, she would be available and at your wish would come to Washington as convenient for you.

"Third point you have already covered. She did request that she be given a copy of these proceedings, which I told her she would receive, and of course copies of these exhibits would be attached for her identification and examination.

"And the final point was this: She has been, as you know, under protective custody of the Secret Service from shortly after the assassination. She has been most grateful for this protection. The Secret Service have shown her every courtesy, as everyone has in this matter. She is extremely grateful for this protection they have given her.

"I haven't had personally enough time to think this thing out myself. I don't know. It is her request, however, that at this point she feels the protection is no longer necessary. She feels that at this time she can walk among people with her head held high. She has nothing to hide. She is not afraid.

"She feels that the Secret Service has performed a noble service to her. And this is not meant by way of saying for some action on their part she wants to get rid of them.

"I have noticed that since we have been in Washington, she resents being guided. She feels she can find her way by herself.

"And, if the Commission would give this matter consideration—we don't know whom to go to. I haven't thought about it. I don't know who has suggested the Secret Service continue protecting her. It is a matter, of course, that ought to be considered.

"But it is her request that as soon as it is practical, she would like to be a free agent and out of the confines of this protection."

The Chairman agreed to this request, saying, "We can understand Mrs. Oswald's desire to live a perfectly normal life with her children. Whatever has been done, as you recognize, has been done for her protection and for her help during these terrible days that she has been going through.

"But she may feel from this moment on that she is under no protection, except what she might ask for. And so you are perfectly free, Mrs. Oswald, to live your normal life without any interference from anyone. And should anyone interfere with you, I hope you would call it to the attention of the Commission."

"Thank you very much."

Marina walked out of the Commission room completely free to do as she saw fit. She, her attorney and her business manager remained at the Willard Hotel a day or two, and she was able to go sightseeing like any other Washington tourist. She returned to the Dallas area to live with the Martins as she had for more than two months. Jim Martin expected to continue as her business manager, as they had signed a contract, according to him, for ten years, his percentage of 10 per cent applying only to commercial revenues he could develop. Contributions from citizens and donations were excluded from the agreements in which he, Attorney Thorne and Robert Oswald shared the income. From the cash already in prospect, which Thorne estimated might go as high as half a million dollars (Martin thought this was a high estimate), she could look forward to a secure existence. If in the years ahead she could forget the sorrows she had known, her life had brightened at last. However, not all of her troubles were over.

On Sunday Robert Oswald came to Martin's house and advised her to leave. He took her and the children to his place.

The middle of the next week she fired both Martin and Thorne, despite their contracts, and Robert hired an attorney to instigate proceedings to dissolve the agreements.

As to this new development, which seemed to set a whole new row of dominoes tumbling, Martin testified, "Well, this whole thing, since I got into it, this whole thing seems to me like I have been kind of made a patsy. Robert Oswald wouldn't take her in right after this incident because he was afraid of what might happen, might or might not happen. The Fords also expressed the same opinion."

"What do you mean by the same opinion?"

"That they wouldn't have taken her in at first. Mr. Ford expressed the opinion that he was afraid of what the public reaction might be, and he didn't know what to think.

"We took her in with the full knowledge that anything could happen, and anything might happen, and it was done strictly on an altruistic basis at first, and then this manager thing came in which I wish it hadn't at all.

"But be that as it may, it has happened, and things have been turned upside down.

"But then as soon as the Secret Service was pulled off, then Robert insisted that she move from my home to his home and start proceedings to cancel the contracts that are in existence. She was up there— she came back to the doctor on a Tuesday after she left our home, and stopped in at the house and said she wanted to come back to live with us.

"She left my home on Sunday, went to Denton to live with Robert, came back to the doctor, Dr. Bishop, on Tuesday, and came over to the house to pick up some of her belongings, and—"

"Excuse me, just so the Commission has the date straight, the Sunday you are referring to when she left is the Sunday after her appearance before this Commission?"

"Yes."

"That would be the ninth of February, is that correct?"

"Right. Then on Tuesday, which would be the eleventh, she came back to the house and wanted to move back in."

Whatever the cause for the falling-out between Thorne and Martin as opposed to Marina and Robert, this new disagreement caused Jim Martin to wonder about Marina's motives. The seed of a new plot theory sprouted, but although it survived only momentarily, it apparently created enough pressure to force other matters to the surface.

Martin continued with his version of the split:

"It just seemed strange to me that a sudden move should be made like that and then within two days after that, it was Tuesday, and Wednesday. Thursday I received a letter from her discharging me as her manager, or attempting to discharge me."

"I was asking you about intelligence, and that sort of thing.

"This would not indicate that sort of thing to you, would it?"

"No, but the whole thing seemed to be a kind of a preplanned thing."

"Will you spell that out in more detail, because when Congressman Boggs asked you questions as to whether Mrs. Oswald might be part of Soviet intelligence, you replied you are now beginning to wonder, and you also replied you wonder if you have been made a patsy.

"Could you, in your own words, explain that answer in greater detail?"

"Of course, not knowing how a spy would work or anything, I have no knowledge of anything of this sort. This whole thing shows a lack of gratefulness or something, and actually she showed the same thing with Mrs. Paine. She lived with Mrs. Paine for quite some time. Then Mrs. Paine has been trying to contact her consistently for, well, ever since the assassination, and we have passed letters to her, letters from Mrs. Paine to Marina, wherein she has asked Marina to at least call her or do something, and Marina doesn't want to have anything to do with her."

"Has Marina given you a reason for that?"

"She said she doesn't like her."

"Do you know why it was that Robert Oswald advised her not to go back to the Paines, or did you know that he did?"

"I knew that he did."

"Do you know the reason for that?"

"No. He said he just didn't like her."

"He gave no reasons?"

"No."

"And Mrs. Oswald, Marina Oswald, gave no reason to you as to why she didn't like the Paines?"

"No, I think it is because Robert didn't. That is a thought."

"You said that—"

"She has expressed that."

"You said that you were beginning to wonder whether this is a preplanned affair. What do you mean by that?"

"Well, I don't mean preplanned from the very beginning, but I think probably sometime in December, from then on it might have been planned.

"We have accumulated for her a considerable amount of money in story rights."

"How much?"

"Well, on advances—this is not the ultimate or the end result—but just on advances, it is one hundred and thirty-two thousand dollars."

The FBI was continuing to probe all the facts they could unearth regarding the assassination. A major development in the living arrangements and business affairs of Marina was certain to raise a question in their minds. Inasmuch as Robert had at least for that moment taken over the active management of Marina's affairs, they were impelled to go back to him for further interviews.

On February 19, the FBI interviewed Robert Oswald again. The Commission received the information from the FBI on February 21. The story broke in the Houston *Post* a day later.

Lee Oswald, according to Marina, was not only the would-be killer of General Walker; one morning in April 1963 he had started to go out of the Neely Street house, pistol in his belt, with the avowed intention of shooting former Vice President Richard M. Nixon!

As a member of the Commission I can only say that I was astounded to get the report of this latest development. Could it be possible that Marina had simply forgotten this incident and failed to tell it to the Commission for that reason? Even allowing for the obvious pressure she had endured in the past three months, it was indeed perplexing that she would have failed to consider this important enough to recall. The many-sided Marina now had another side. When Senator Russell was quoted at the time of the publication of the Commission's report that he found Marina's behavior "baffling," he may have had this development in mind. The way the story had finally come out, Marina was said to have told Jim Martin about this on January 30. Martin in turn told Robert within the next few days, and all this time the information had been held back for reasons that may have seemed justified in the minds of those who knew it, but it certainly struck me as a strange way to serve the truth. Robert decided to tell the FBI on February 19, 1964.

Jim Martin was queried on the facts:

"I want to ask you about a particular incident that was referred to in the Houston *Post*, an article in the paper and the source was given as you and that is in regard to Mr. Nixon, Richard Nixon, former Vice President of the United States.

"Did Marina ever say anything to you about Lee Oswald planning any violent action or assassination of Richard M. Nixon?"

"Yes."

"When did you first learn about that?"

"I don't remember the date. It was some time in January, and she mentioned it, said that he had come home one night and said, one evening, and said that he had waited for Nixon to shoot him."

"Where was this?"

"In Dallas."

"What time was it that he came home that night?"

"I didn't question her too much about the time. I assumed that it was after work."

"At about what time of the day was it?"

"Five or six o'clock. She said they were living on Neely Street, and he came home that night and told her about it. So the next morning he got up—Nixon had not come into town, so he said that he would be in the next day—and so he got up the next morning and got dressed with a suit, I believe she said, and she locked him in the bathroom and kept him there all day, they said."

"Did she say how she locked him in the bathroom?"

"No."

"Did you ask her how she could do that, whether there was a lock on the inside of the bathroom or outside?"

"No, I thought it was a little—I thought the story was a little farfetched myself."

"Was this brought up in connection with anything in particular, or just come out of the blue, blurted out?"

"It just came out of the blue."

"There was no prior conversation that led up to this or any background to it?"

"Not that I recall. It was just a statement that she made. I think she was talking about Oswald—"

"Was she prone to come out with these kinds of comments or was this an unusual circumstance?"

"No. She at times referred to some particular incident in Russia or various things like that. And they would be completely unattached to anything that we had been talking about."

"What more did you say to her about this incident when she brought it up?"

"Well, the only time I recall Nixon being in Dallas was in November. Now, she was not living with Oswald in November and—"

"Did you say that to her?"

"No. I just let the thing go."

"You didn't even ask her how she locked him in the bathroom?"

"No. I thought about it, because I know the only bathroom doors I have seen lock from the inside and they swing in."

"Did you ask her what he did after he was locked in the bathroom?"

"Yes."

"What did she say about that?"

"She said he didn't do anything. When she let him out that night, and I suppose he would be pretty mad at her, and she said no, he wasn't."

"Did she say she kept him in the bathroom all day?"

"Yes."

"Was anybody else present at the time of this statement by her to you?"

"My wife."

"Did your wife make any inquiry?"

"No. We thought it was some kind of a story."

"You mean you thought it was an untrue story?"

"Yes, and why, I don't know. It didn't sound logical."

"Were there other conversations with Marina that you had where you thought she was telling you things that were untrue?"

"She would relate stories about Russia that I would listen to, but they didn't sound right."

"Do you recall any?"

"Well, they mostly dealt with boy friends."

"What did she say in that regard?"

"Oh, she would talk about some individual boy friends, usually a non-Russian, someone from Rumania or Germany or from some other country."

"What did she say?"

"Oh, I don't know about specific incidents. She would remark about she knew—I am trying to think of a specific—one was, let's see, she left Leningrad and went to Minsk because of an association with a married man there."

"In Leningrad?"

"It was either she left Leningrad to go to Minsk or vice versa."

"But she left one or the other to go to the other because of an association with a married man?"

"Yes."

"Where was the association, in Leningrad or in Minsk?"

"Well, it was in the city that she left."

"She was getting away from that association, was she?"

"Yes."

"By going to the other city?"

"Yes."

"Do you recall any other conversation when she told you something that you don't believe?"

"Oh, she remarked about people that she knew in Russia that had, we will say, lovers—"

"Did she tell anything about a letter that she wrote to a boy friend in Minsk?"

"After she was here in New Orleans?"

"Yes."

"Yes."

"What did she say about that?"

"Let's see, she said she wrote the letter, and I believe what it was she told the boy that she wasn't—she wanted to come back to Russia, to him, she loved him, and the letter was returned, I believe, for lack of postage, and Oswald got hold of the letter, and he asked her about it, and I think he asked her either to read it or he would read it. I believe she read it to him. This caused quite a bit of difficulty. Now, that is when she was in New Orleans."

"When she was telling you about these people that had lovers in Russia, you didn't believe these stories? Is that what you are saying?"

"Well, of course, I know nothing about Russian life."

"Yes."

"So I more or less took it with a grain of salt. I didn't put any credibility to it or any doubt to it. It was just something that was said and I didn't either accept it or reject it."

"Now, on the Nixon matter, when that came to your attention, did you tell anyone else about it?"

"I discussed it with my wife and with John Thorne."

"Will you tell us about the conversation when you related this to someone else?"

"It was on the telephone, and I was quite shocked at first about it and then, thinking it over, it didn't sound logical."

"You believed it at first?"

"Yes. I guess I didn't see any reason for it not to be true. But then I didn't see any reason for it to be a lie, either, and I supposed it was possible."

"When did you tell Mr. Thorne about it with reference to when Marina told you?"

"The same day. I don't recall the date at all."

"What did you say to Mr. Thorne about it?"

"I just related the incident, what she had told me."

"Did you say anything to him about telling the Commission about it?"

"No."

"Did he say anything about telling the Commission about it?"

"No, I don't believe so."

"Was there anything else said in this telephone conversation with Mr. Thorne except relating what Marina had said?"

"I remarked what a big bombshell that would be as far as publicity was concerned if the newspapers ever got hold of something like that."

"That it would be helpful in regard to Marina's story, did you say that?"

"No, I did think it would be harmful."

"Did you say that to him?"

"I believe so."

"Why would it be harmful?"

"Well, this purportedly took place after the Walker incident, and she had made a statement that if Oswald repeated anything of a similar nature as the Walker incident she would turn him over to the police, and this was a repeat or similar, he actually didn't shoot at him but threatened to, and she did not report it to the police."

"I see. The Walker incident took place on April 10, 1963, according to our records."

Many versions of the story of how Lee Oswald had gone out to kill Richard Nixon blossomed in the press. The Commission obtained all the information they could from the FBI and other witnesses, but knowing they would want to ask other questions, they waited until June 11 to call Marina back to Washington. Then she told the story in her own words:

"It was early in the morning and my husband went out to get a newspaper, then he came in and sat reading the newspaper. I didn't pay any attention to him because I was occupied with the housework.

"Then he got dressed and put on a good suit. I saw that he took a pistol. I asked him where he was going and why he was getting dressed.

"He answered, 'Nixon is coming. I want to go and have a look.'

"I said, 'I know how you look,' or rather, 'I know how you customarily look, how you customarily take a look,' because I saw he was taking the pistol with him, rather than I know how you look in the sense that you are dressed, how you look at things is what I mean."

"Had it come to your attention, Mrs. Oswald, that Mr. Nixon was going to be in Dallas prior to that time?"

"No, I did not."

"Had you seen anything in the newspapers or heard anything over the radio or television?"

"No, we didn't have TV. I didn't see that in the newspaper.

"I did not think up this incident with Nixon myself."

"What do you mean by that, Mrs. Oswald?"

"I had forgotten entirely about the incident with Vice President Nixon when I was here the first time. When you asked me the questions about it, then I remembered it. I wasn't trying to deceive you the first time."

"What did your husband say that day when he got this gun and dressed up about Richard Nixon, did he tell you anything about him?"

"No, I just didn't know what to do, you know."

"How did you know he was interested in doing something about Mr. Nixon at that time?"

"My husband just said that Nixon is coming to Dallas."

"Then what did you do?"

"First I didn't know what to do. I wanted to prevent him from going out."

"Did you say anything to him?"

"I called him into the bathroom and I closed the door and I wanted to prevent him and then I started to cry. And I told him that he shouldn't do this, that he had promised me."

"Are you referring to his promise to you that you have described in your prior testimony after the Walker incident?"

"Yes, that was the promise."

"Do you recall the bathroom, how the door closes? Does it close into the bathroom on Neely Street or from the outside in?"

"I don't remember now. I don't remember. I only remember that it was something to do with the bathroom."

"Did you lock him into the bathroom?"

"I can't remember precisely."

"Do you recall how the locks were on the bathroom door there?"

"I can't recall. We had several apartments and I might be confusing one apartment with the other."

"Is it your testimony that you made it impossible for him to get out if he wanted to?"

"I don't remember."

"Did he try to get out of the bathroom?"

"I remember that I held him. We actually struggled for several minutes and then he quieted down. I remember that I told him that if he goes out it would be better for him to kill me than to go out."

"He is quite a big man and you are a small woman."

"No, he is not a big man, he is not strong."

"Well, he was five feet nine, and you are how tall?"

"When he is very upset, my husband is very upset, he is not strong, and when I want to and when I collect all my forces and want to do something very badly I am stronger than he is."

472

"You meant mentally or physically?"

"I am not strong but, you know, there is a certain balance of forces between us."

"Do you think it was persuasion, your persuasion of him or the physical force or both that prevented him from going?"

"I don't think it was physically, physical prevention because if he—I couldn't keep him from going out if he really wanted to.

"It might have been that he was just trying to test me. He was the kind of person who could try and wound somebody in that way. Possibly he didn't want to go out at all, but was just doing this all as a sort of joke, not really as a joke, but rather to simply wound me, to make me feel bad.

"I might be mistaken about some of the details of this incident, but it is very definite he got dressed, took a gun and then didn't go out. The reason why there might be some confusion in my mind about the details because it happened in other apartments in which we lived that we quarreled and then I would shut him in the bathroom, and in this particular case it may not have happened quite that way, but there is no doubt that he got dressed and had a gun."

"Do you remember what you said to him and what he said to you at that time?"

"I don't remember now, but I told the FBI precisely."

"And were your reports to the FBI in regard to this incident accurate, truthful and correct?"

"They were correct as far as I could remember. The only detail as far as my memory served me—the only detail which might be confused is the one with the bathroom."

"Had your husband said anything before or did he say anything at that time in regard to Mr. Nixon showing any hostility, friendship, or anything else?"

"Showing any hostility or friendship toward Mr. Nixon?"

"Yes, toward Nixon."

"I don't remember him saying anything—I don't remember but he didn't tell me. I don't remember him saying anything of that sort. I only remember the next day he told me that Nixon did not come.

"The FBI suggested that possibly I was confused between Johnson and Nixon, but there is no question that in this incident it was a question of Mr. Nixon.

"I remember distinctly the name Nixon because I read from the

473

Presidential elections that there was a choice between President Kennedy and Mr. Nixon."

"Where did your husband get the pistol that morning, do you remember?"

"What, where?"

"Where."

"My husband had a small room where he kept all that sort of thing. It is a little larger than a closet."

"Did you see him go in and get the pistol?"

"I didn't see him go into the room. I only saw him standing before the open door and putting the pistol in his pocket."

"Do you recall which pocket he put the pistol in?"

"It was not in a pocket. He put it in his belt."

"What else happened about this incident beyond what you have told us?"

"He took off his suit and stayed home all day reading a book. He gave me the pistol and I hid it under the mattress."

"Did you say anything more than you have told us to him about this matter at that time?"

"I closed the front door to the building that day and when we were quarreling about—when we were struggling over the question of whether or not he should go out I said a great deal to him."

"What did you say to him then?"

"I don't remember."

"Just tell us in substance."

"I really don't remember now. I only remember that I told him that I am sorry of all these pranks of his and especially after the one with General Walker, and he had promised me, I told him that he had promised me—"

"Did he say anything in answer to that?"

"I don't remember."

"As I recall, in your previous testimony there was some indication that you had said that if he did the Walker type of thing again you would notify the authorities.

"Did that conversation come up at this time with your husband?"

"Yes, I said that. But he didn't go at that time and after all he was my husband."

"Does—do you mean you said it again at the time of the Nixon incident?"

"Yes, I told him that, but you must understand that I don't speak English very well, and for that reason I used to keep a piece of paper with me, and I had it, you know what piece of paper I am talking about.

"At that time I didn't know how to go in police station, I don't know where it was."

"When you put the pistol under the mattress, what happened to the pistol from then on?"

"That evening he asked for it and said that nothing was going to happen, and that he said he wouldn't do anything and took the pistol back. And put it into his room."

"Now, when you talked to him about the Nixon incident and persuaded him not to go out and do anything to Mr. Nixon, did you say anything about your pregnancy in trying to persuade him?"

"Yes."

"What did you say about that?"

"Yes, I told him that I was pregnant."

"Did you observe his action at the time of this Nixon incident, how he acted?"

"How he reacted to this?"

"How he reacted to your interfering with him."

"At first he was extremely angry, and he said, 'You are always getting in my way.' But then rather quickly he gave in, which was rather unusual for him.

"At the time I didn't give this any thought, but now I think it was just rather a kind of nasty joke he was playing with me.

"Sometimes Lee was—he had a sadistic—my husband had a sadistic streak in him and he got pleasure out of harming people, and out of harming me, not physically but emotionally and mentally."

"Have you told us substantially all that happened about this Nixon incident?"

"That is all I can remember."

"Can you tell us why you didn't mention this incident to the Commission when you appeared before?"

"There were an awful lot of questions at that time, and I was very tired and felt that I had told everything and I don't remember, I can't understand why I didn't mention this. It would have been better for me to mention it the first time than to make you all do more work on it."

"At the time of this incident did you threaten to go to the authorities in case your husband did not desist in his intention?"

"Yes, I said that."

"Did you ask him if he intended to use the pistol against Mr. Nixon?"

"I told him that 'You have already promised me not to play any more with that thing.' Not really play, but you know—I didn't mean, of course, just playing but using the pistol.

"Then he said, 'I am going to go out and find out if there will be an appropriate opportunity and if there is I will use the pistol.'

"I just remembered this and maybe I didn't say this in my first testimony, and now it just has occurred to me that he said this."

"How much time elapsed, if you can remember, from the time he first told you that he was going out and when he finally became pacified?"

"That was maybe thirty minutes. The whole incident took maybe twenty minutes. It was about ten minutes I took—fifteen minutes maybe. Fifteen minutes, it took maybe ten minutes for him to be prepared to go out and then the incident in the bathroom took maybe five minutes until he quieted down.

"It doesn't mean I held him in the bathroom for five minutes because I couldn't do that."

"You said he stayed at the house the remainder of the day. During the remainder of the day did you discuss again with him the incident?"

"No, no."

"Did you have some fear that he would use these weapons against someone else?"

"Of course, I was afraid."

"What?"

"Of course, I was afraid."

"You thought that he might use his weapons against someone?"

"After the incident with Nixon I stopped believing him."

"You what?"

"I stopped believing him."

"Why?"

"Because he wasn't obeying me any longer, because he promised and then he broke his promise."

"I remember you testified before and I asked you if you had heard

476

him threaten any official or other person and your answer was no."

"Because I forgot at that time about the incident with Nixon."

"I want to ask you again: In view of the fact that you knew—in view of the fact that he had threatened Walker by shooting at him, and he threatened Vice President Nixon, can you not tell this Commission whether after that he threatened to hurt, harm any other person?"

"Nobody else. Perhaps I should be punished for not having said anything about all this, but I was just a wife and I was trying to keep the family together, at that time, I mean to say. I am talking, of course, of the time before President Kennedy's death. And if I forget to say anything now I am not doing it on purpose."

"Did the Nixon incident have anything to do with your decision to go to New Orleans to live?"

"After the incident with Walker it became clear to me that it would be a good idea to go away from Dallas and after the incident with Nixon insisted—I insisted on it."

"Did you ever consider telling the police about the Walker and Nixon incidents?"

"I thought of this but then Lee was the only person who was supporting me in the United States, you see. I didn't have any friends, I didn't speak any English and I couldn't work, and I didn't know what would happen if they locked him up and I didn't know what would happen to us.

"Of course, my reason told me that I should do it but because of circumstances I couldn't do it."

"Did anyone at any time advise you or tell you not to tell the Commission about this incident?"

"Martin told me that it is not necessary to mention this, but when they were asking me here in the Commission whether I had anything to add to my testimony, I really forgot about it. When Martin and I were talking about it he said, 'Well, try not to think about these things too much.' "

"Did he say anything about why it wasn't necessary to tell about this incident?"

"I don't remember. I don't think he told me why. Maybe he told me and I just didn't understand because I didn't understand English very well."

"When you were telling about the Nixon incident you referred to your husband's sadistic streak.

"Do you recall that?"

"Yes."

"Can you tell us a little more about that, how it showed?"

"Any time I did something which didn't please him he would make me sit down at a table and write letters to the Russian Embassy stating that I wanted to go back to Russia. He liked to tease me and torment me in this way. He knew that this—he just liked to torment me and upset me and hurt me, and he used to do this especially if I interfered in any of his political affairs, in any of his political discussions."

There were many details of the Nixon incident Marina was unable to recall with any degree of certainty. The date of this occurrence appears to have been three or four days before Lee fled to New Orleans at her urging. That was April 24, 1963. Inasmuch as no public announcement of a planned visit by Nixon in this period could be found, nor according to the Commission's report any invitation to come to Dallas, it was thought possible that Marina had confused two Vice Presidents. Could she have meant Lyndon Johnson, who did visit on April 23? She thought not, and then again perhaps.

After the Commission had explored every possible source of information bearing on this incident and was able to add very little to Marina's account, it had to take the attitude that the incident could not be said to have any direct bearing on proof that Lee Oswald did or didn't kill the President. Although additional proof was hardly needed, if one takes the story at its face value, it would seem to add a considerable weight to the strong evidence that Lee Oswald's mind turned to murder whenever he wanted to impress Marina with his strength. And although in this incident it could only have been Marina he was directly trying to impress, had he been able to carry out his threat would he not have imagined he was proving it to the whole world as he finally tried to do seven months later?

Among the witnesses closely associated in his lifetime with Lee Oswald there was only one who persisted in the belief in his innocence. John Pic, Lee's half brother, joined the other witnesses in expressing his conclusion that Oswald was the assassin. He also had some revealing things to say about his associations with Marguerite, the lone member of the family who stuck stubbornly to her claims.

478

"When I attempted to talk to Lee about this, he ignored me, and I was never able to get to the kid again after that. He didn't care to hear anything I had to say to him. So in a matter of a few days they packed up and left, sir. They moved to the Bronx somewhere."

"Well, at this point . . . I would like to ask you this: You hadn't seen them from October of 1950 until the summer of 1952. Did you notice any change in him, his over-all attitude, his relations with his mother, his demeanor, his feelings toward others, his actions toward others?"

"He was definitely the boss."

"Now, tell us on what you base that?"

"I mean if he decided to do something, regardless of what my mother said, he did it. She had no authority whatsoever with him. He had no respect for her at all."

From that time on not only the relationship between Lee and John Pic remained cold but also the relationship between John and his mother. While Marguerite remained in New York, Pic saw her occasionally.

"Whenever I would meet her it would be the same old song and dance, like hinting around I should help support her, which I couldn't afford to do."

The money problem Marguerite stressed was an old story to the children.

"Every time she met anyone she would remind them she was a widow with three children. I didn't feel she had it any tougher than a lot of people walking around."

Pic decided to re-enlist and was transferred to the Norfolk, Virginia, area. He and his family left New York.

"When I did finally get transferred from the ship to Portsmouth, Virginia, I did not make known to my mother our whereabouts or our address."

Lee Oswald was not the only member of the family who, when he moved, would deliberately fail to give his mother his forwarding address.

The final break, however, between Marguerite and John Pic came six years after the knife incident when Lee and Pic became estranged. According to his account, Marguerite took the opportunity to pay him back for evicting her from the apartment in New York. Pursuant to orders of transfer, he was crossing the country en route to Japan. He stopped in Fort Worth, where his mother was now living, and stayed at her place for a few days.

"When we got there, my mother informed us she had no food in the house, so my wife and I went and bought a whole bunch of groceries for our stay which we expected to do. I got in contact with some old friends, and they invited me over for Sunday dinner the following Sunday at their house, and being I was pressed for time I had another Sunday dinner invitation at my brother Robert's house. My mother was invited to this dinner."

"At your brother's?"

"Yes, sir."

"Yes."

"He then resided at 7313 Davenport Street, I believe. Well, it seems that my mother declined her part of the invitation, and was quite put out that my wife and I did not decline our part because she decided that we should spend Sunday dinner eating with her. So my wife and I and two children drove off to my brother Robert's house to go eat. After we were there for about a half hour, she called us up and told me to come get our bags, that we would have to leave.

"So my wife and I, we left the kids at my brother Robert's because we knew there would be a big scene with all the trimmings, and we went back and we walked in, didn't say nothing, just packed up our bags and she was yelling and screaming, reminding us about the time we threw her out of the apartment in New York and she was getting even with us for this when we threw her and Lee out.

"I then informed her that I wanted nothing more to do with her and that every time she and my wife got together that she had nothing but bad things to say about her. And I let her know that our relationship ends right then and there, and since that time, sir, I have not written her, talked to her, anything."

"Or seen her."

"Or have seen her, except in magazines and stuff. She has sent me a bunch of junk in the mail. During this conversation when we was getting thrown out, I reminded her that she made nothing but trouble for us and especially my wife, she was always on my wife. And so I owed her a few dollars for the phone call I had made, so I gave her ten dollars and this seemed to satisfy, well, probably accomplished what she set out to do, get some money off of me one way or the other. This is how I looked at it. This didn't upset her, after we left, after I gave her ten dollars. So we went to my brother Robert's, we ate, we stayed at their house until Tuesday morning, and we left and then went to Japan, sir."

It was a harsh judgment John Pic's testimony passed on Marguerite. He felt that Lee may have been deeply affected by her continual talk about her money problems. This might well help to account for Lee's impression that the capitalist world was nothing but a system of exploitation of the have-nots by the haves.

"Were you of the opinion from time to time that on these occasions when she talked about what appears to be, that she was *in extremis* with respect to finances when in fact she was not, she was overstating this condition or status?"

"Yes, I believe she overstated it most of the time."

"Because there were purchases of houses, at least on the installment plan, and she seemed to have capital to do that, did she not?"

"Yes, sir; she could always buy and sell a house some way or other."

"What was your impression as to why she was doing this—to impress you boys or was that just her fixation or personality trait?"

"It is my impression that she did it in order to make a profit on every deal she got involved with."

"I am not thinking of a house sale as such. But that question was more directed to her talking about her financial circumstances. Was she attempting to impress you boys that she was working herself to the bone to support you and you should be more grateful than you appeared to be, and that sort of thing?"

"That is practically verbatim, sir."

"Were you under the impression that she was overstating in that respect?"

"Yes, sir."

"Was that likewise the feeling of your brother Robert?"

"Yes, I am sure it was."

"What was your impression as to whether your mother was always sincere and straightforward with respect to that subject matter?"

"My opinion, sir, at the time was all she cared about was getting hold of and making some money in some form or another. This is her god, so to speak, was to get money. And to get as much out of me as she could and as much out of Robert as she could."

"And as much out of anybody else as she could?"

"Yes, sir."

"Was your mother an extravagant person money-wise?"

"I don't know what she did with the money, sir. She bought very little as far as clothes and things. We didn't eat steak every day. We didn't eat that good. In fact, when I joined the service in 1950 I was a hundred and eighteen pounds, and my weight prior to that was usually about a hundred and thirty, forty. I think within a month or two after I joined the service I was up to a hundred and forty-five and none of my uniforms fit me. I was—there is a picture of me in the Pasqual High School thing, and I am very thin. People couldn't recognize me from that picture. I lost a lot of weight working, and not eating too good. I would come home and have to fix my own meals."

"Was your mother attentive in that respect? Did she go out of her way to have meals ready for you boys when you returned to home either after work or after school or otherwise?"

"If there was a majority eating there was usually something set aside for the lesser, which was kept warm in the oven."

"You mean the member of the family who was absent at mealtime, she would save something for him?"

"Yes, sir."

"Did you get the feeling, you and your brother, in due course, that your mother's references to these financial needs at times, at least when to use the vernacular, she was crying wolf?"

"Yes, sir."

"These continued references by her to her financial needs, did you think that had an effect on Lee as well as on yourself and your brother?"

"It didn't affect me that much. I ignored most of them. If I had money I sent it. If I didn't, that was it. Lee was brought up in this atmosphere of constant money problems, and I am sure it had quite an effect on him and also Robert."

John Pic felt that all of Marguerite's sons had joined the service for the same reason. Speaking of Lee's enlistment in the Marine Corps, he said, "My mother told me some way or another, I don't remember, sir. This is how I learned about it, either by phone call or by letter or some way. Of course, I knew he would do it as soon as he reached the age."

"All right. Why did you know he would do it and tell us the circumstances upon which you—the facts upon which you base that observation?"

"He did it for the same reasons that I did it and Robert did it, I assume, to get from out and under."

"Out and under what?"

"The yoke of oppression from my mother."

"Had that been a matter of discussion between you and, for example, between you and your brother Robert?"

"No, sir, it was just something we understood about and never discussed."

"And that would include Lee as well as your brother Robert; that is, you were all aware of it?"

"I know this includes my brother Robert. Of course, when I was eighteen years old I didn't discuss things like this with Lee, who was much younger."

John Pic's testimony goes deep into the family history. He tells how even after ten years when he met Lee for Thanksgiving dinner at Robert's in 1962 he had the feeling Lee's hostility toward him remained. He resented Lee's introducing him to others as his half brother. As youngsters they always regarded themselves just as brothers. Was Lee still standing off because of the knife incident?

He felt that Lee had changed. He really did not know him. As to Lee's reasons for not letting Marina learn English, he was asked, "Was there any conversation during the course of the day in which you participated or overheard as to Marina's undertaking to learn English?"

"Well, my sister-in-law, Vada—"

"That is Robert's wife?"

"Wife. Of course, she had, she and my wife had a lot to say to each other, and through my wife I found out what Vada had said to her, that Lee did not permit Marina to wear any lipstick, he did not permit her to learn English. My wife, she thought this was really absurd and said the best thing to do was to get them a TV set and let her sit home and learn English. My wife thought it was terrible the way her conditions were as far as this was concerned. The girls seemed to gather in the dinette and we sat around in the living room, talking."

"Was anything said by Vada or your wife on that occasion as to the reason why Lee was not permitting Marina to learn English and speak it and write it?"

"Well, my wife assumed that if she did ever learn English she would wise up, being we had seen the Japanese wives with their husbands. For example, while they were living over in Japan and the wife is usually meek and mild but when they get over here they change, you see, she gets her American ways, and lowers the boom on the husband like all the other American wives do. And my wife was under the impression that this would happen if once she did learn English and everything."

This was a somewhat new but plausible theory of why Lee didn't encourage Marina to learn English.

"Did you have the impression when you saw him on Thanksgiving of 1962 that in the meantime he had become embittered, resentful of his station?"

"Well, sir, the Lee Harvey Oswald I met in November of 1962 was not the Lee Harvey Oswald I had known ten years previous. This person struck me as someone with a chip on his shoulder."

John Pic completed his testimony by expressing himself totally unsympathetic to Marguerite's theories of Lee's innocence. His final impressions in New York were of a willful and unruly youngster brandishing a jackknife, threatening people with weapons to get his own way. There did not seem to be anything to mitigate Lee's guilt.

He volunteered this opinion: "I think, I believe that Lee Oswald did the crime that he is accused of. I think that anything he may have done was aided with a little extra push from his mother in the living conditions that she presented to him. I also think that his reason for leaving the Marine Corps is not true and accurate. I mean I don't think he cared to get out of the Marine Corps to help his mother. He probably used this as an excuse to get out and go to his defection.

"I know myself I wouldn't have gotten out of the service because of her, and I am sure Robert wouldn't either, and this makes me believe that Lee wouldn't have."

"Was your mother loving and affectionate toward you boys?"

"I would say for myself, sir, I wasn't to her."

"What is that?"

"I was not toward her."

"Why?"

"I had no motherly love feeling toward her. Like I say, I think I first became resentful to her when she informed me I would not return to the military school and from then my hostilities toward her grew."

"Well, up to that point, what had been your feeling toward your mother?"

"We had never been in a very affectionate family, sir."

"That is affectionate with respect to the boys toward your mother?"

"That is right, sir, kissing her, and things like this. It is my own opinion that she is out right now to make as much money as she can on her relationship with Lee Harvey Oswald. That is the only thing —I don't really believe she really believes he is innocent. I think she is out to make money than if she has to say he is guilty. I think she is a phony in the whole deal."

CHAPTER 37

THE LONER

JOHN PIC MADE VIVID how remote the relationship of brothers could become, how far members of a family could depart from the ties of flesh and blood.

Marguerite had need for the solace her children might have given her, but she seemed to make it impossible for them to do so. The pattern of their lives drove them apart. Their temperaments were toxic. None had much to give the other. Here was a family in fragments, a relatively meaningless accident of birth and propagation.

Lee's half brother had always gone by the name of John Edward Pic. On the other hand, John Pic's father went by the name of Edward John Pic, Jr. The father's testimony and his affidavit stating his feeling toward Marguerite was like a fresh breath of air in the midst of a miasma. He had had no personal contacts with Marguerite for thirty years, and yet he had some kind things to say about her:

"When Marguerite Claverie Pic and I separated after we had lived together a year, we resided in a house on Genois Street, south of Canal Street, in New Orleans. This was a rented house. The rent was either twenty-eight or thirty dollars per month. At no time prior to our separation did Marguerite work. During all of that period she was a housewife.

"I neither refused nor failed to support her either during or after our marriage. There were personality and incompatibility difficulties between us commencing at an early stage of our marriage. We just couldn't get along. Things kept getting worse and worse. Marguerite was aware of my earning capacity at the time we married. There were difficulties between us respecting money and household financial management, but this was only one of the sources of the difficulties. My financial situation did not worsen after our marriage.

"Marguerite's pregnancy with my son John Edward Pic was not the cause of our separation. I had no objection to children. It was a coincidence that about that time we had reached the point that we could not make a go with each other any more. Our separation, which was amicable and which was arranged through an attorney, would have taken place irrespective of Marguerite's pregnancy with my son John Edward Pic.

"As I testified in my deposition, Marguerite was a nice girl. I haven't anything whatsoever adverse to say against her, it is just that we couldn't get along. Our dispositions would not jell. I do not mean to imply that the fault, if any, lay with either of us. We just didn't get along.

"My distinct recollection is that I had no difficulty maintaining the household and supporting my family though there was some difference between Marguerite and me as to the manner, style and the level on which our household should be maintained."

What Edward Pic, Jr., had to say about his respect for Marguerite and sense of duty in supporting his son's upbringing stands in sharp contrast to the comments of other members of the family. Without coercion he appears to have recognized an obligation, and he appears to have been able to put aside petty grievances and say a good word for someone he had not seen in three decades. Among the witnesses before the President's Commission, gratuitous "good words" of one party for another were somewhat limited. It was pleasant not to find Marguerite's first husband vindictive and unforgiving. Whatever the limitations of Edward Pic, Jr., in the eyes of his first wife, the record shows that he recognized an obligation and apparently met it. In this bizarre saga of an assassin how did the others meet that standard? Each reader must be judge for himself. It is hoped that many Americans will see fit to go far beyond the pages of this volume and delve into the expansive record of the Commission as spread out in twenty-six volumes of testimony and exhibits. The monumental record of the President's Commission will stand like a Gibraltar of factual literature through the ages to come. Although not intended as such, it is perhaps the most significant sociological study ever made.

The Commission investigating President Kennedy's assassination was charged with a number of sober responsibilities:

(1) to ascertain, evaluate and report upon the facts relating to the assassination of the late President John F. Kennedy and the subsequent violent death of the man charged with the assassination;

(2) to examine the evidence developed by the Federal Bureau of

Investigation and any additional evidence that might thereafter come to light or be uncovered by federal or state authorities;

(3) to make such further investigation as the Commission found desirable, and to report to President Johnson its findings and conclusions.

In addition to the specific charges was an implied obligation to attempt to determine Lee Harvey Oswald's motivation in murdering a President, assuming the record pointed emphatically in that direction. What were Oswald's reasons? Why would he do such a heartless thing? Why would he murder a man who had never injured him and whom in many ways he apparently admired? The Commission labored over this question with soul-searching thoroughness. Before agreement was reached by the Commission, each sentence had to measure up to the unofficially adopted motto of the Commission, "Truth is our only client here." To the best of the ability of seven dedicated public servants and a staff of valiant workers, that ideal was fulfilled.

The report stated:

The Commission could not make any definitive determination of Oswald's motives. It has endeavored to isolate factors which contributed to his character and which might have influenced his decision to assassinate President Kennedy. These factors were:

(a) His deep-rooted resentment of all authority which was expressed in a hostility toward every society in which he lived;

(b) His inability to enter into meaningful relationships with people, and a continuous pattern of rejecting his environment in favor of new surroundings;

(c) His urge to try to find a place in history and despair at times over failures in his various undertakings;

(d) His capacity for violence as evidenced by his attempt to kill General Walker;

(e) His avowed commitment to Marxism and communism, as he understood the terms and developed his own interpretation of them; this was expressed by his antagonism toward the United States, by his defection to the Soviet Union, by his failure to be reconciled with life in the United States even after his disenchantment with the Soviet Union, and by his efforts, though frustrated, to go to Cuba.

Each of these contributed to his capacity to risk all in cruel and irresponsible actions.

Can there be any question that Lee Oswald had the "capacity to risk all in cruel and irresponsible actions"? As the witnesses wrote this biography of an assassin, time and again they highlighted his heartless behavior. In Lee Oswald's own writings, his letters, essays and diary, he shouted this theme—I am not afraid to smash anything, even myself, if it serves my willful wishes. He implied to his brother Robert that as an American, if Russia and the United States ever came to grips in war, he would shoot him as an enemy as quickly as a stranger. In Moscow he slashed his wrist, inviting death to get his own way. Secretly but with cool premeditation he plotted to rid the world of General Walker: photographs of the general's house, apparent rehearsals of his intended crime, even the forethought to know where he would bury the rifle afterward so the dogs couldn't pick up the scent! Less criminal perhaps but equally as cruel were his repeated threats to Marina. He would beat her, tell her coldly she would have to go back to Russia, order her around like a quarry slave. It was his instinct to kill not just for the purpose of getting his own way but for the sense of power and command it gave him. The Nixon incident seems absurd in view of the futility of his threat and the fact that he probably had little chance of carrying out his stated purpose. Nevertheless, if true, it was further evidence that here was a man whose mind repeatedly turned to murder as a way of venting his frustrations. What petty provocation had brought on that bluster? Marina did not recall any reason. But "reason" was not always necessary where it involved Lee Oswald's actions.

Lee's deep-rooted resentment of all authority, which was expressed in a hostility toward every society in which he lived, would appear to have had its beginnings far back in his youth. John Pic first noted that Marguerite seemed to have lost control of him when they had gone to live in New York. Lee was nearly thirteen. He was a truant and actually confined at Youth House for psychiatric study for three weeks, April 16-May 7, 1953. He was then placed on parole with a recommendation that a referral be made to the Community Service Society for treatment. Just prior to that, the incident had taken place which prompted John Pic to insist on Marguerite's and Lee's leaving his home. The incident of Lee's pulling a knife and the estrangement of Lee and John was at least significant enough to have resulted in a long-standing coolness of Lee toward his half brother. But Lee's resentment of authority became more and more apparent in his adult years. His performance at the American Embassy in Moscow when he made the gesture of giving up his citizenship; his contempt for the very bureaucrats whose assent he depended on for permission to remain in Russia; his eventual annoyance with the photograph of Lenin staring down at him in the factory where he worked in Minsk; and, when he had finally decided to return to the United States, his accusation that his hosts were stealing from him things mailed from the States—these were a few examples of his increasing contempt for any authority. "Only on the moon," as Marina had expressed it; there perhaps he would find contentment, but only then, it would seem, if he were the "Commissar" and no one dared contradict his personal authority. No one enjoys the unreasonable exercise of authority by a superior. Although his mother may have been demanding during the years he lived with her, she was by no means oppressing him twenty-four hours a day. She worked and he was left alone countless hours to do as he saw fit, and he apparently spent a good deal of his time reading inflammatory literature and nursing grievances he had never personally experienced. In many ways the ability of Lee Oswald to fabricate grievances is striking. There is no evidence that he went hungry at night when he was a youngster, and yet he visualized American economic life as poverty-ridden. Marguerite's reminders of their straitened circumstances may have given him an exaggerated sense of deprivation, but on the other hand he was quite upset when Aline Mosby in her article about his defection implied he had spent his youth in dire straits. Many an American youngster has overcome economic adversity far worse than anything Lee Oswald experienced in his lifetime. It would appear that at times he was indulged by his mother rather than disciplined. He was not called on to face reality.

Perhaps the most significant finding of the President's Commission was Lee Oswald's inability to enter into meaningful relationships with people, and a continuous pattern of rejecting his environment in favor of new surroundings. What are meaningful relationships as applied to the normal human being?

The first "meaningful relationship" most of us experience in our lives is the relationship with our family. Throughout the centuries the family has provided the muscle and sinew of most civilized cultures. Lee's family relationships were blighted from the beginning. His mother described this situation herself:

"You have to understand this. As a family we separated—not maybe for any particular reason. It is just the way we live. I am not a mother that has a home that the children can come to and feed them and so on. I am a working mother. I do twenty-four-hour duty. So I am not that type mother, where I am a housewife with money, that the children have a home to come to."

It was perhaps unfortunate that Lee Oswald married a young woman whose background was also less than ideal. First, she had not had a full family life herself. What family concept Marina had was apparently inherited mostly from her grandmother and to some extent kept alive by her aunt and uncle in Minsk after her mother died and left her with a stepfather. Marina expressed her distress at not finding a way of encouraging Lee to get along with his mother. She also expressed regret that to live with Marguerite after Lee's death seemed impossible.

Lee confided that he deliberately avoided forming any attachments—friends, close associates or Marine friends—because he did not want any ties with the past when he defected to Russia. This was a key to Lee Oswald's outlook on life: to be obligated to others was to be subject to restraint; to have friends might mean having to acknowledge debts to pay; to be responsible to anyone was anathema to his brash sense of individuality. John Pic said he thought that all the children wanted to get out from under Marguerite's "yoke." Lee wanted more than to get out from under Marguerite's yoke; he wanted to get out from under any responsibility, a selfish, egocentric attitude which if carried to extremes could well end where it did in self-destruction. In the end, can any individual successfully deny all social obligations or responsibilities and survive anywhere? Even Robinson Crusoe found and recognized his obligation to Friday.

Lee's marriage to Marina failed to give him what he was seeking. Marriage, after all, is a "meaningful" human relationship, perhaps the most delicate of all, requiring patience and consideration. It would appear that neither Marina nor Lee was able to deal successfully with this relationship. Lee apparently made it impossible for Marina to find a solution. She appears to have dealt with him the best way she knew how to the very end, but he assassinated a President just hours after his last quarrel with Marina. She said about that last night, "I was smiling inside. I of course wanted to make up with him"—words that took a grim turn a few hours later.

The Commission found that Lee's urge to try to find a place in history and his despair at times over failures in his various undertakings were factors leading to his heinous crime. There will be those who read this biography of an assassin who will single this out as the overriding consideration. As a member of the Commission I feel sure that this was indeed a consuming drive behind Lee Oswald's motley career, but at the same time this seems related to the previous point —the absence of meaningful personal human relationships.

Perhaps on this point an elected political figure is qualified to speak. It is generally assumed that some part of the motivation that leads human beings to seek public office is a desire for recognition. It would seem to me that Lee Oswald never could understand that fame without concern for the basic values of humanity is an absurdity. History makes heroes and it is well that it should. Without the example before us of the achievement of great men of the past, would we not lack motivation for the accomplishments of the future? But the man who sets out to become famous irrespective of the sound values of society, irrespective of a real love for his fellow human being, irrespective of the consequences of his acts upon other human beings is a special kind of criminal. He gets and deserves the total contempt of history and mankind. Lee Oswald was that kind of a person. Even if he wasn't aware that it was recognition and fame he was seeking when he committed the most craven crime in history, all his pretensions of reforming the world, creating a better society, protesting injustices to mankind were as empty as anything could be. He murdered a man whose life was full of "meaningful human relationships," a man who in the eyes of the American public symbolized affection for his fellow men.

That Lee Oswald did indeed have the capacity for the kind of violence he was guilty of in Dallas is well established by the witnesses. However, I would like to say a few words about the last of the points in regard to his motivation brought out in the Commission report—namely that Lee's avowed commitment to Marxism and communism was an important factor in explaining his behavior. There will be some who will scoff at this factor.

Few can deny that many of the great traditions of modern free government, of democracy indeed, find their origins deep in the traditions of Christian ethics. Alexis de Tocqueville, that incisive observer of American institutions, pointed out well over a hundred years ago that self-government and personal freedom flourished in America because of the tradition among settlers, "Do unto others as you would have them do unto you." Freedom and democracy depend on self-restraint. They depend on voluntary consideration of the other fellow.

In my judgment, if one were to stress the thing I consider most deceptive about communism, it is the failure of its advocates to recognize the importance of reasonable human relationships. To my mind here lies the treacherous fallacy of the creed Lee Oswald embraced. Lee Oswald was not an ordinary assassin whose brutal act was the product of an addled head. It was not just his head that was addled. It was his heart as well. In his life he had had no meaningful human relationships.

When one meddles with a social institution as basic to meaningful human relationships as the "family," or even inadvertently does something that weakens this fundamental social unit, I for one believe we are on unsafe ground. Or if one thinks that through an act of Congress some government agency can supplant the responsibilities of the individual with an appropriation or a law, I for one look at the proposal with a critical eye.

The witnesses have recorded in the archives their biography of an assassin. They have recorded more than that. They have etched on the stones of history a unique and comprehensive picture of human nature in mid-passage of the twentieth century. Hardly any of what the 552 witnesses had to say in 25,000 pages of testimony is totally insignificant. The quotations in this volume are a fraction of the whole record, and it has been one of the writer's aims to convey the broad picture of the events surrounding a sorrowful day in our history. The conclusions of these final remarks are personal observations. If there is one outstanding conviction that has been confirmed for me by the death of the 35th President of the United States it is that meaningful personal relations are still the most important elements in any society and the most precious possession of an individual. Thus the witnesses spoke to me. "To each his own" may be a fine poetic concept, but we do not live alone, and neither a Lee Oswald nor anyone else can succeed in so doing.

INDEX

A MEMBER OF CONGRESS since January 3, 1949, Representative Gerald R. Ford was elected Minority Leader of the House of Representatives at the opening of the 89th Congress on January 4, 1965. He has been a member of the Joint Senate-House Republican Leadership since January 1963. In November 1963 he was appointed by President Johnson to the seven-member board known as the Warren Commission, to investigate the assassination of President Kennedy.

Representative Ford was born July 14, 1913, in Omaha, Nebraska, but spent his childhood in Grand Rapids, Michigan, where he attended school. At the University of Michigan, he was a member of the undefeated national football championship teams of 1932 and 1933. In 1934, he was selected Michigan's most valuable player. Ford received his law degree in 1941 from the Yale University Law School, where, in addition to pursuing his scholastic activities, he acted as assistant varsity football coach. Following his admission to the Michigan State bar in June of that year, he became a partner in the law firm of Ford and Buchen in Grand Rapids.

In 1942 Ford entered the U. S. Navy where he served 47 months on active duty in World War II. He was released in January of 1946 with the rank of Lieutenant Commander.

Returning to Grand Rapids, Ford resumed the practice of law. In the 1948 primary election, he defeated the Republican incumbent and became the Representative from the Fifth Congressional District of Michigan.

In 1949 he was selected by the United States Junior Chamber of Commerce as one of "America's Ten Outstanding Young Men" and received its Distinguished Service Award. In 1959 the judges for *Sports Illustrated* selected him to receive the magazine's Silver Anniversary All-American Award as one of 25 football players of 25 years before who had contributed most to their fellow citizens in the quarter-century.

Representative Ford is married to the former Elizabeth Bloomer of Grand Rapids and they have four children.

JOHN R. STILES served as Gerald Ford's first campaign manager in 1948, when Ford unseated the incumbent. The two men have been friends for many years, and it was a natural result of their close association that Mr. Stiles became Congressman Ford's special assistant throughout the Congressman's ten-month service on the Warren Commission. Theirs was more than a literary collaboration on *Portrait of the Assassin*—it was the product of their daily work together over that period.

Mr. Stiles served in 1960 as Field Director of the Nixon-for-President campaign and continues to be active in Republican politics.